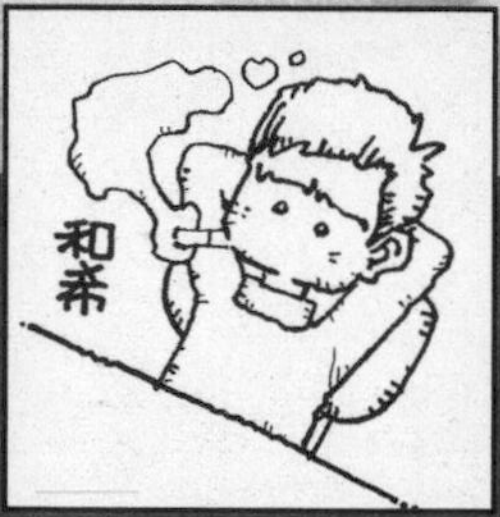
和希

KAZUKI TAKAHASHI

Astral's character design was the first I completed for *ZEXAL*. He's the character I have the greatest attachment to. And Miyoshi-kun's Astral looks great!

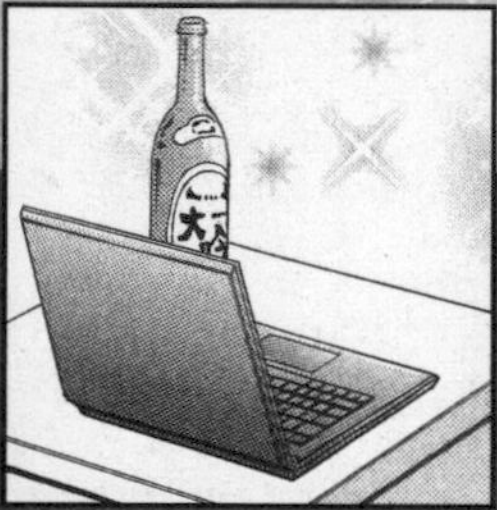

SHIN YOSHIDA

With the anime over, I have a bit more time, so I put together a deck for a staff tournament and got whooped! I'm going to study up and get revenge!

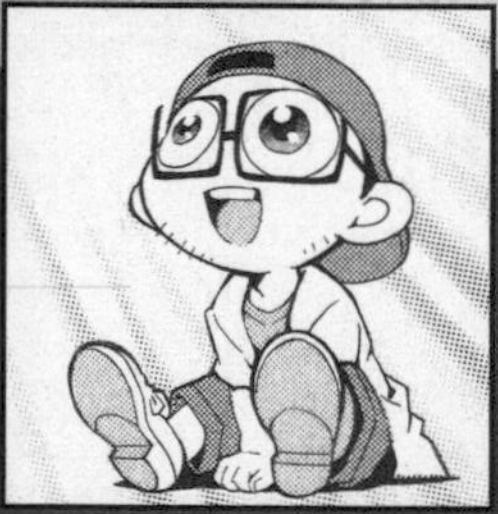

NAOHITO MIYOSHI

My right hand has been sore, and it turns out I have tendinitis! I didn't think I was overworking it, but... Anyway, I can still hold a pen without any problem! Guess that means I have to get back to work! Haha!

Volume 7
SHONEN JUMP Manga Edition

Original Concept by **KAZUKI TAKAHASHI**
Production Support: STUDIO DICE
Story by **SHIN YOSHIDA**
Art by **NAOHITO MIYOSHI**

Translation & English Adaptation TAYLOR ENGEL AND IAN REID, HC LANGUAGE SOLUTIONS
Touch-up Art & Lettering JOHN HUNT
Designer STACIE YAMAKI
Editor MIKE MONTESA

Printed in the U.S.A.

Published by VIZ Media, LLC
P.O. Box 77010
San Francisco, CA 94107

10 9 8 7 6 5 4 3 2 1
First printing, September 2015

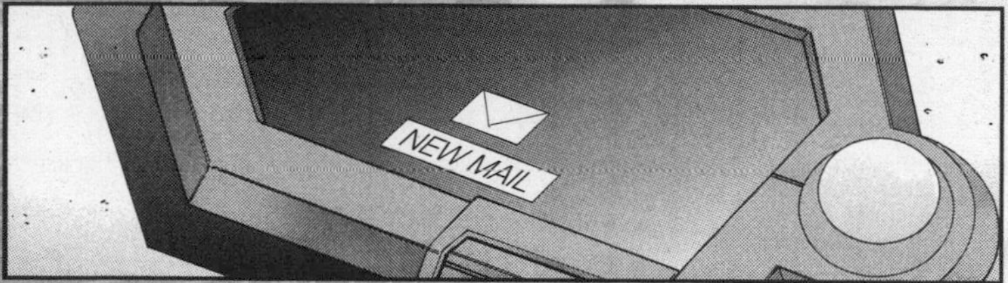
NEW MAIL

Yu-Gi-Oh! ZEXAL

VOLUME 7:
Just One Hope!!

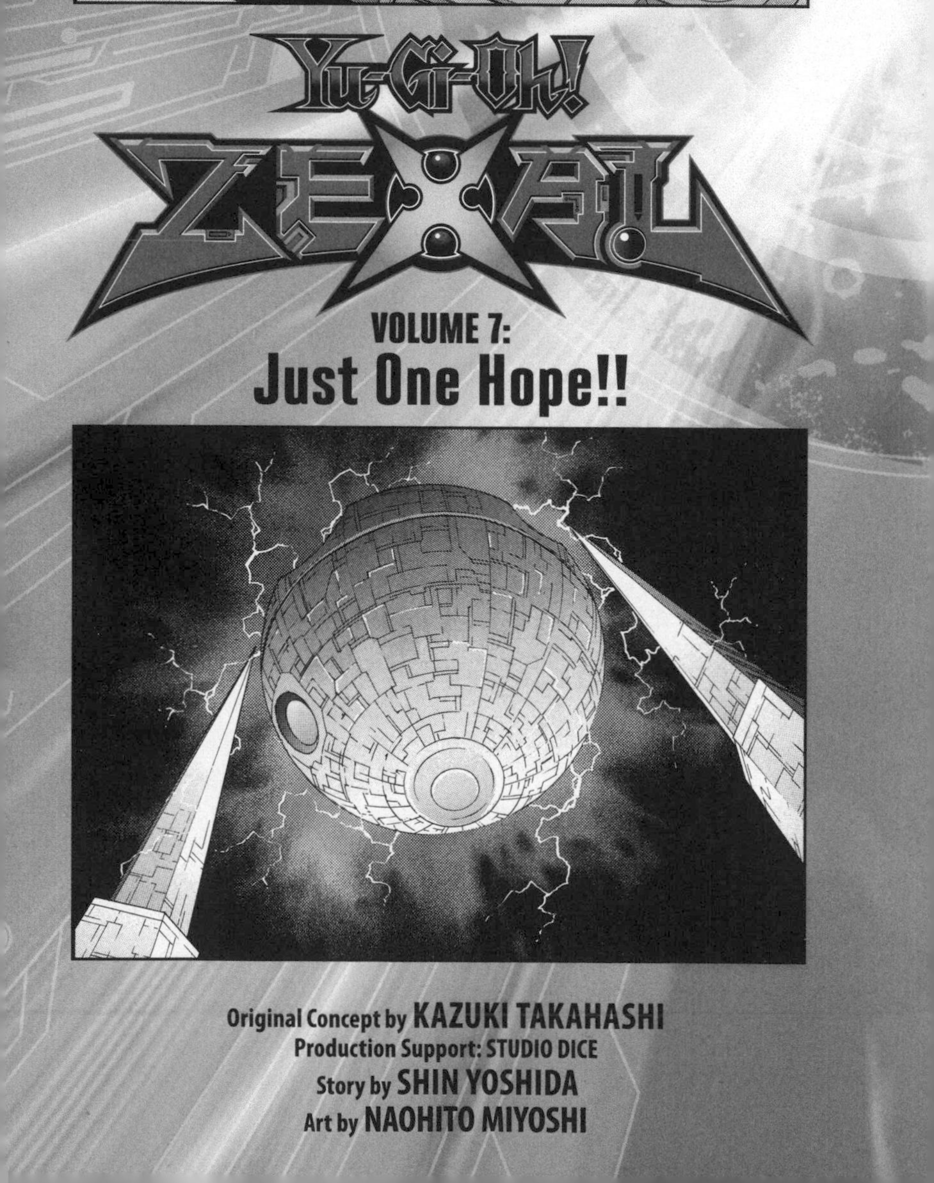

Original Concept by KAZUKI TAKAHASHI
Production Support: STUDIO DICE
Story by SHIN YOSHIDA
Art by NAOHITO MIYOSHI

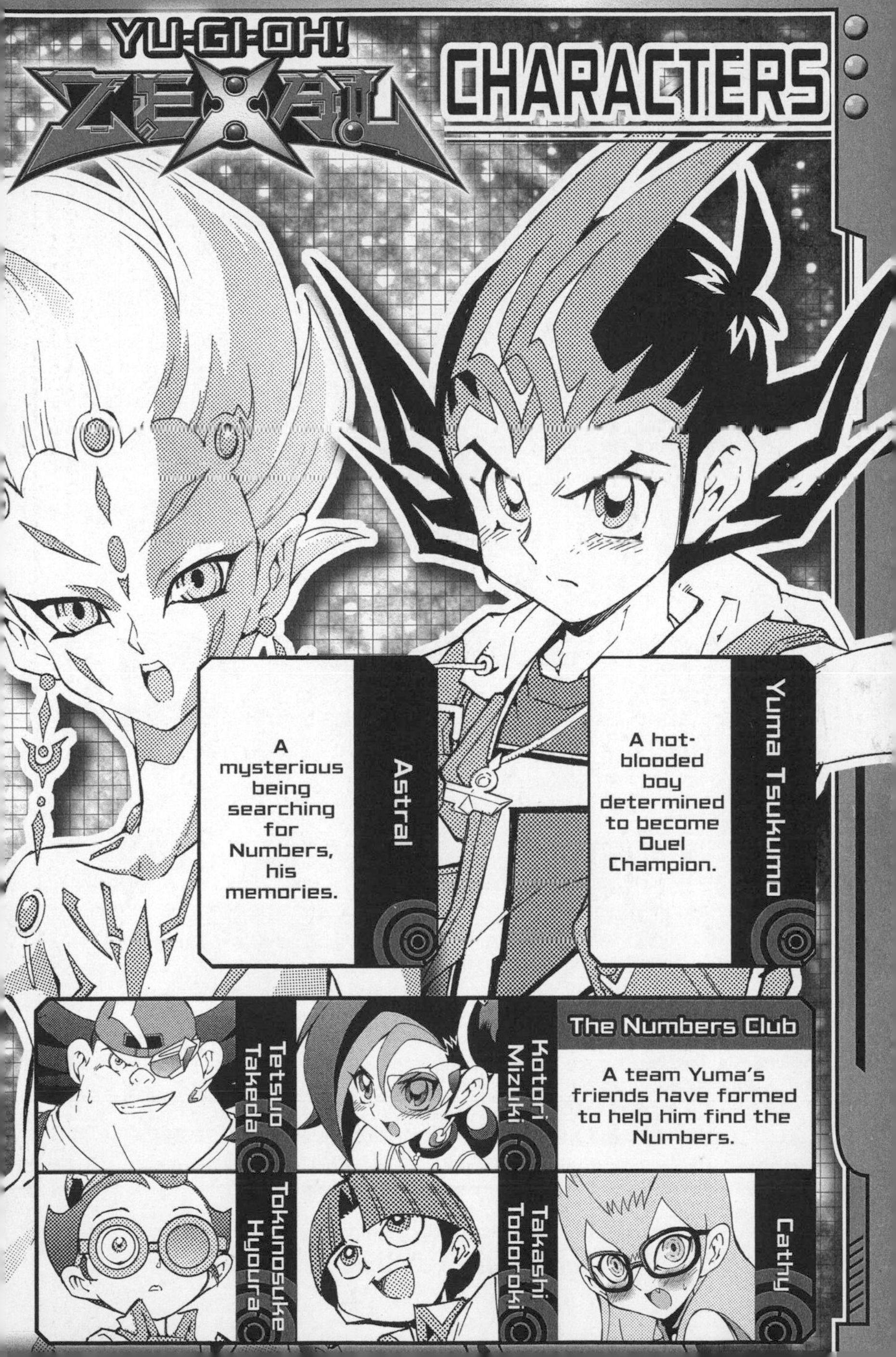
YU-GI-OH! ZEXAL
CHARACTERS
Yuma Tsukumo
A hot-blooded boy determined to become Duel Champion.
Astral
A mysterious being searching for Numbers, his memories.
The Numbers Club
A team Yuma's friends have formed to help him find the Numbers.
Kotori Mizuki
Tetsuo Takeda
Cathy
Takashi Todoroki
Tokunosuke Hyoura

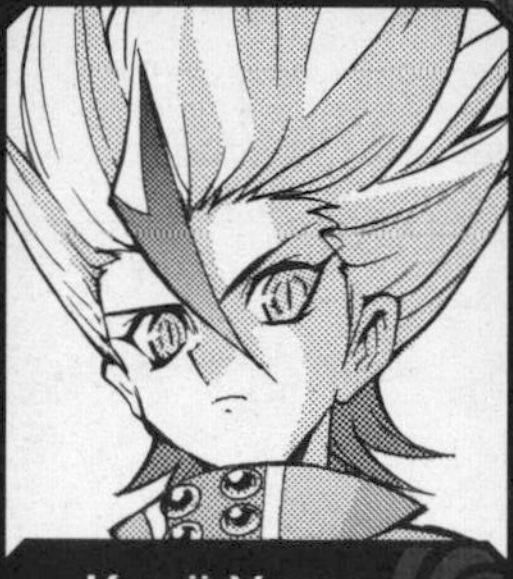

Kyoji Yagumo

Kyoji hunts the Numbers cards for Dr. Faker.

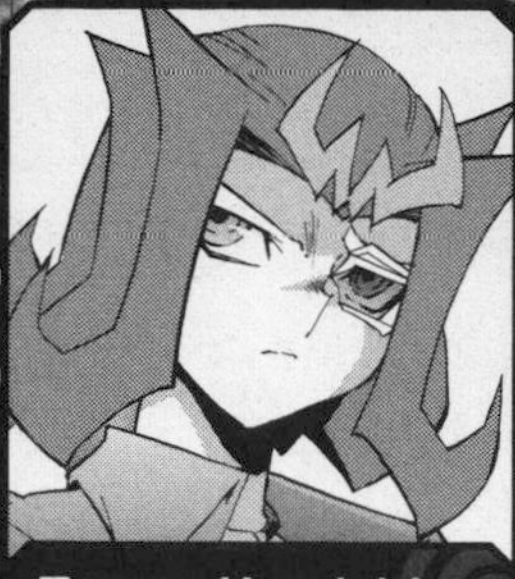

Ryoga Kamishiro

Goes by the nickname "Shark." His fate is tied to Yagumo's.

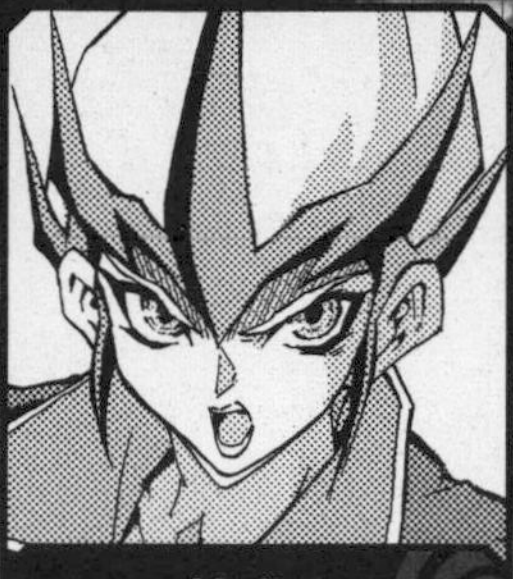

Kaito

A Numbers Hunter who is searching for Numbers to save his little brother.

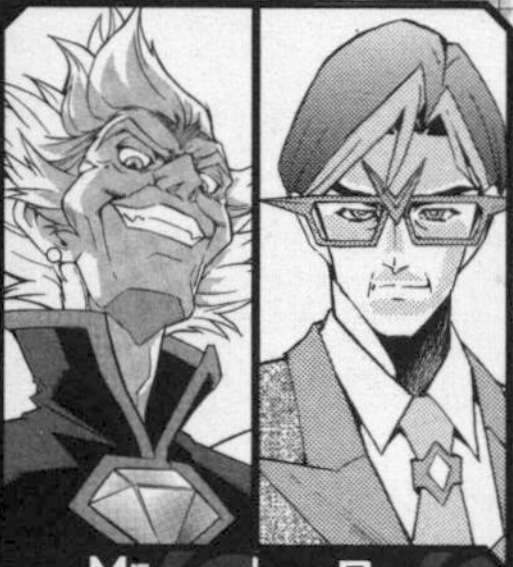

Mr. Heartland | Dr. Faker

These two villains are collecting Numbers to destroy the Astral world.

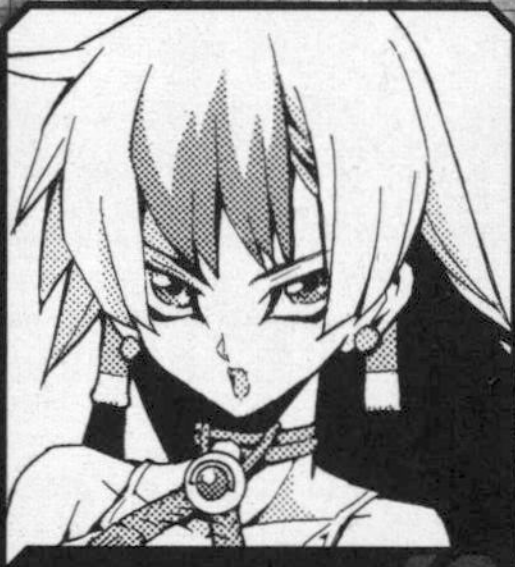

Luna

She is trying to destroy the Numbers cards along with Ryoga.

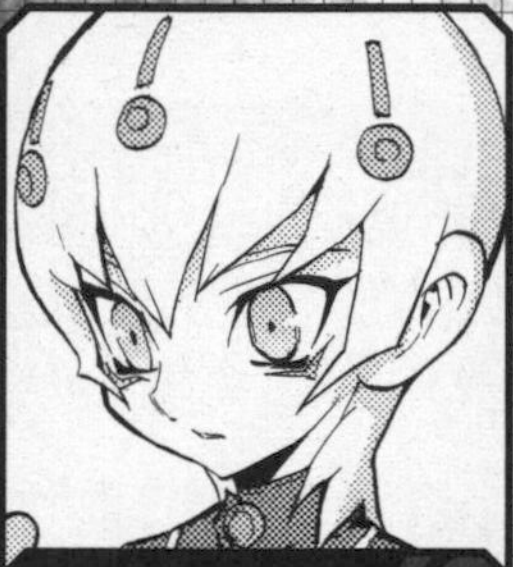

Haruto

He possesses the power to destroy the Astral world.

Previously...

Yuma Tsukumo is crazy about dueling. One day, during a duel, the charm his parents had left him—"the Emperor's Key"—triggered an encounter with a strange being who called himself Astral. Astral was a genius duelist, but his memories had turned into special cards called "Numbers" and were lost. Yuma began working with Astral to find them!

Standing in their way are Dr. Faker, who's trying to use the power of the Numbers cards to destroy the Astral World, and Kaito, who's hunting the Numbers to help his little brother! Ryoga and Luna are also working to wipe out the Numbers. Meanwhile, Yagumo joins forces with Dr. Faker and declares war on Yuma and friends! The Numbers War begins.

Yuma's power of believing in people saves Kaito and Ryoga, and a bond begins to form between them. Just then, Yagumo takes Haruto hostage and forces Kaito to fight on his side. Yagumo lures Yuma to a stadium, where Yuma and Kaito must face each other as enemies!!

Yu-Gi-Oh! ZEXAL

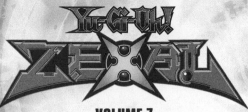

VOLUME 7
Just One Hope!!

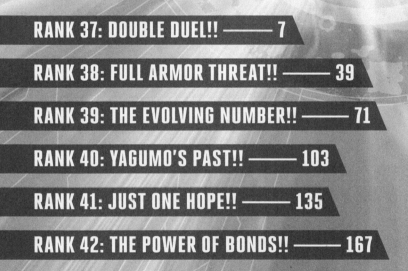

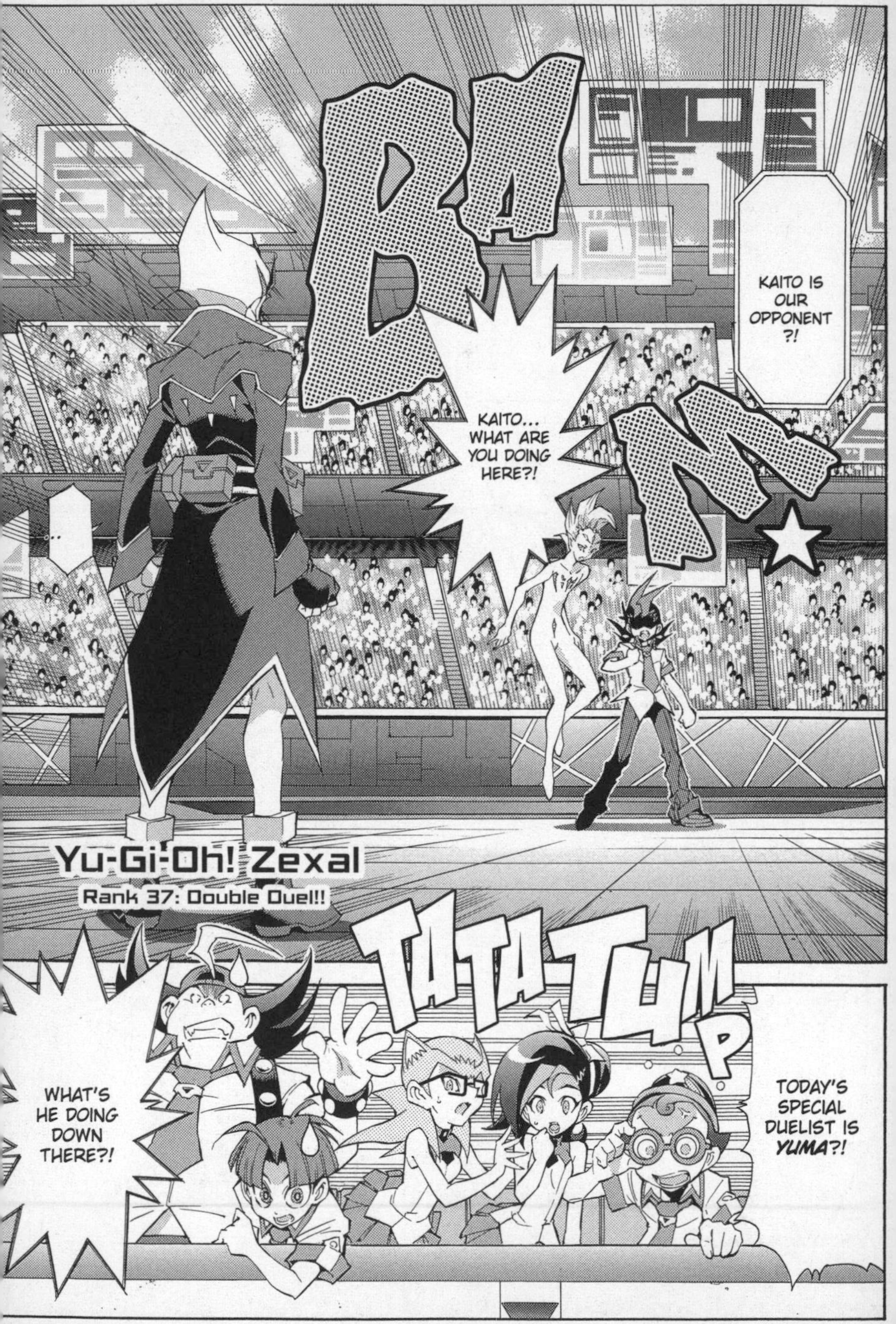
KAITO IS OUR OPPONENT?!
BAM★
KAITO... WHAT ARE YOU DOING HERE?!
...
Yu-Gi-Oh! Zexal
Rank 37: Double Duel!!
TODAY'S SPECIAL DUELIST IS *YUMA*?!
TATATUMP
WHAT'S HE DOING DOWN THERE?!

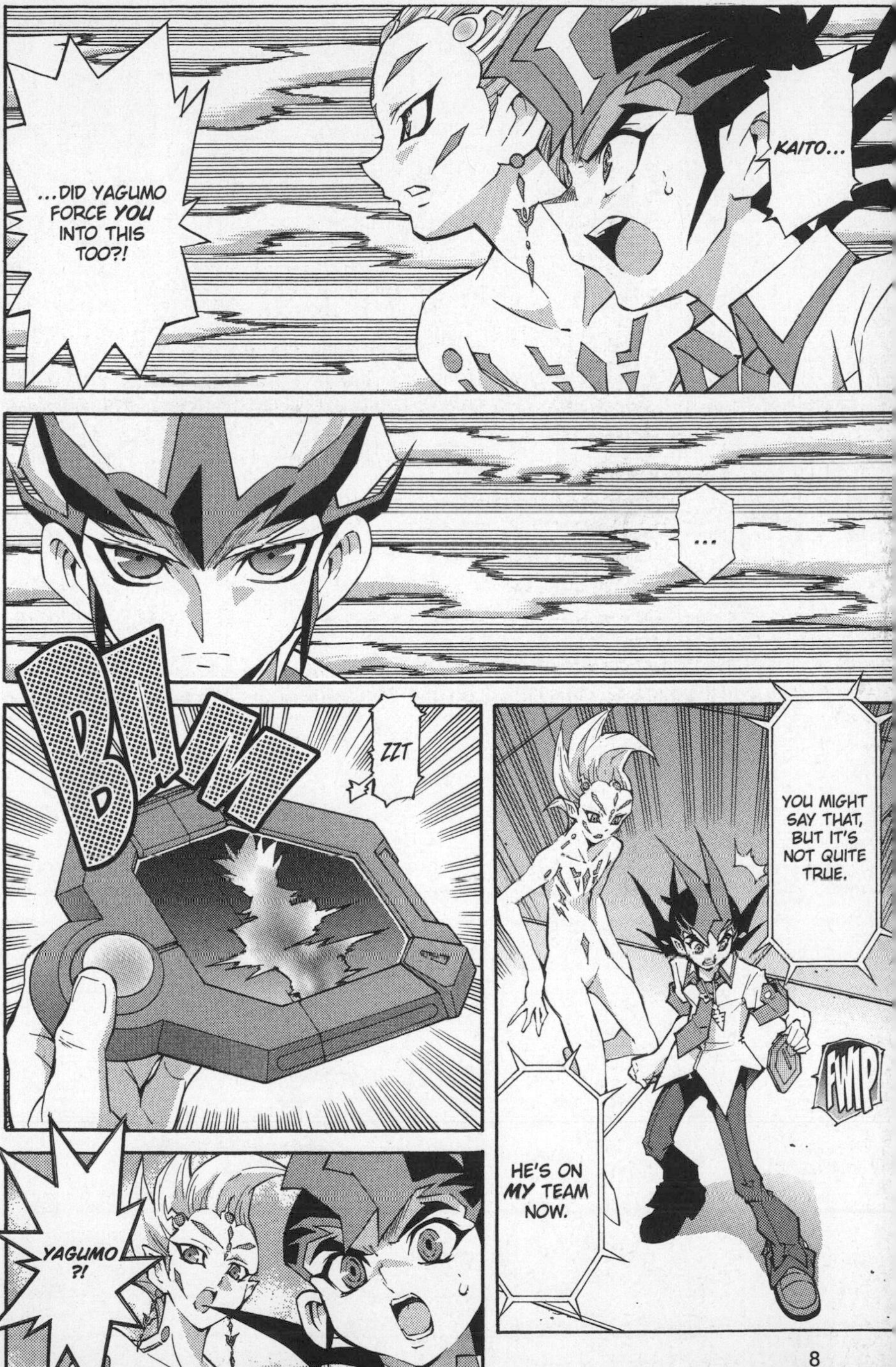
KAITO...
...DID YAGUMO FORCE YOU INTO THIS TOO?!
...
YOU MIGHT SAY THAT, BUT IT'S NOT QUITE TRUE.
HE'S ON MY TEAM NOW.
FWIP
BAM
ZZT
YAGUMO?!

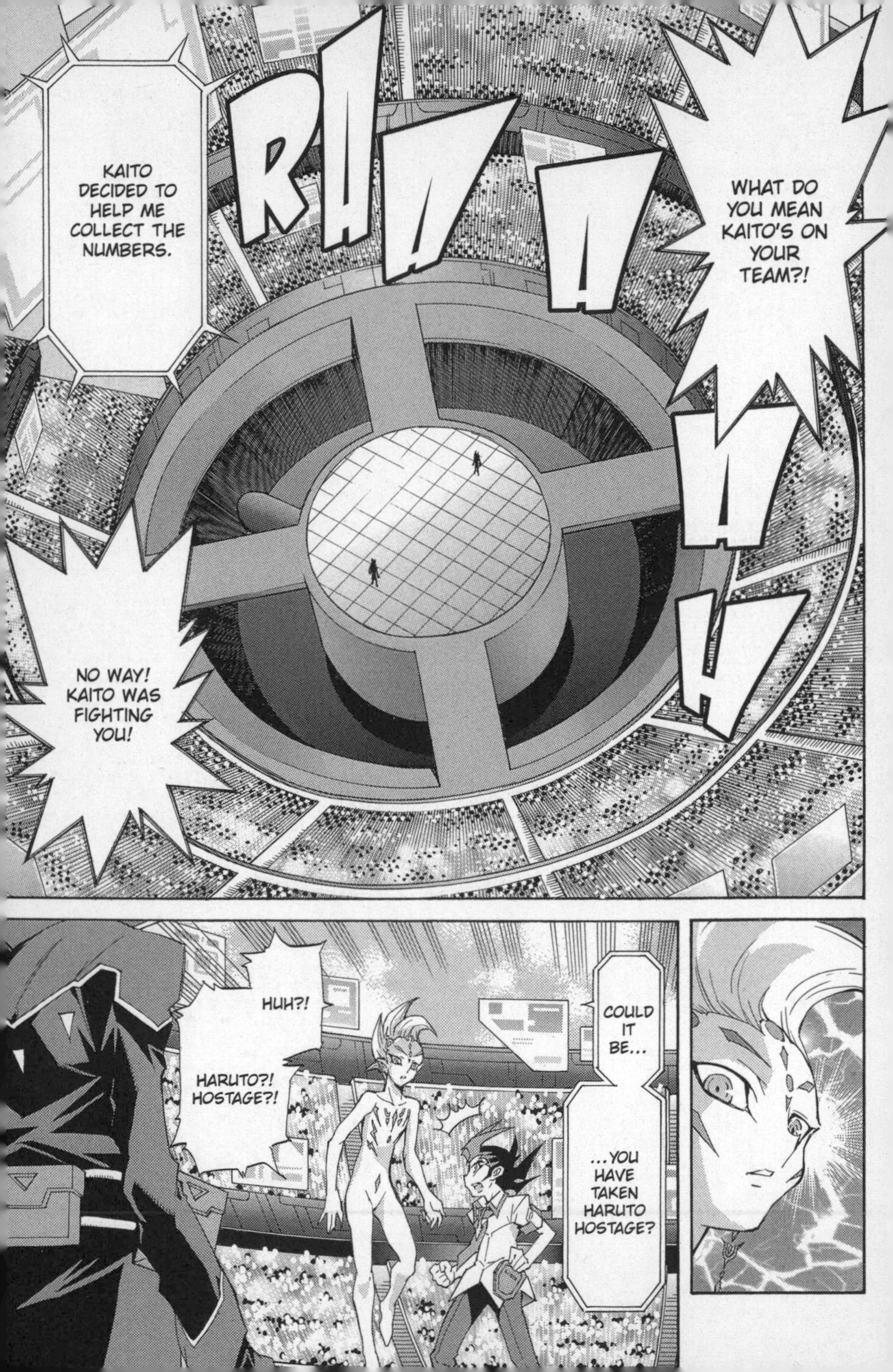
WHAT DO YOU MEAN KAITO'S ON YOUR TEAM?!
KAITO DECIDED TO HELP ME COLLECT THE NUMBERS.
NO WAY! KAITO WAS FIGHTING YOU!
COULD IT BE...
...YOU HAVE TAKEN HARUTO HOSTAGE?
HUH?!
HARUTO?! HOSTAGE?!

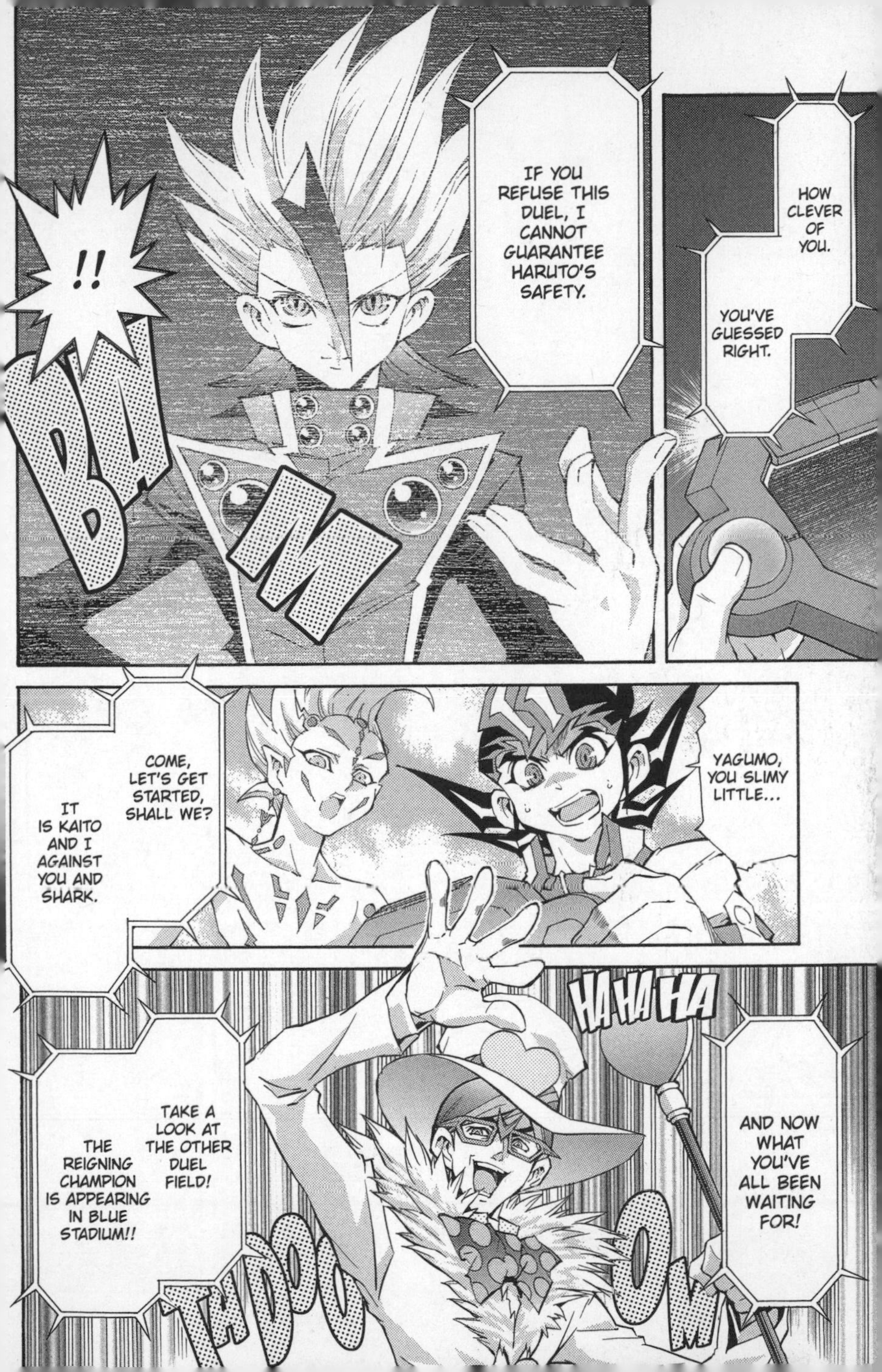
HOW CLEVER OF YOU.
YOU'VE GUESSED RIGHT.
IF YOU REFUSE THIS DUEL, I CANNOT GUARANTEE HARUTO'S SAFETY.
!!
BAM
YAGUMO, YOU SLIMY LITTLE...
COME, LET'S GET STARTED, SHALL WE?
IT IS KAITO AND I AGAINST YOU AND SHARK.
HA HA HA
AND NOW WHAT YOU'VE ALL BEEN WAITING FOR!
TAKE A LOOK AT THE OTHER DUEL FIELD!
THE REIGNING CHAMPION IS APPEARING IN BLUE STADIUM!!
THDOOOM

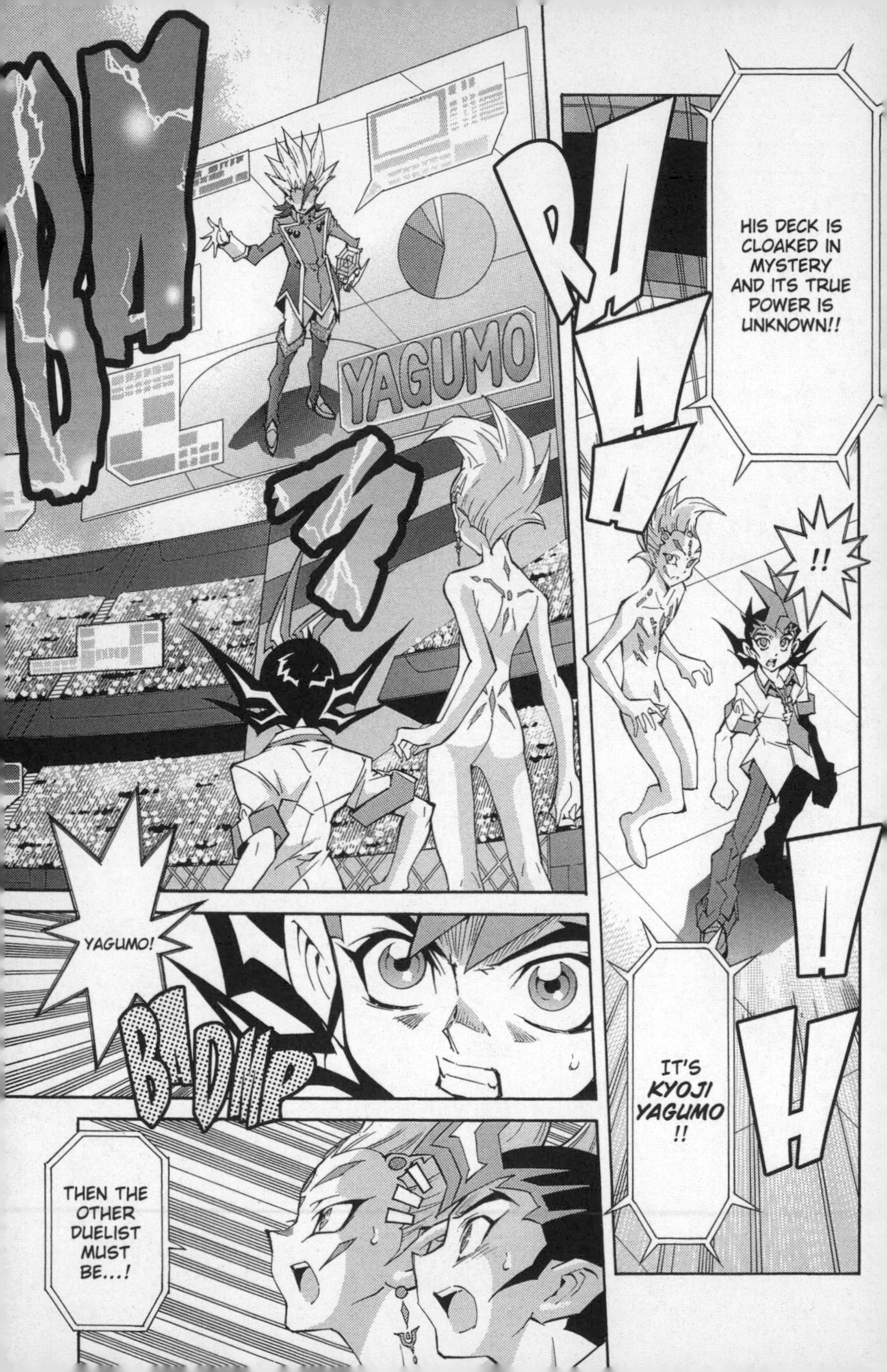
BAM
YAGUMO
YAGUMO!
BA-DMP
THEN THE OTHER DUELIST MUST BE...!
RAAAAH
HIS DECK IS CLOAKED IN MYSTERY AND ITS TRUE POWER IS UNKNOWN!!
!!
IT'S *KYOJI YAGUMO*!!

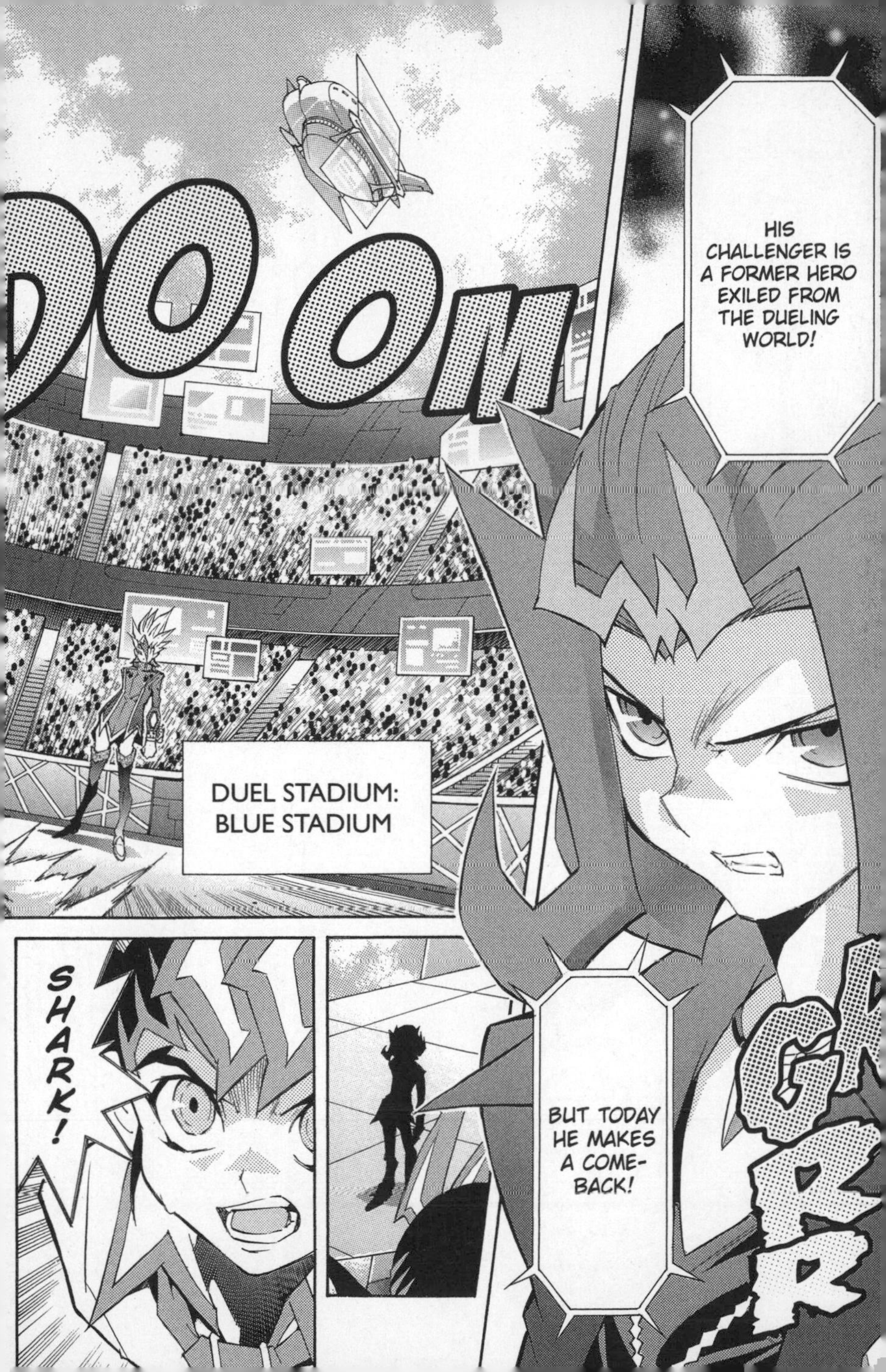
HIS CHALLENGER IS A FORMER HERO EXILED FROM THE DUELING WORLD!
BUT TODAY HE MAKES A COME-BACK!
GRR
DOOM
DUEL STADIUM: BLUE STADIUM
SHARK!

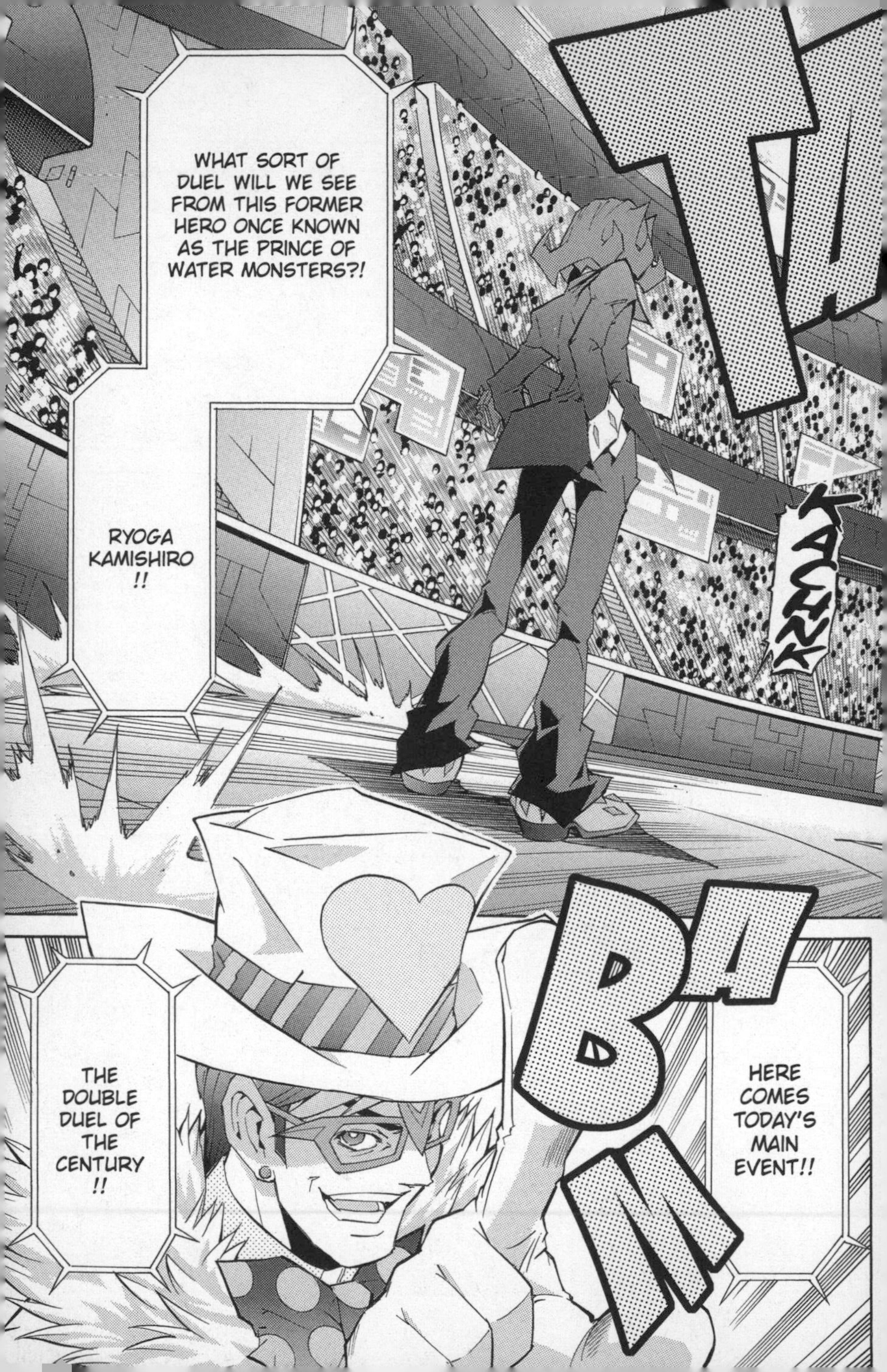
KACHNK
WHAT SORT OF DUEL WILL WE SEE FROM THIS FORMER HERO ONCE KNOWN AS THE PRINCE OF WATER MONSTERS?!
RYOGA KAMISHIRO !!
BAM
HERE COMES TODAY'S MAIN EVENT!!
THE DOUBLE DUEL OF THE CENTURY !!

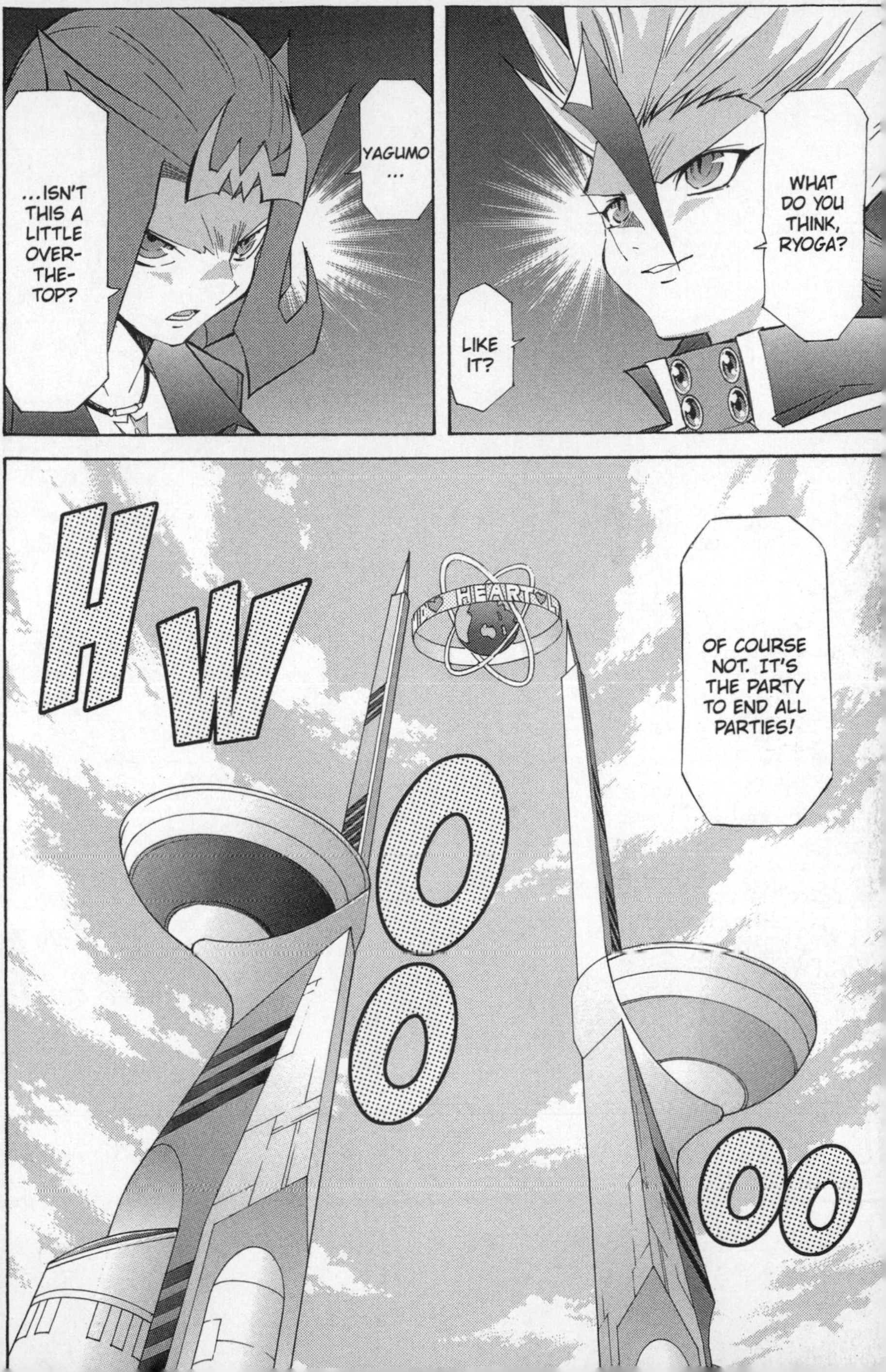
WHAT DO YOU THINK, RYOGA?
LIKE IT?
YAGUMO...
...ISN'T THIS A LITTLE OVER-THE-TOP?
OF COURSE NOT. IT'S THE PARTY TO END ALL PARTIES!
HEART
HWOOOOO

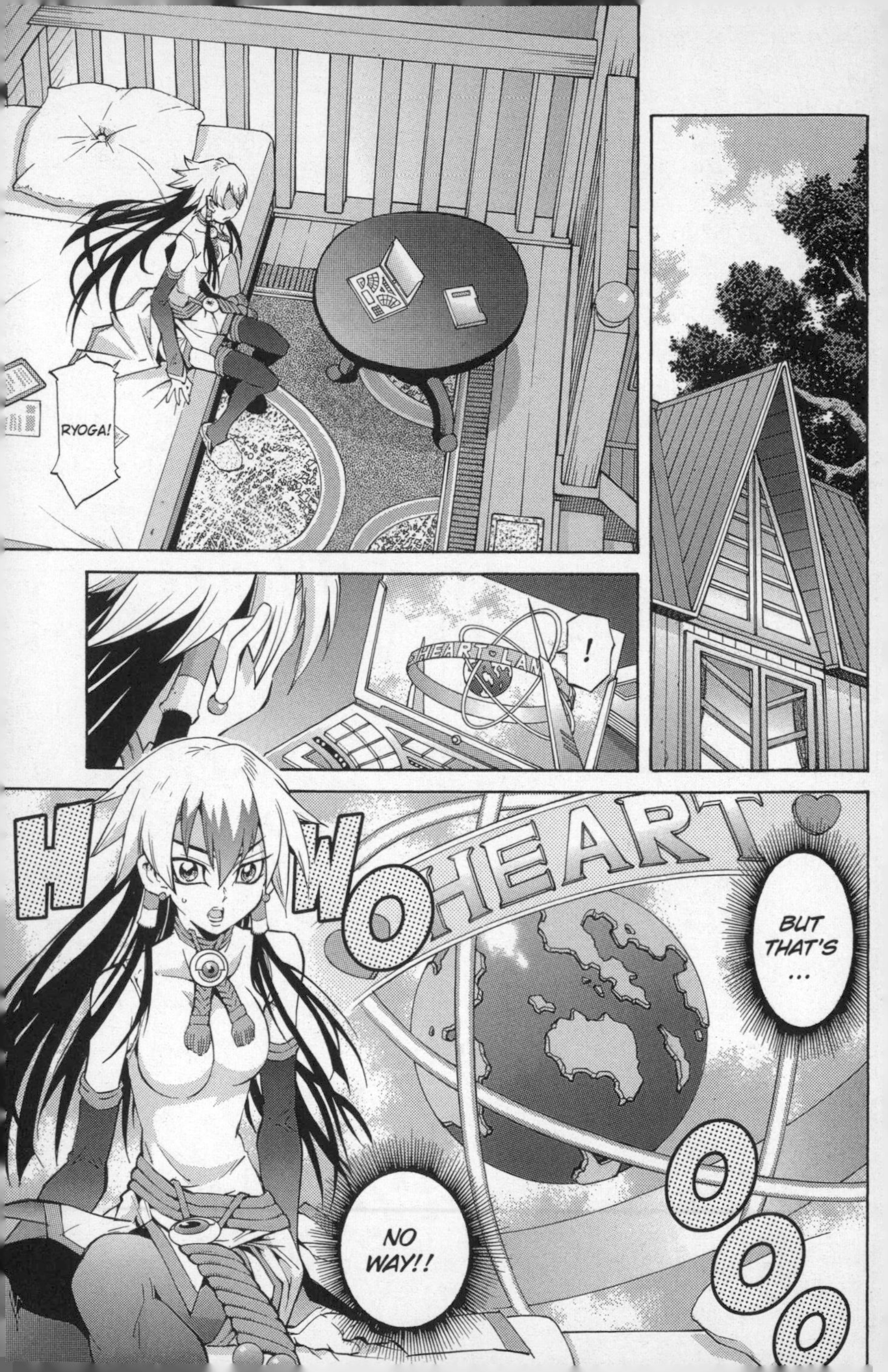
RYOGA!
!
HEART
BUT THAT'S ...
NO WAY!!
HWOOOOO

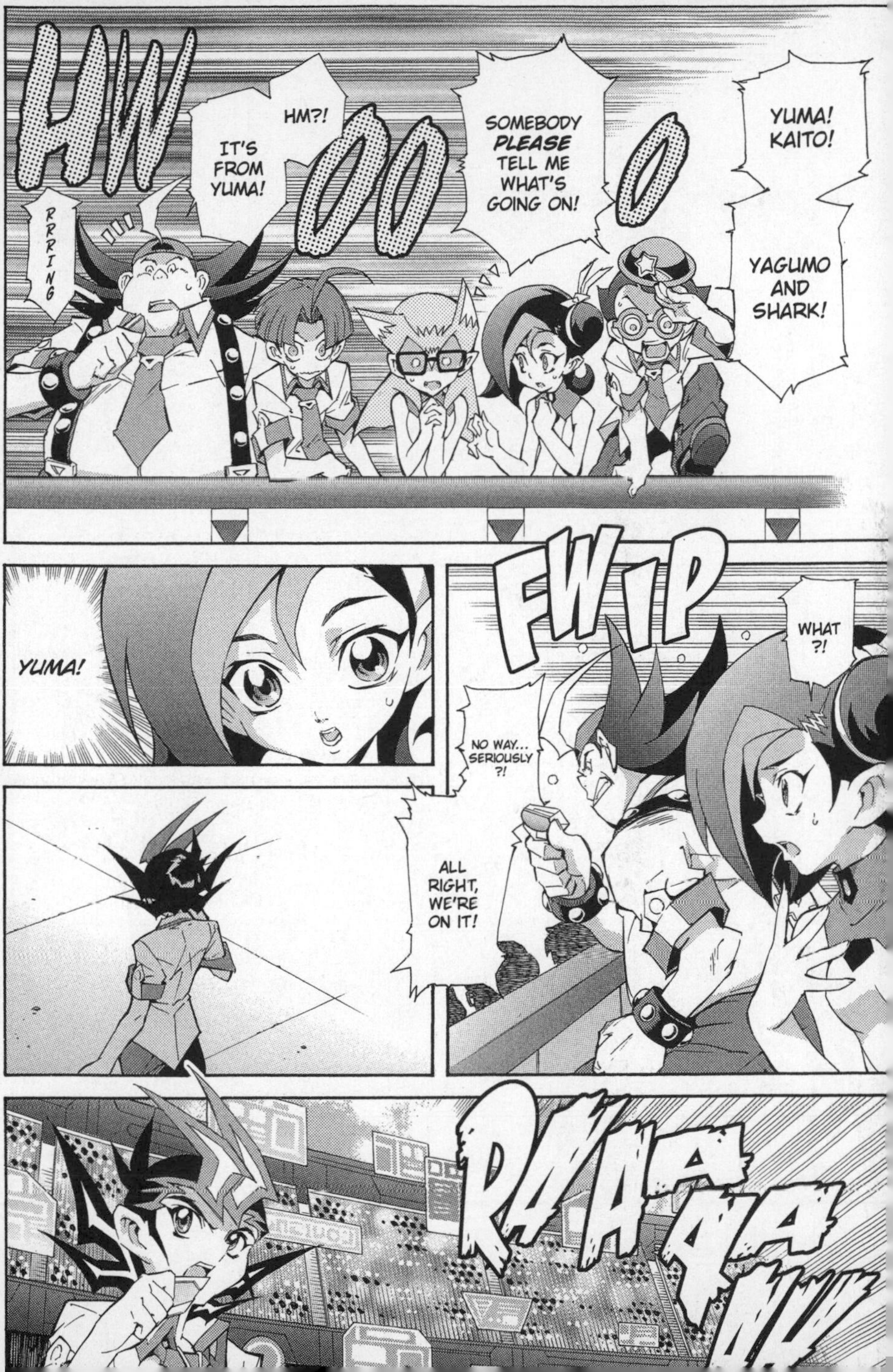
YUMA! KAITO!
YAGUMO AND SHARK!
SOMEBODY PLEASE TELL ME WHAT'S GOING ON!
HM?!
IT'S FROM YUMA!
RRRING
HWOOOO
FWIP
WHAT?!
NO WAY... SERIOUSLY?!
ALL RIGHT, WE'RE ON IT!
YUMA!
RAAAAH

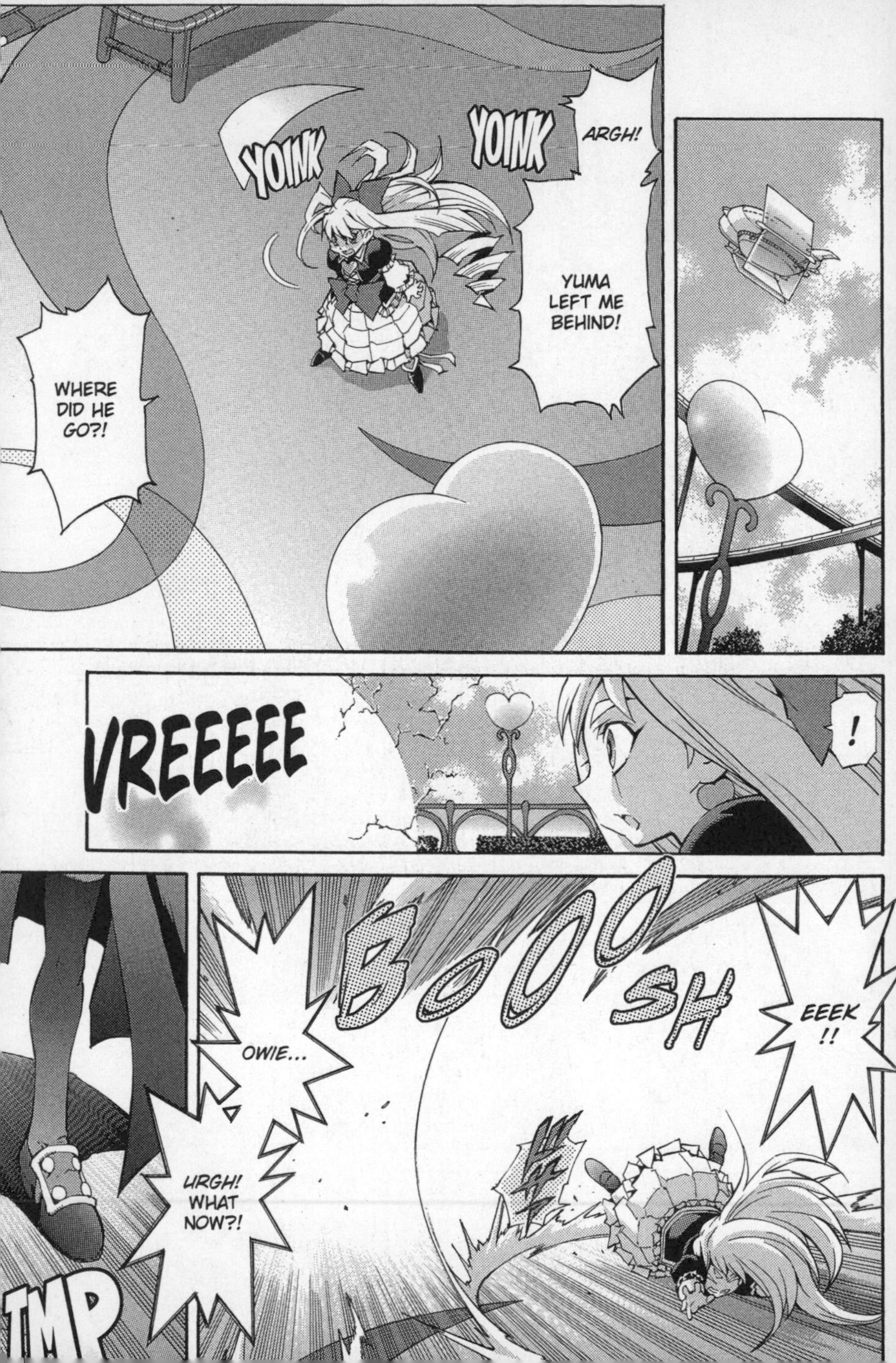
ARGH!
YOINK
YOINK
YUMA LEFT ME BEHIND!
WHERE DID HE GO?!
!
VREEEEE
BOOOOSH
EEEK !!
OWIE...
URGH! WHAT NOW?!
TMP

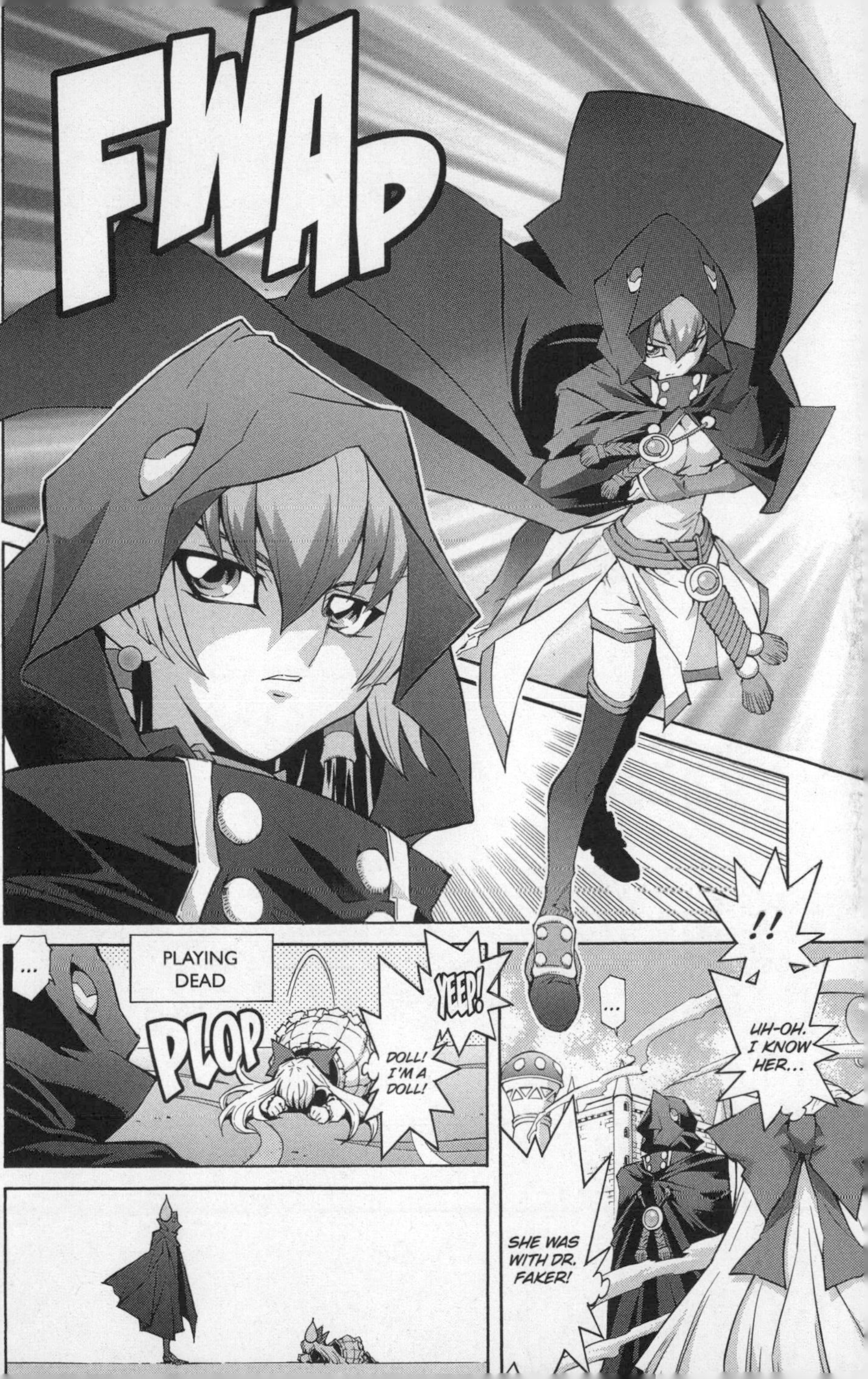
FWAP
!!
...
UH-OH. I KNOW HER...
SHE WAS WITH DR. FAKER!
YEEP!
PLAYING DEAD
...
PLOP
DOLL! I'M A DOLL!

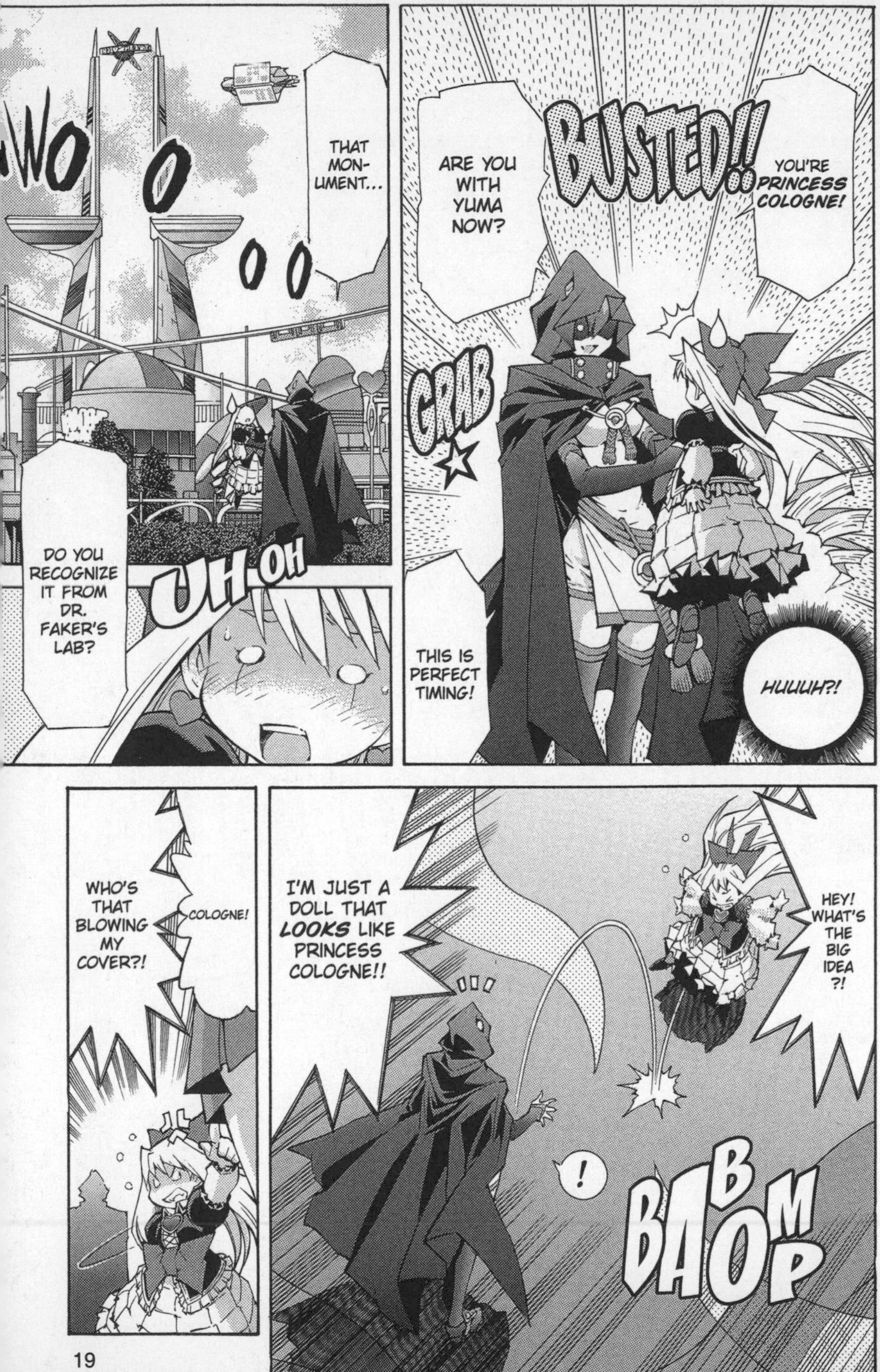
BUSTED!!
YOU'RE PRINCESS COLOGNE!
ARE YOU WITH YUMA NOW?
GRAB
THIS IS PERFECT TIMING!
HUUUH?!
WOOOOO
THAT MONUMENT...
DO YOU RECOGNIZE IT FROM DR. FAKER'S LAB?
UH OH
HEY! WHAT'S THE BIG IDEA?!
I'M JUST A DOLL THAT LOOKS LIKE PRINCESS COLOGNE!!
!
BABOMP
COLOGNE!
WHO'S THAT BLOWING MY COVER?!

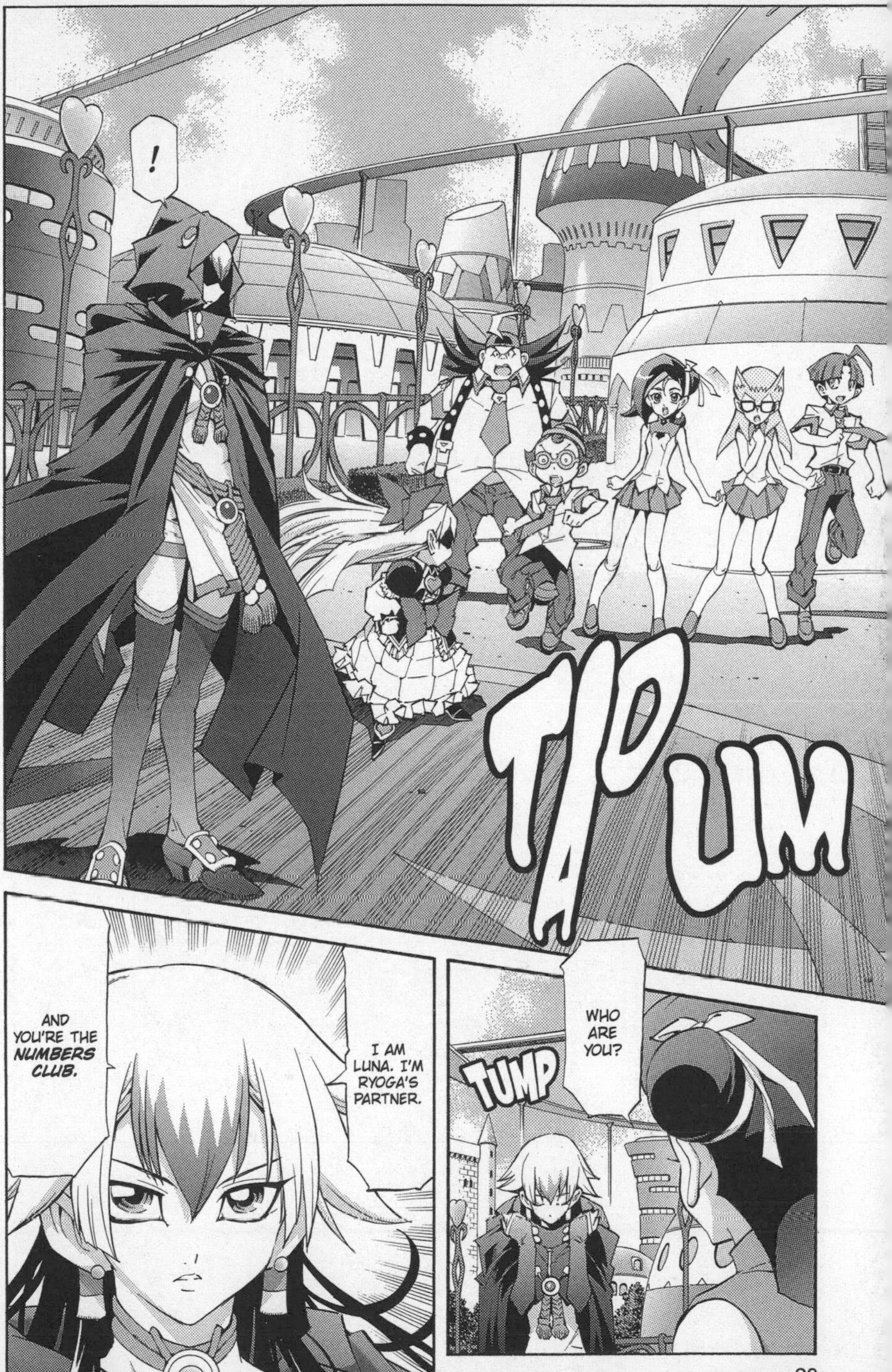
!
TADUM
WHO ARE YOU?
TUMP
I AM LUNA. I'M RYOGA'S PARTNER.
AND YOU'RE THE **NUMBERS CLUB**.

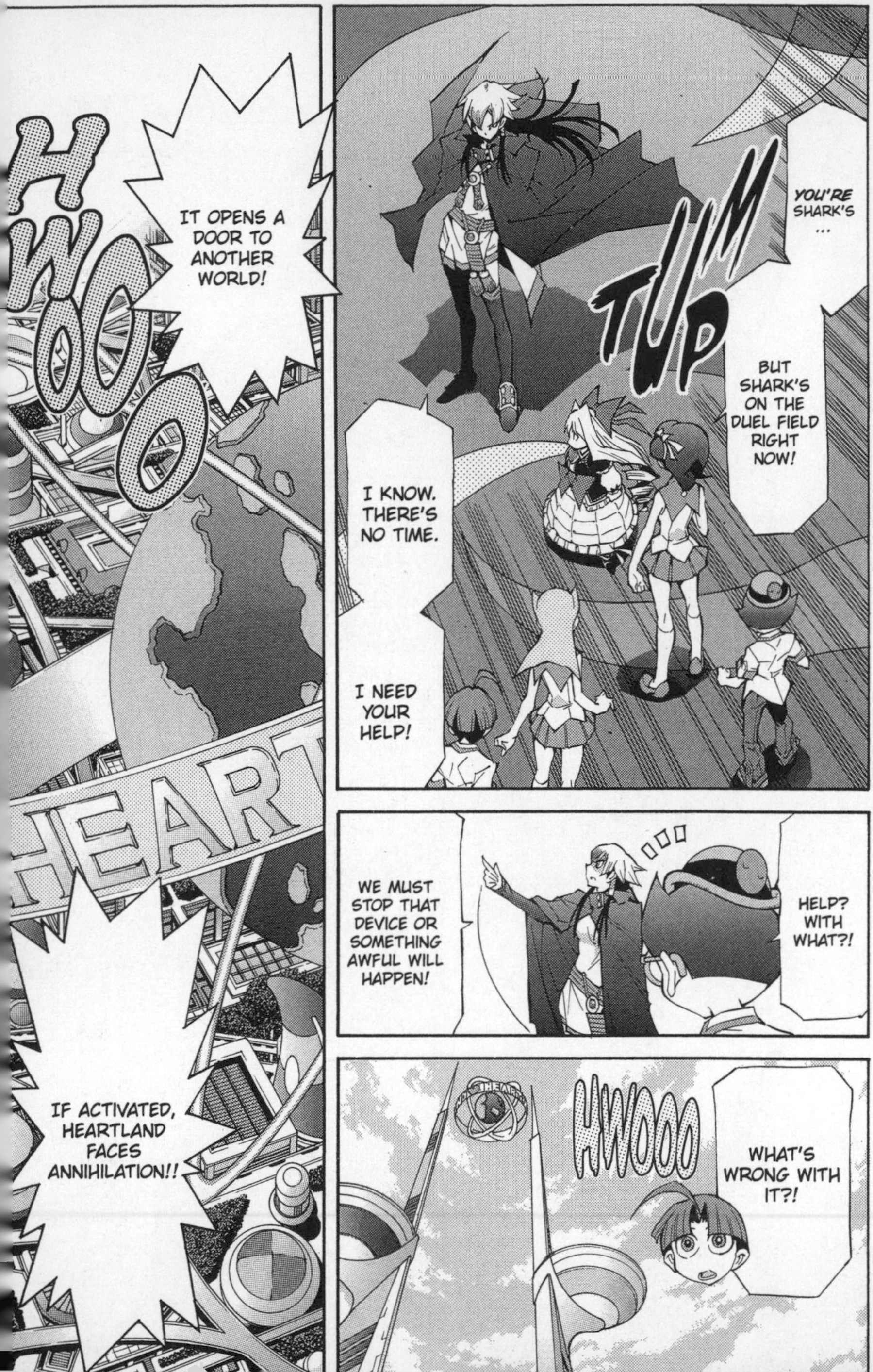
YOU'RE SHARK'S ...
TUMP
BUT SHARK'S ON THE DUEL FIELD RIGHT NOW!
I KNOW. THERE'S NO TIME.
I NEED YOUR HELP!
HELP? WITH WHAT?!
WE MUST STOP THAT DEVICE OR SOMETHING AWFUL WILL HAPPEN!
WHAT'S WRONG WITH IT?!
HWOOO
HWOOO
IT OPENS A DOOR TO ANOTHER WORLD!
HEART
IF ACTIVATED, HEARTLAND FACES ANNIHILATION!!

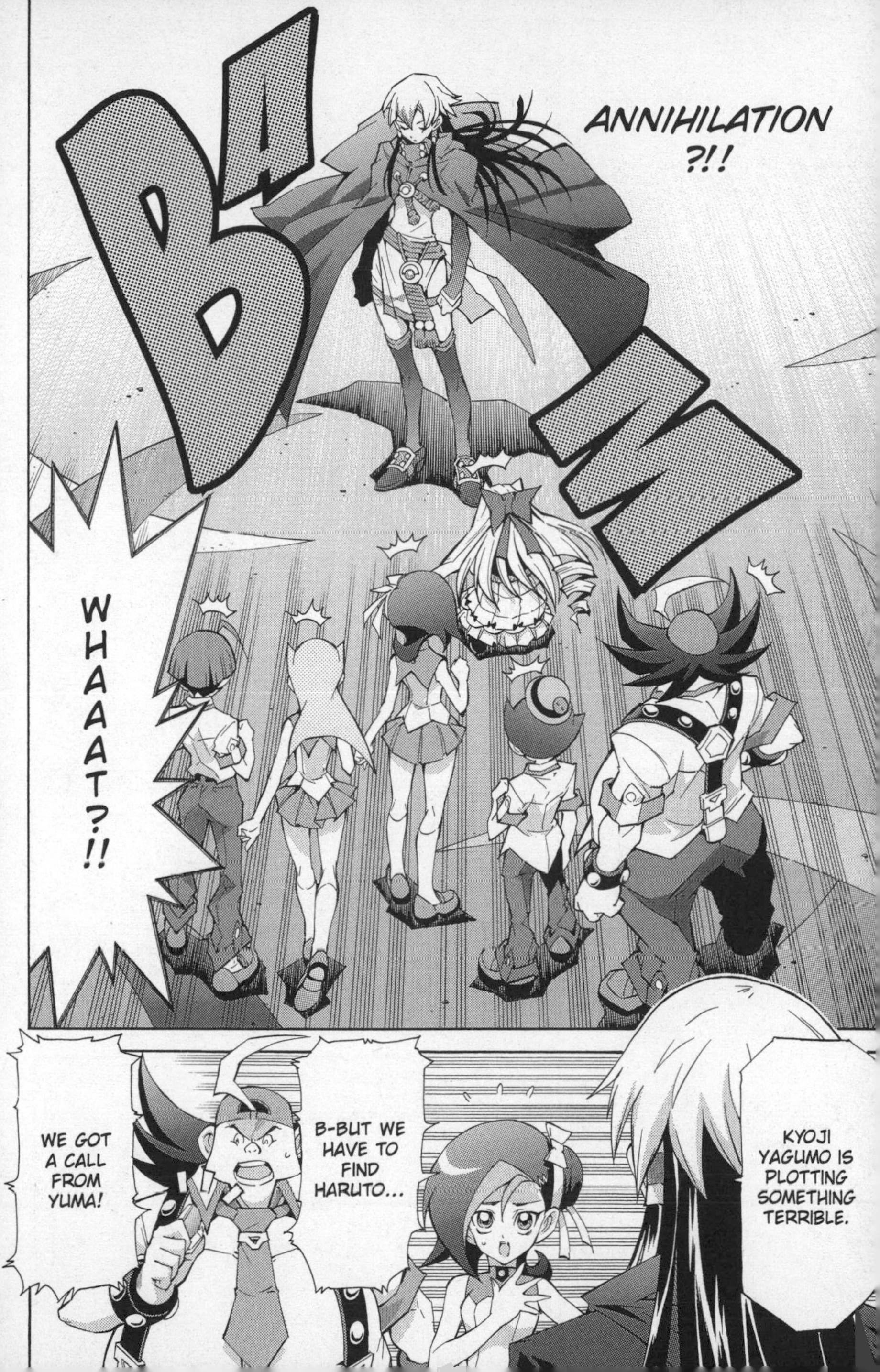
ANNIHILATION ?!!
BAM
WHAAAAT?!!
KYOJI YAGUMO IS PLOTTING SOMETHING TERRIBLE.
B-BUT WE HAVE TO FIND HARUTO...
WE GOT A CALL FROM YUMA!

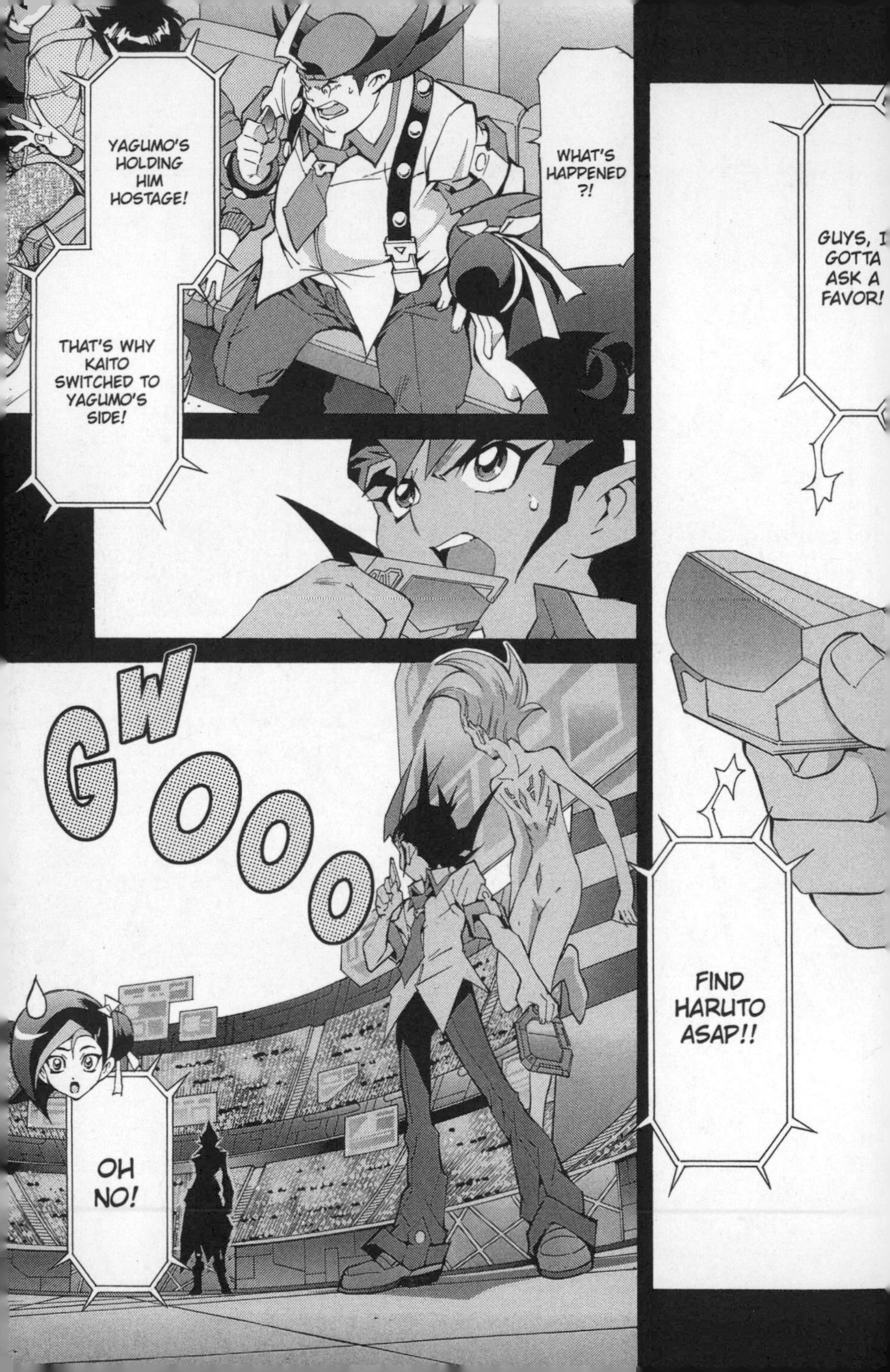

GUYS, I GOTTA ASK A FAVOR!
FIND HARUTO ASAP!!
WHAT'S HAPPENED?!
YAGUMO'S HOLDING HIM HOSTAGE!
THAT'S WHY KAITO SWITCHED TO YAGUMO'S SIDE!
GWOOOO
OH NO!

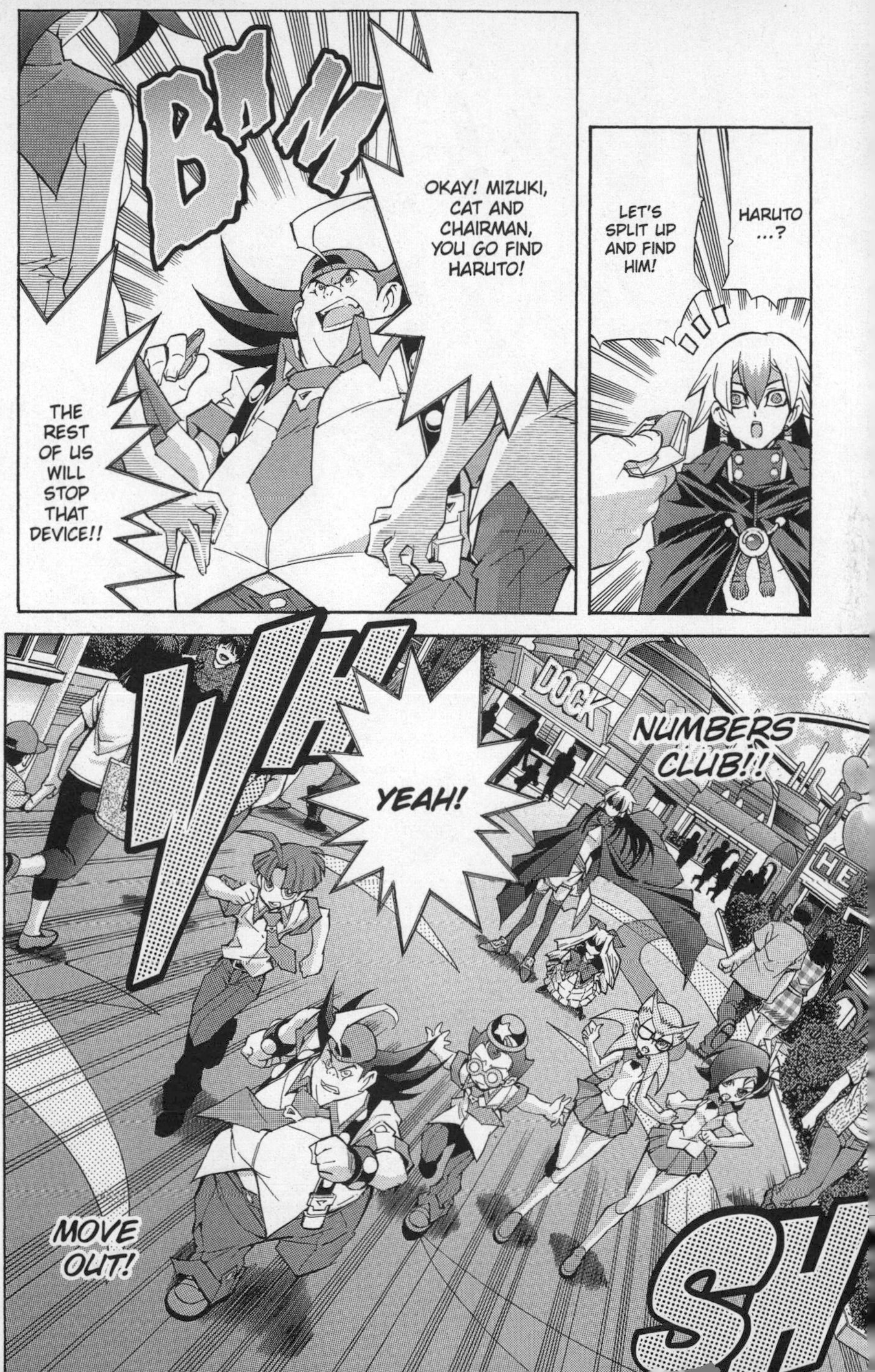
HARUTO ...?
LET'S SPLIT UP AND FIND HIM!
BAM
OKAY! MIZUKI, CAT AND CHAIRMAN, YOU GO FIND HARUTO!
THE REST OF US WILL STOP THAT DEVICE!!
DOCK
NUMBERS CLUB!!
YEAH!
MOVE OUT!

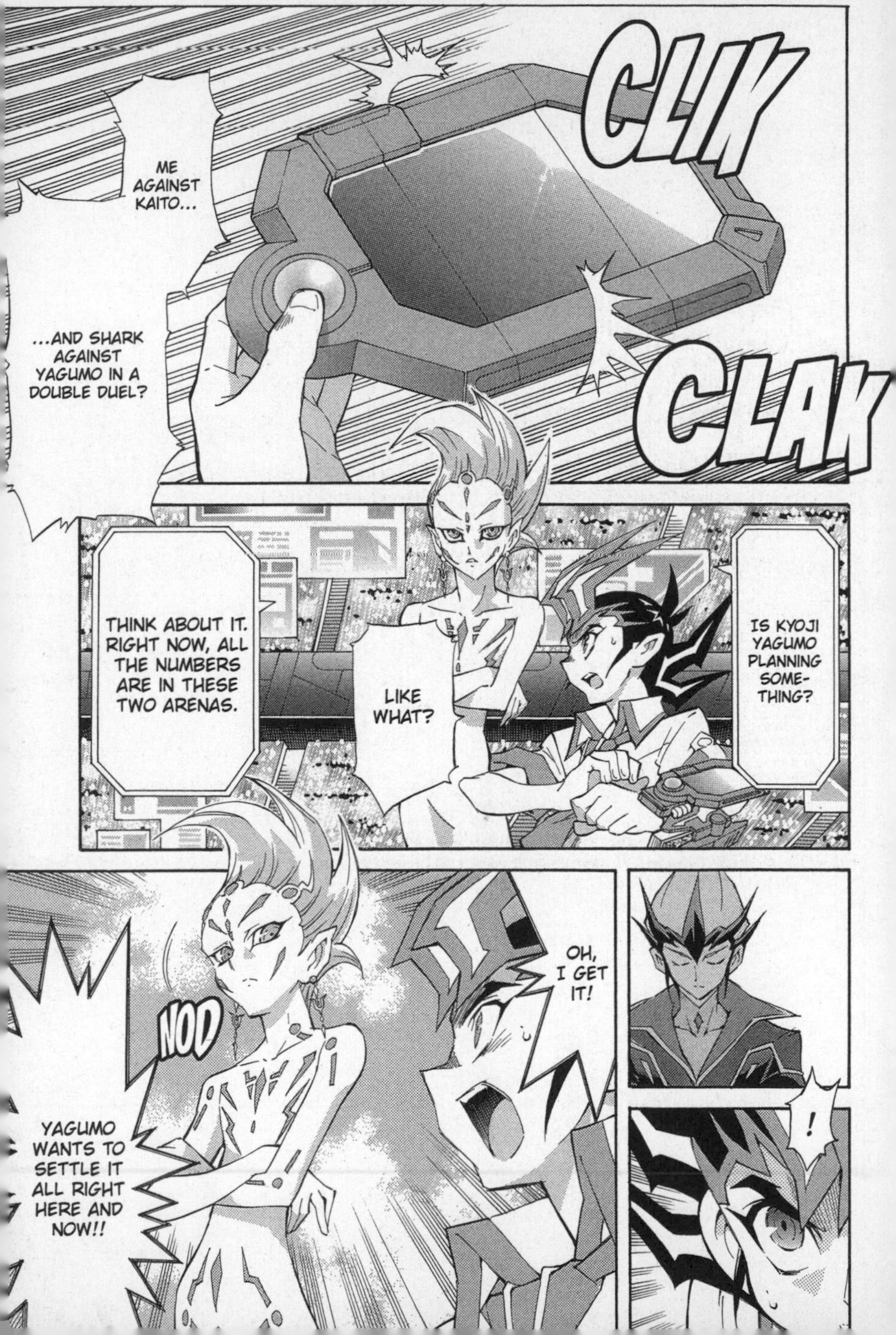
CLIK
CLAK
ME AGAINST KAITO...
...AND SHARK AGAINST YAGUMO IN A DOUBLE DUEL?
IS KYOJI YAGUMO PLANNING SOME-THING?
LIKE WHAT?
THINK ABOUT IT. RIGHT NOW, ALL THE NUMBERS ARE IN THESE TWO ARENAS.
!
OH, I GET IT!
NOD
YAGUMO WANTS TO SETTLE IT ALL RIGHT HERE AND NOW!!

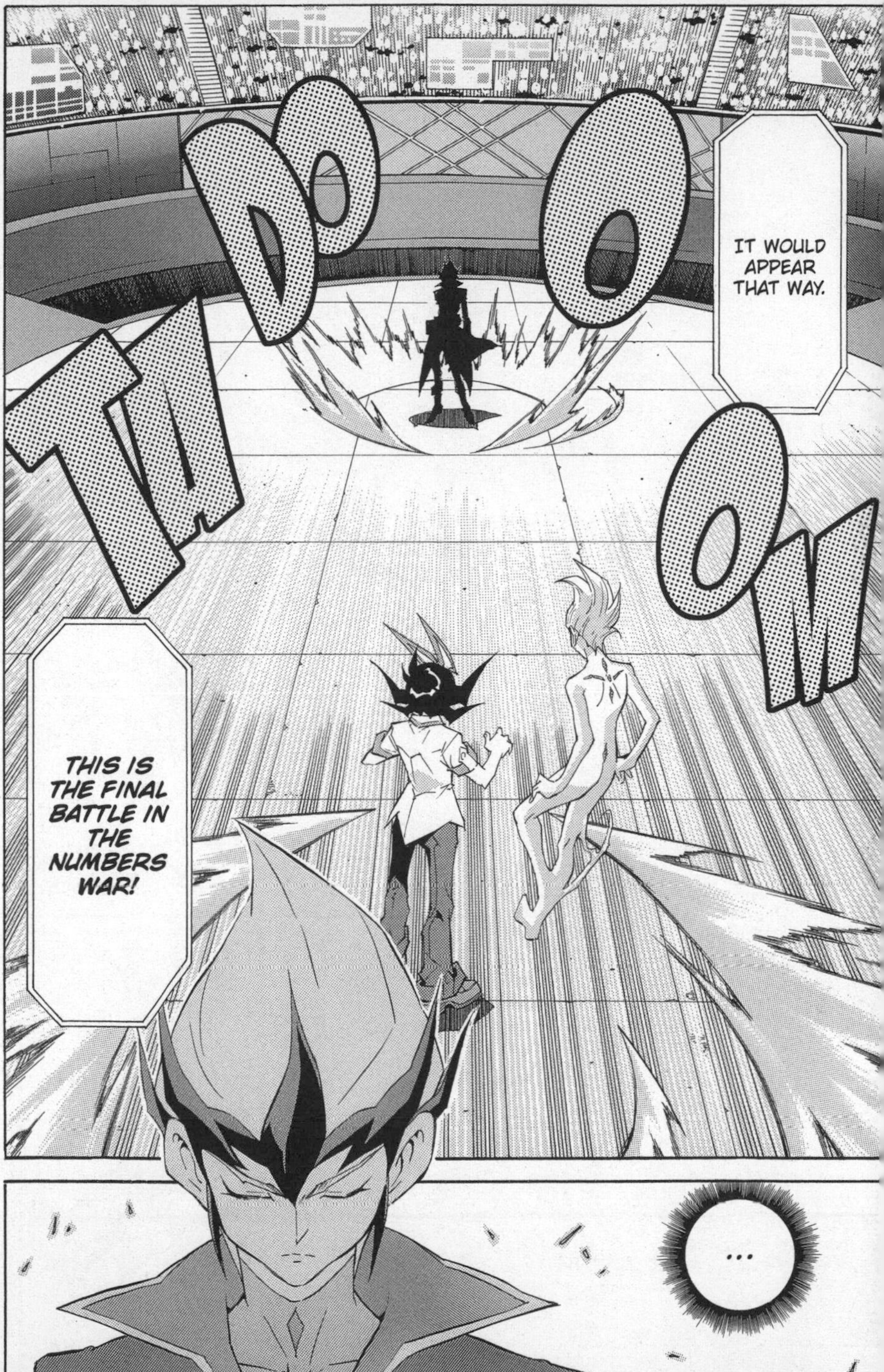
IT WOULD APPEAR THAT WAY.
TADOOOOM
THIS IS THE FINAL BATTLE IN THE NUMBERS WAR!
...

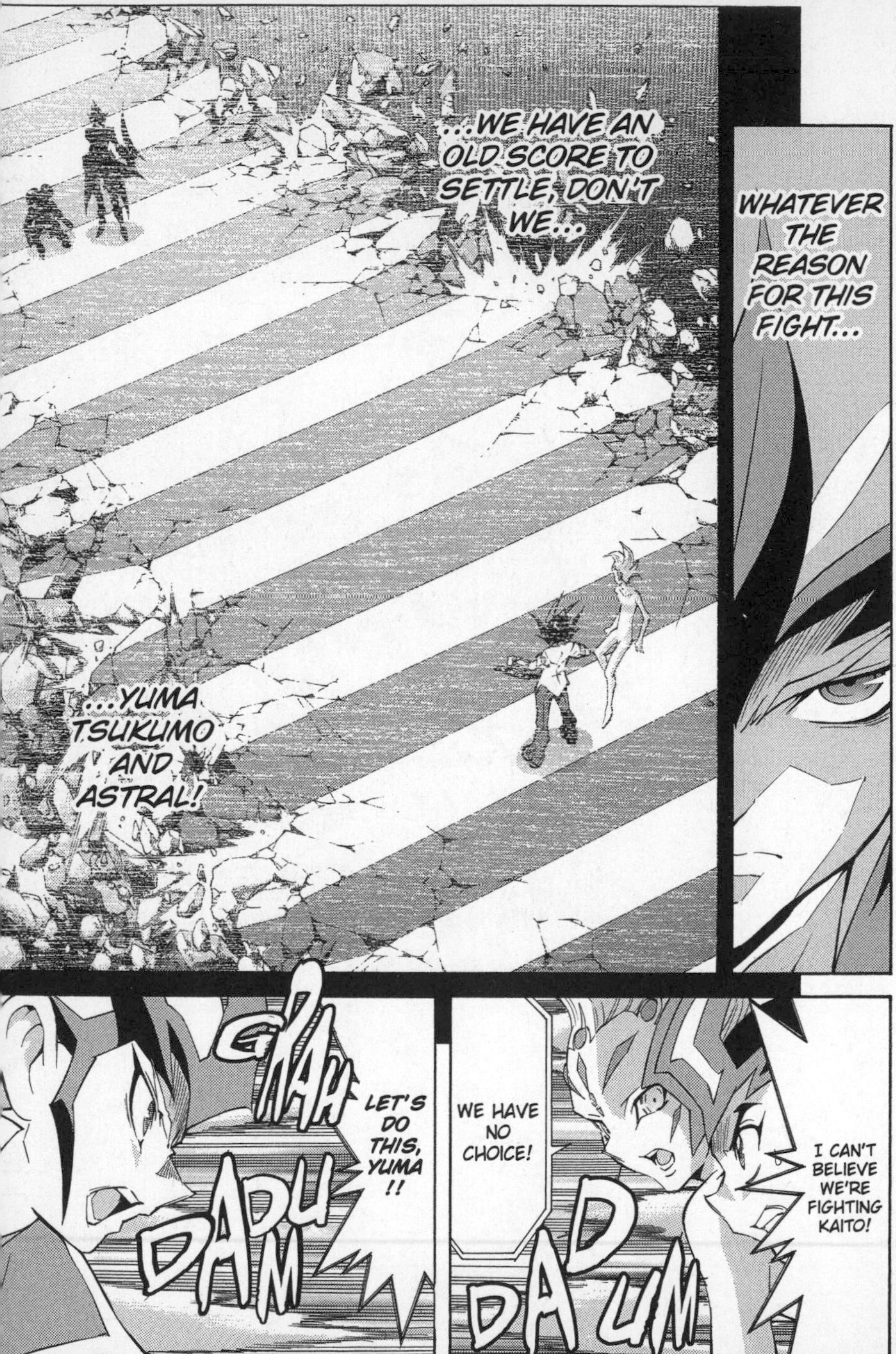
WHATEVER THE REASON FOR THIS FIGHT...
...WE HAVE AN OLD SCORE TO SETTLE, DON'T WE...
...YUMA TSUKUMO AND ASTRAL!
I CAN'T BELIEVE WE'RE FIGHTING KAITO!
WE HAVE NO CHOICE!
DADUM
LET'S DO THIS, YUMA!!
DADUM

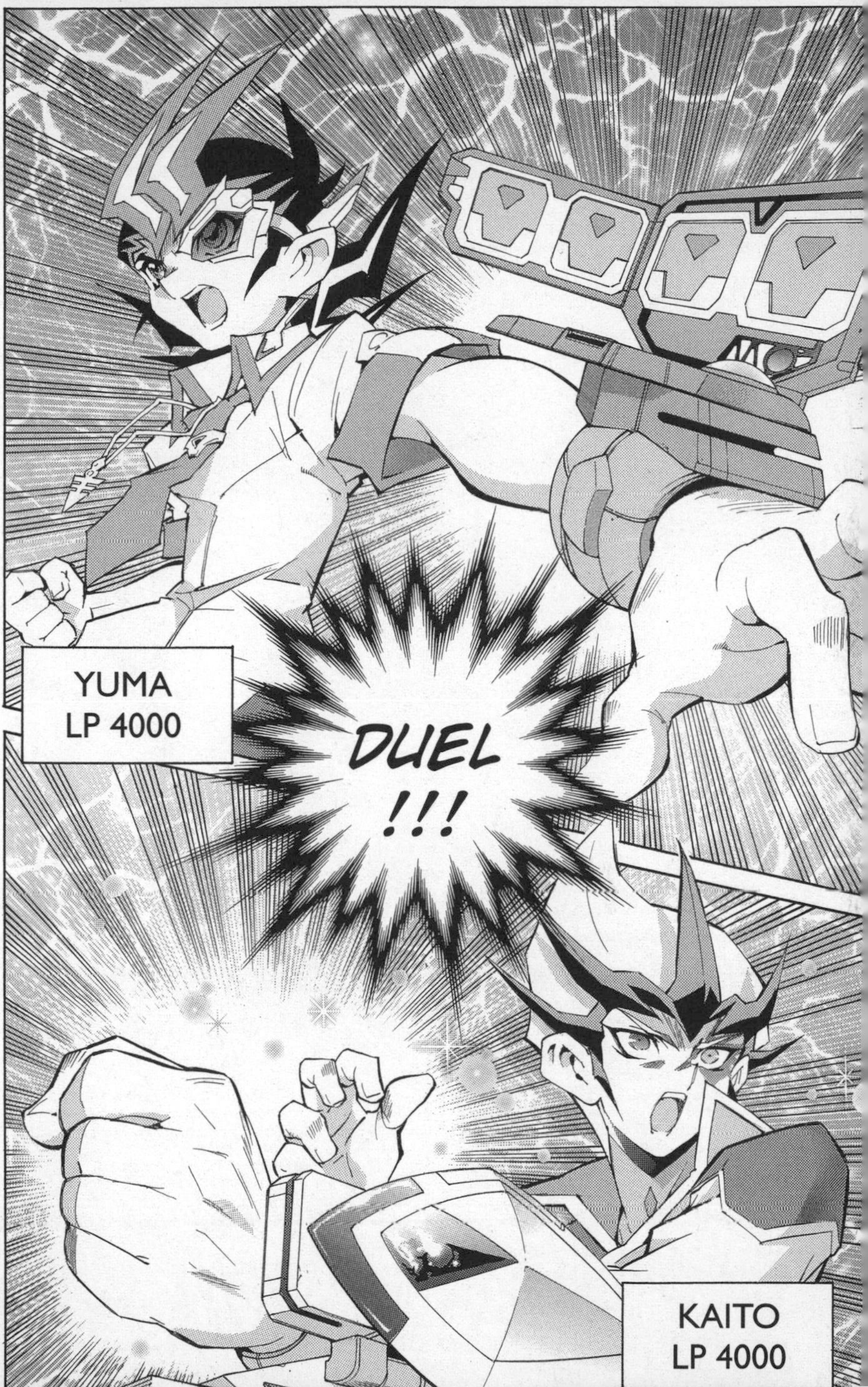
YUMA
LP 4000
DUEL !!!
KAITO
LP 4000

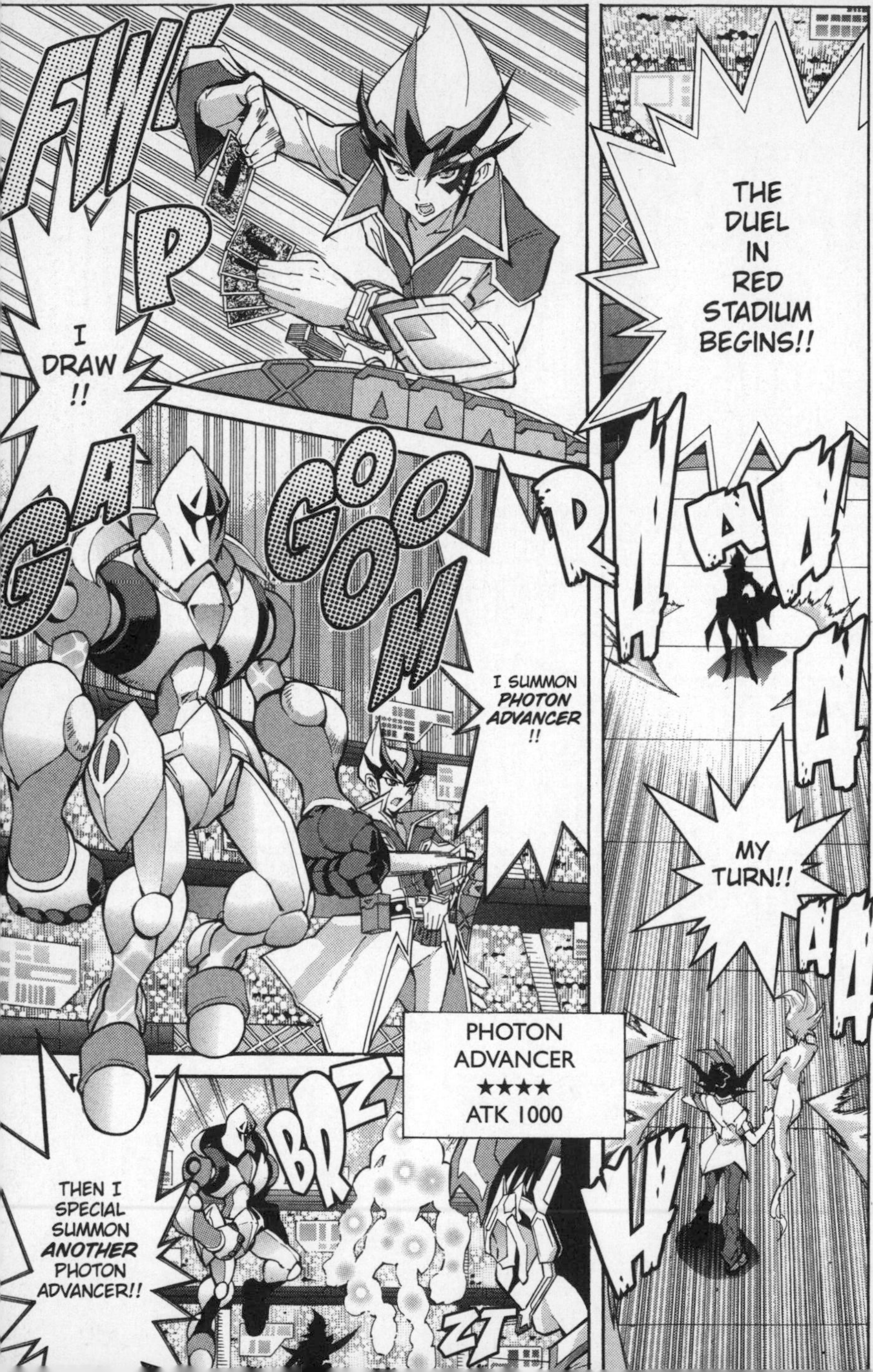
THE DUEL IN RED STADIUM BEGINS!!
MY TURN!!
FWIP
I DRAW!!
GA
GOOOOM
I SUMMON PHOTON ADVANCER!!
PHOTON ADVANCER ★★★★ ATK 1000
BRZ
THEN I SPECIAL SUMMON ANOTHER PHOTON ADVANCER!!
ZT

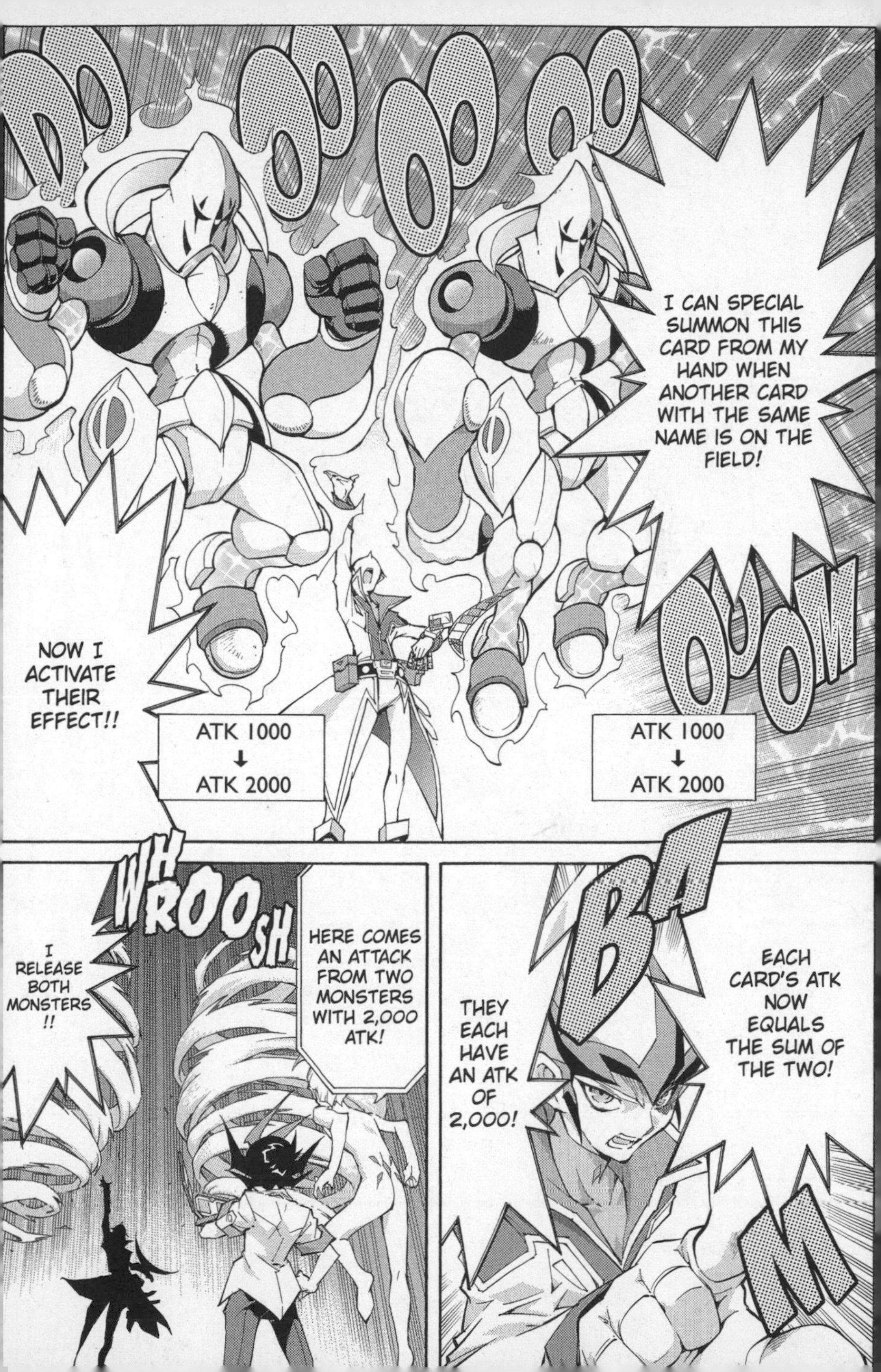
I CAN SPECIAL SUMMON THIS CARD FROM MY HAND WHEN ANOTHER CARD WITH THE SAME NAME IS ON THE FIELD!
ATK 1000 ↓ ATK 2000
NOW I ACTIVATE THEIR EFFECT!!
ATK 1000 ↓ ATK 2000
BA
EACH CARD'S ATK NOW EQUALS THE SUM OF THE TWO!
THEY EACH HAVE AN ATK OF 2,000!
M
HERE COMES AN ATTACK FROM TWO MONSTERS WITH 2,000 ATK!
WHROOSH
I RELEASE BOTH MONSTERS !!

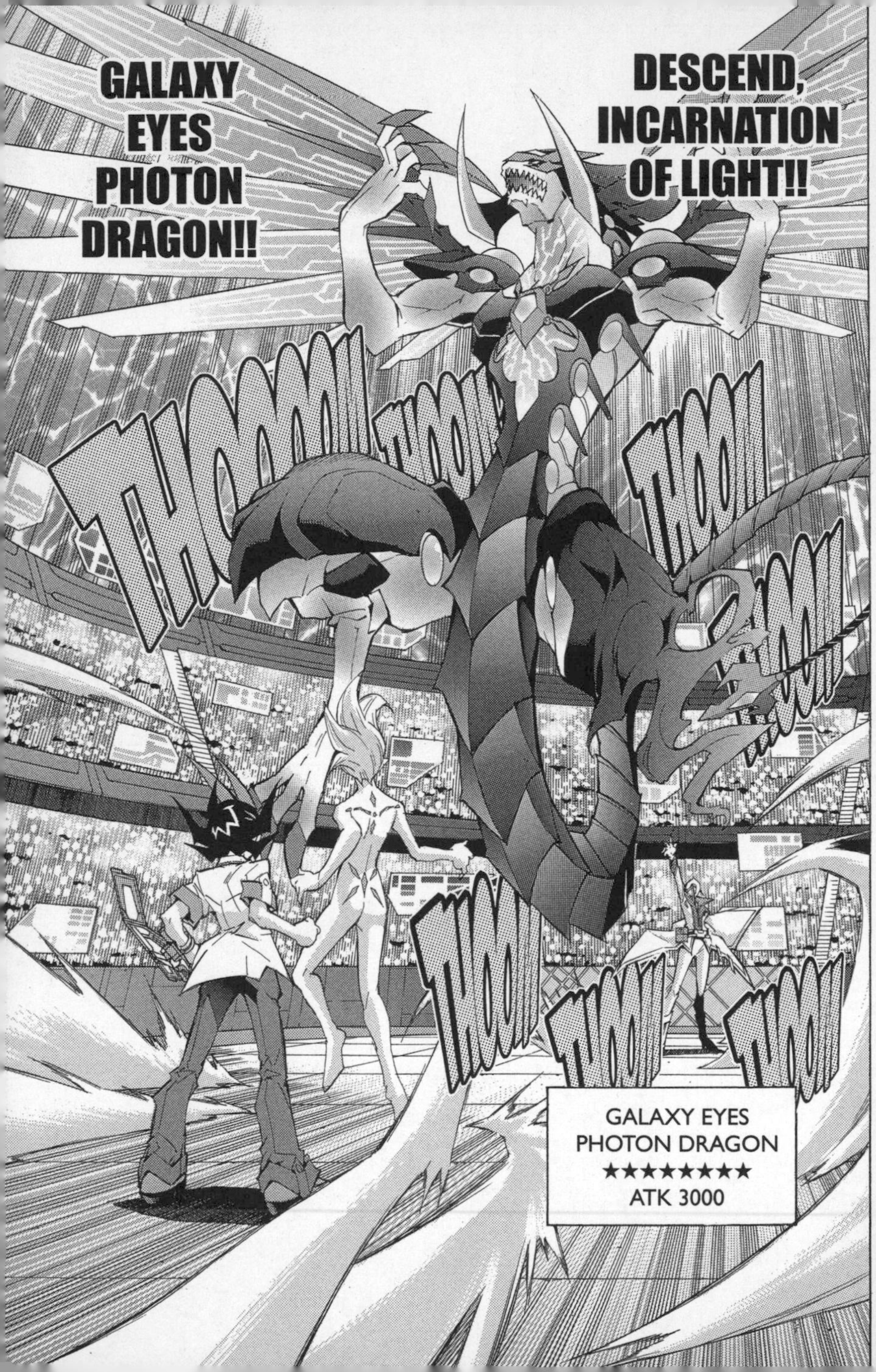
DESCEND, INCARNATION OF LIGHT!!
GALAXY EYES PHOTON DRAGON!!
THOOM!!
THOOM!!
THOOM!!
THOOM!!
THOOM!!
GALAXY EYES PHOTON DRAGON
★★★★★★★★
ATK 3000

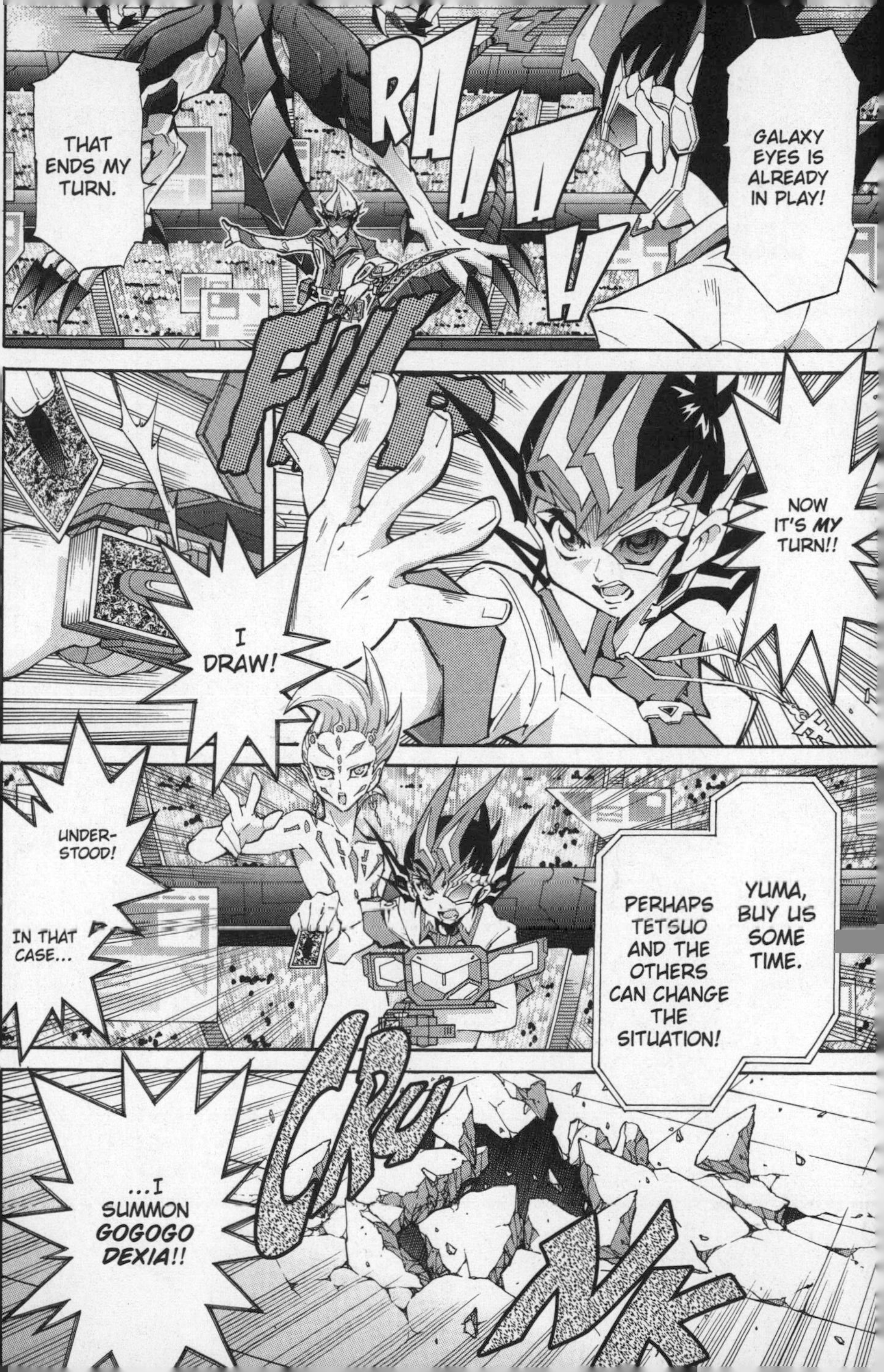
GALAXY EYES IS ALREADY IN PLAY!
RAAAAH
THAT ENDS MY TURN.
NOW IT'S *MY* TURN!!
I DRAW!
YUMA, BUY US SOME TIME.
PERHAPS TETSUO AND THE OTHERS CAN CHANGE THE SITUATION!
UNDER-STOOD!
IN THAT CASE...
...I SUMMON *GOGOGO DEXIA*!!

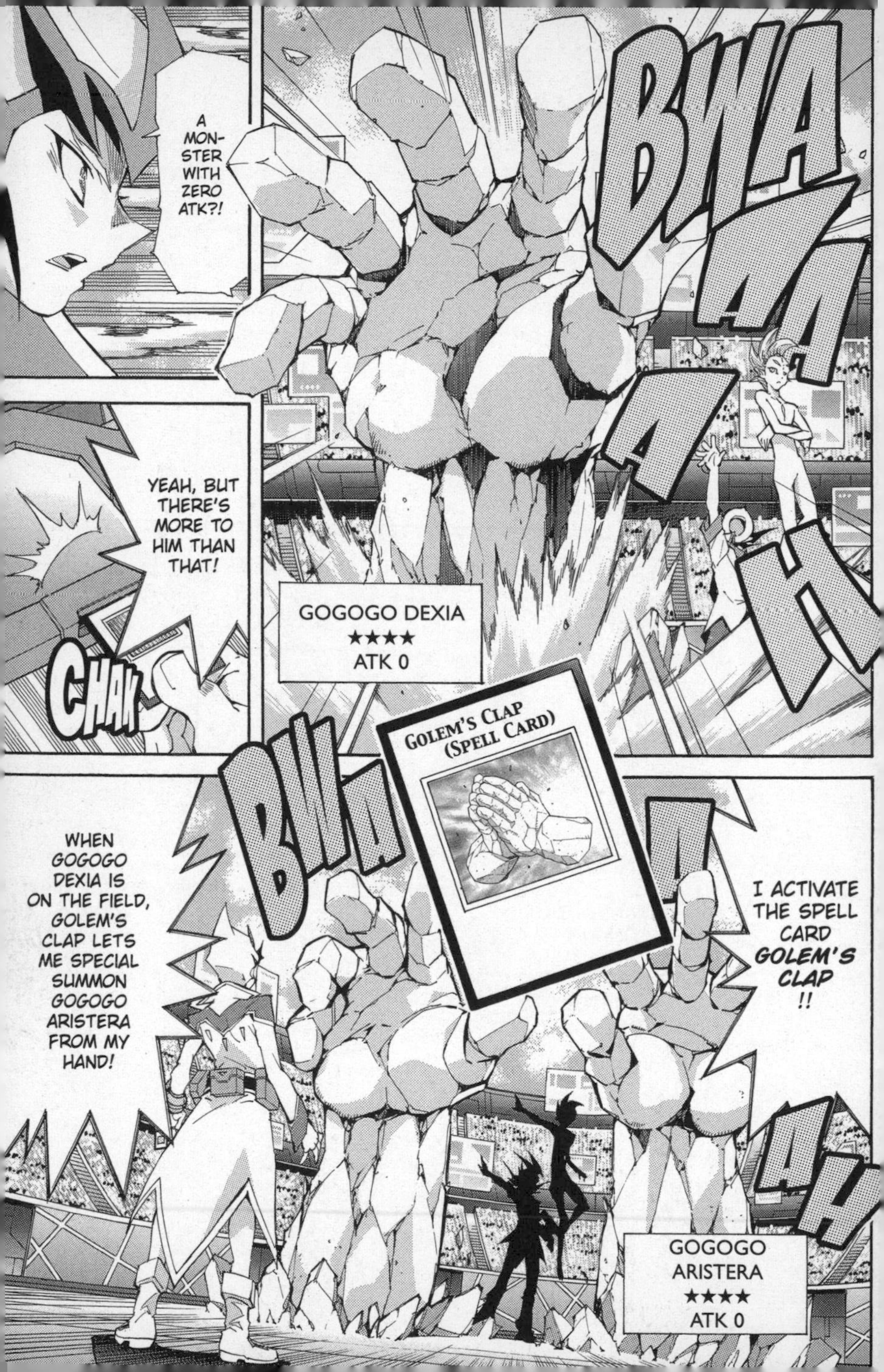
BWAAAAH
GOGOGO DEXIA ★★★★ ATK 0
A MONSTER WITH ZERO ATK?!
YEAH, BUT THERE'S MORE TO HIM THAN THAT!
CHAK
I ACTIVATE THE SPELL CARD GOLEM'S CLAP!!
GOLEM'S CLAP (SPELL CARD)
BWAAAH
WHEN GOGOGO DEXIA IS ON THE FIELD, GOLEM'S CLAP LETS ME SPECIAL SUMMON GOGOGO ARISTERA FROM MY HAND!
GOGOGO ARISTERA ★★★★ ATK 0

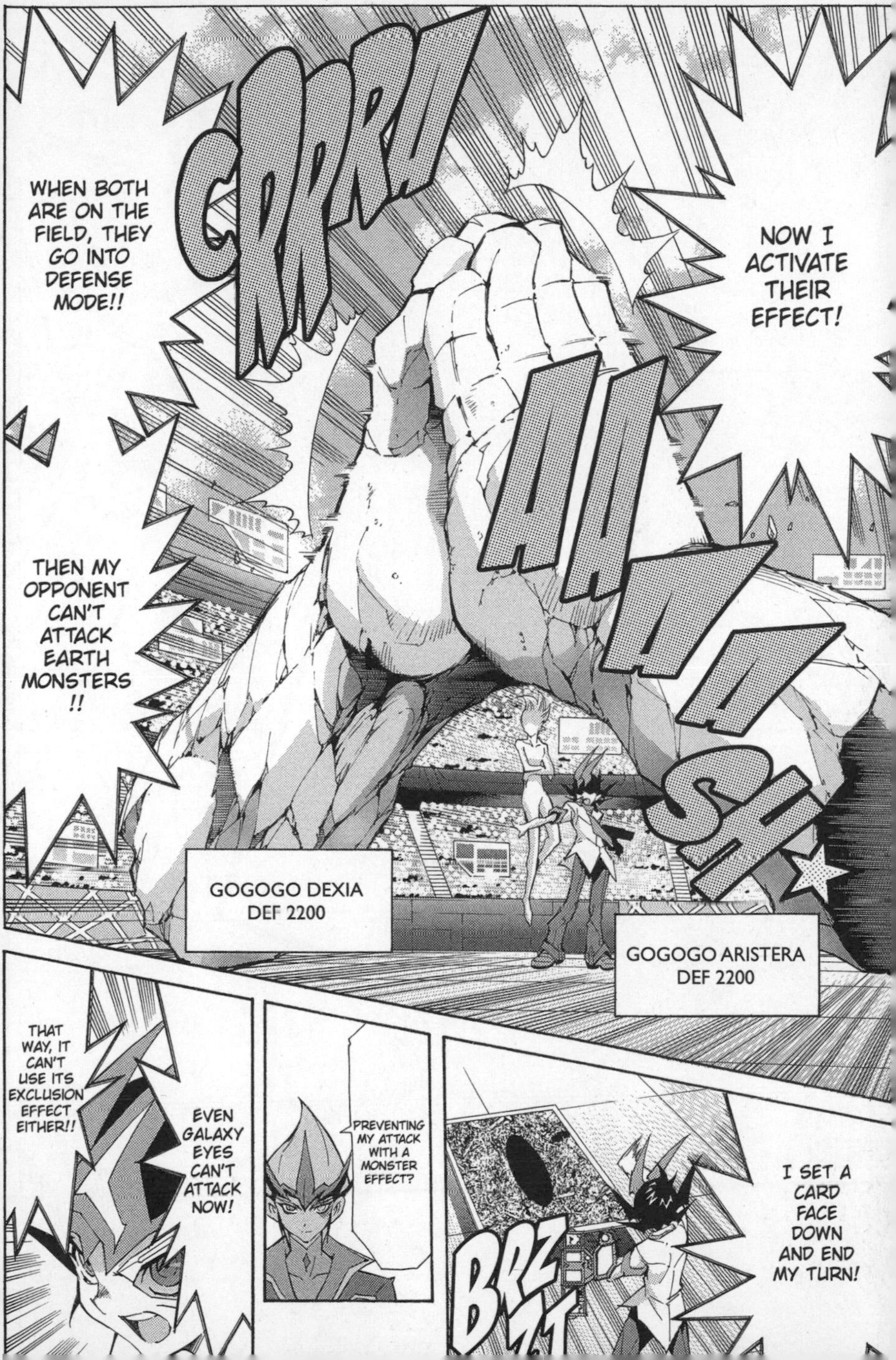
NOW I ACTIVATE THEIR EFFECT!
WHEN BOTH ARE ON THE FIELD, THEY GO INTO DEFENSE MODE!!
CRRRAAAASH
THEN MY OPPONENT CAN'T ATTACK EARTH MONSTERS!!
GOGOGO ARISTERA DEF 2200
GOGOGO DEXIA DEF 2200
I SET A CARD FACE DOWN AND END MY TURN!
BRZZT
PREVENTING MY ATTACK WITH A MONSTER EFFECT?
EVEN GALAXY EYES CAN'T ATTACK NOW!
THAT WAY, IT CAN'T USE ITS EXCLUSION EFFECT EITHER!!

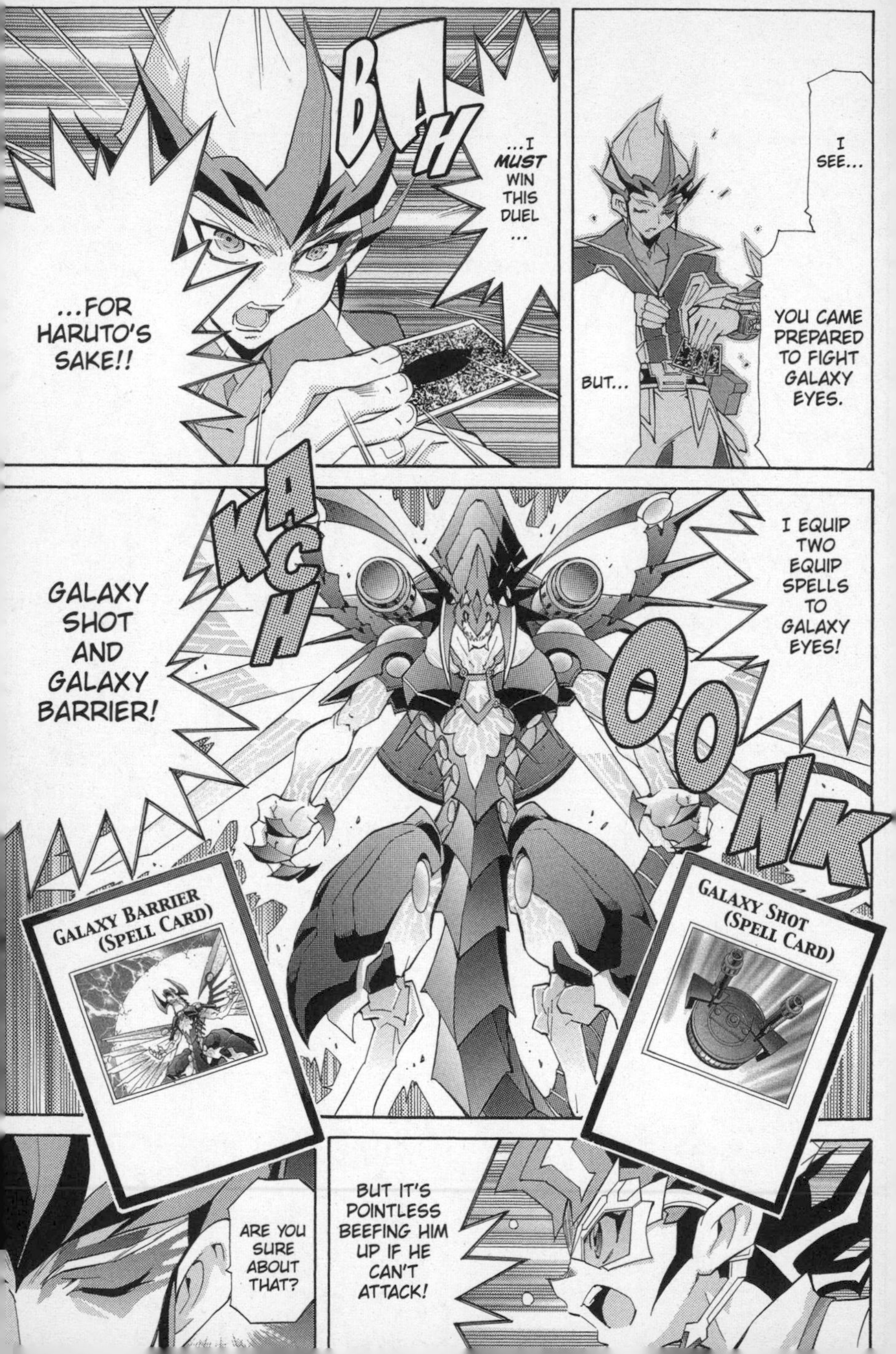
I SEE...
YOU CAME PREPARED TO FIGHT GALAXY EYES.
BUT...
BAH
...I MUST WIN THIS DUEL ...
...FOR HARUTO'S SAKE!!
I EQUIP TWO EQUIP SPELLS TO GALAXY EYES!
OONK
KACH
GALAXY SHOT AND GALAXY BARRIER!
GALAXY SHOT (SPELL CARD)
GALAXY BARRIER (SPELL CARD)
BUT IT'S POINTLESS BEEFING HIM UP IF HE CAN'T ATTACK!
ARE YOU SURE ABOUT THAT?

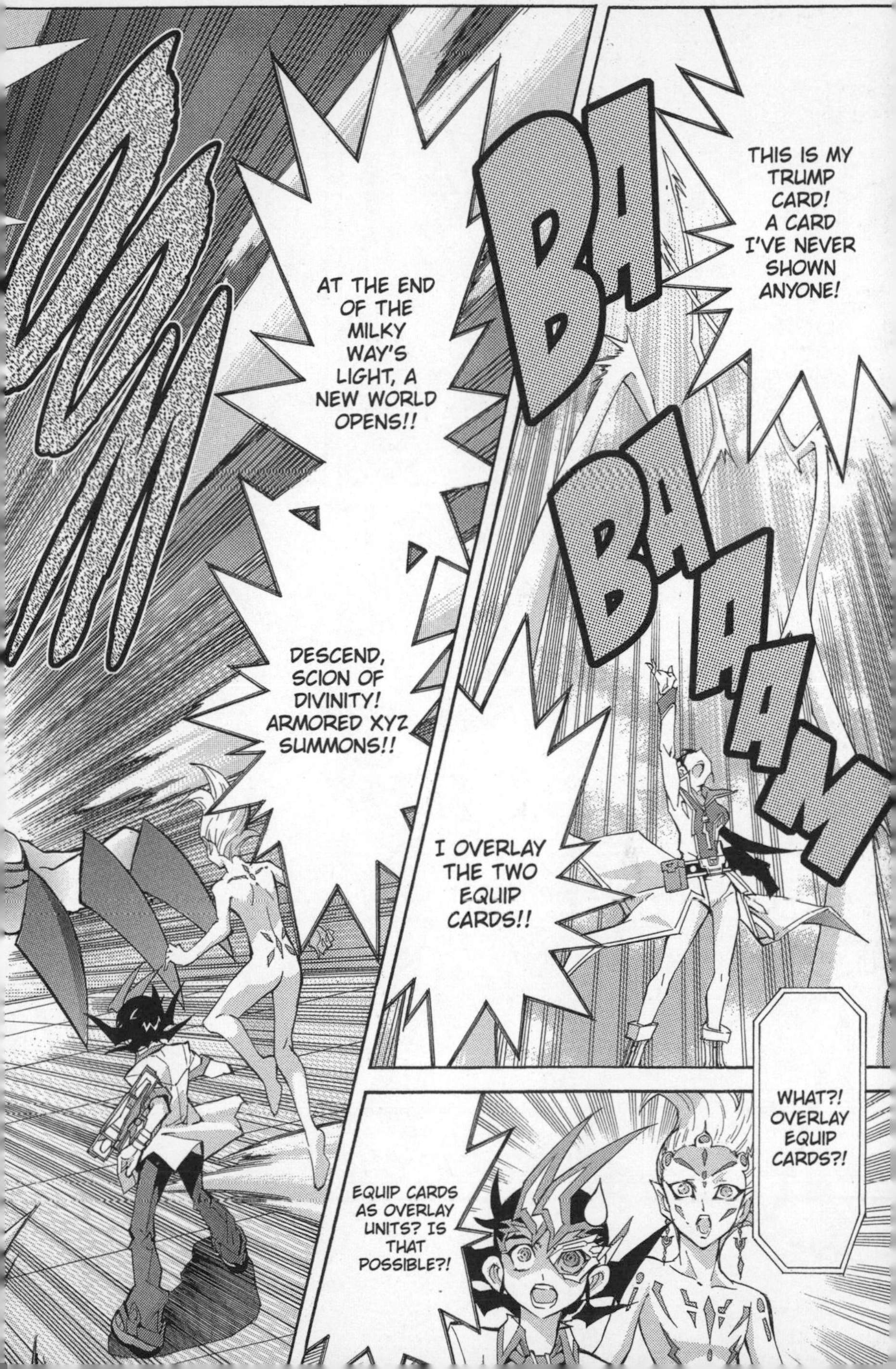
THIS IS MY TRUMP CARD! A CARD I'VE NEVER SHOWN ANYONE!
BA
BAAAAM
I OVERLAY THE TWO EQUIP CARDS!!
WHAT?! OVERLAY EQUIP CARDS?!
EQUIP CARDS AS OVERLAY UNITS? IS THAT POSSIBLE?!
AT THE END OF THE MILKY WAY'S LIGHT, A NEW WORLD OPENS!!
DESCEND, SCION OF DIVINITY! ARMORED XYZ SUMMONS!!

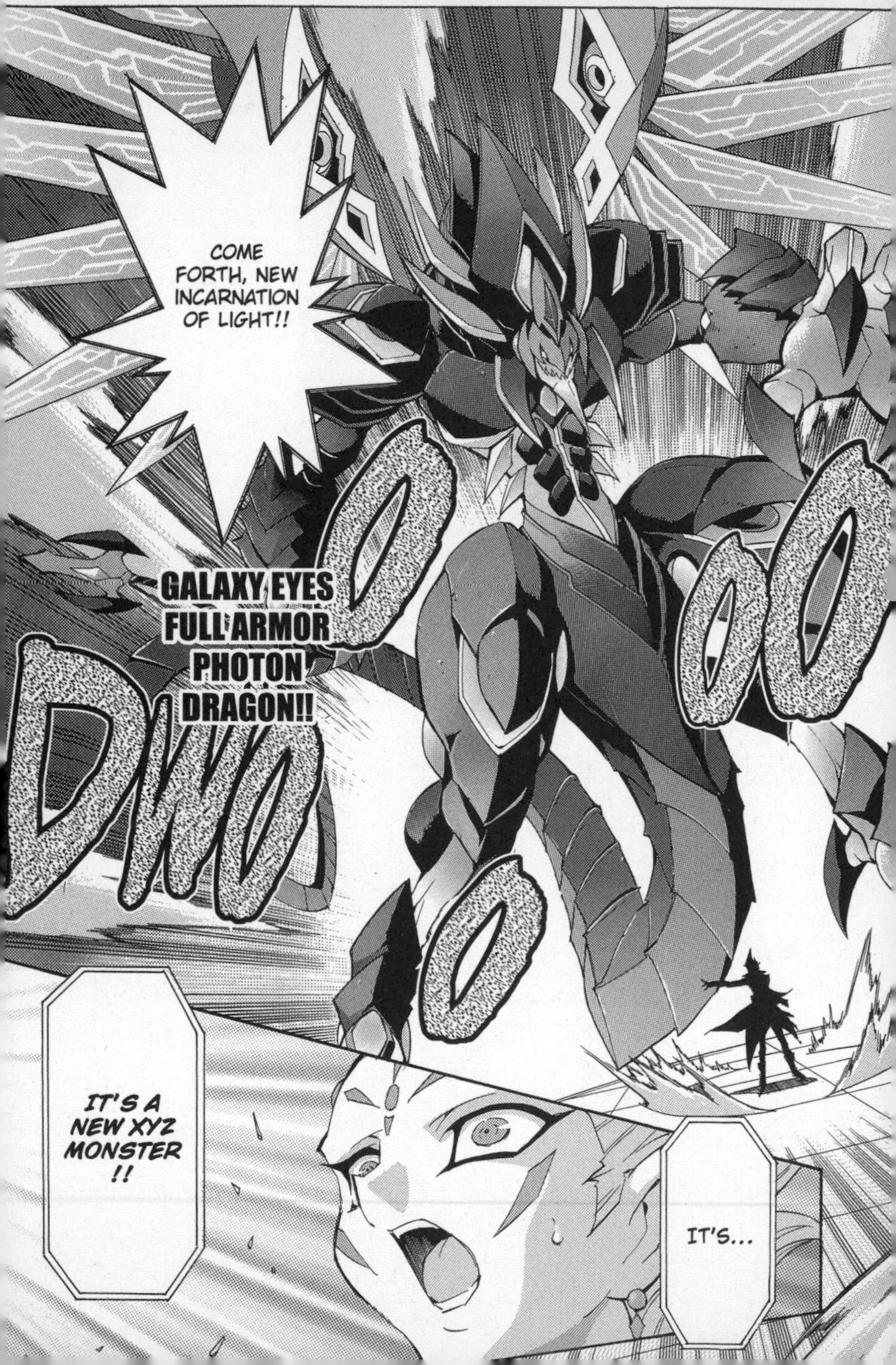
COME FORTH, NEW INCARNATION OF LIGHT!!
GALAXY EYES FULL ARMOR PHOTON DRAGON!!
DWOOOOO
IT'S...
IT'S A NEW XYZ MONSTER!!

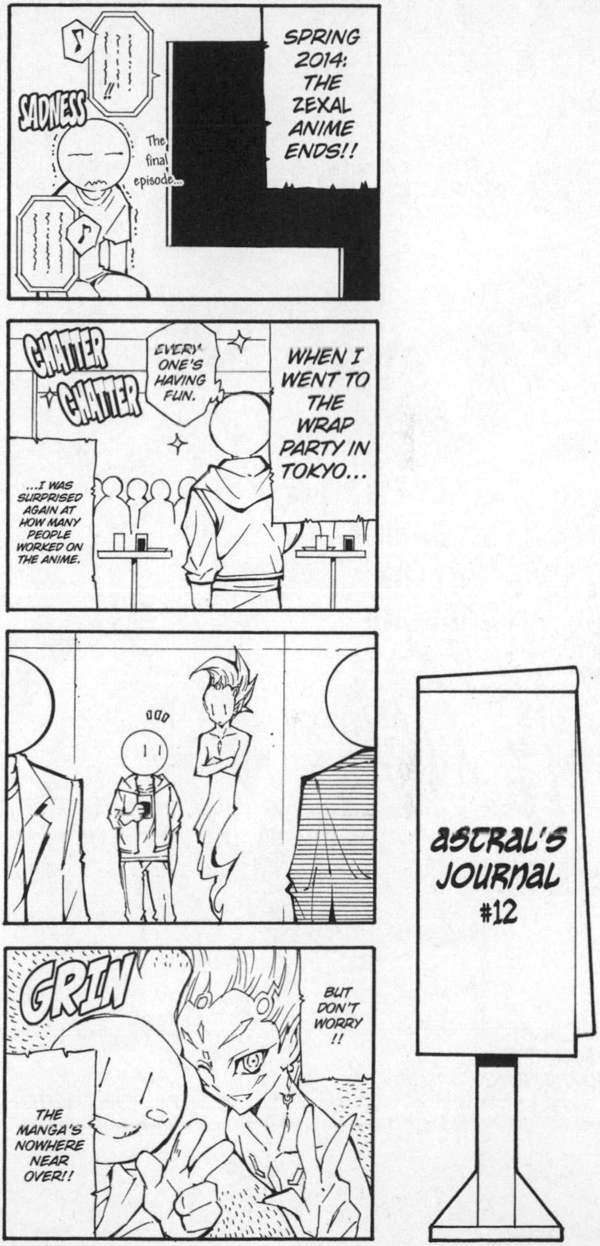
ASTRAL'S JOURNAL #12
SPRING 2014: THE ZEXAL ANIME ENDS!!
SADNESS
The final episode...
WHEN I WENT TO THE WRAP PARTY IN TOKYO...
EVERYONE'S HAVING FUN.
CHATTER CHATTER
...I WAS SURPRISED AGAIN AT HOW MANY PEOPLE WORKED ON THE ANIME.
BUT DON'T WORRY!!
GRIN
THE MANGA'S NOWHERE NEAR OVER!!

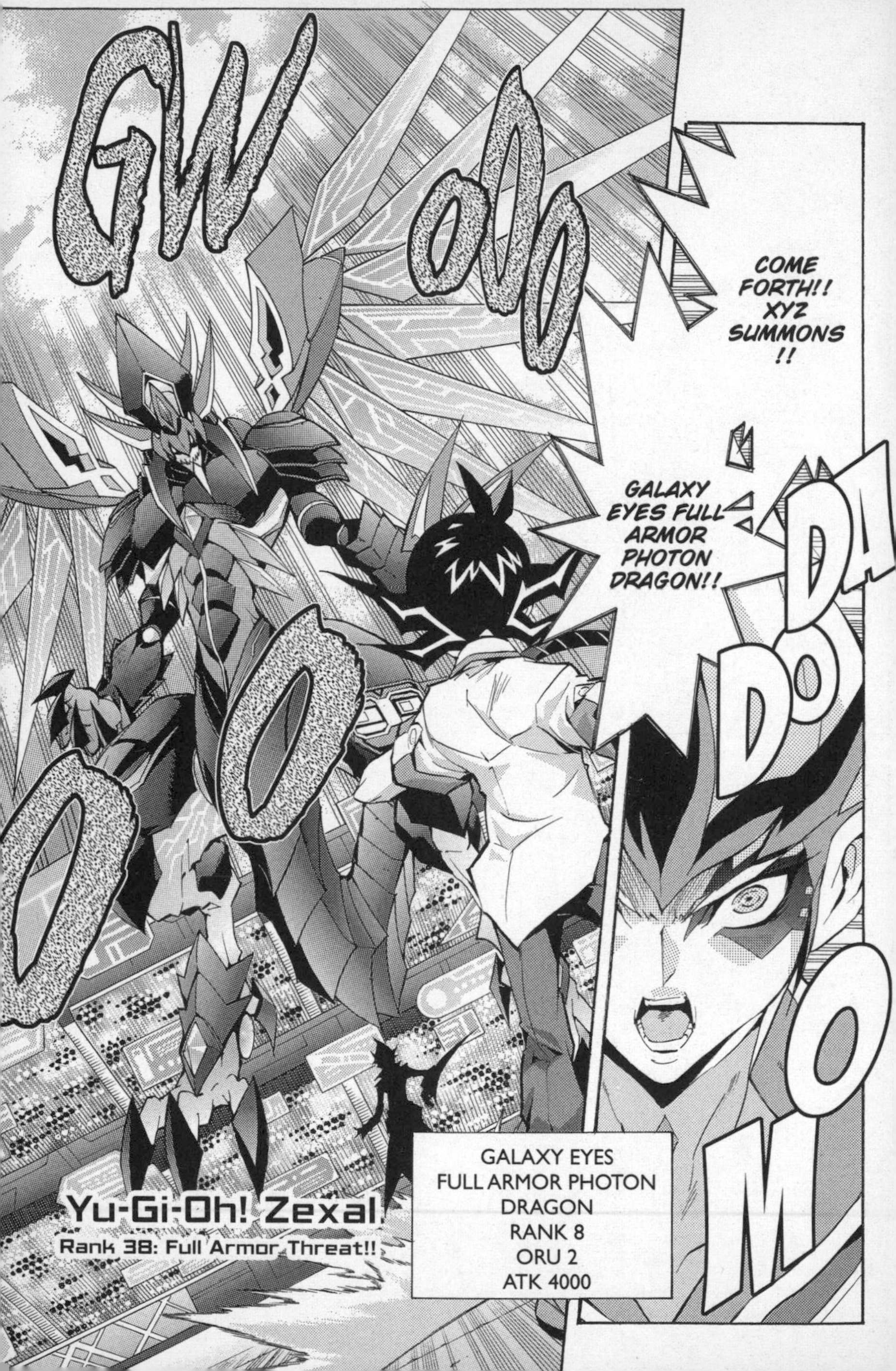
COME FORTH!! XYZ SUMMONS!!
GALAXY EYES FULL ARMOR PHOTON DRAGON!!
GALAXY EYES FULL ARMOR PHOTON DRAGON RANK 8 ORU 2 ATK 4000
Yu-Gi-Oh! Zexal
Rank 38: Full Armor Threat!!

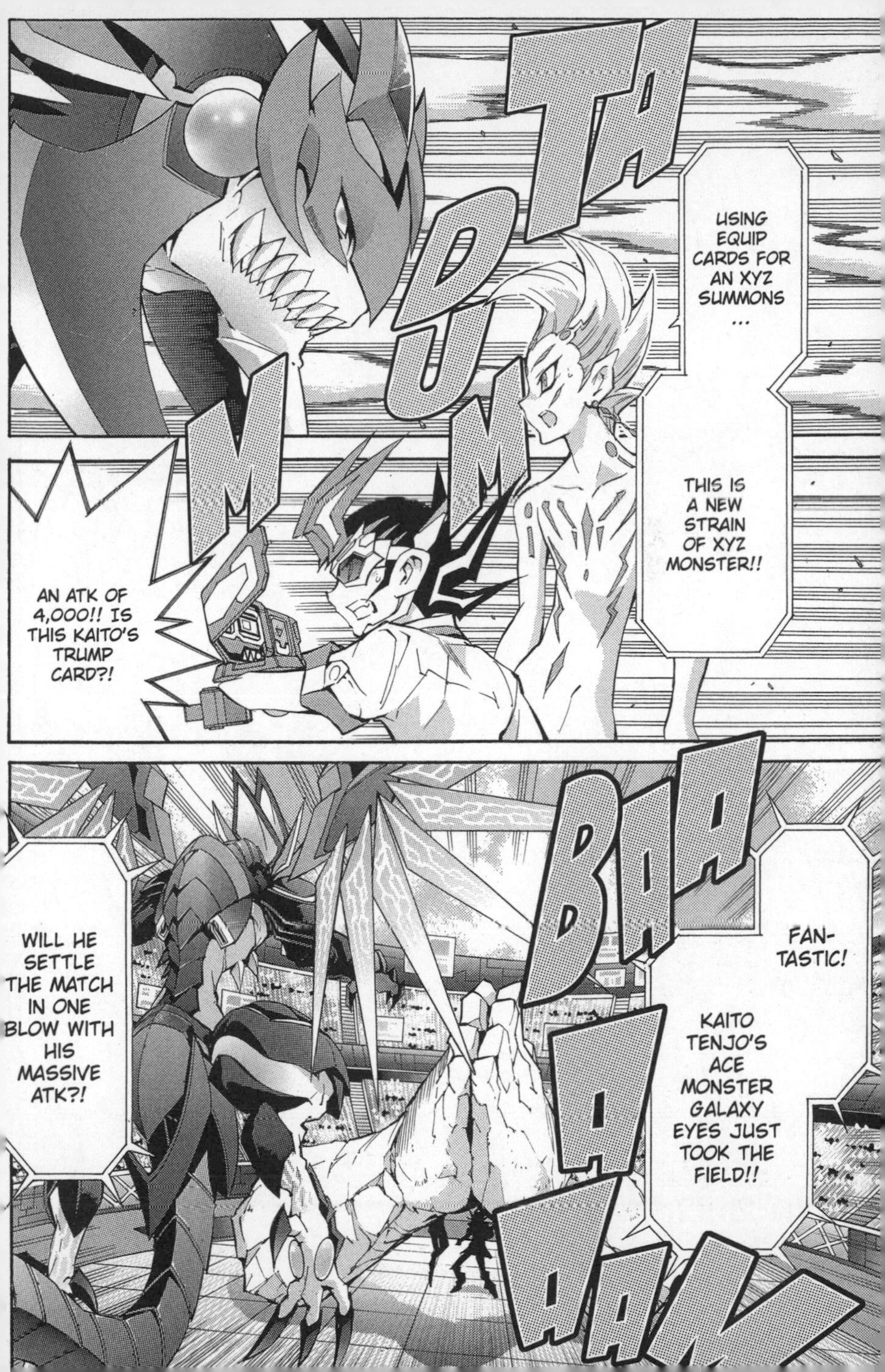
USING EQUIP CARDS FOR AN XYZ SUMMONS ...
THIS IS A NEW STRAIN OF XYZ MONSTER!!
TADUMMM
AN ATK OF 4,000!! IS THIS KAITO'S TRUMP CARD?!
FAN-TASTIC!
KAITO TENJO'S ACE MONSTER GALAXY EYES JUST TOOK THE FIELD!!
BAAAAAN
WILL HE SETTLE THE MATCH IN ONE BLOW WITH HIS MASSIVE ATK?!

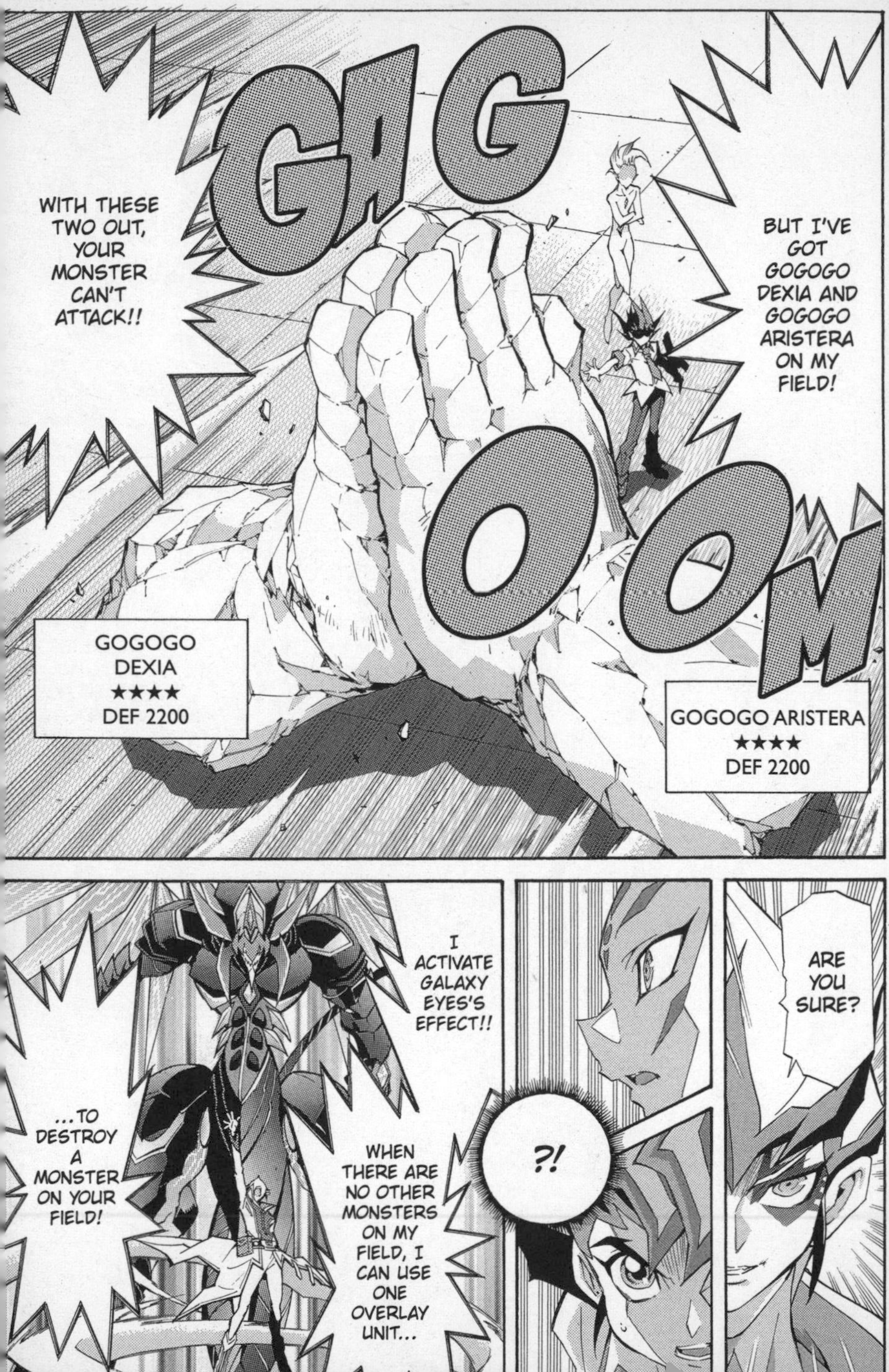
BUT I'VE GOT GOGOGO DEXIA AND GOGOGO ARISTERA ON MY FIELD!
GAG
WITH THESE TWO OUT, YOUR MONSTER CAN'T ATTACK!!
OOM
GOGOGO ARISTERA ★★★★ DEF 2200
GOGOGO DEXIA ★★★★ DEF 2200
ARE YOU SURE?
?!
I ACTIVATE GALAXY EYES'S EFFECT!!
WHEN THERE ARE NO OTHER MONSTERS ON MY FIELD, I CAN USE ONE OVERLAY UNIT...
...TO DESTROY A MONSTER ON YOUR FIELD!

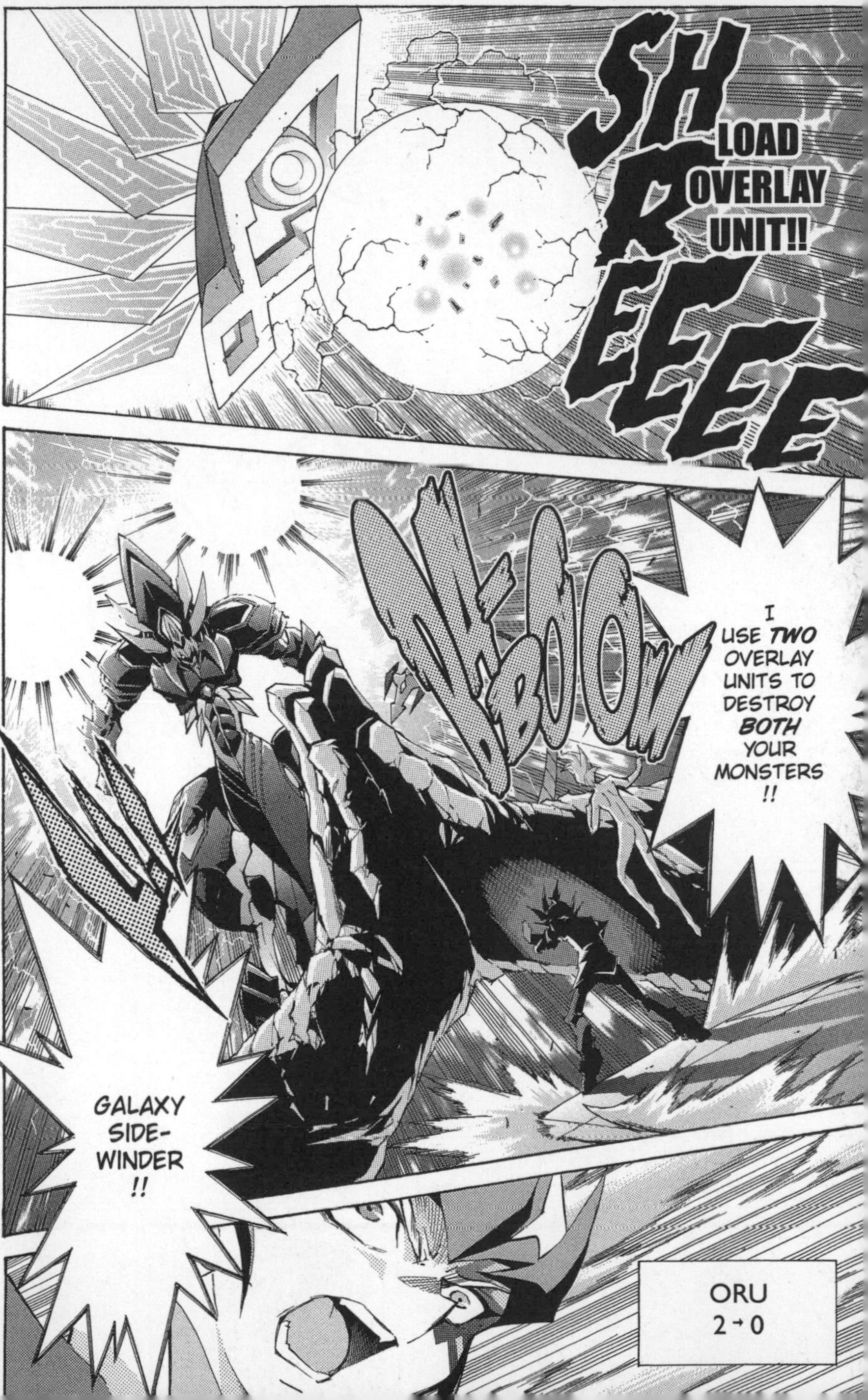
SHREEEE
LOAD OVERLAY UNIT!!
I USE TWO OVERLAY UNITS TO DESTROY BOTH YOUR MONSTERS!!
GALAXY SIDE-WINDER!!
ORU 2→0

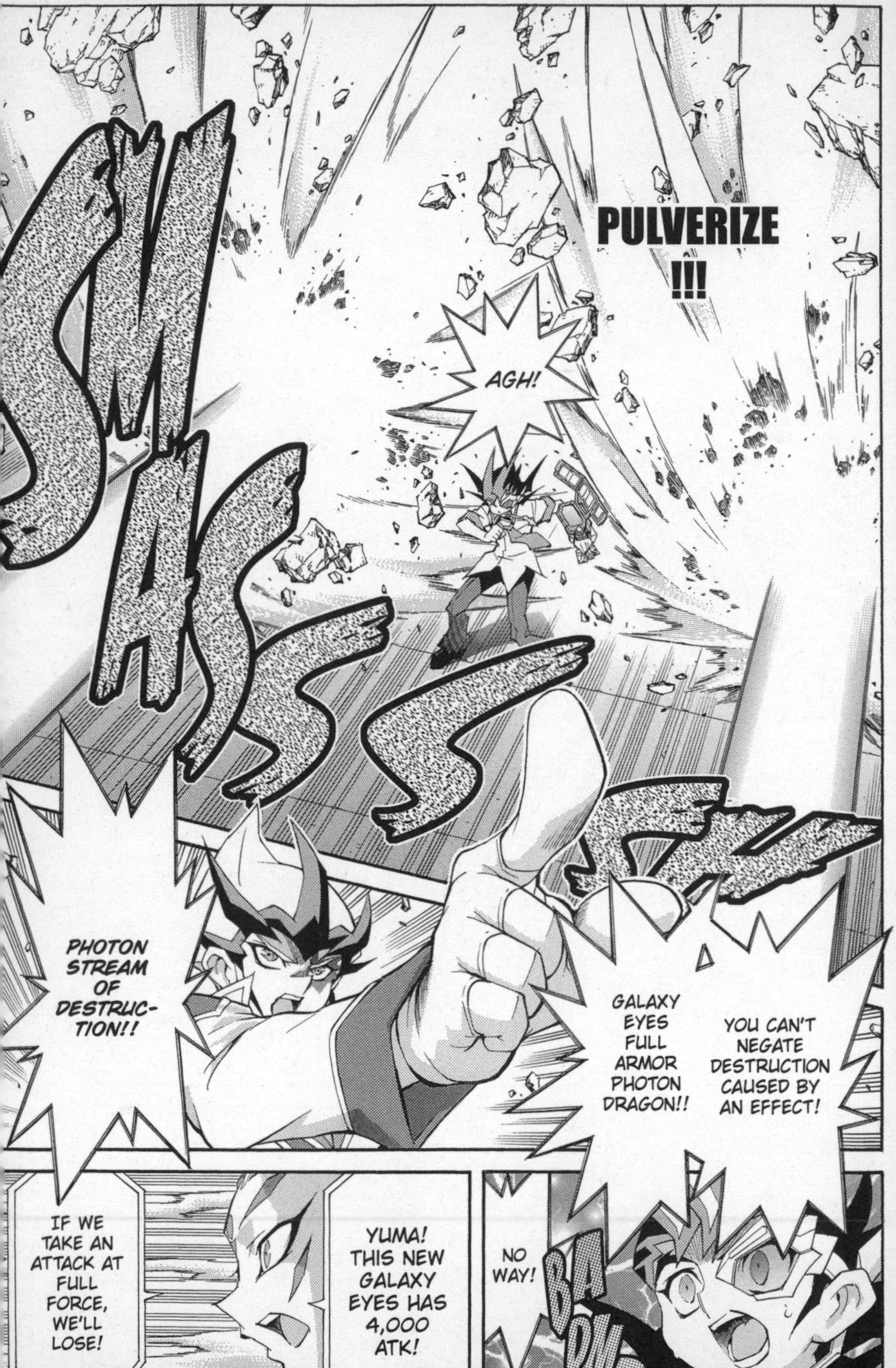
PULVERIZE !!!
AGH!
YOU CAN'T NEGATE DESTRUCTION CAUSED BY AN EFFECT!
GALAXY EYES FULL ARMOR PHOTON DRAGON!!
PHOTON STREAM OF DESTRUC-TION!!
NO WAY!
YUMA! THIS NEW GALAXY EYES HAS 4,000 ATK!
IF WE TAKE AN ATTACK AT FULL FORCE, WE'LL LOSE!

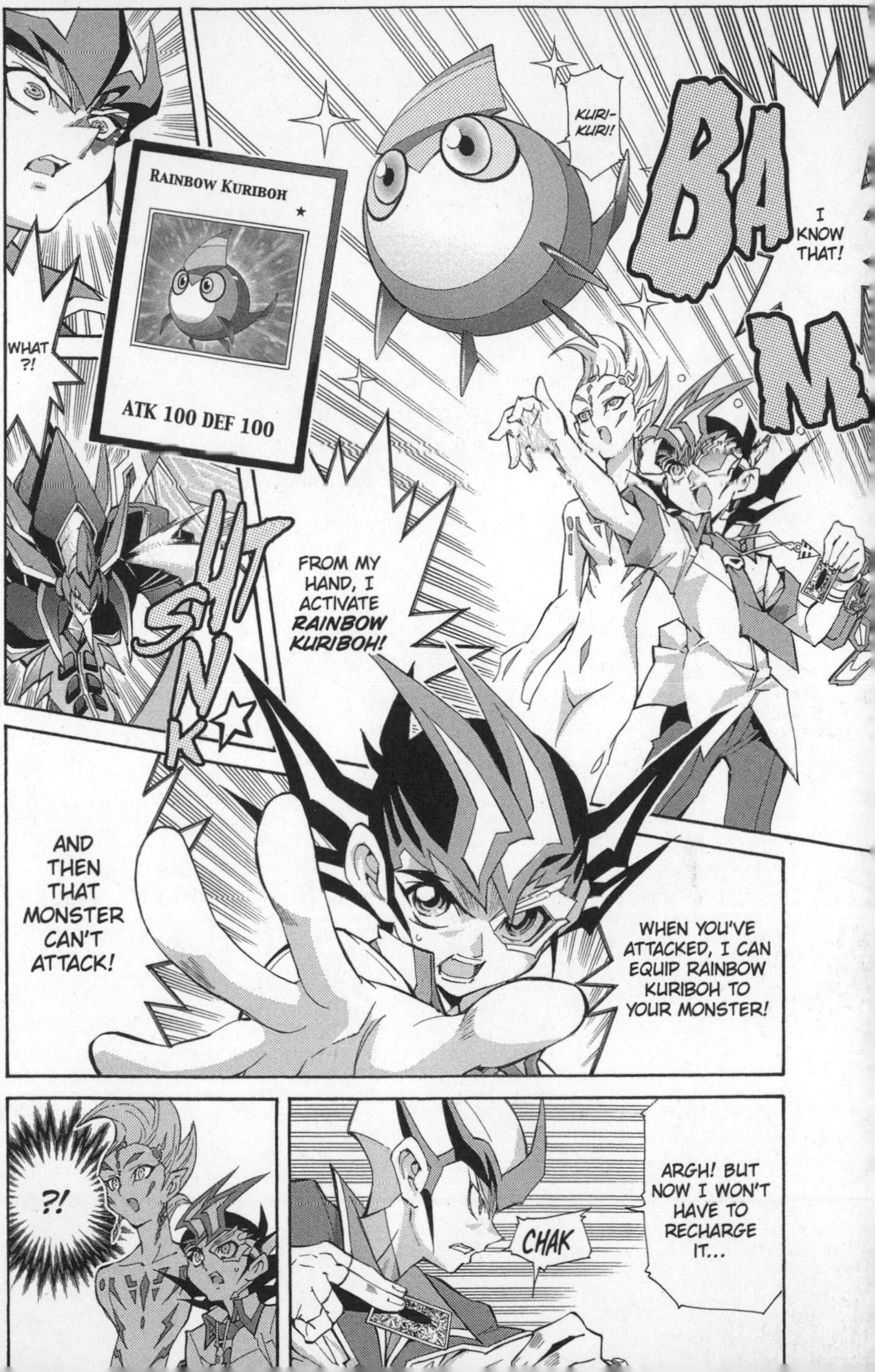
KURI-KURI!
BAM
I KNOW THAT!
FROM MY HAND, I ACTIVATE RAINBOW KURIBOH!
RAINBOW KURIBOH
ATK 100 DEF 100
WHAT ?!
WHEN YOU'VE ATTACKED, I CAN EQUIP RAINBOW KURIBOH TO YOUR MONSTER!
AND THEN THAT MONSTER CAN'T ATTACK!
ARGH! BUT NOW I WON'T HAVE TO RECHARGE IT...
CHAK
?!

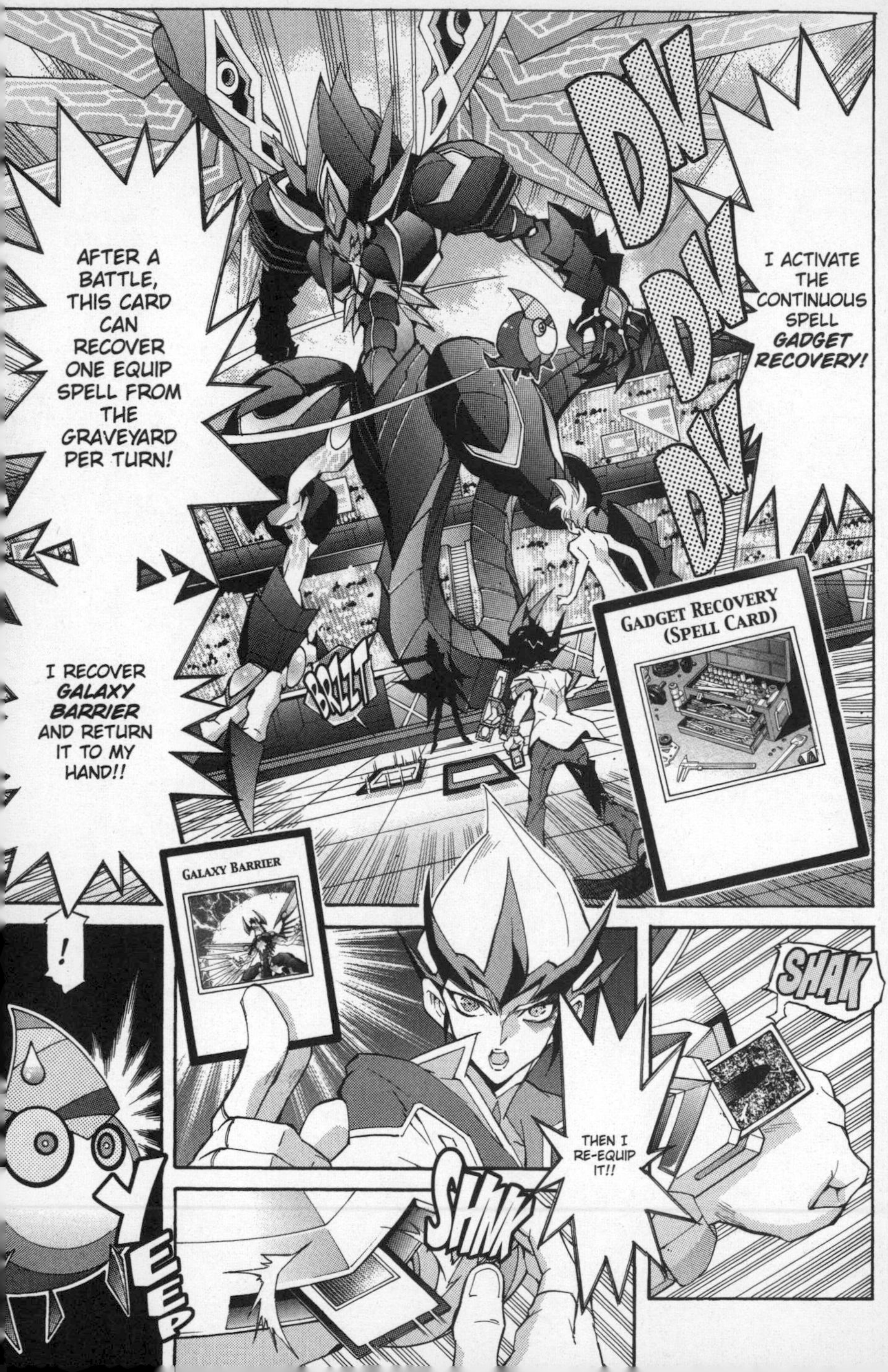
I ACTIVATE THE CONTINUOUS SPELL GADGET RECOVERY!
DN DN DN DN
AFTER A BATTLE, THIS CARD CAN RECOVER ONE EQUIP SPELL FROM THE GRAVEYARD PER TURN!
GADGET RECOVERY (SPELL CARD)
BRZZT
I RECOVER GALAXY BARRIER AND RETURN IT TO MY HAND!!
GALAXY BARRIER
SHAK
THEN I RE-EQUIP IT!!
SHNK
!
YEEEP

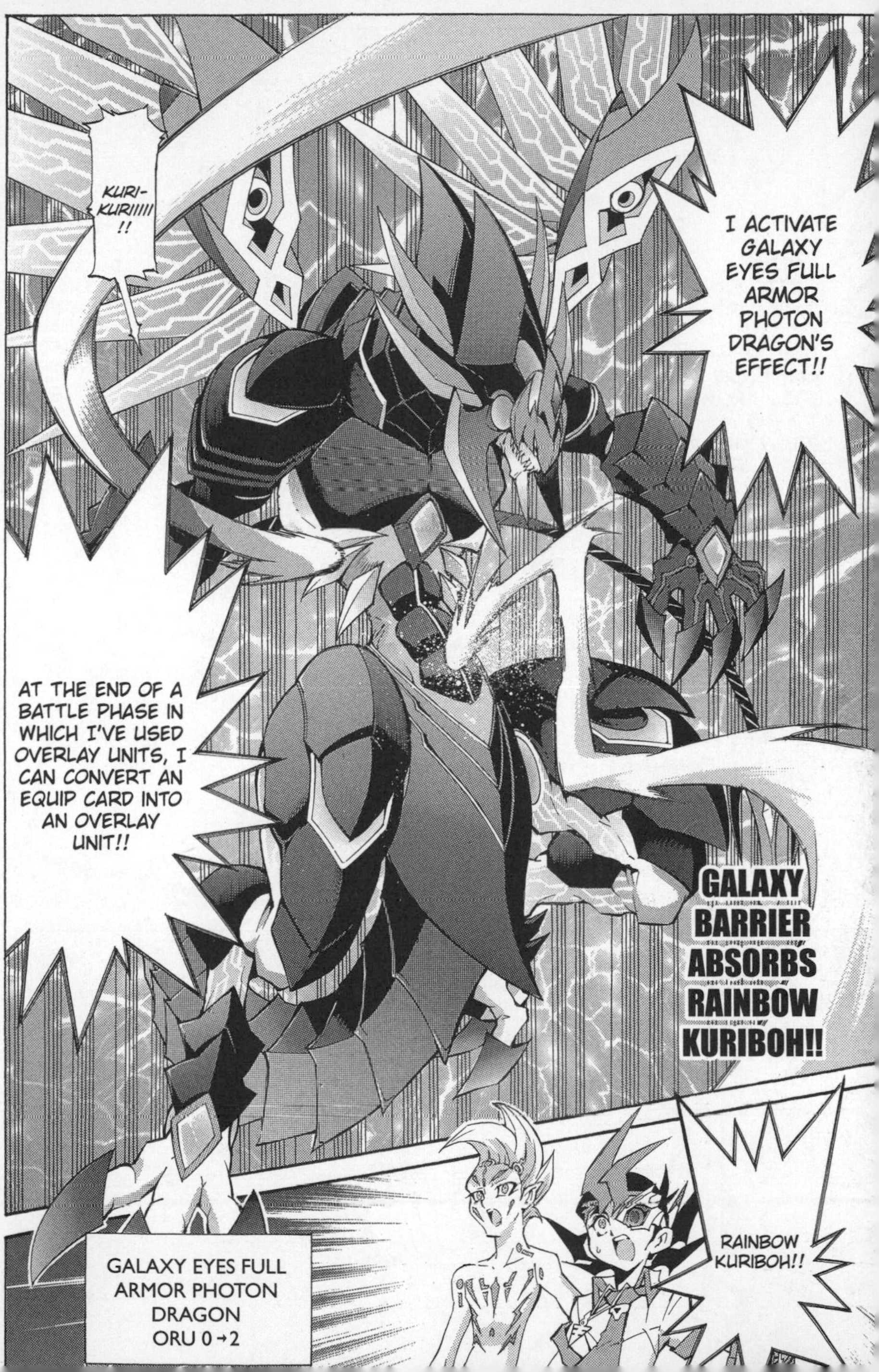
I ACTIVATE GALAXY EYES FULL ARMOR PHOTON DRAGON'S EFFECT!!
KURI-KURI!!!!!! !!
AT THE END OF A BATTLE PHASE IN WHICH I'VE USED OVERLAY UNITS, I CAN CONVERT AN EQUIP CARD INTO AN OVERLAY UNIT!!
GALAXY BARRIER ABSORBS RAINBOW KURIBOH!!
RAINBOW KURIBOH!!
GALAXY EYES FULL ARMOR PHOTON DRAGON ORU 0→2

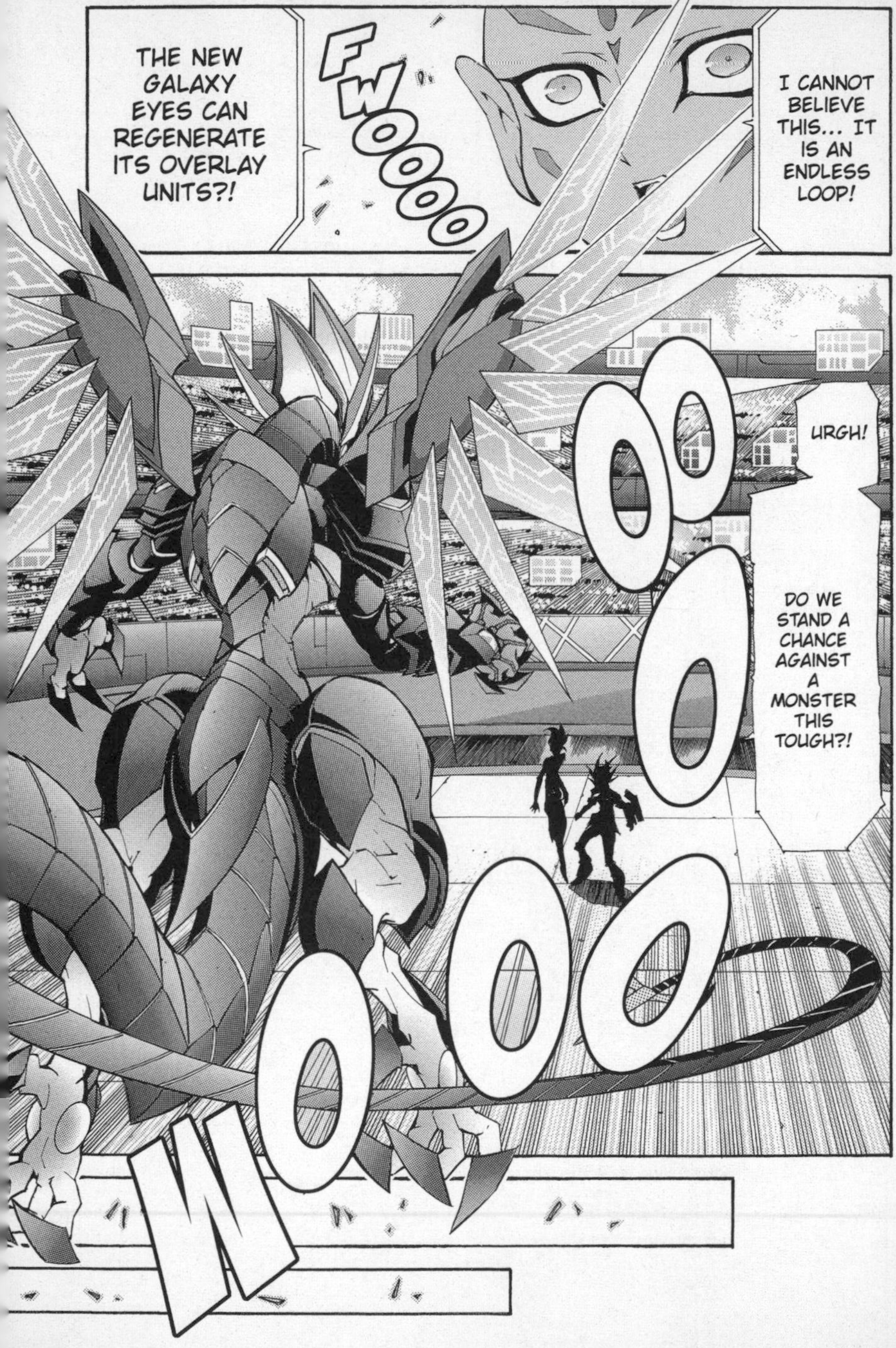
I CANNOT BELIEVE THIS... IT IS AN ENDLESS LOOP!
FWOOOO
THE NEW GALAXY EYES CAN REGENERATE ITS OVERLAY UNITS?!
URGH!
DO WE STAND A CHANCE AGAINST A MONSTER THIS TOUGH?!
WOOOOOOO

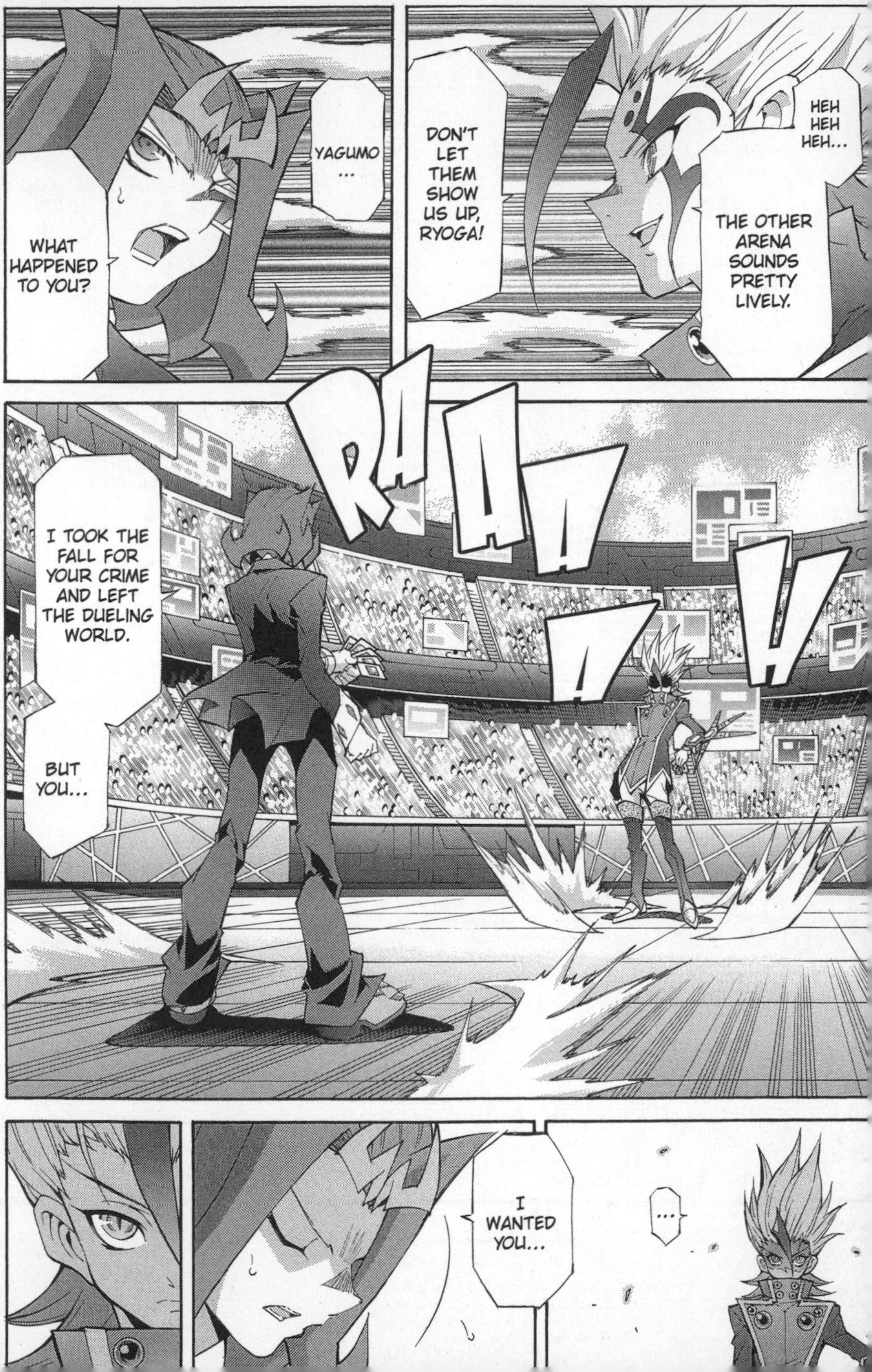
HEH HEH HEH...
THE OTHER ARENA SOUNDS PRETTY LIVELY.
DON'T LET THEM SHOW US UP, RYOGA!
YAGUMO...
WHAT HAPPENED TO YOU?
RAAAAH
I TOOK THE FALL FOR YOUR CRIME AND LEFT THE DUELING WORLD.
BUT YOU...
...
I WANTED YOU...

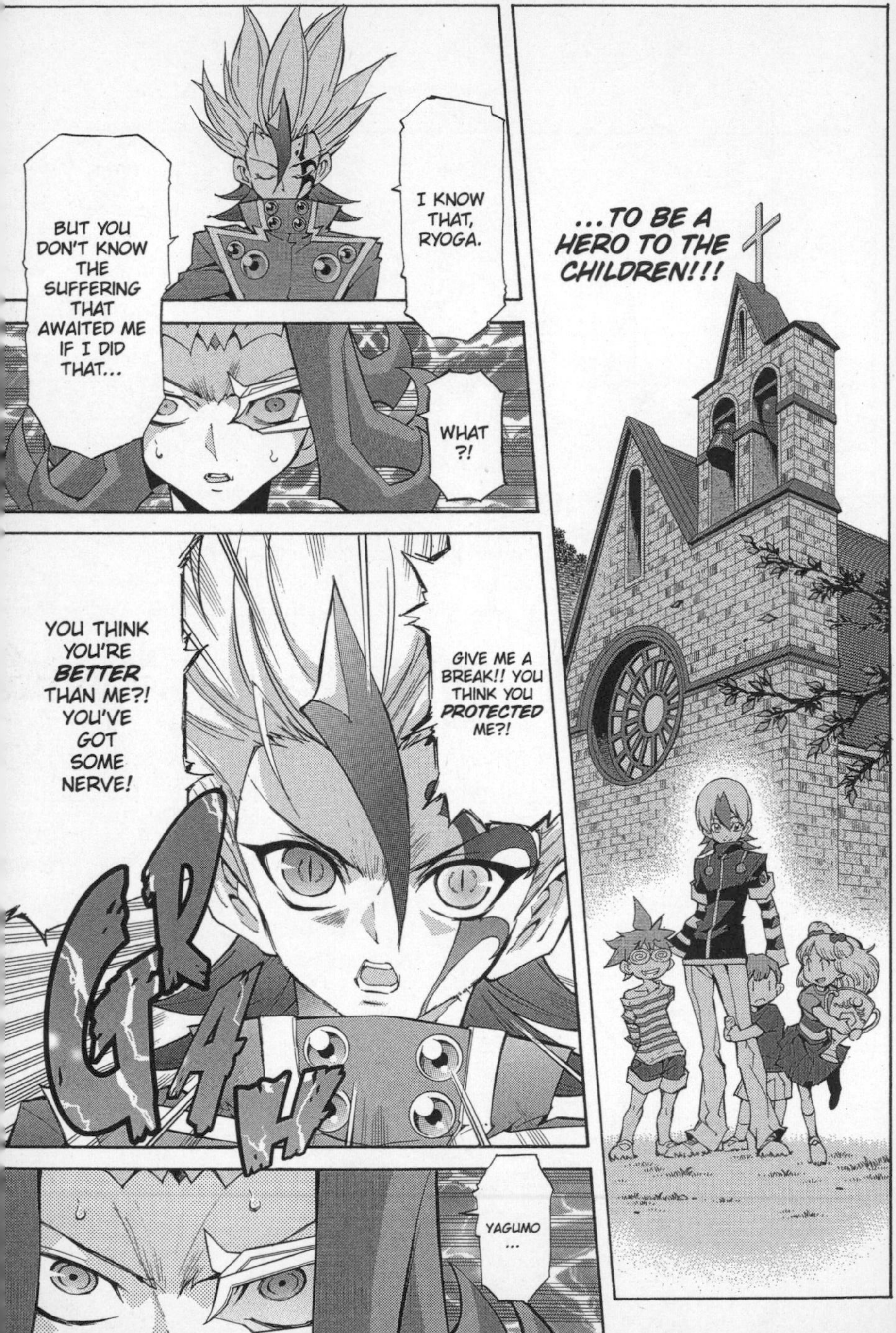
...TO BE A HERO TO THE CHILDREN!!!
I KNOW THAT, RYOGA.
BUT YOU DON'T KNOW THE SUFFERING THAT AWAITED ME IF I DID THAT...
WHAT?!
GIVE ME A BREAK!! YOU THINK YOU *PROTECTED* ME?!
YOU THINK YOU'RE ***BETTER*** THAN ME?! YOU'VE GOT SOME NERVE!
YAGUMO...

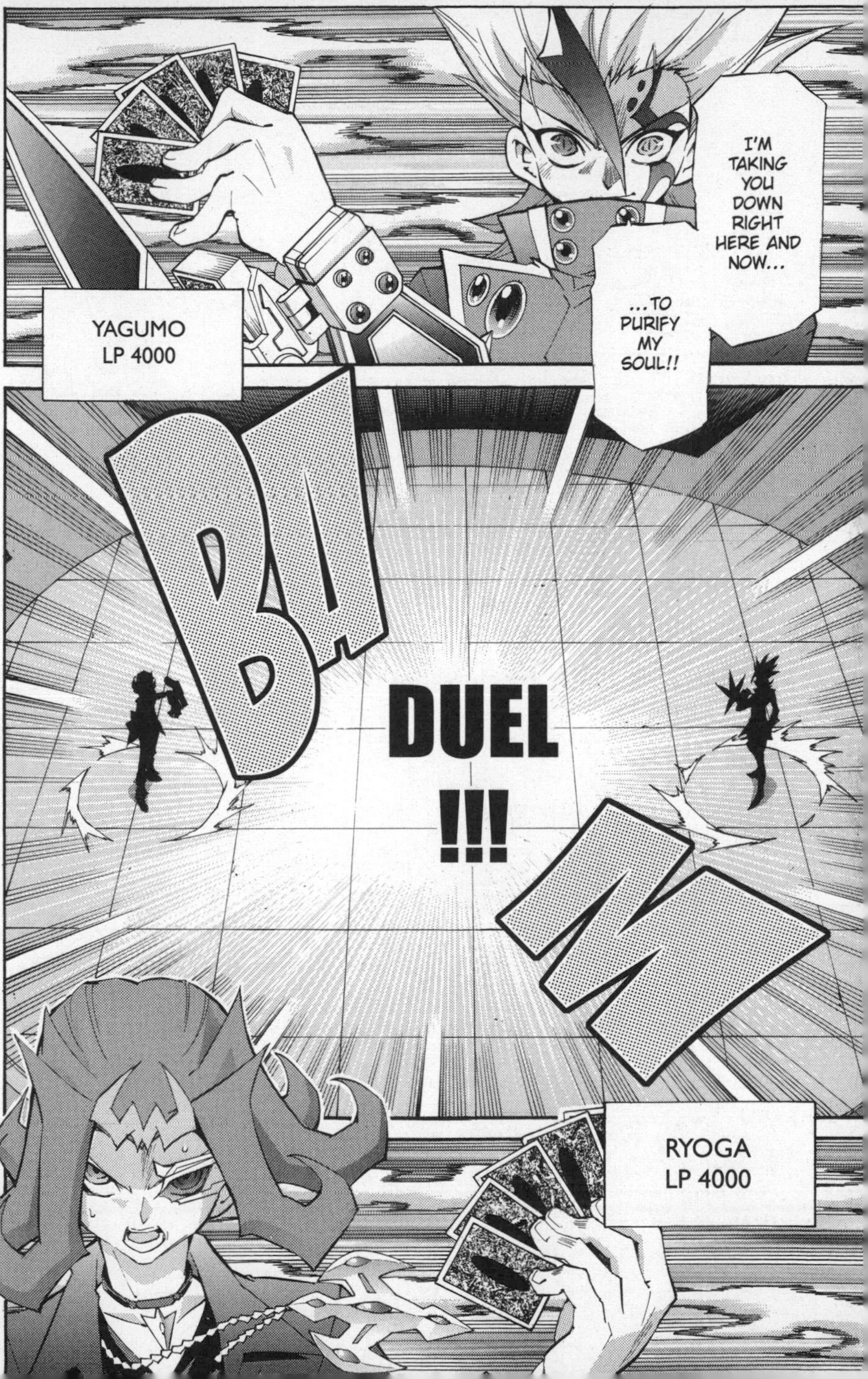
I'M TAKING YOU DOWN RIGHT HERE AND NOW...
...TO PURIFY MY SOUL!!
YAGUMO LP 4000
BA
DUEL !!!
M
RYOGA LP 4000

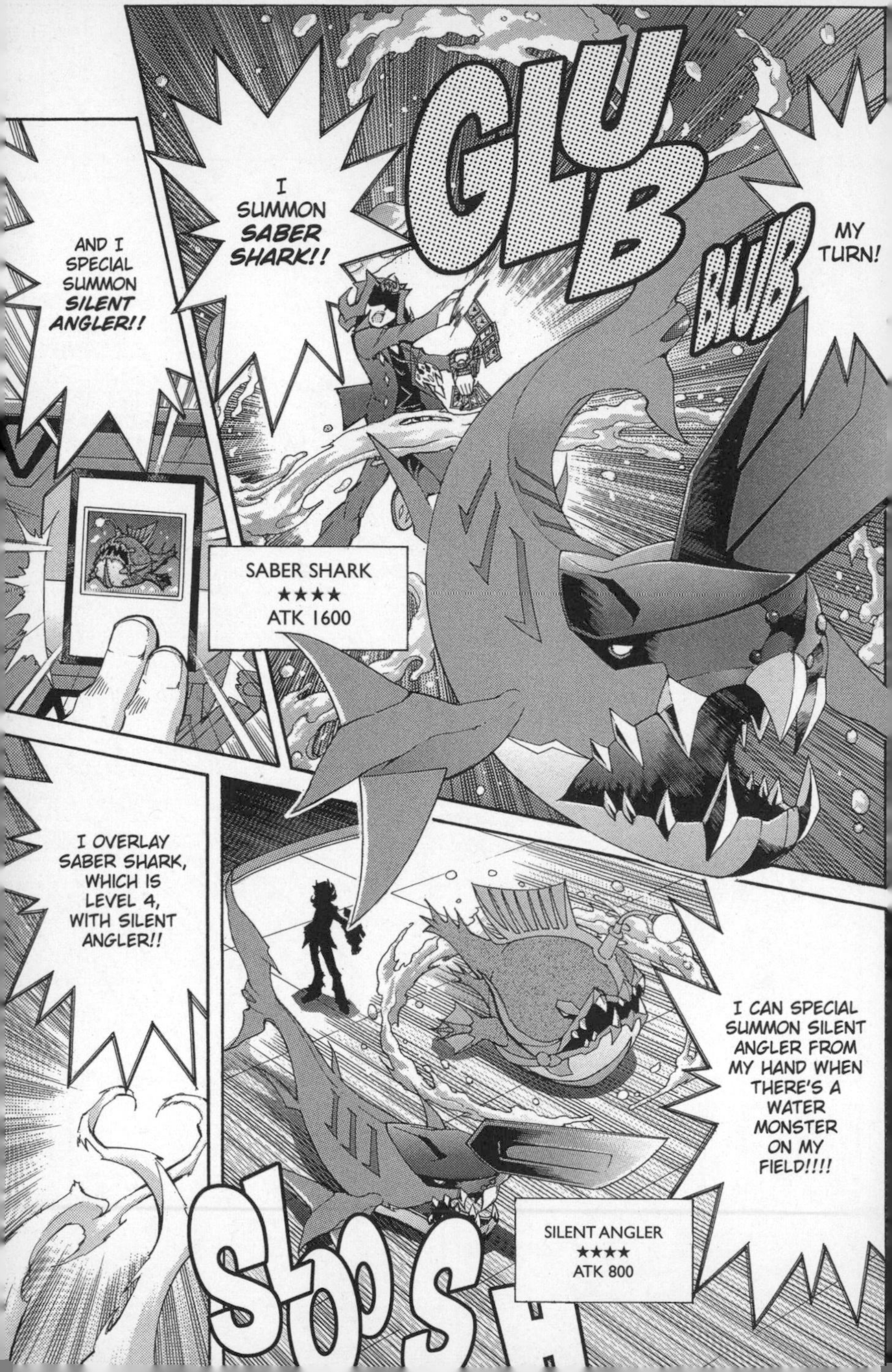
MY TURN!
GLUB
BLUB
I SUMMON SABER SHARK!!
SABER SHARK
★★★★
ATK 1600
AND I SPECIAL SUMMON SILENT ANGLER!!
I CAN SPECIAL SUMMON SILENT ANGLER FROM MY HAND WHEN THERE'S A WATER MONSTER ON MY FIELD!!!!
SILENT ANGLER
★★★★
ATK 800
SLOOSH
I OVERLAY SABER SHARK, WHICH IS LEVEL 4, WITH SILENT ANGLER!!

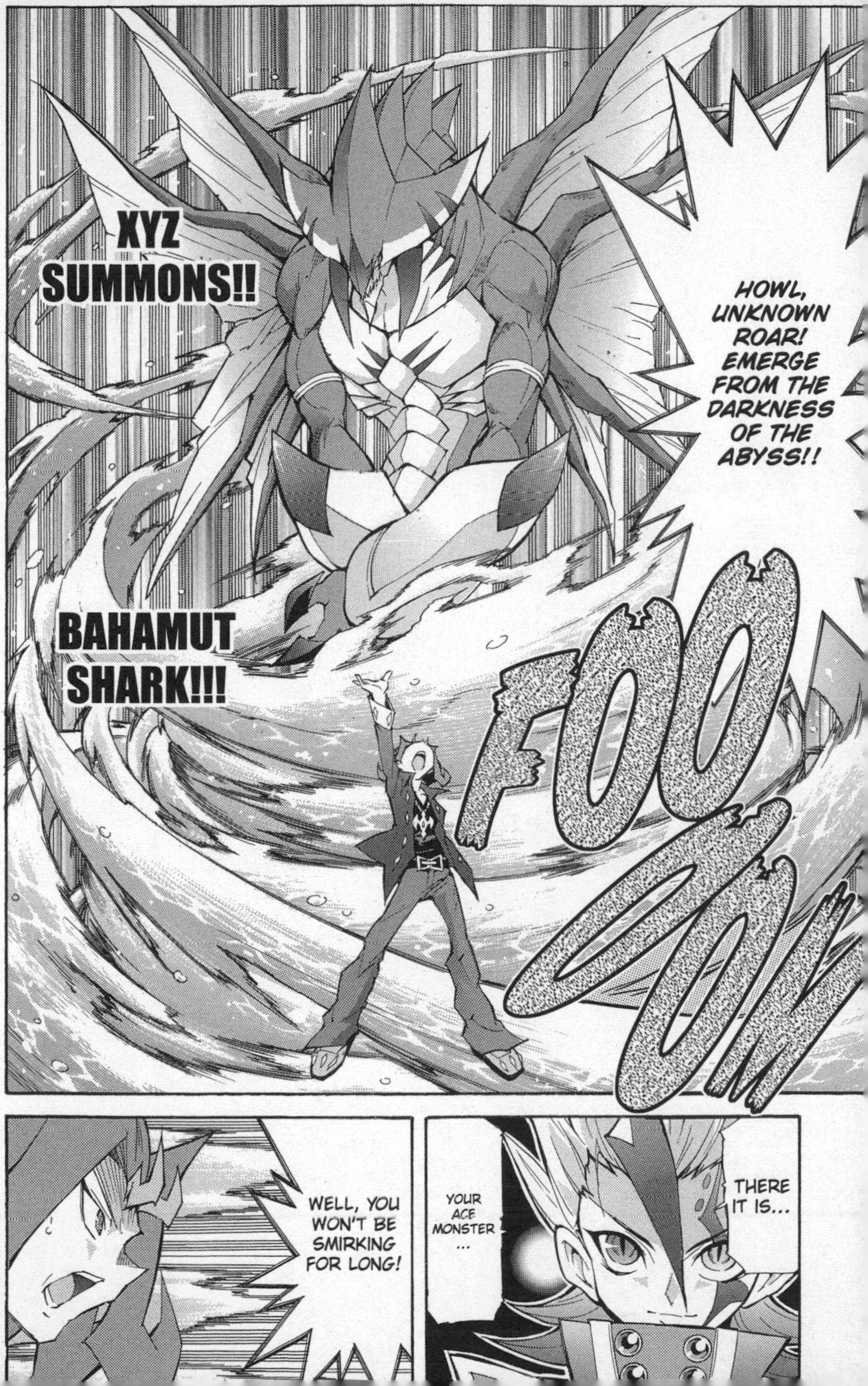
HOWL, UNKNOWN ROAR! EMERGE FROM THE DARKNESS OF THE ABYSS!!
XYZ SUMMONS!!
BAHAMUT SHARK!!!
FOOOM
THERE IT IS...
YOUR ACE MONSTER ...
WELL, YOU WON'T BE SMIRKING FOR LONG!

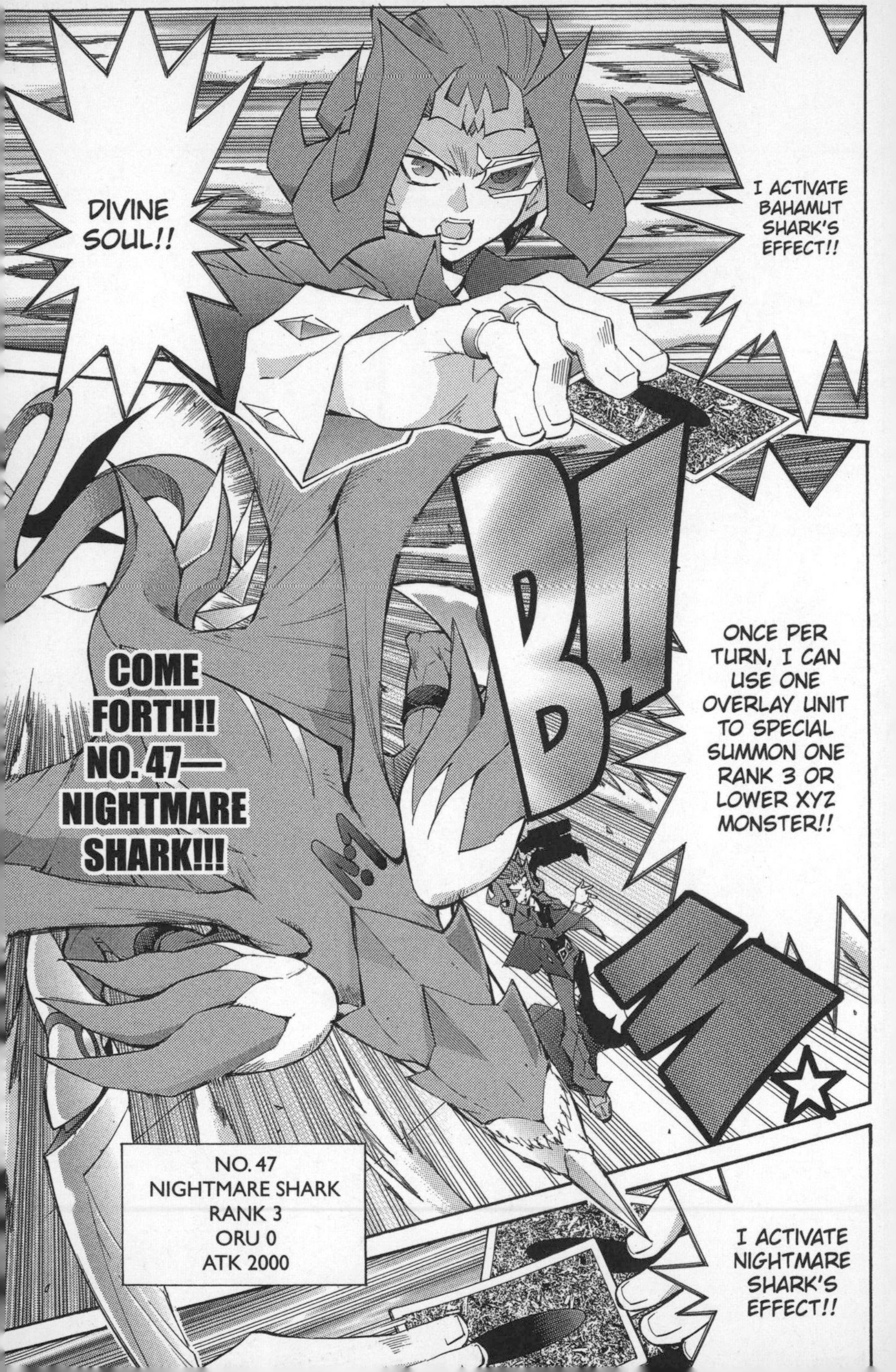
I ACTIVATE BAHAMUT SHARK'S EFFECT!!
DIVINE SOUL!!
ONCE PER TURN, I CAN USE ONE OVERLAY UNIT TO SPECIAL SUMMON ONE RANK 3 OR LOWER XYZ MONSTER!!
BAM
COME FORTH!! NO. 47— NIGHTMARE SHARK!!!
I ACTIVATE NIGHTMARE SHARK'S EFFECT!!
NO. 47
NIGHTMARE SHARK
RANK 3
ORU 0
ATK 2000

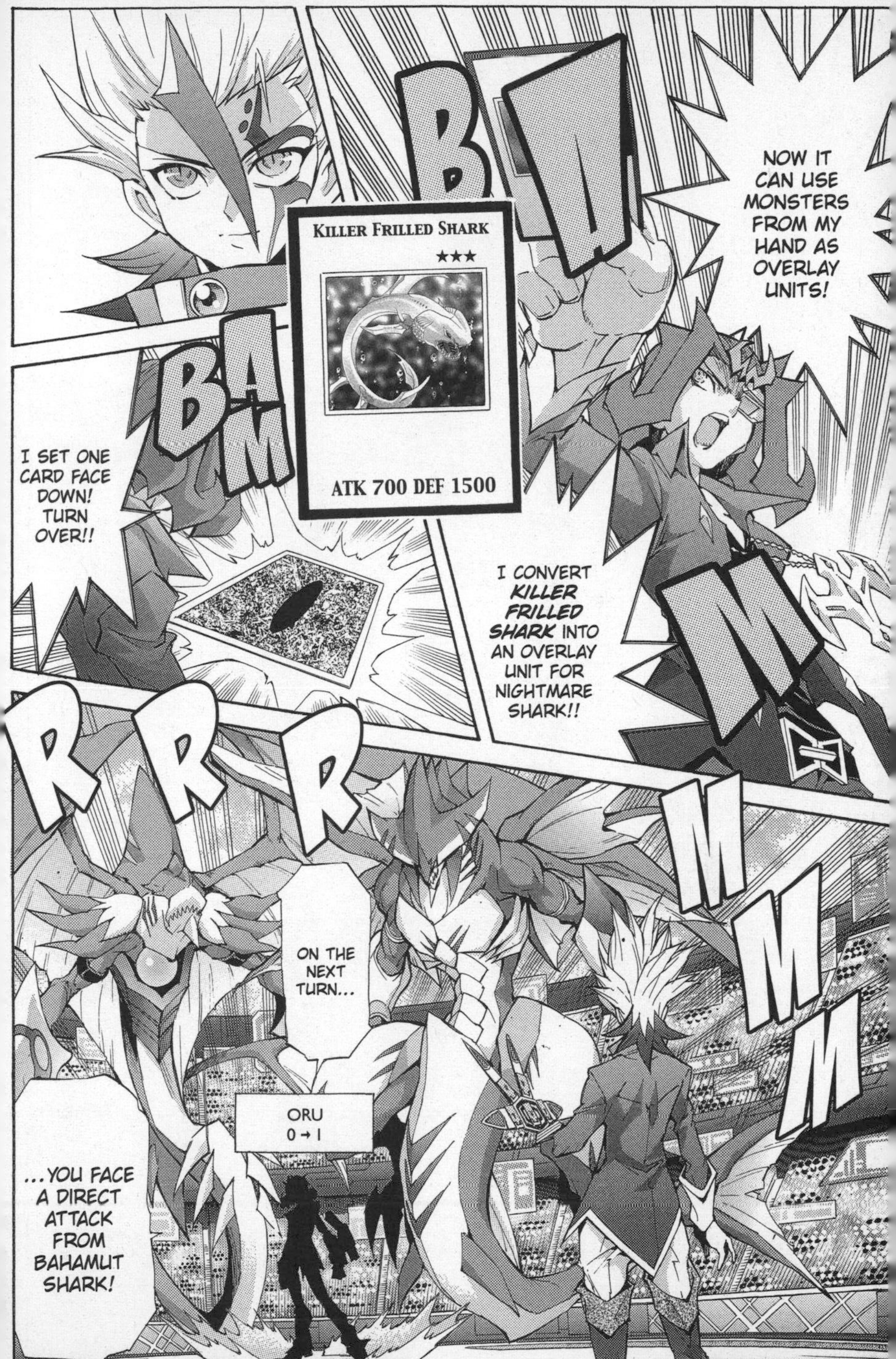
BAM
NOW IT CAN USE MONSTERS FROM MY HAND AS OVERLAY UNITS!
KILLER FRILLED SHARK
★★★
ATK 700 DEF 1500
I CONVERT *KILLER FRILLED SHARK* INTO AN OVERLAY UNIT FOR NIGHTMARE SHARK!!
MM
BAM
I SET ONE CARD FACE DOWN! TURN OVER!!
RRR
MMMM
ON THE NEXT TURN...
ORU 0→1
...YOU FACE A DIRECT ATTACK FROM BAHAMUT SHARK!

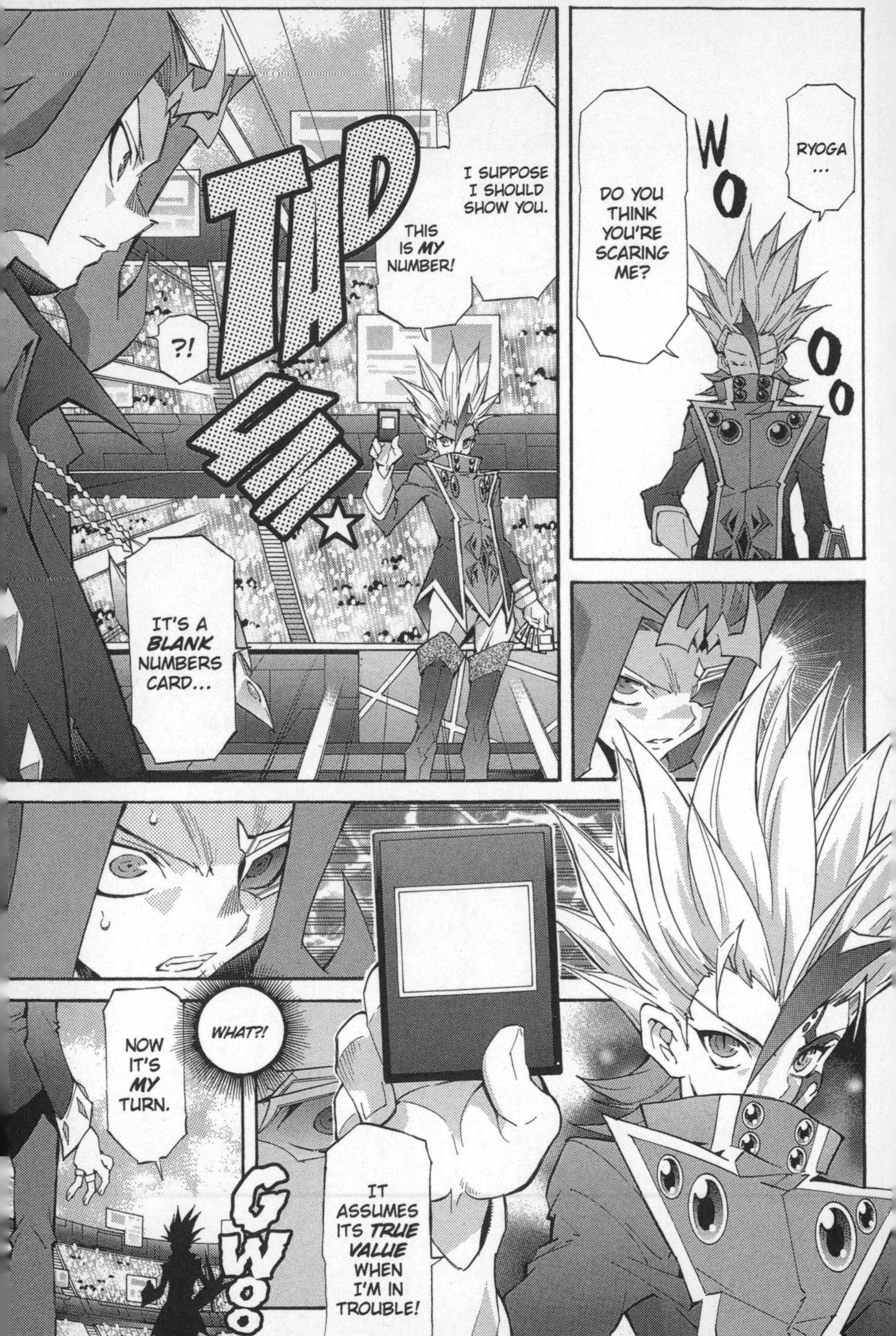
RYOGA ...
DO YOU THINK YOU'RE SCARING ME?
WOOO
I SUPPOSE I SHOULD SHOW YOU.
THIS IS MY NUMBER!
TAP
?!
IT'S A BLANK NUMBERS CARD...
NOW IT'S MY TURN.
WHAT?!
IT ASSUMES ITS TRUE VALUE WHEN I'M IN TROUBLE!
GWOO

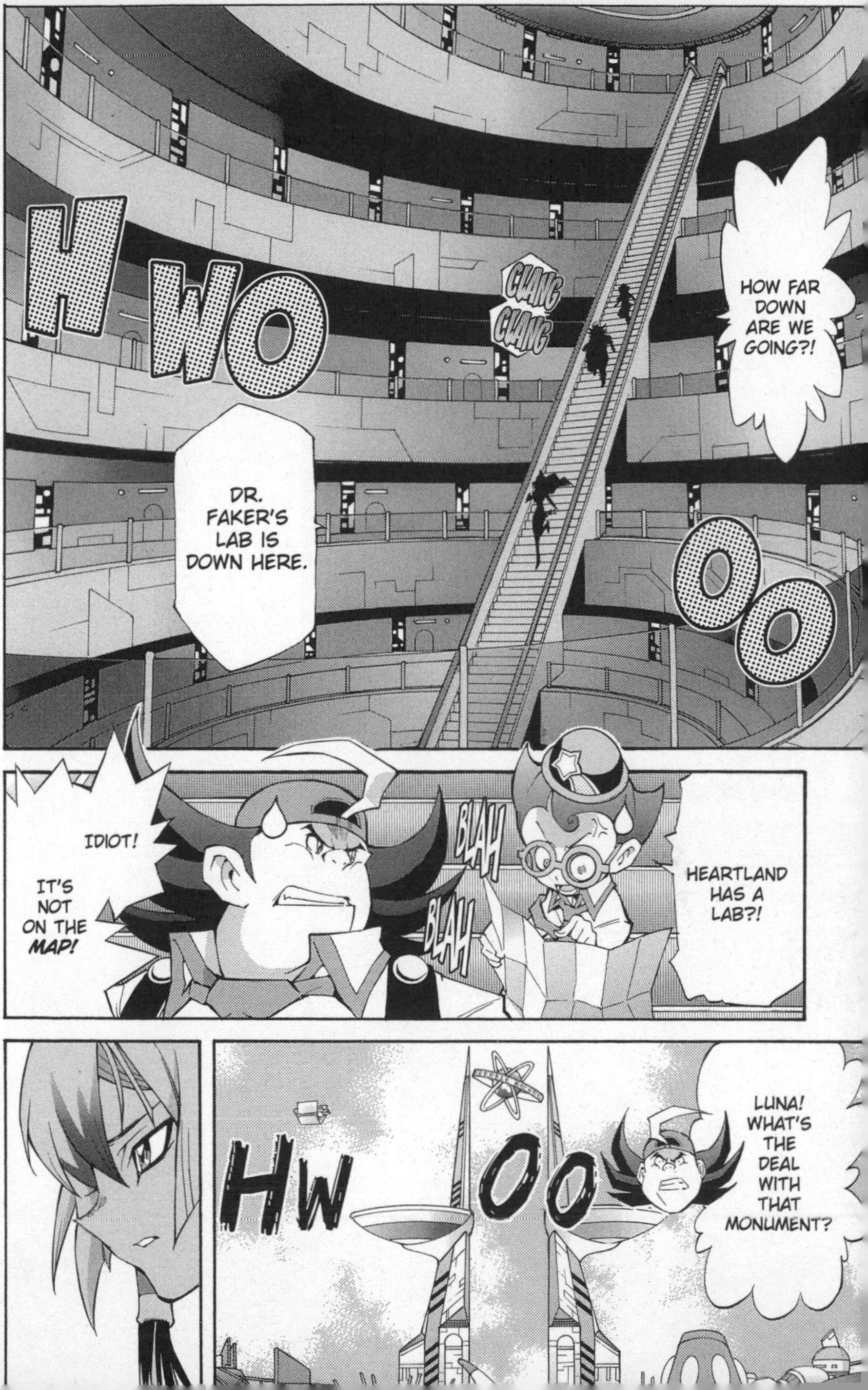
HOW FAR DOWN ARE WE GOING?!
CLANG CLANG
HWOOOO
DR. FAKER'S LAB IS DOWN HERE.
HEARTLAND HAS A LAB?!
BLAH BLAH
IDIOT!
IT'S NOT ON THE MAP!
LUNA! WHAT'S THE DEAL WITH THAT MONUMENT?
HWOO

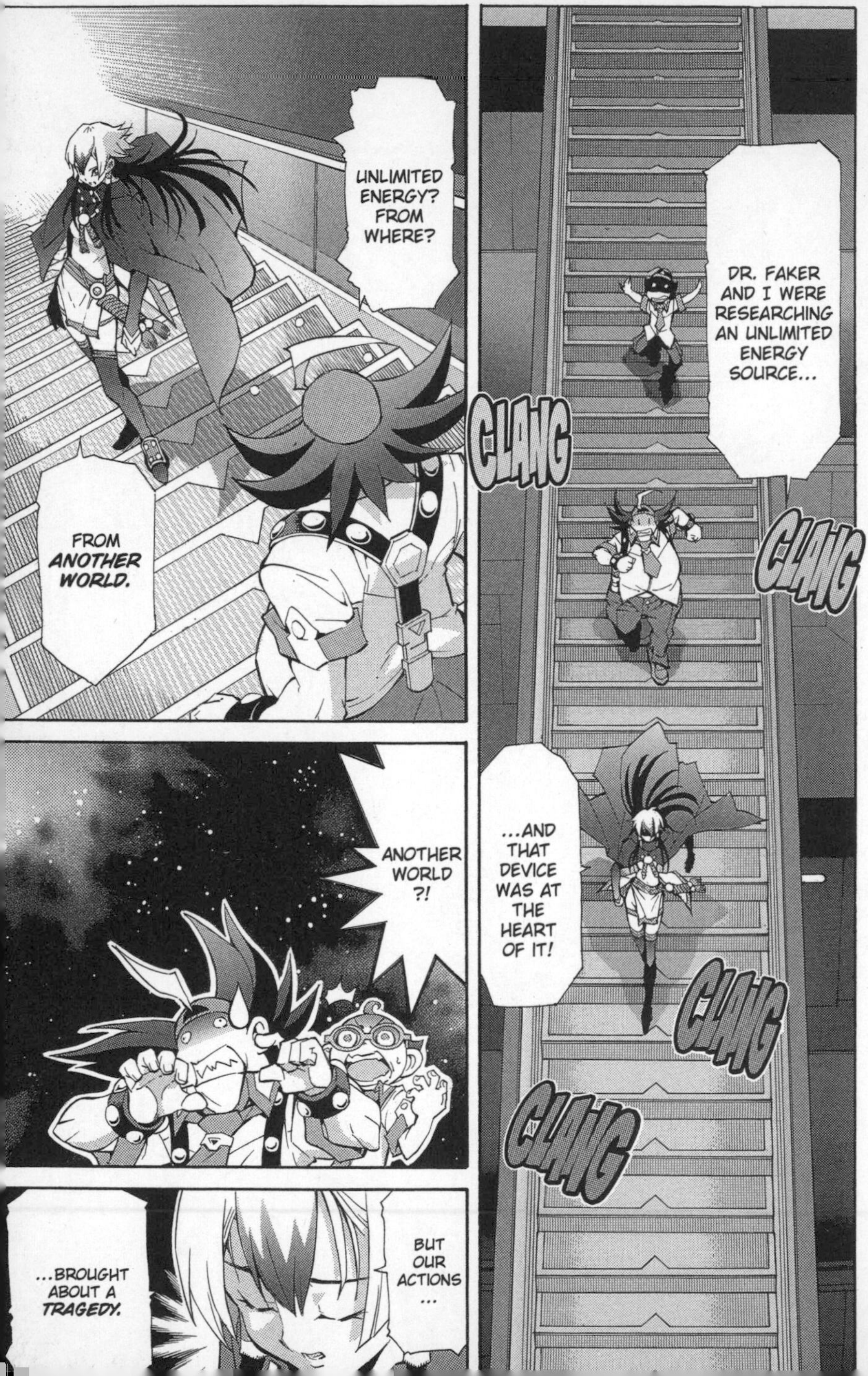
DR. FAKER AND I WERE RESEARCHING AN UNLIMITED ENERGY SOURCE...
CLANG
CLANG
...AND THAT DEVICE WAS AT THE HEART OF IT!
CLANG
CLANG
UNLIMITED ENERGY? FROM WHERE?
FROM ANOTHER WORLD.
ANOTHER WORLD ?!
BUT OUR ACTIONS ...
...BROUGHT ABOUT A TRAGEDY.

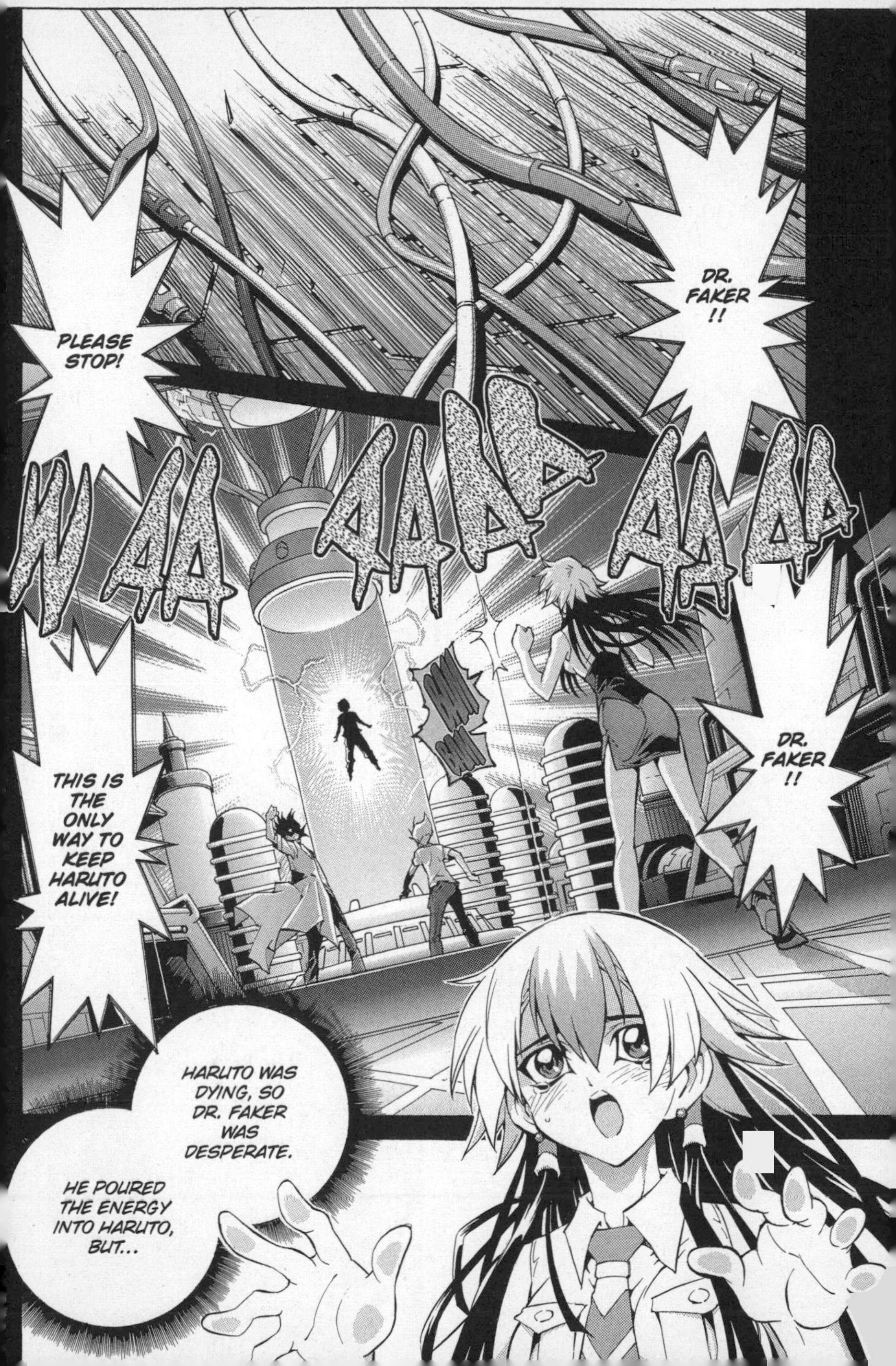
DR. FAKER !!
PLEASE STOP!
DR. FAKER !!
THIS IS THE ONLY WAY TO KEEP HARUTO ALIVE!
HARUTO WAS DYING, SO DR. FAKER WAS DESPERATE.
HE POURED THE ENERGY INTO HARUTO, BUT...

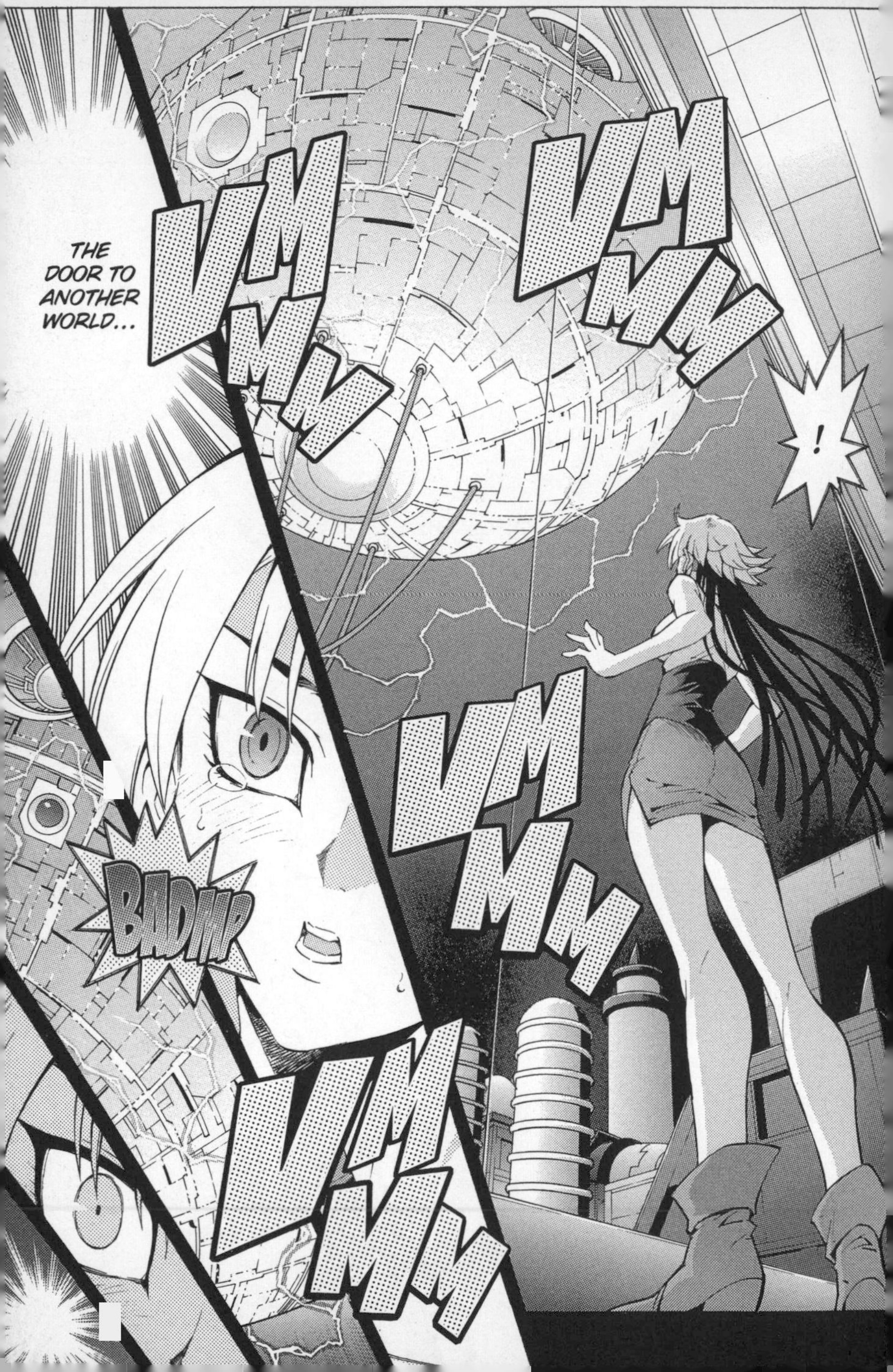
VMMMM
VMMMM
!
VMMMM
VMMMM
THE DOOR TO ANOTHER WORLD...
BADMP

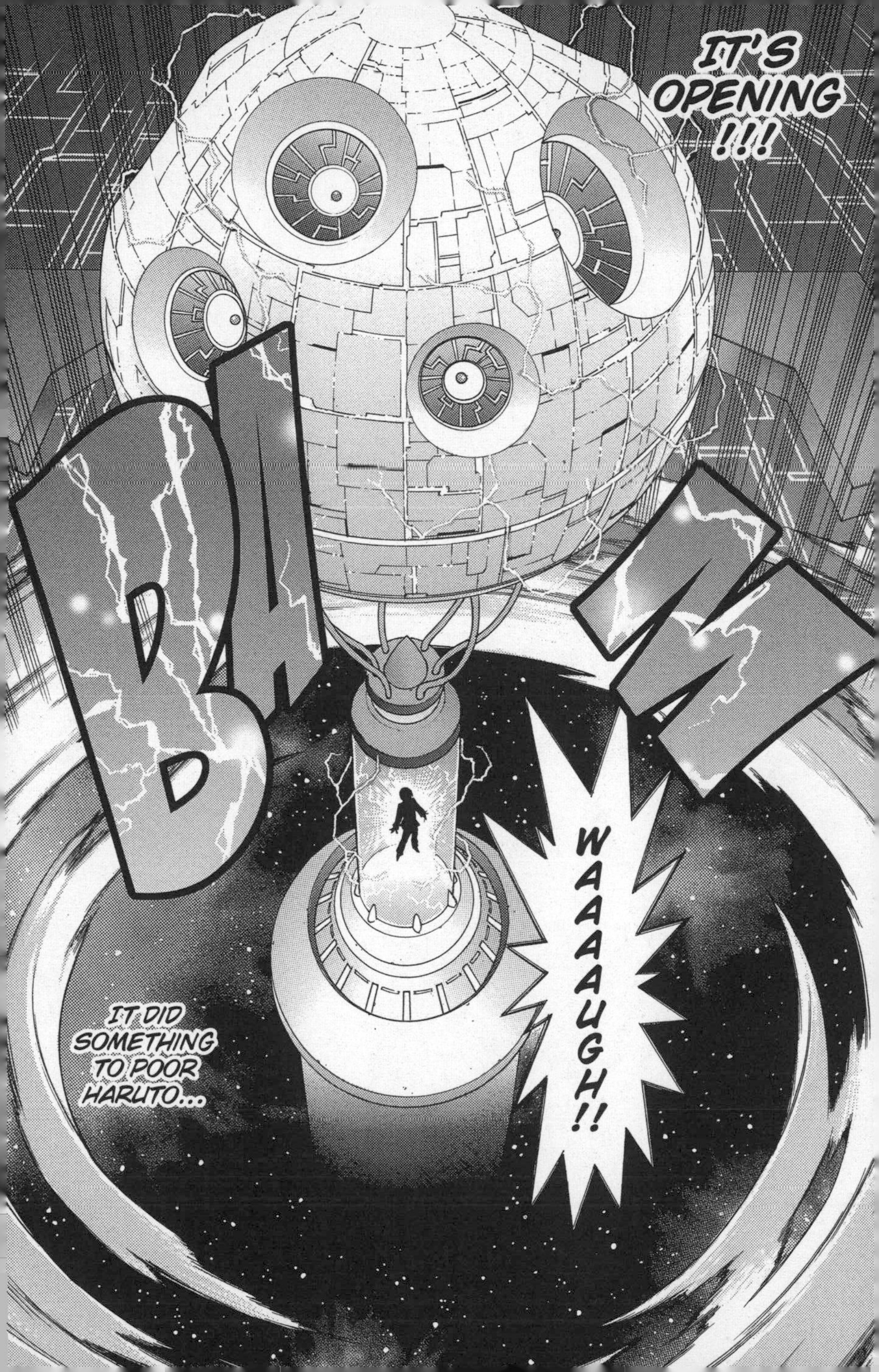
IT'S OPENING !!!
BAM
WAAAAUGH!!
IT DID SOMETHING TO POOR HARUTO...

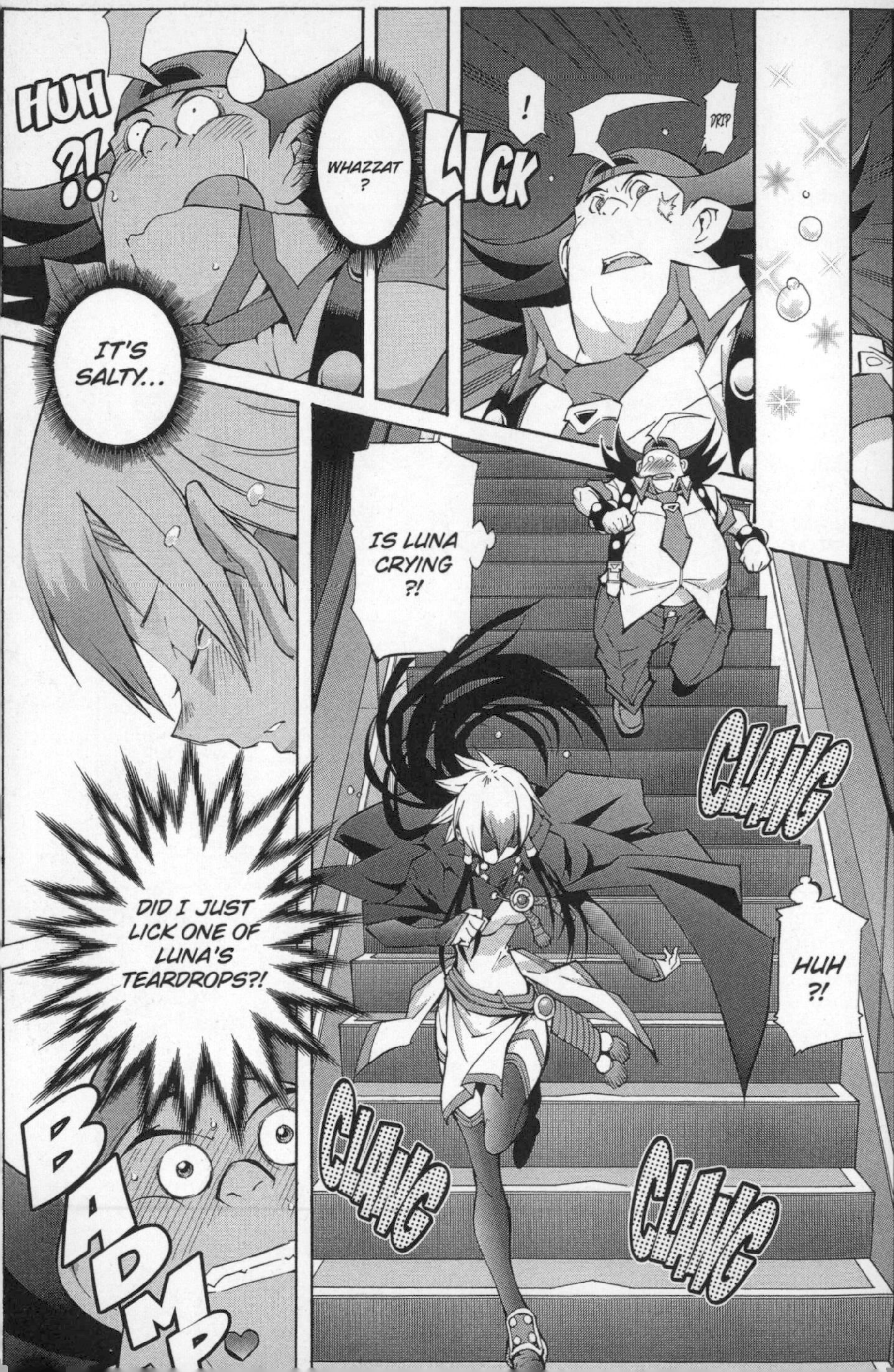
DRIP
!
LICK
WHAZZAT ?
HUH ?!
IT'S SALTY...
IS LUNA CRYING ?!
CLANG
HUH ?!
CLANG
CLANG
DID I JUST LICK ONE OF LUNA'S TEARDROPS?!
BADUMP

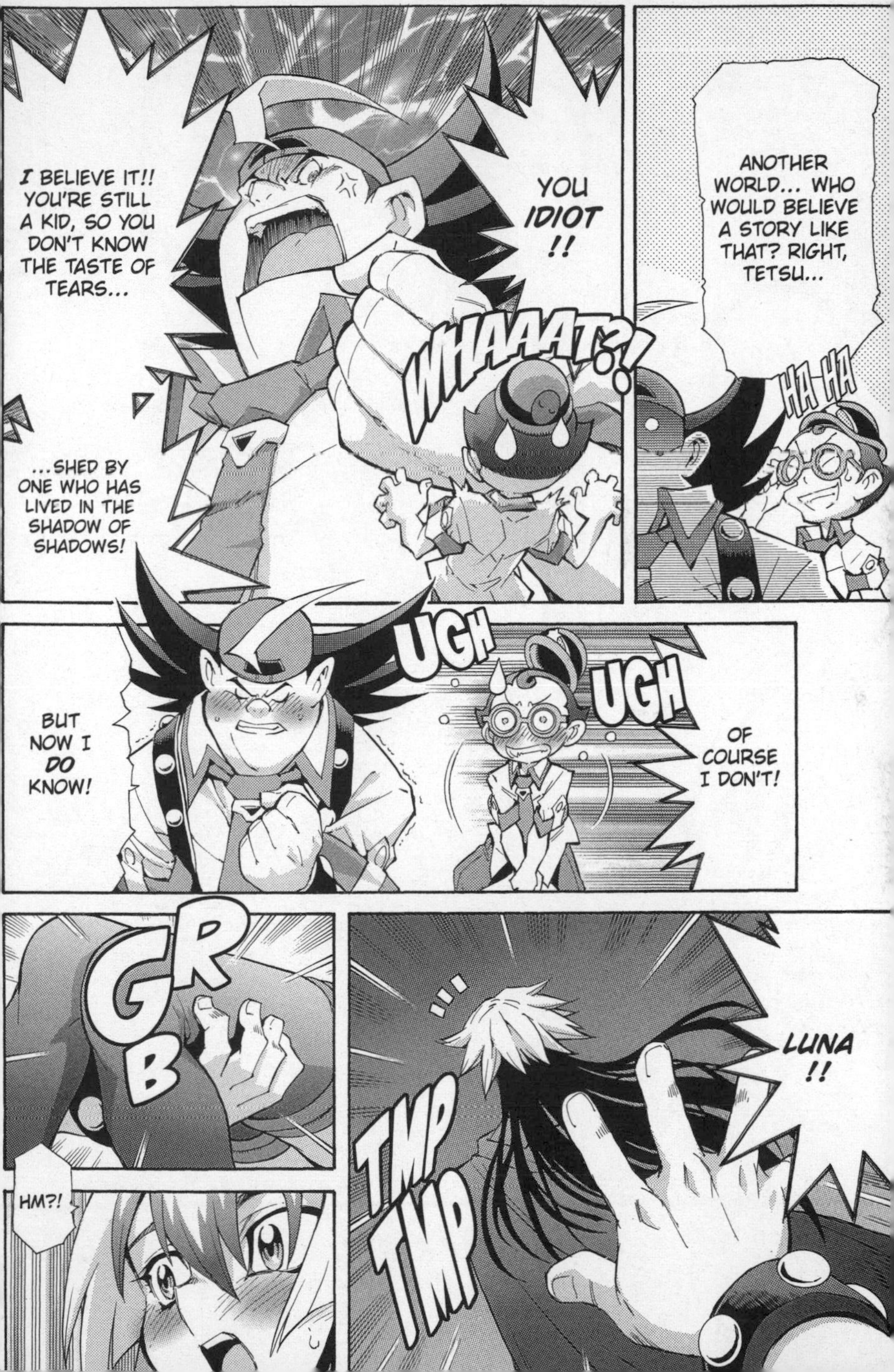
ANOTHER WORLD... WHO WOULD BELIEVE A STORY LIKE THAT? RIGHT, TETSU...
HA HA
YOU IDIOT!!
I BELIEVE IT!! YOU'RE STILL A KID, SO YOU DON'T KNOW THE TASTE OF TEARS...
WHAAAT?!
...SHED BY ONE WHO HAS LIVED IN THE SHADOW OF SHADOWS!
OF COURSE I DON'T!
UGH
UGH
BUT NOW I DO KNOW!
LUNA!!
...
TMP
TMP
GR
B
HM?!

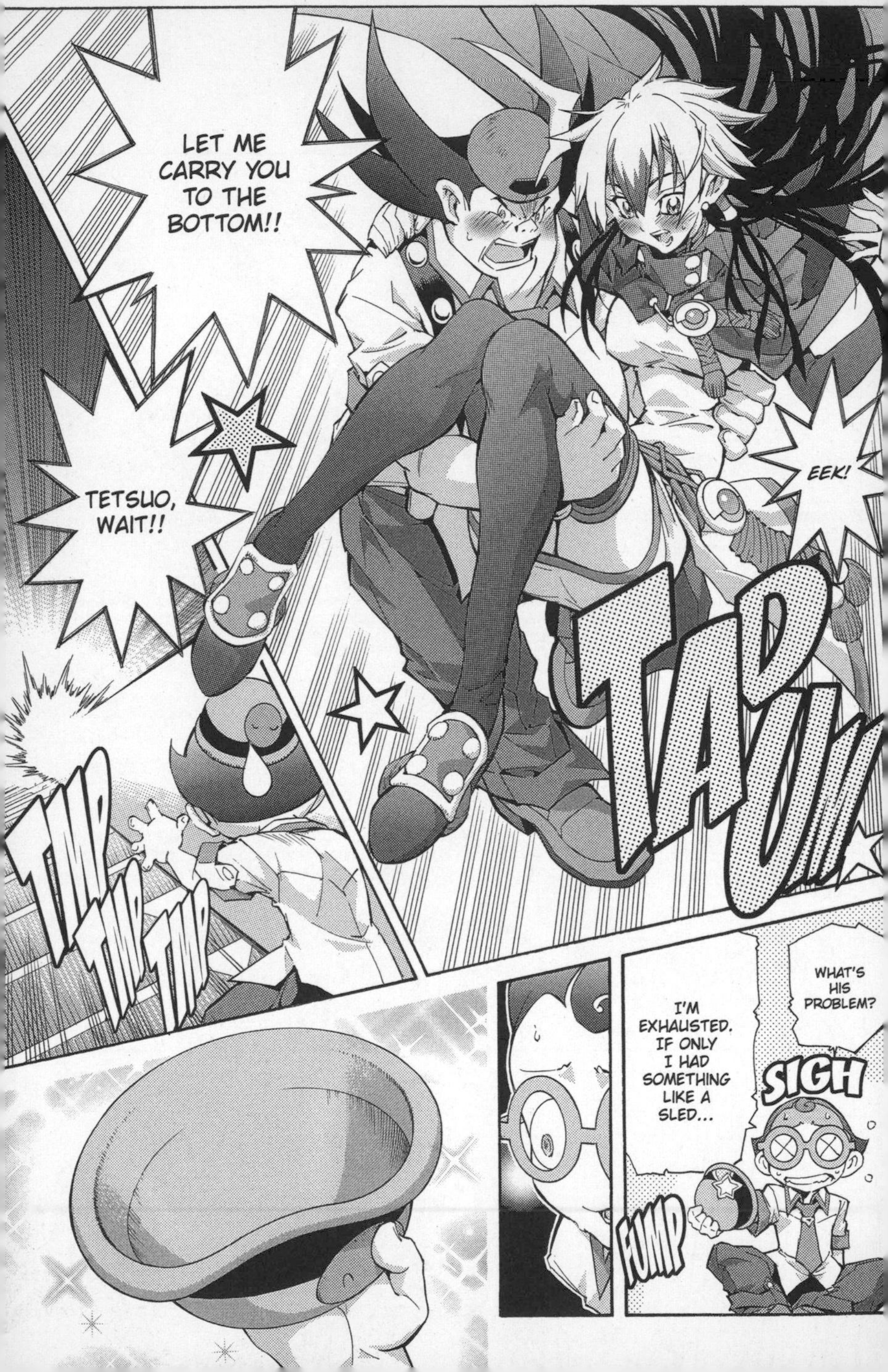

LET ME CARRY YOU TO THE BOTTOM!!
EEK!
TETSUO, WAIT!!
TADUM
TMP TMP TMP
WHAT'S HIS PROBLEM?
I'M EXHAUSTED. IF ONLY I HAD SOMETHING LIKE A SLED...
SIGH
FUMP

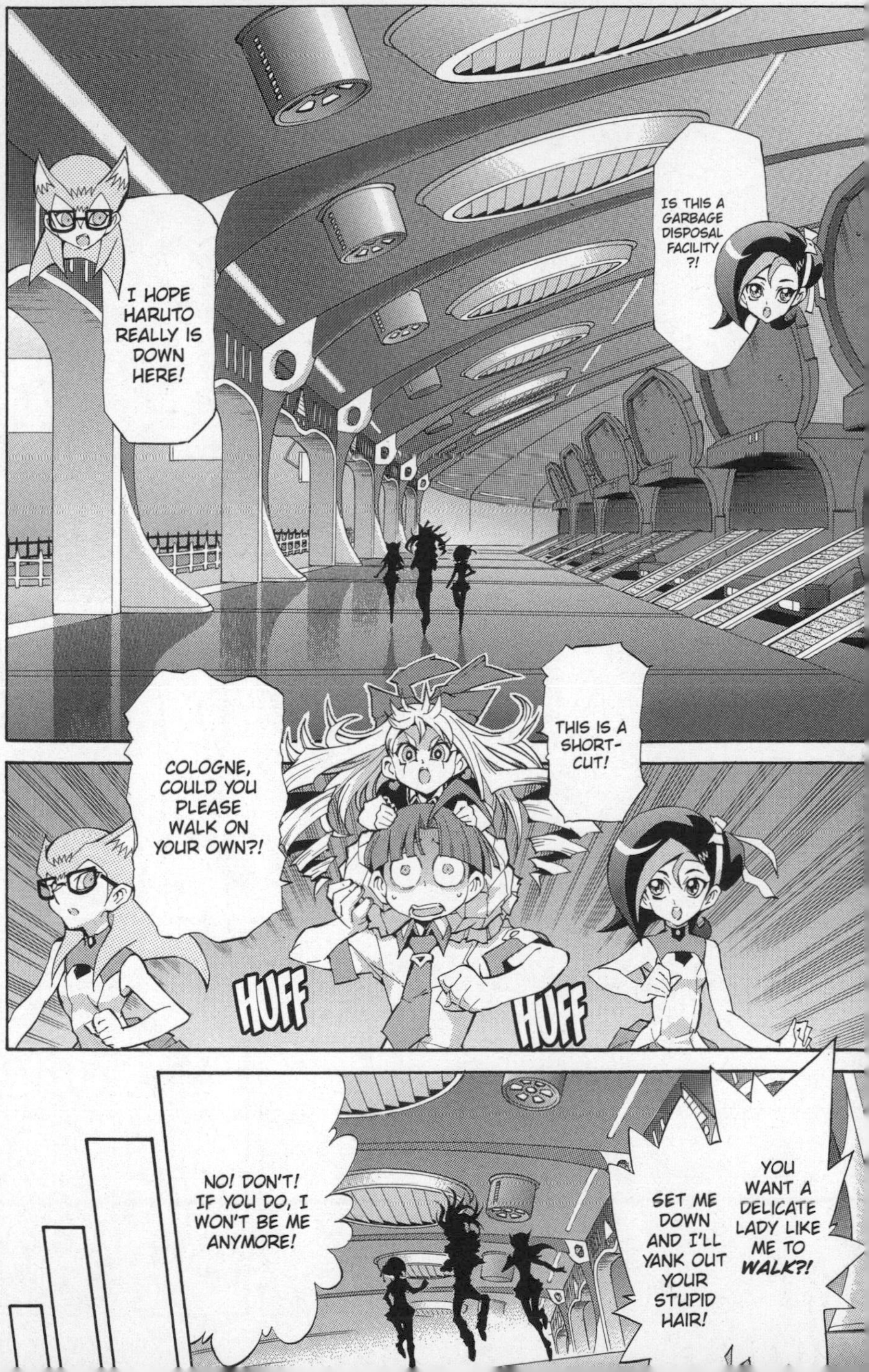
IS THIS A GARBAGE DISPOSAL FACILITY?!
I HOPE HARUTO REALLY IS DOWN HERE!
THIS IS A SHORT-CUT!
COLOGNE, COULD YOU PLEASE WALK ON YOUR OWN?!
HUFF
HUFF
YOU WANT A DELICATE LADY LIKE ME TO *WALK?!*
SET ME DOWN AND I'LL YANK OUT YOUR STUPID HAIR!
NO! DON'T! IF YOU DO, I WON'T BE ME ANYMORE!

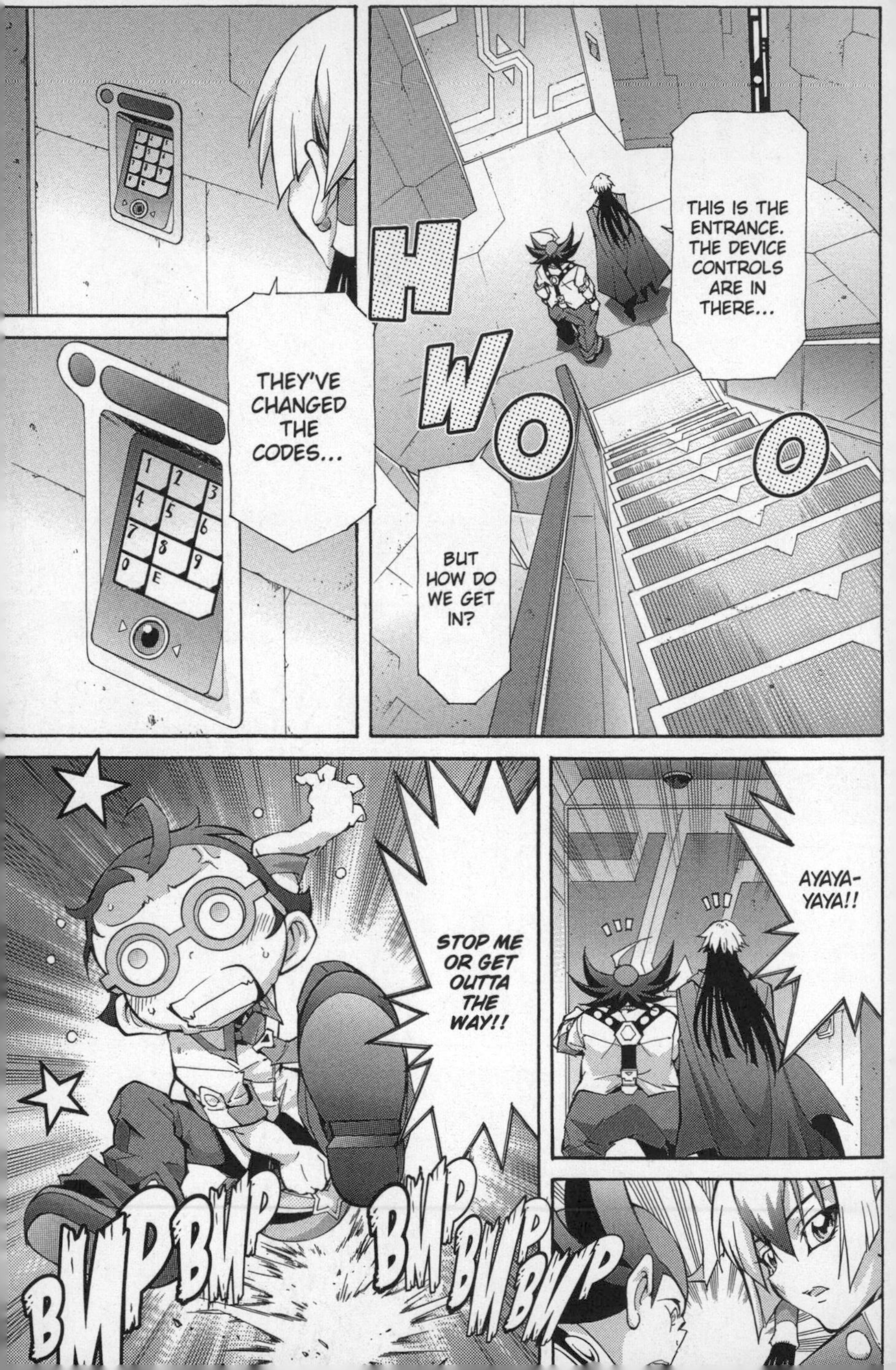
THIS IS THE ENTRANCE. THE DEVICE CONTROLS ARE IN THERE...
HWOOO
BUT HOW DO WE GET IN?
THEY'VE CHANGED THE CODES...
AYAYA-YAYA!!
STOP ME OR GET OUTTA THE WAY!!
BMP BMP
BMP BMP BMP

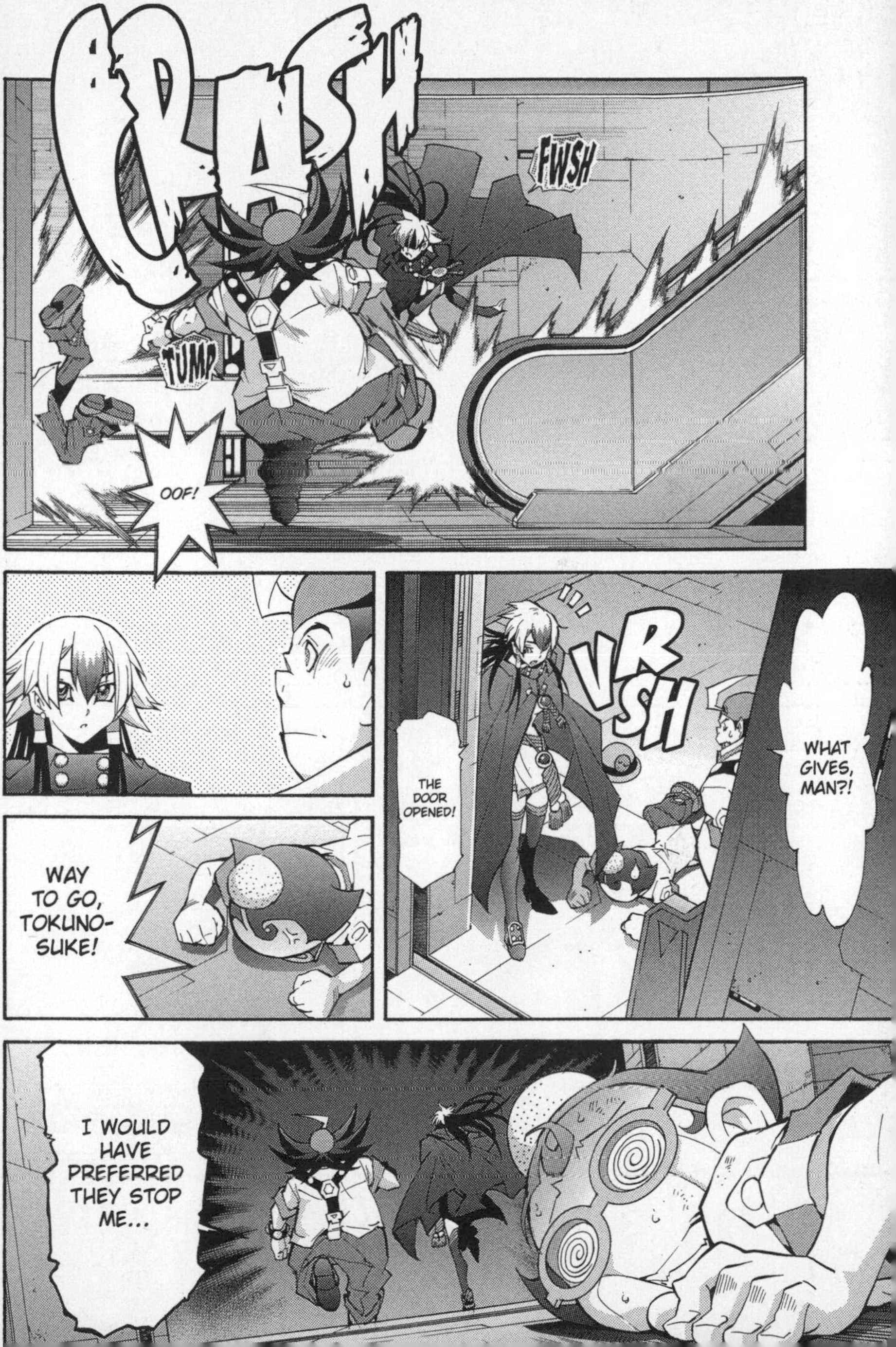
FWSH
CRASH
TUMP
OOF!
WHAT GIVES, MAN?!
VRSH
THE DOOR OPENED!
WAY TO GO, TOKUNOSUKE!
I WOULD HAVE PREFERRED THEY STOP ME...

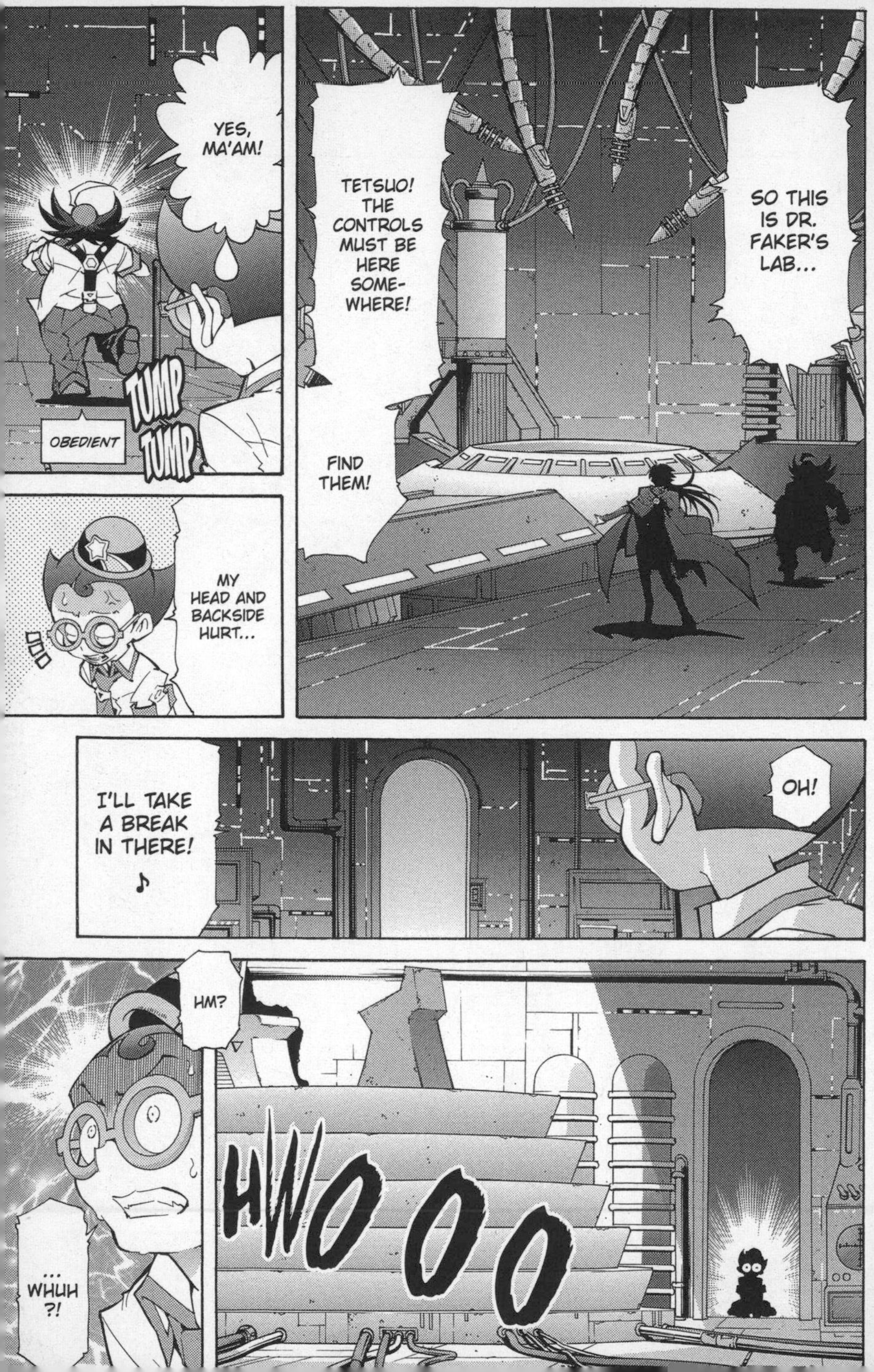
SO THIS IS DR. FAKER'S LAB...
TETSUO! THE CONTROLS MUST BE HERE SOME-WHERE!
FIND THEM!
YES, MA'AM!
TUMP TUMP
OBEDIENT
MY HEAD AND BACKSIDE HURT...
OH!
I'LL TAKE A BREAK IN THERE! ♪
HM?
HWOOOO
...WHUH?!

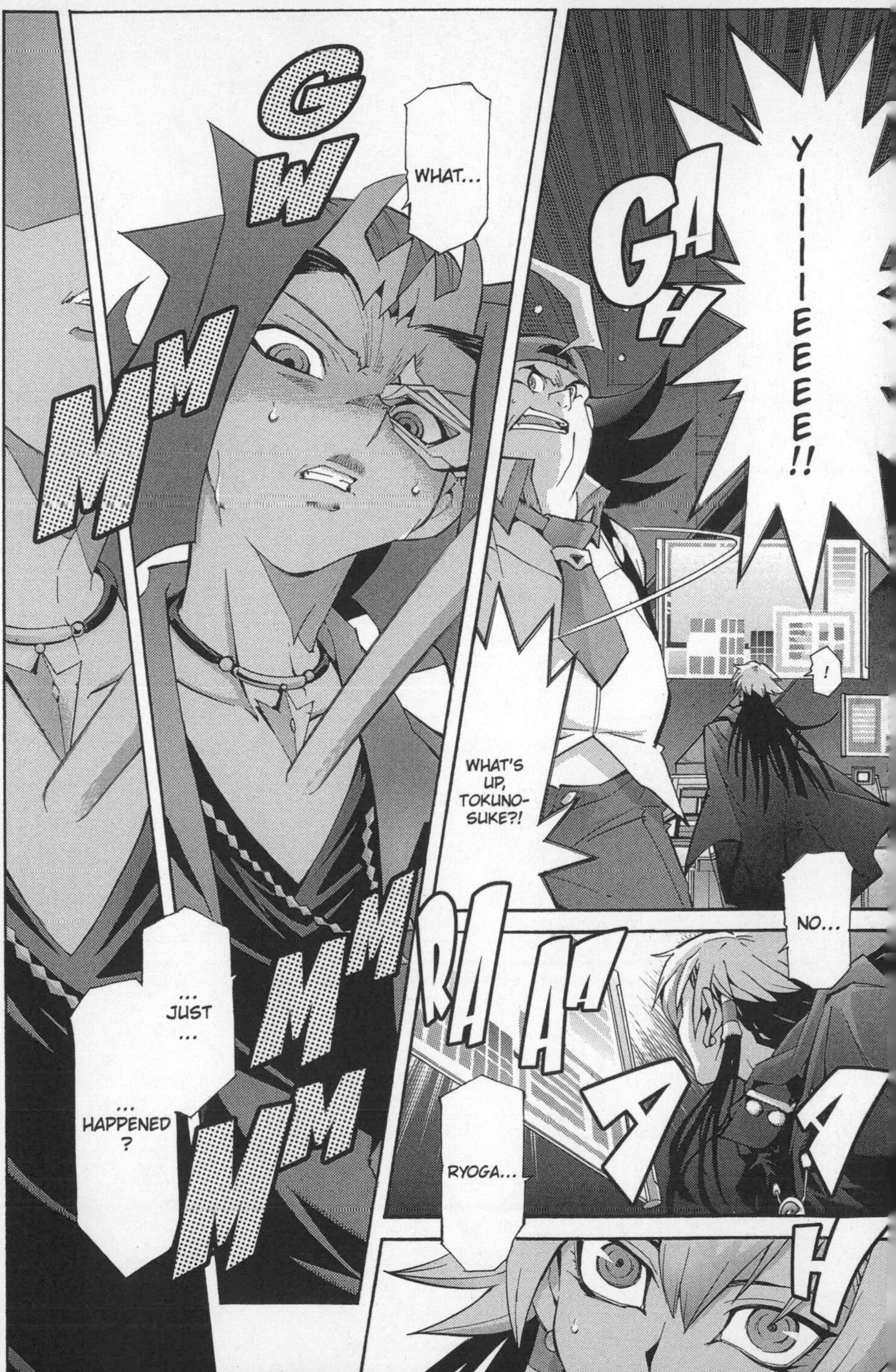
GAH
YIIIIEEEE!!
!
WHAT'S UP, TOKUNOSUKE?!
RAAAAAH
NO...
RYOGA...
GWMMM
WHAT...
...JUST...
...HAPPENED?
MMMMM

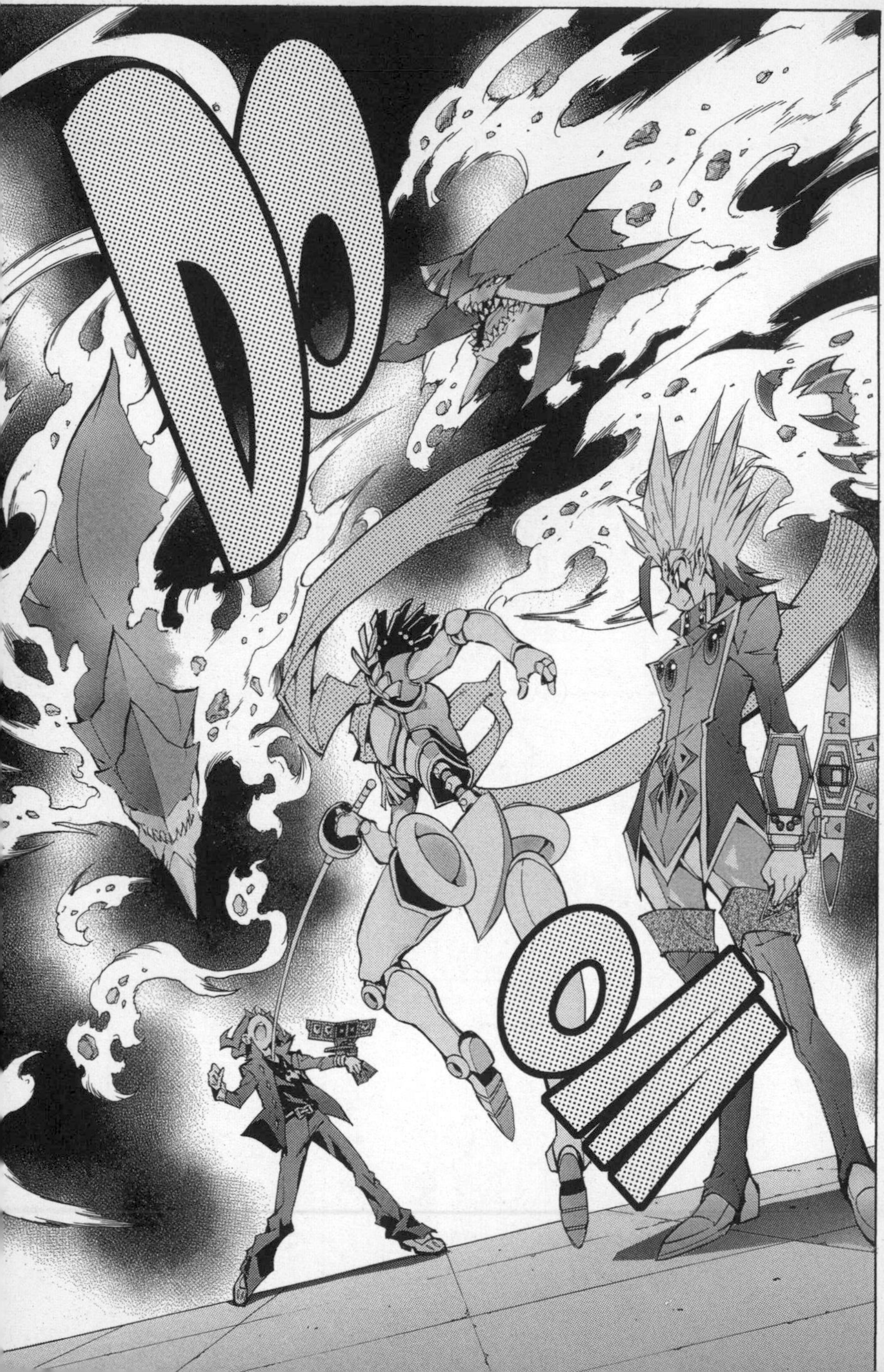
DO
O!!

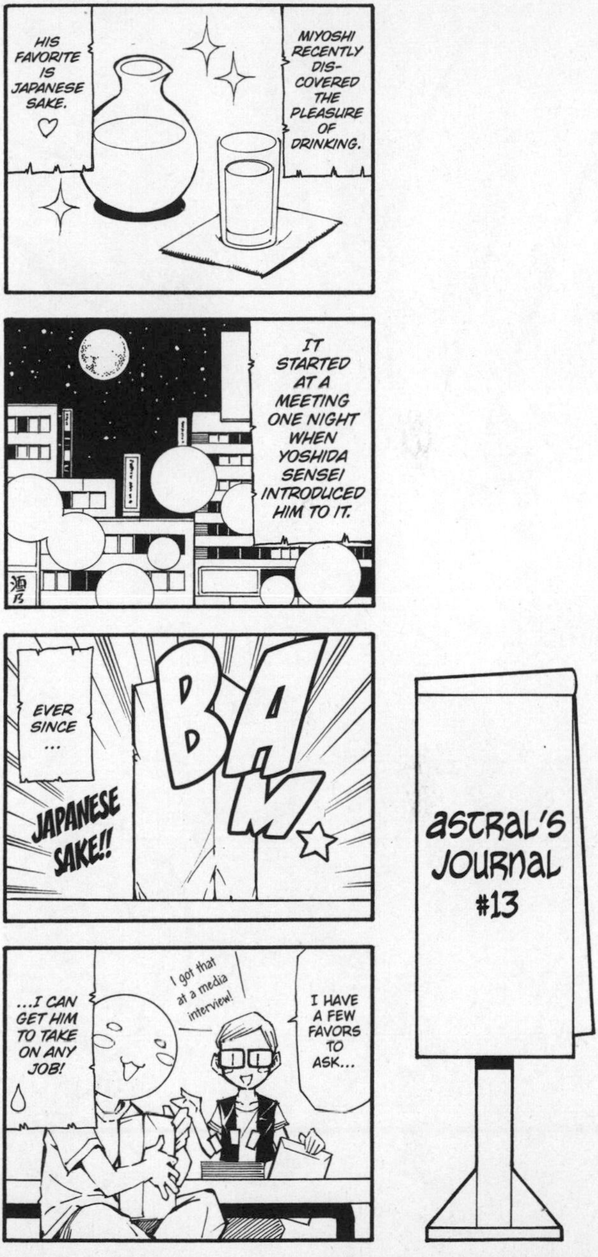
ASTRAL'S JOURNAL #13
MIYOSHI RECENTLY DIS-COVERED THE PLEASURE OF DRINKING.
HIS FAVORITE IS JAPANESE SAKE. ♥
IT STARTED AT A MEETING ONE NIGHT WHEN YOSHIDA SENSEI INTRODUCED HIM TO IT.
BAM
EVER SINCE...
JAPANESE SAKE!!
I HAVE A FEW FAVORS TO ASK...
I got that at a media interview!
...I CAN GET HIM TO TAKE ON ANY JOB!

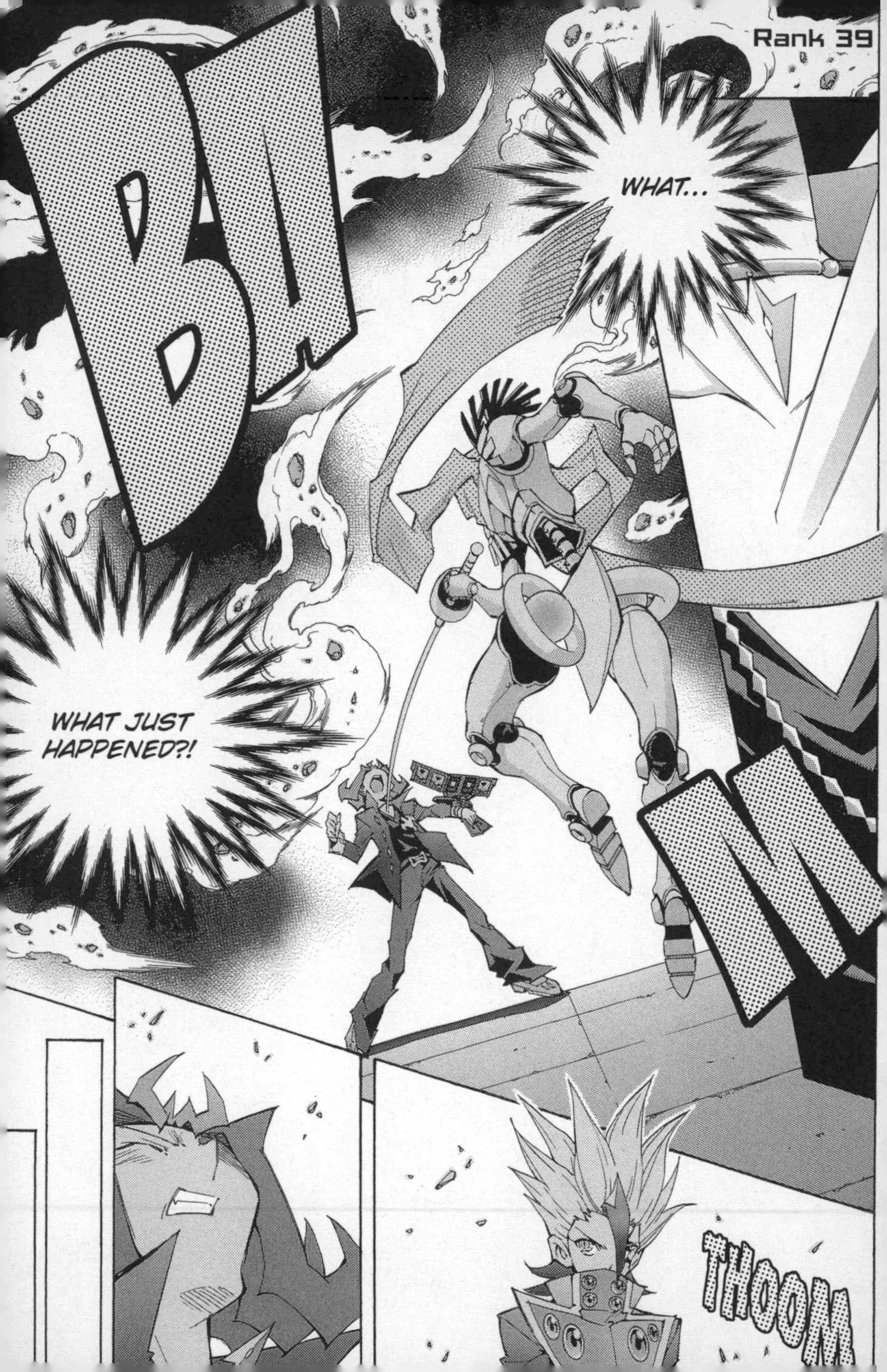
WHAT...
WHAT JUST HAPPENED?!
THOOM

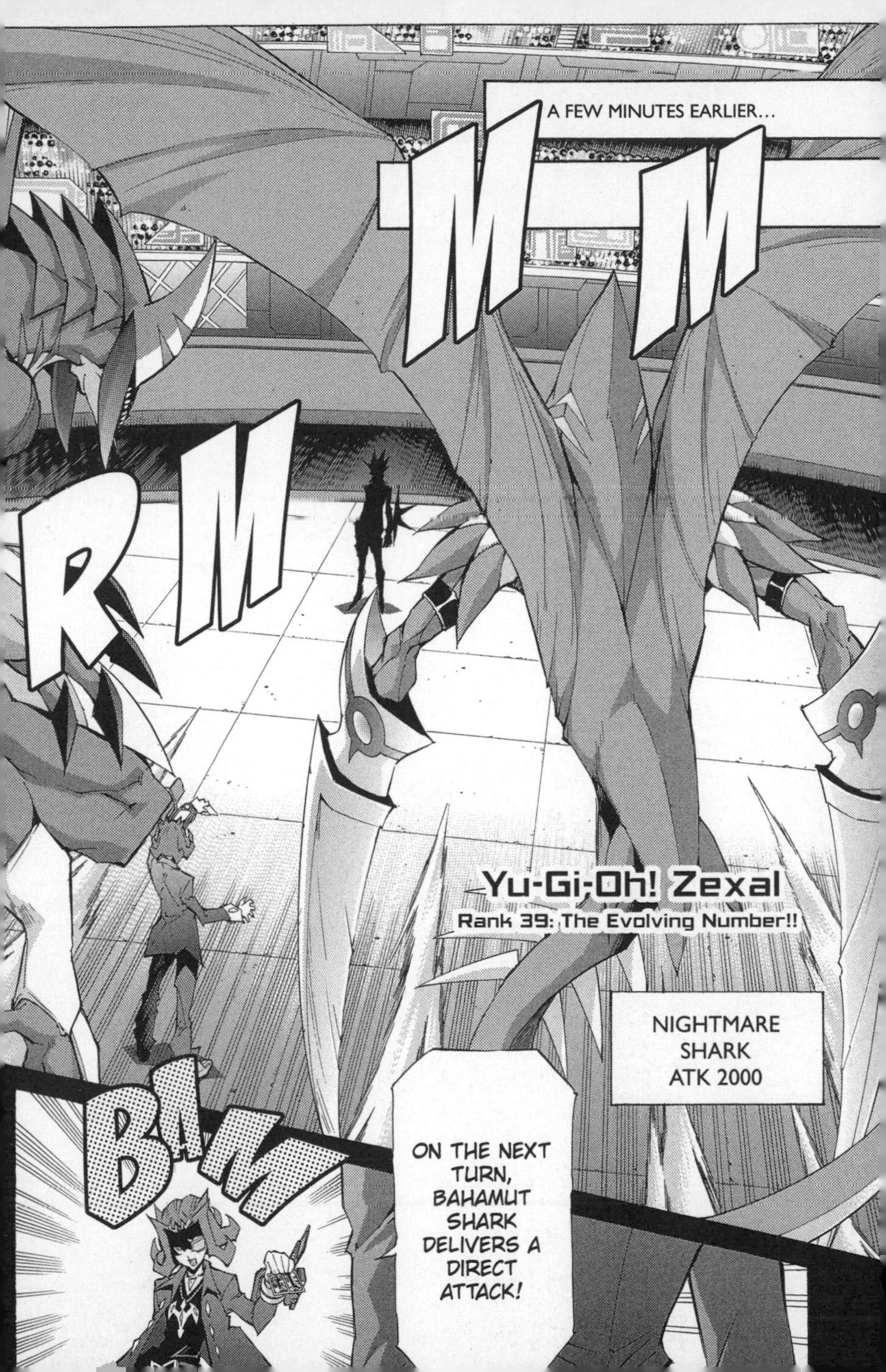

A FEW MINUTES EARLIER…
MM
RM
Yu-Gi-Oh! Zexal
Rank 39: The Evolving Number!!
NIGHTMARE SHARK ATK 2000
ON THE NEXT TURN, BAHAMUT SHARK DELIVERS A DIRECT ATTACK!
BAM

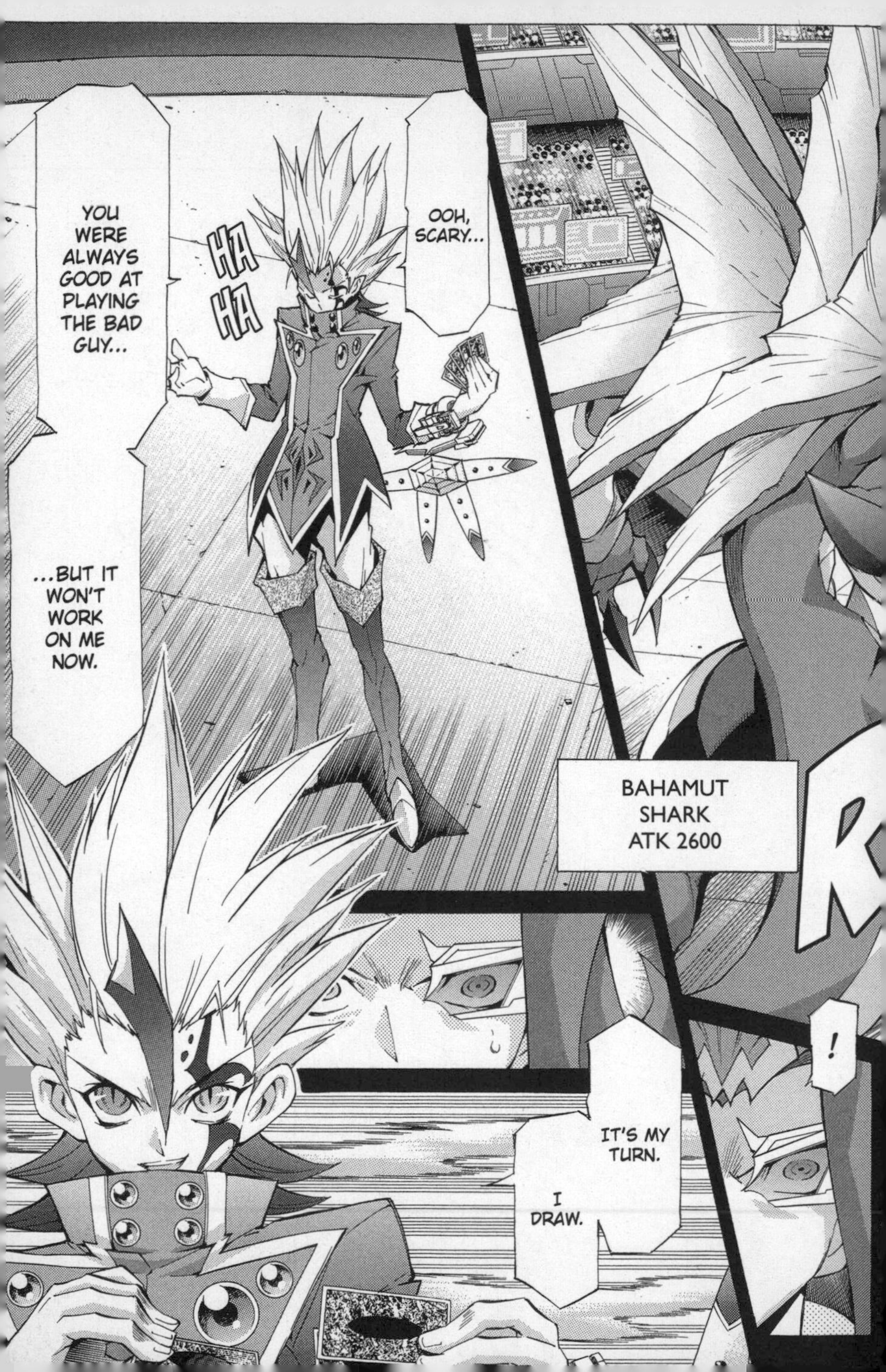
BAHAMUT SHARK ATK 2600
OOH, SCARY...
HA HA
YOU WERE ALWAYS GOOD AT PLAYING THE BAD GUY...
...BUT IT WON'T WORK ON ME NOW.
!
IT'S MY TURN.
I DRAW.

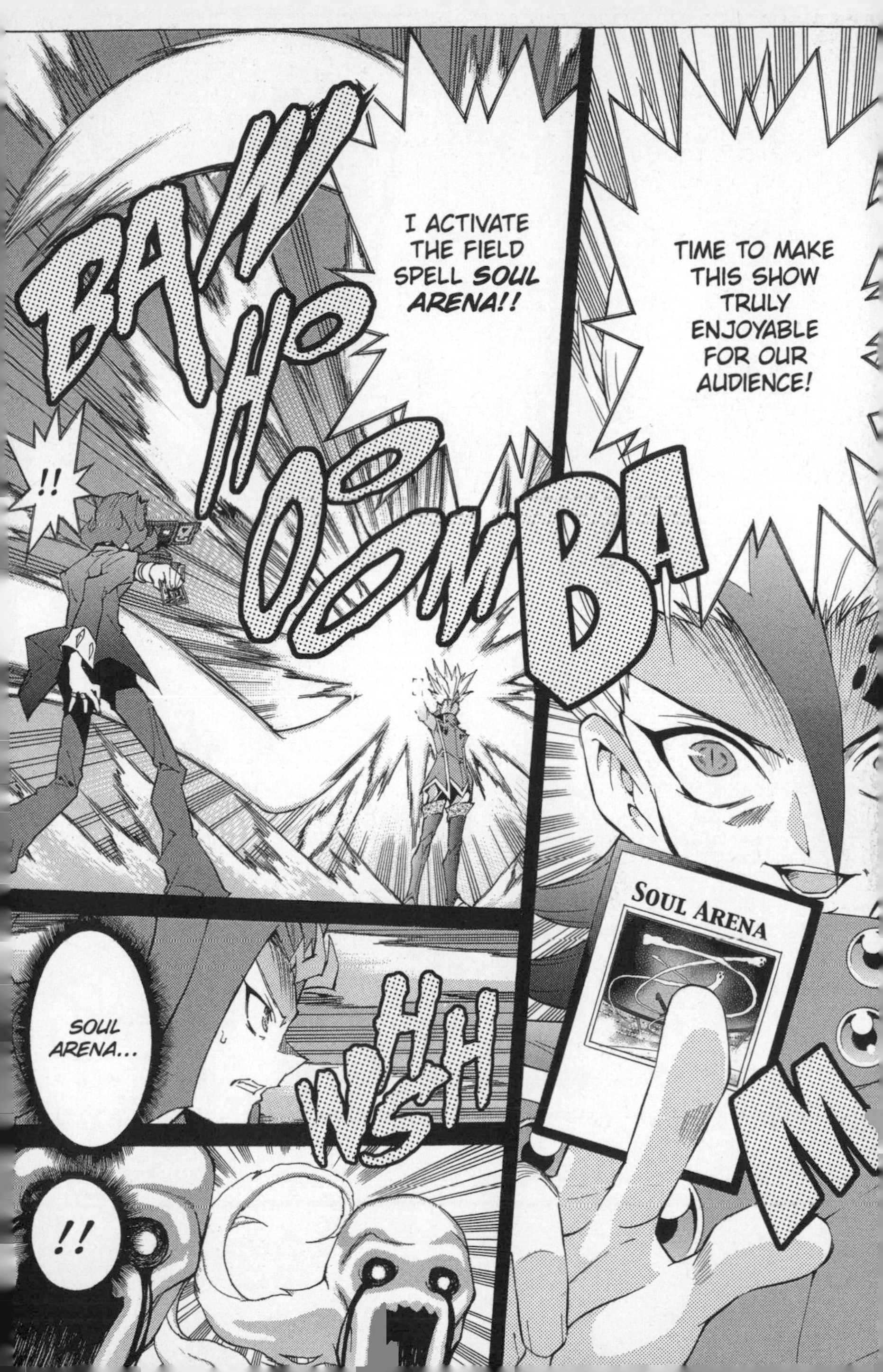
TIME TO MAKE THIS SHOW TRULY ENJOYABLE FOR OUR AUDIENCE!
SOUL ARENA
I ACTIVATE THE FIELD SPELL SOUL ARENA!!
!!
SOUL ARENA...
!!

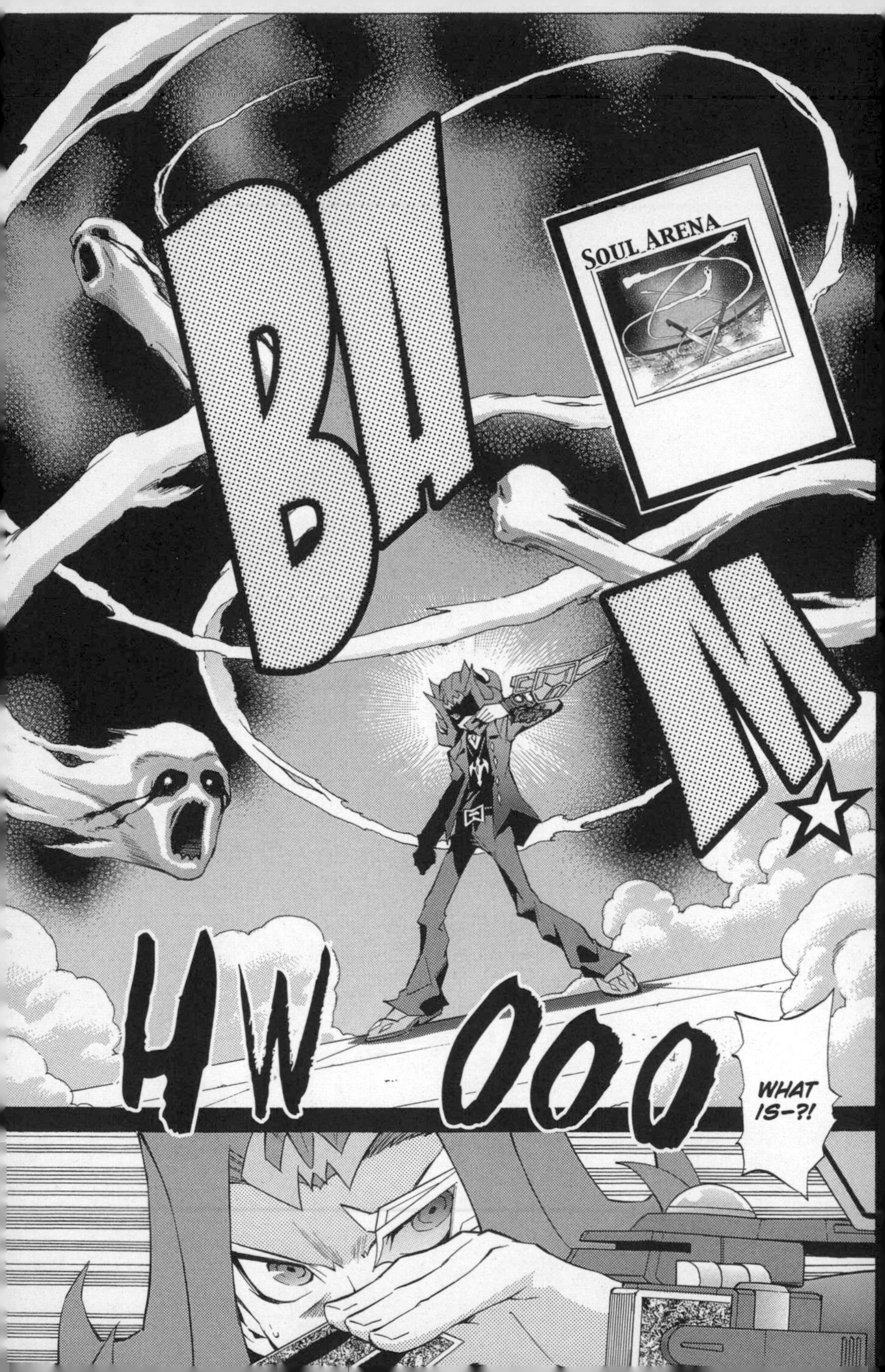
SOUL ARENA
BAM
HWOOO
WHAT IS-?!

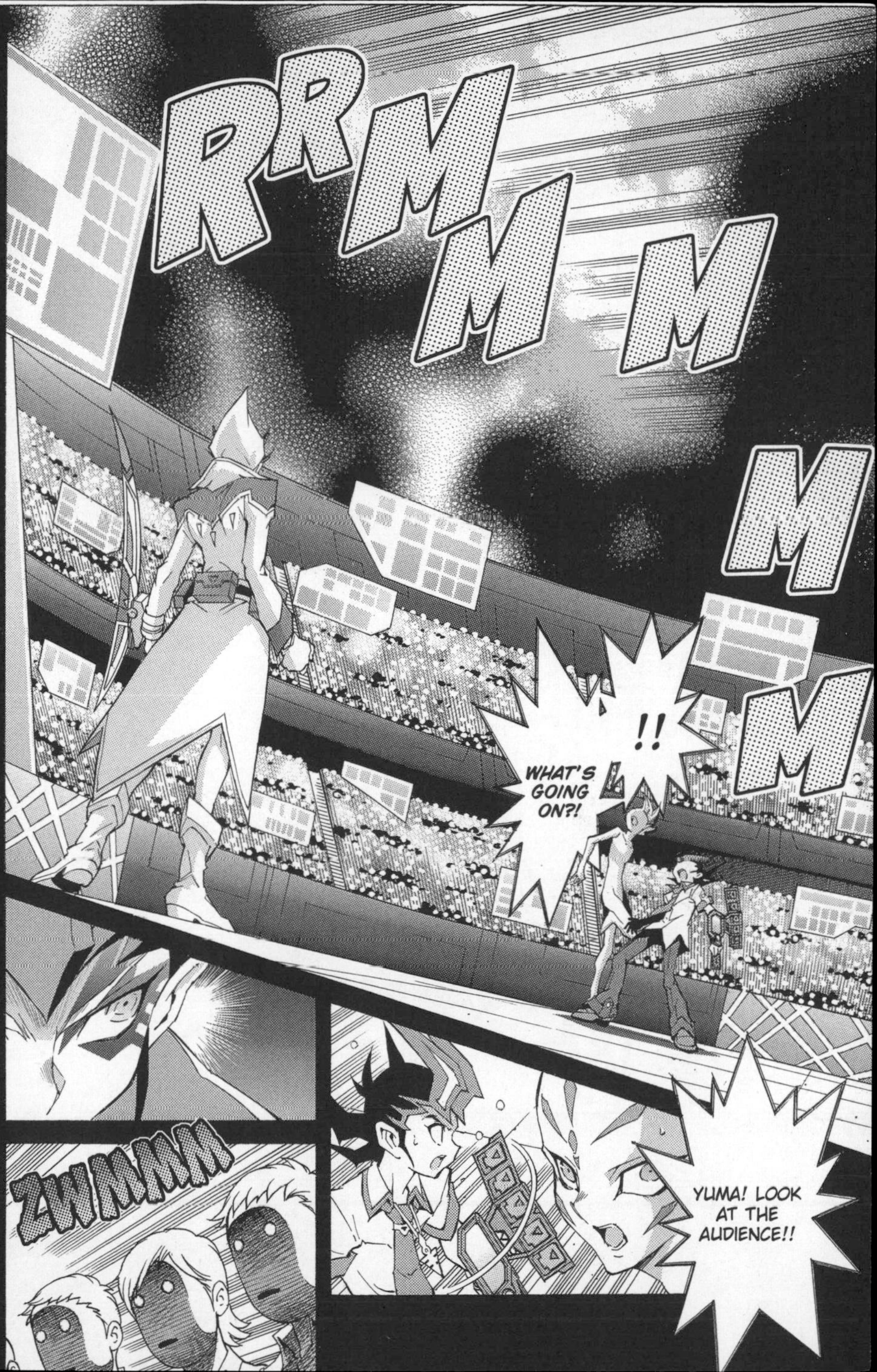
RRMMMMM
!!
WHAT'S GOING ON?!
YUMA! LOOK AT THE AUDIENCE!!
ZWMMM

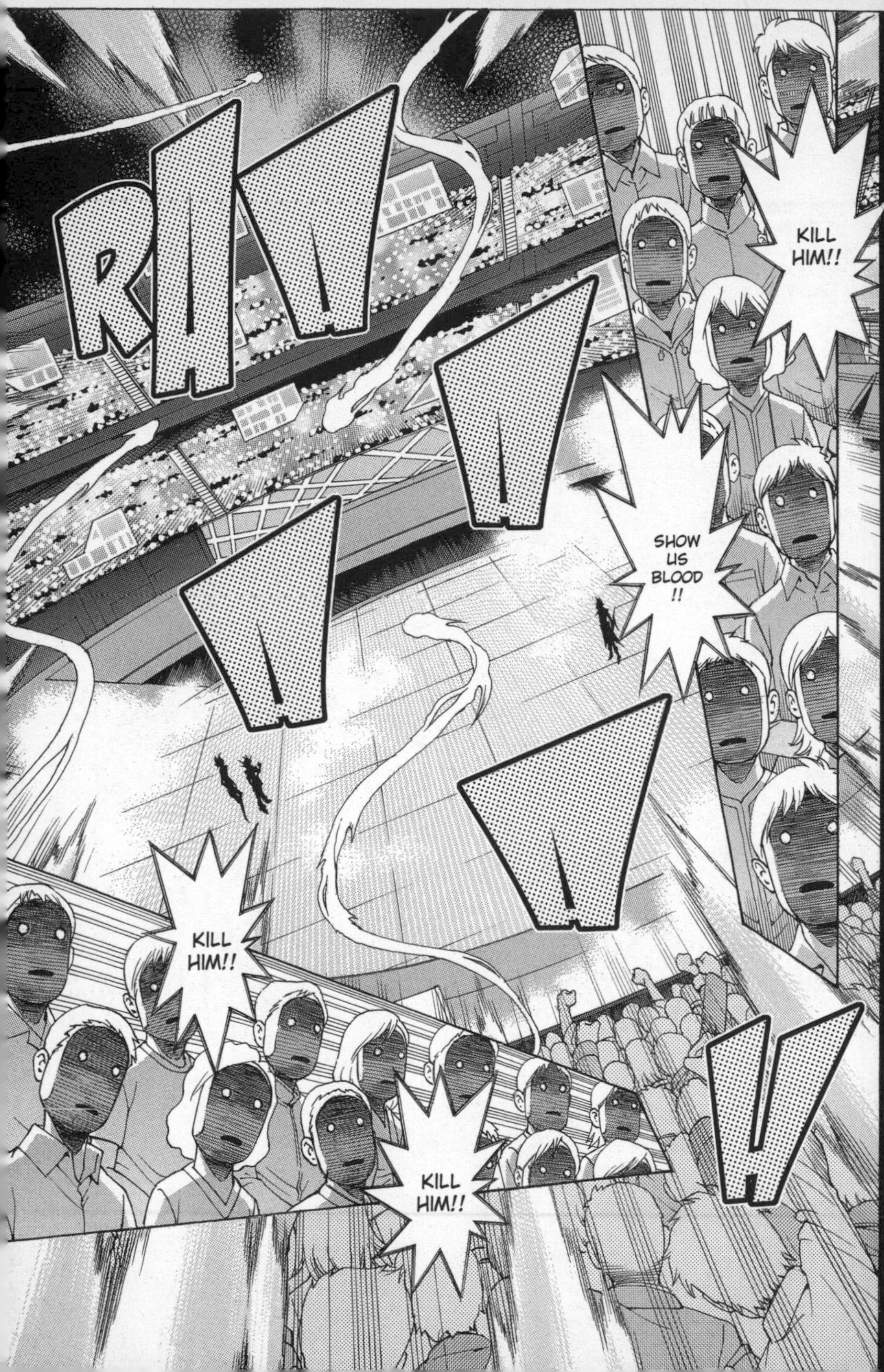
KILL HIM!!
SHOW US BLOOD !!
RAAAAH!
KILL HIM!!
KILL HIM!!

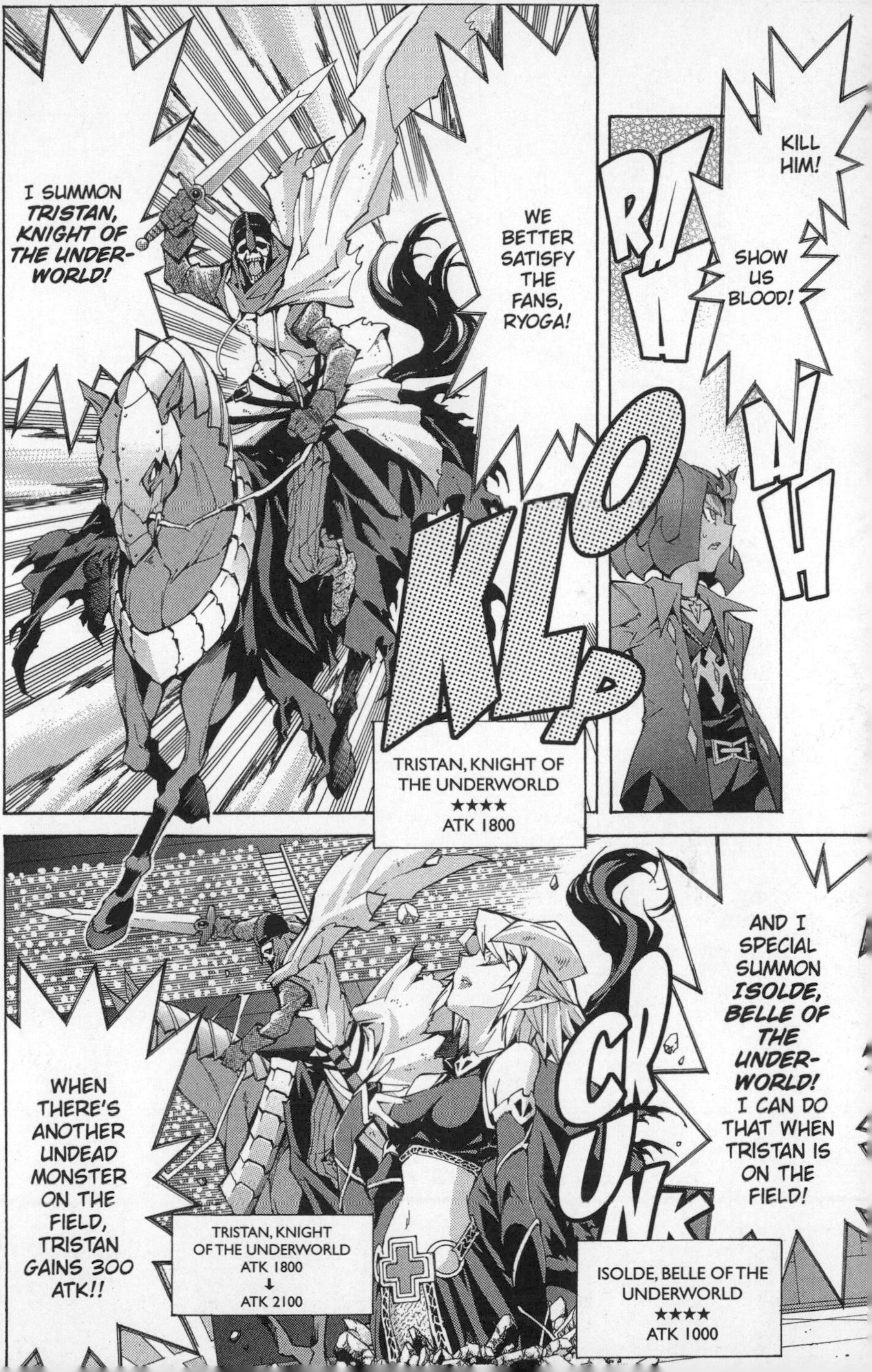
KILL HIM!
SHOW US BLOOD!
WE BETTER SATISFY THE FANS, RYOGA!
I SUMMON *TRISTAN, KNIGHT OF THE UNDERWORLD!*
KLOP
TRISTAN, KNIGHT OF THE UNDERWORLD ★★★★ ATK 1800
AND I SPECIAL SUMMON *ISOLDE, BELLE OF THE UNDERWORLD!* I CAN DO THAT WHEN TRISTAN IS ON THE FIELD!
ISOLDE, BELLE OF THE UNDERWORLD ★★★★ ATK 1000
WHEN THERE'S ANOTHER UNDEAD MONSTER ON THE FIELD, TRISTAN GAINS 300 ATK!!
TRISTAN, KNIGHT OF THE UNDERWORLD ATK 1800 ↓ ATK 2100

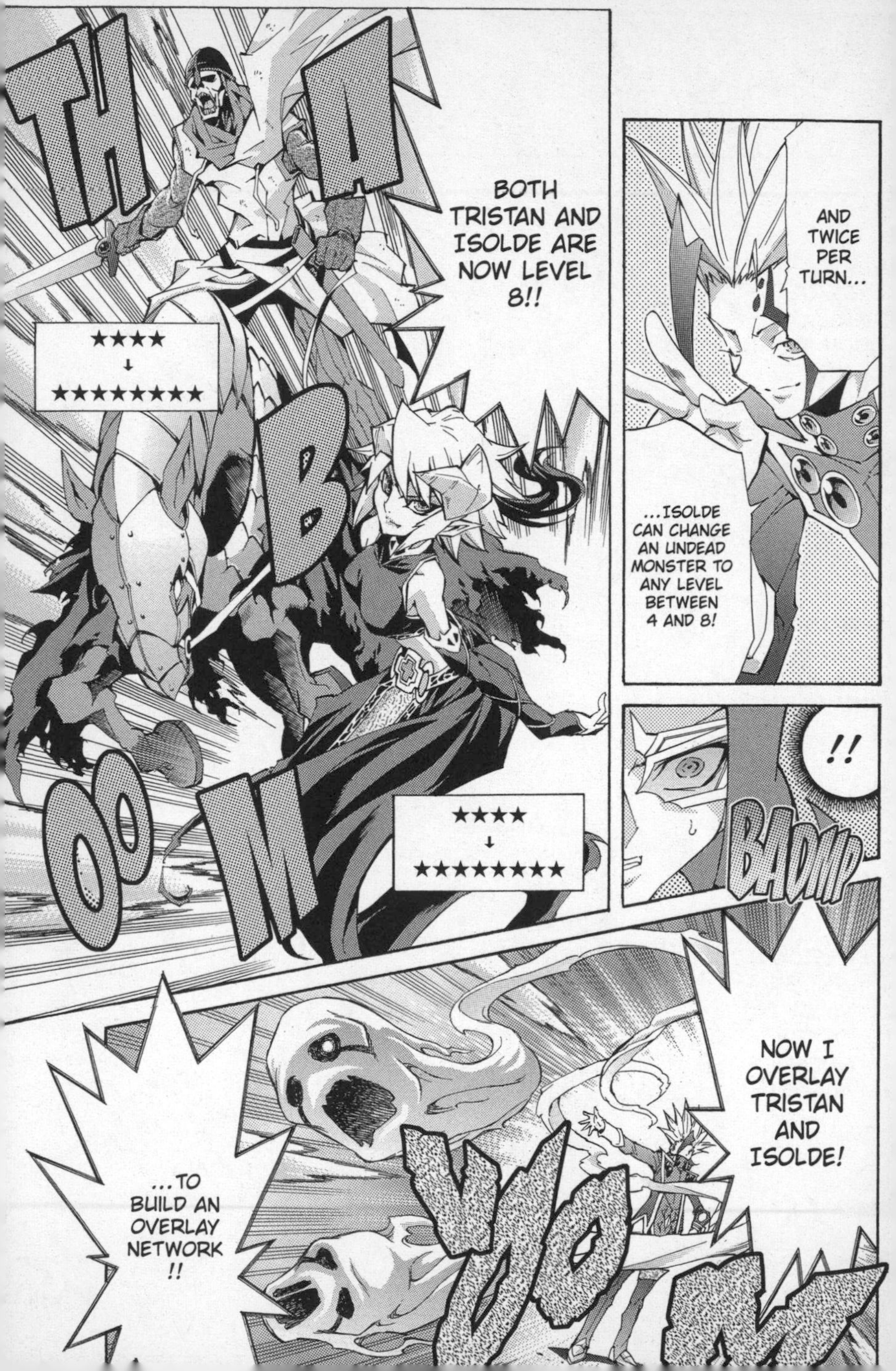
AND TWICE PER TURN...
...ISOLDE CAN CHANGE AN UNDEAD MONSTER TO ANY LEVEL BETWEEN 4 AND 8!
!!
BOTH TRISTAN AND ISOLDE ARE NOW LEVEL 8!!
★★★★ ↓ ★★★★★★★★
★★★★ ↓ ★★★★★★★★
NOW I OVERLAY TRISTAN AND ISOLDE!
...TO BUILD AN OVERLAY NETWORK!!

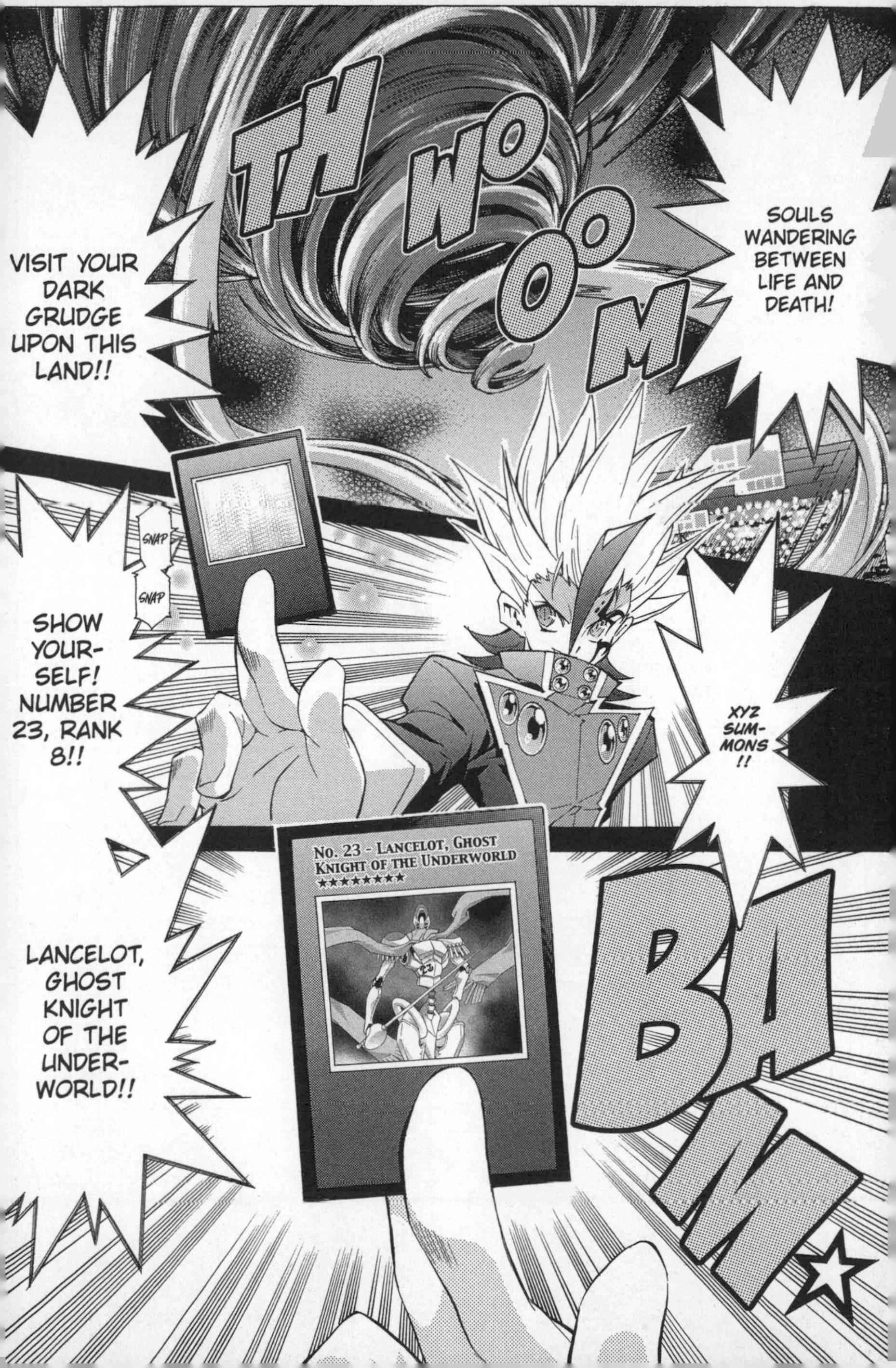
THWOOOM
SOULS WANDERING BETWEEN LIFE AND DEATH!
VISIT YOUR DARK GRUDGE UPON THIS LAND!!
XYZ SUMMONS!!
SNAP
SNAP
SHOW YOURSELF! NUMBER 23, RANK 8!!
BAM
No. 23 - LANCELOT, GHOST KNIGHT OF THE UNDERWORLD
★★★★★★★★
LANCELOT, GHOST KNIGHT OF THE UNDERWORLD!!

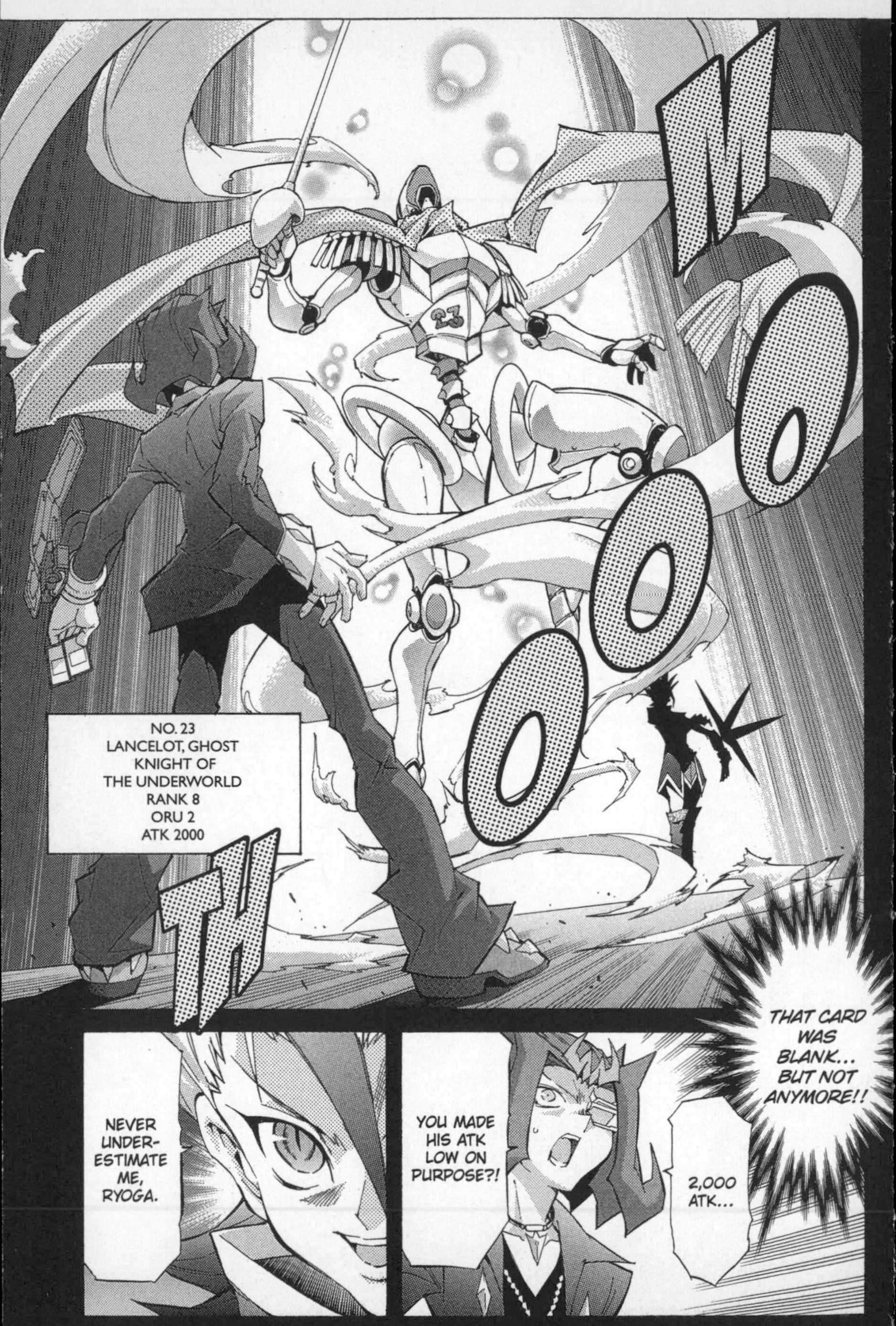
MOOO
NO. 23
LANCELOT, GHOST
KNIGHT OF
THE UNDERWORLD
RANK 8
ORU 2
ATK 2000
TH
THAT CARD WAS BLANK... BUT NOT ANYMORE!!
2,000 ATK...
YOU MADE HIS ATK LOW ON PURPOSE?!
NEVER UNDER-ESTIMATE ME, RYOGA.

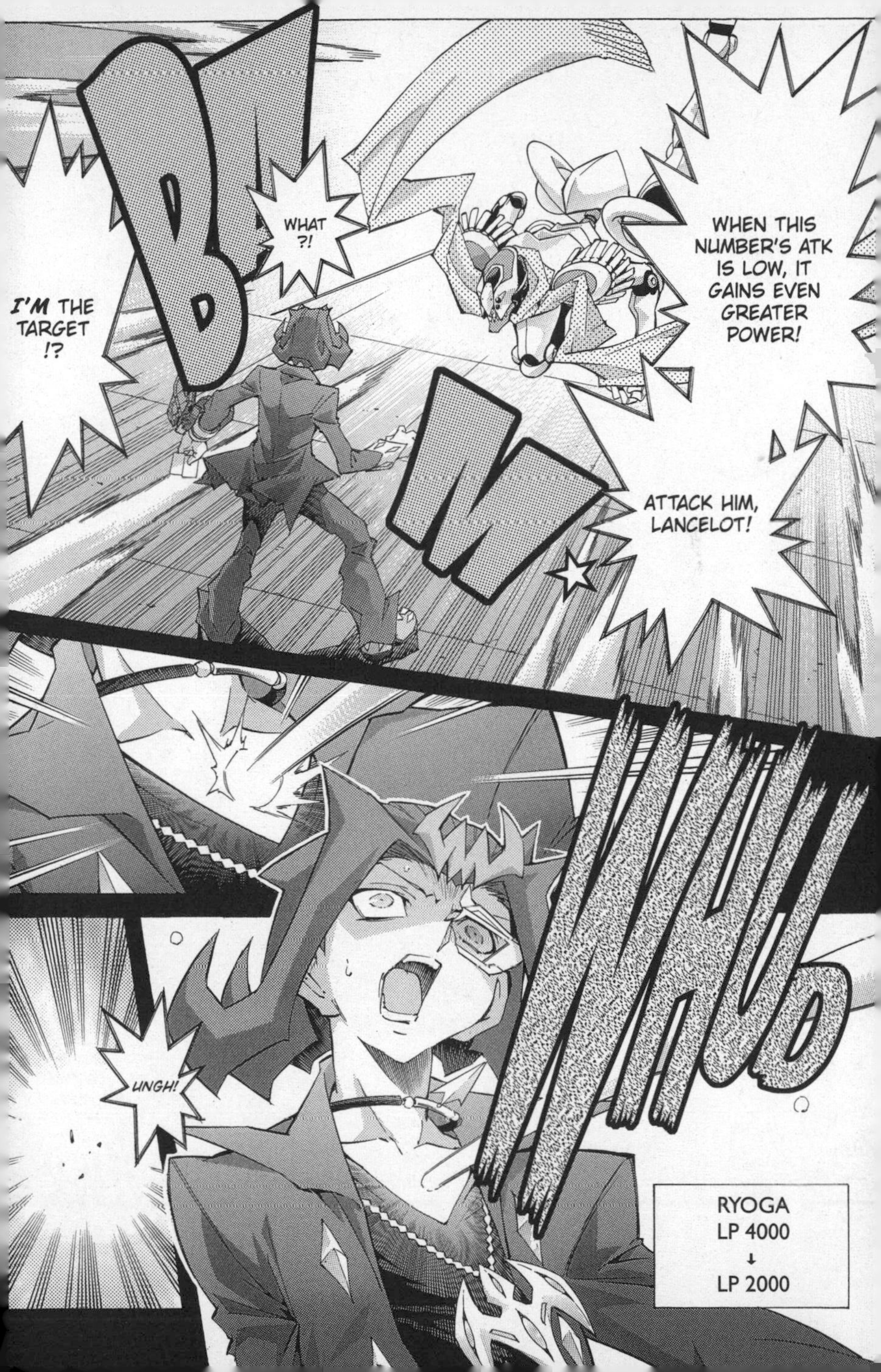
WHEN THIS NUMBER'S ATK IS LOW, IT GAINS EVEN GREATER POWER!
ATTACK HIM, LANCELOT!
WHAT ?!
I'M THE TARGET !?
RYOGA LP 4000 ↓ LP 2000
WHUD
UNGH!

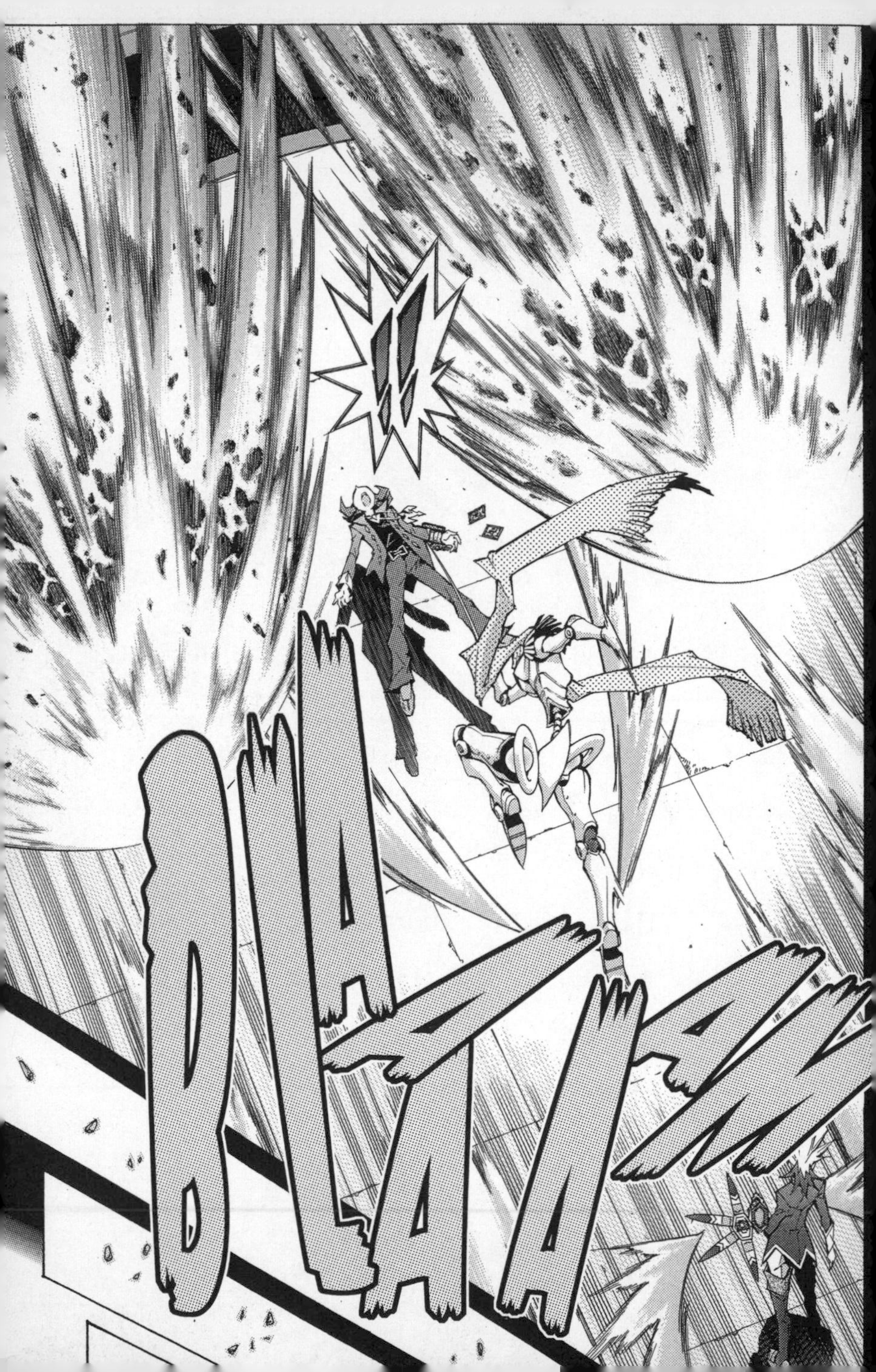
BLAAAM

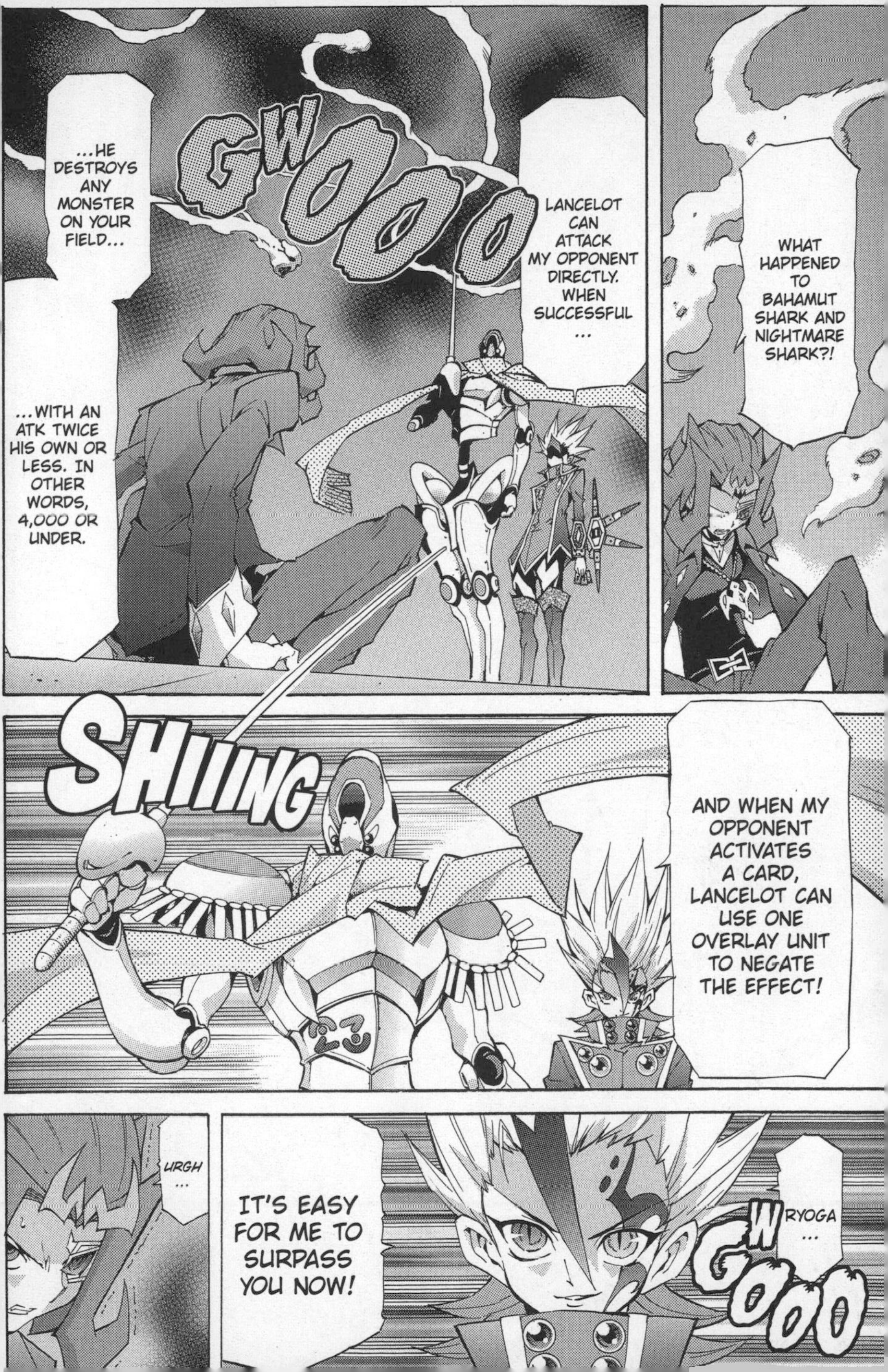
WHAT HAPPENED TO BAHAMUT SHARK AND NIGHTMARE SHARK?!
LANCELOT CAN ATTACK MY OPPONENT DIRECTLY. WHEN SUCCESSFUL ...
GWOOO
...HE DESTROYS ANY MONSTER ON YOUR FIELD...
...WITH AN ATK TWICE HIS OWN OR LESS. IN OTHER WORDS, 4,000 OR UNDER.
AND WHEN MY OPPONENT ACTIVATES A CARD, LANCELOT CAN USE ONE OVERLAY UNIT TO NEGATE THE EFFECT!
SHIIING
RYOGA ...
GWOOO
IT'S EASY FOR ME TO SURPASS YOU NOW!
URGH ...

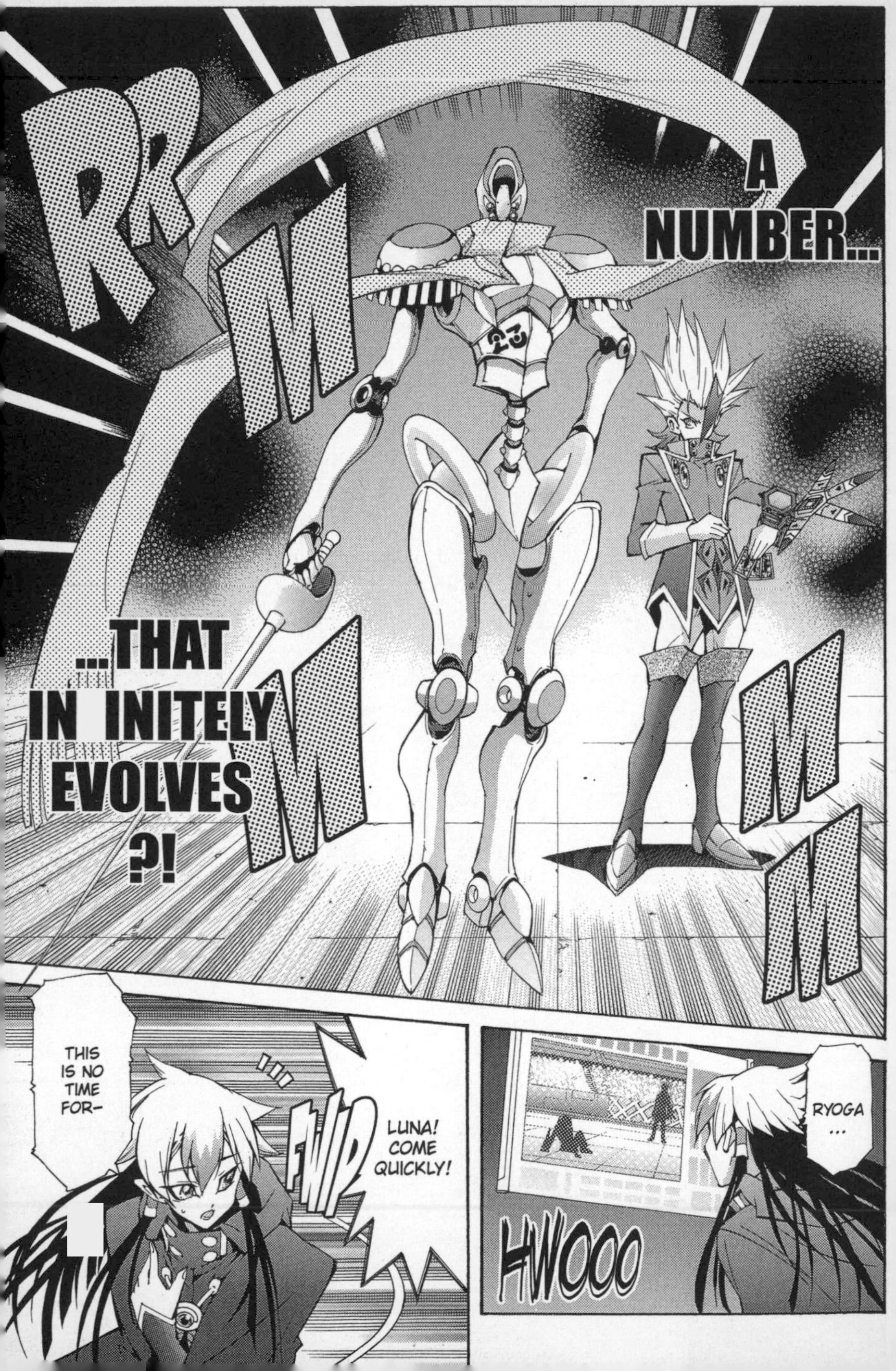
A NUMBER...
RRMMMM
...THAT IN INITELY EVOLVES ?!
RYOGA ...
HWOOO
THIS IS NO TIME FOR–
!!
FWIP
LUNA! COME QUICKLY!

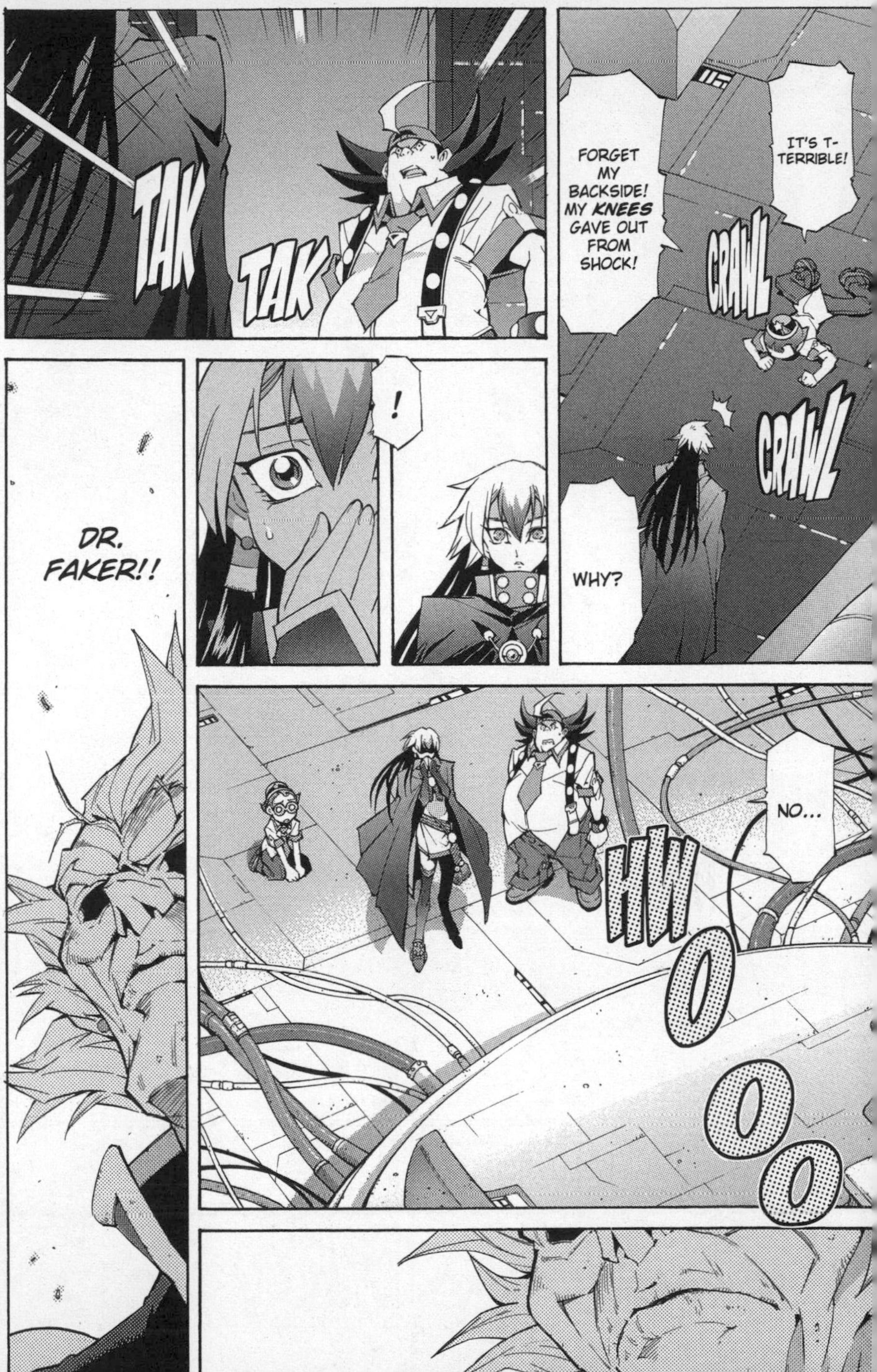
IT'S T-TERRIBLE!
FORGET MY BACKSIDE! MY KNEES GAVE OUT FROM SHOCK!
CRAWL
CRAWL
WHY?
TAK
TAK
!
NO...
HWOOOO
DR. FAKER!!

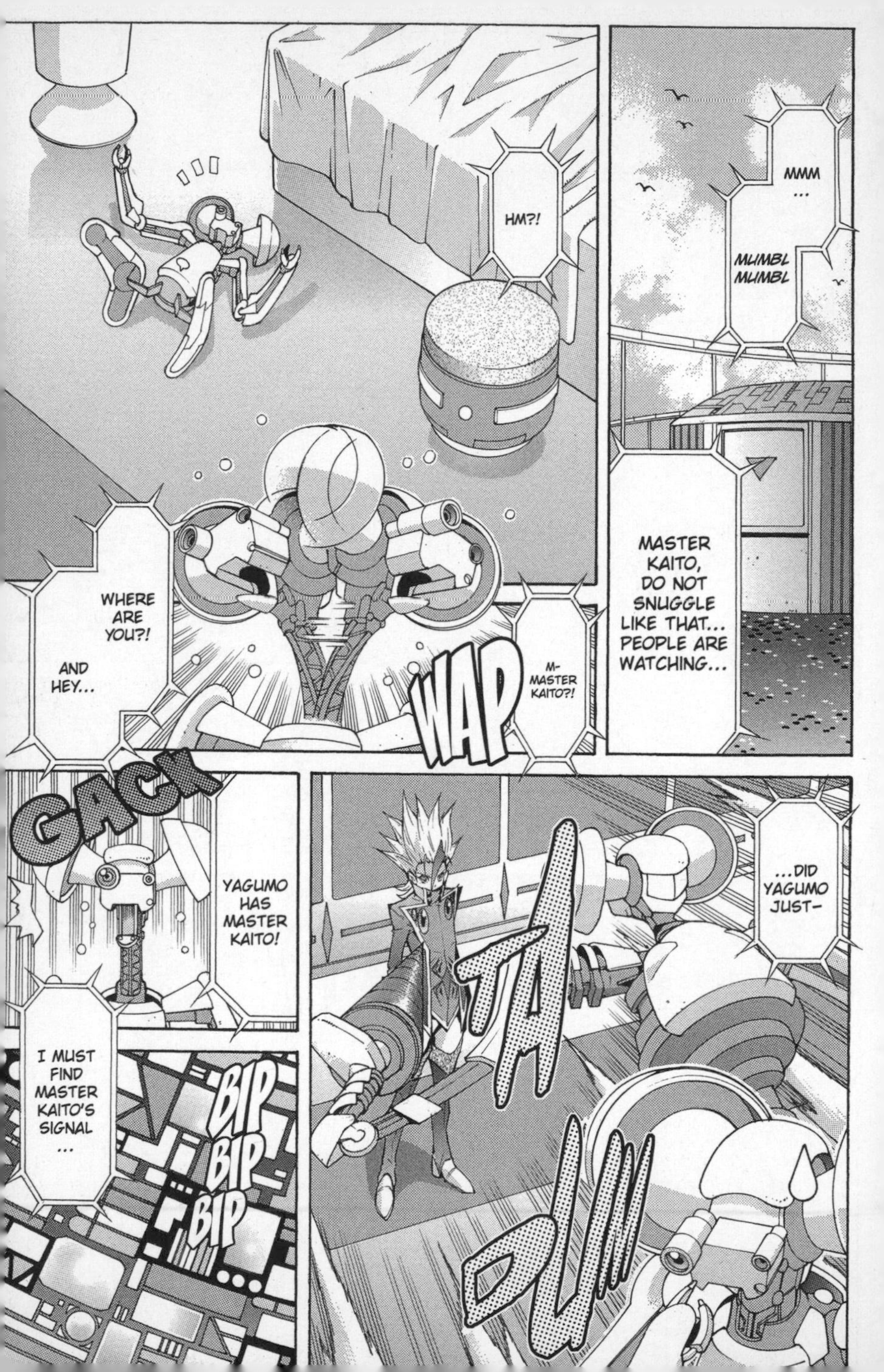
MMM
...
MUMBL
MUMBL
MASTER KAITO, DO NOT SNUGGLE LIKE THAT... PEOPLE ARE WATCHING...
HM?!
M-MASTER KAITO?!
WAP
WHERE ARE YOU?!
AND HEY...
...DID YAGUMO JUST-
TA
GACK
YAGUMO HAS MASTER KAITO!
I MUST FIND MASTER KAITO'S SIGNAL ...
BIP
BIP
BIP
...

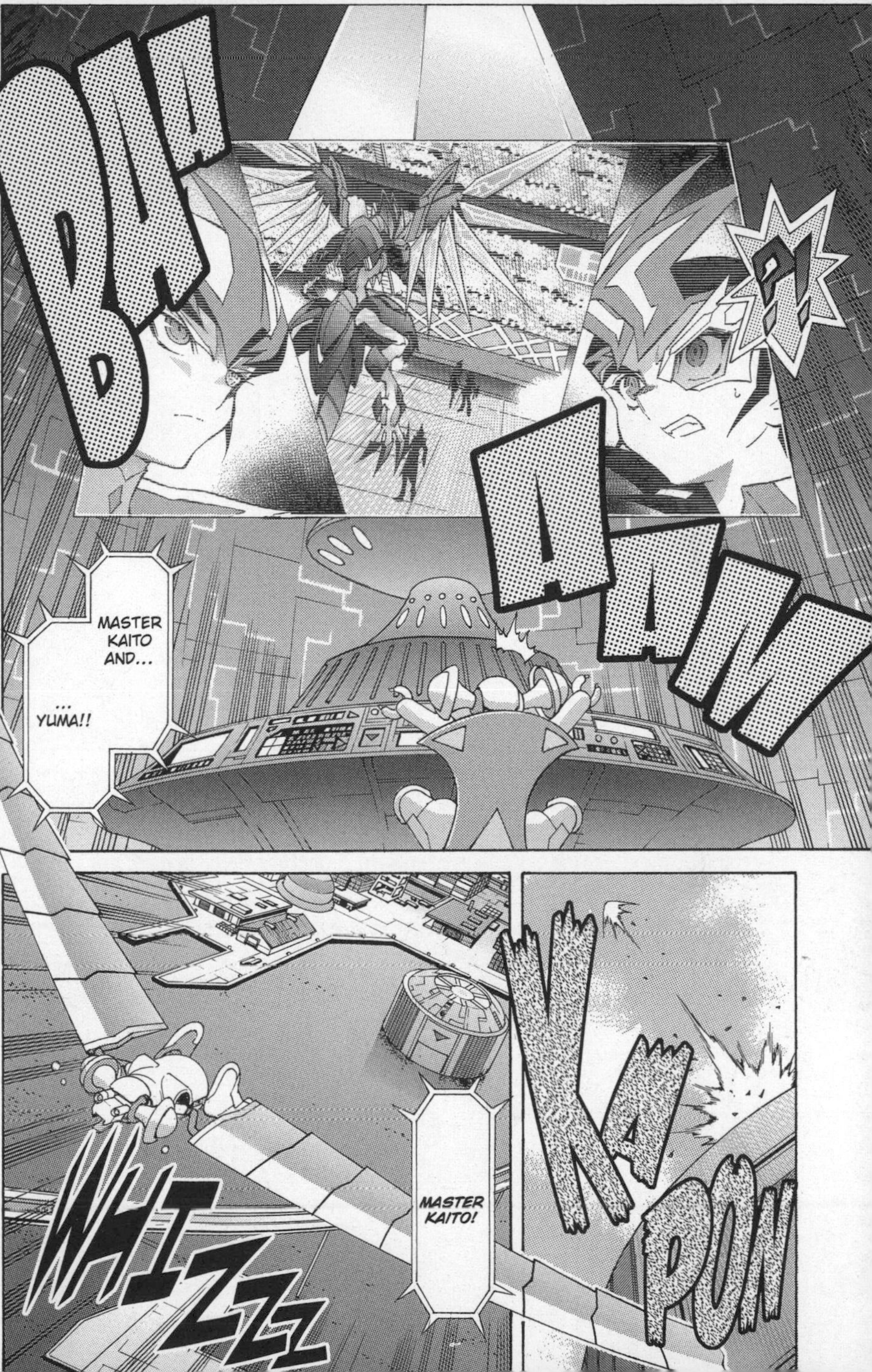
?!
MASTER KAITO AND...
... YUMA!!
KA POW
MASTER KAITO!
WHIZZZ

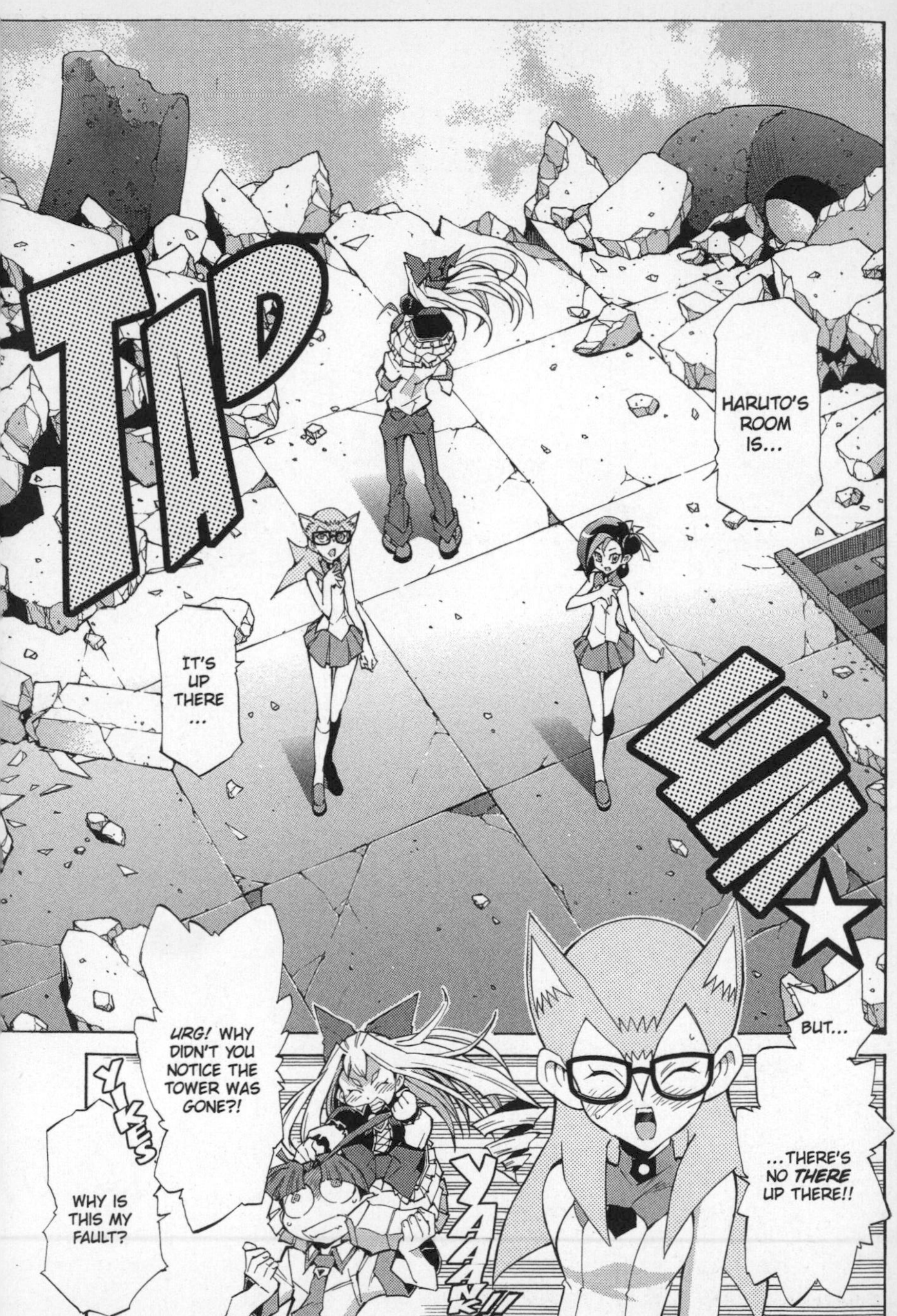
TAP
HARUTO'S ROOM IS...
IT'S UP THERE...
BUT...
...THERE'S NO *THERE* UP THERE!!
YAAANK!!
URG! WHY DIDN'T YOU NOTICE THE TOWER WAS GONE?!
YIKES
WHY IS THIS MY FAULT?

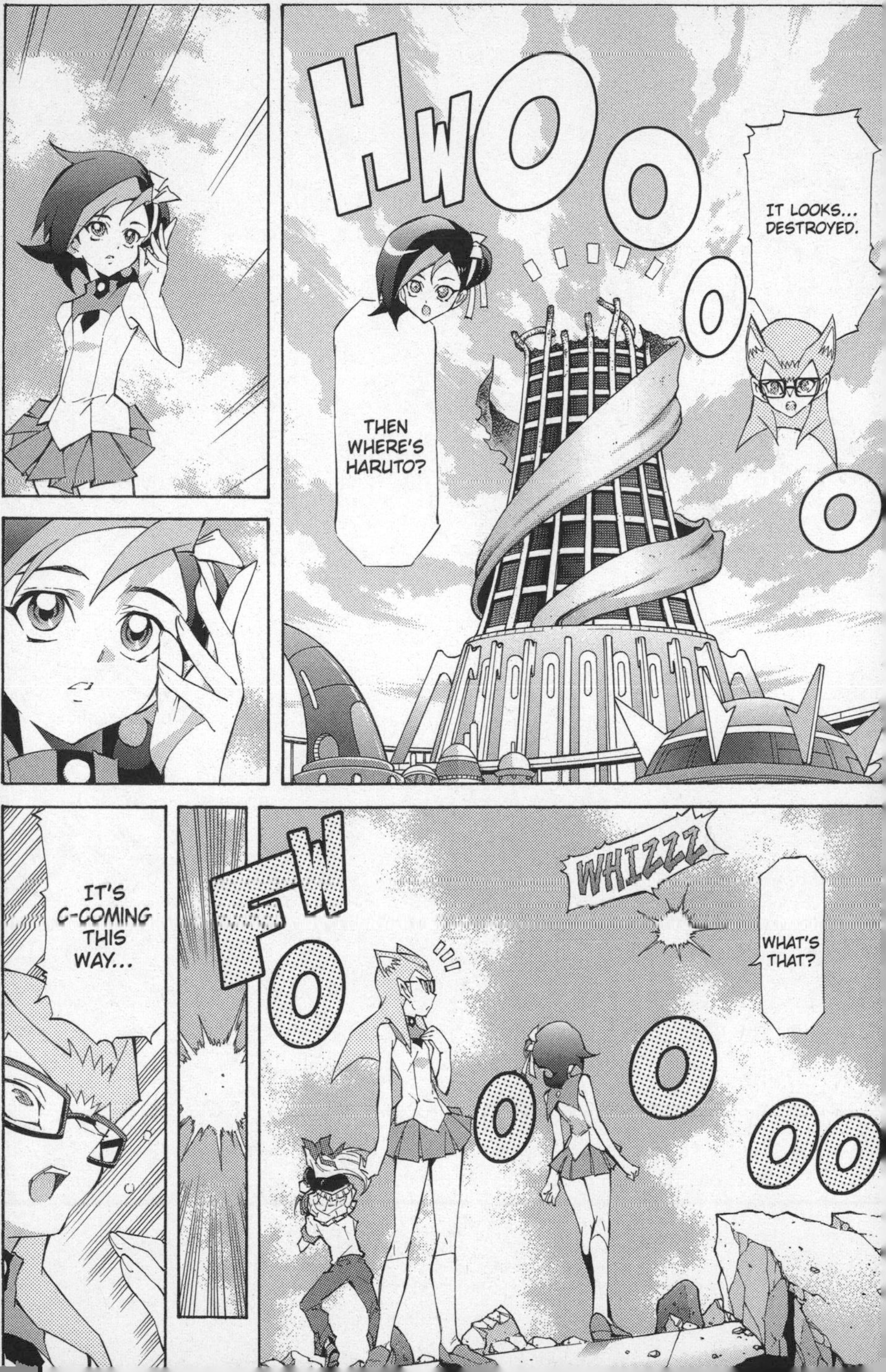
HWOOOO
IT LOOKS... DESTROYED.
THEN WHERE'S HARUTO?
WHIZZZ
WHAT'S THAT?
FWOOOOOO
IT'S C-COMING THIS WAY...

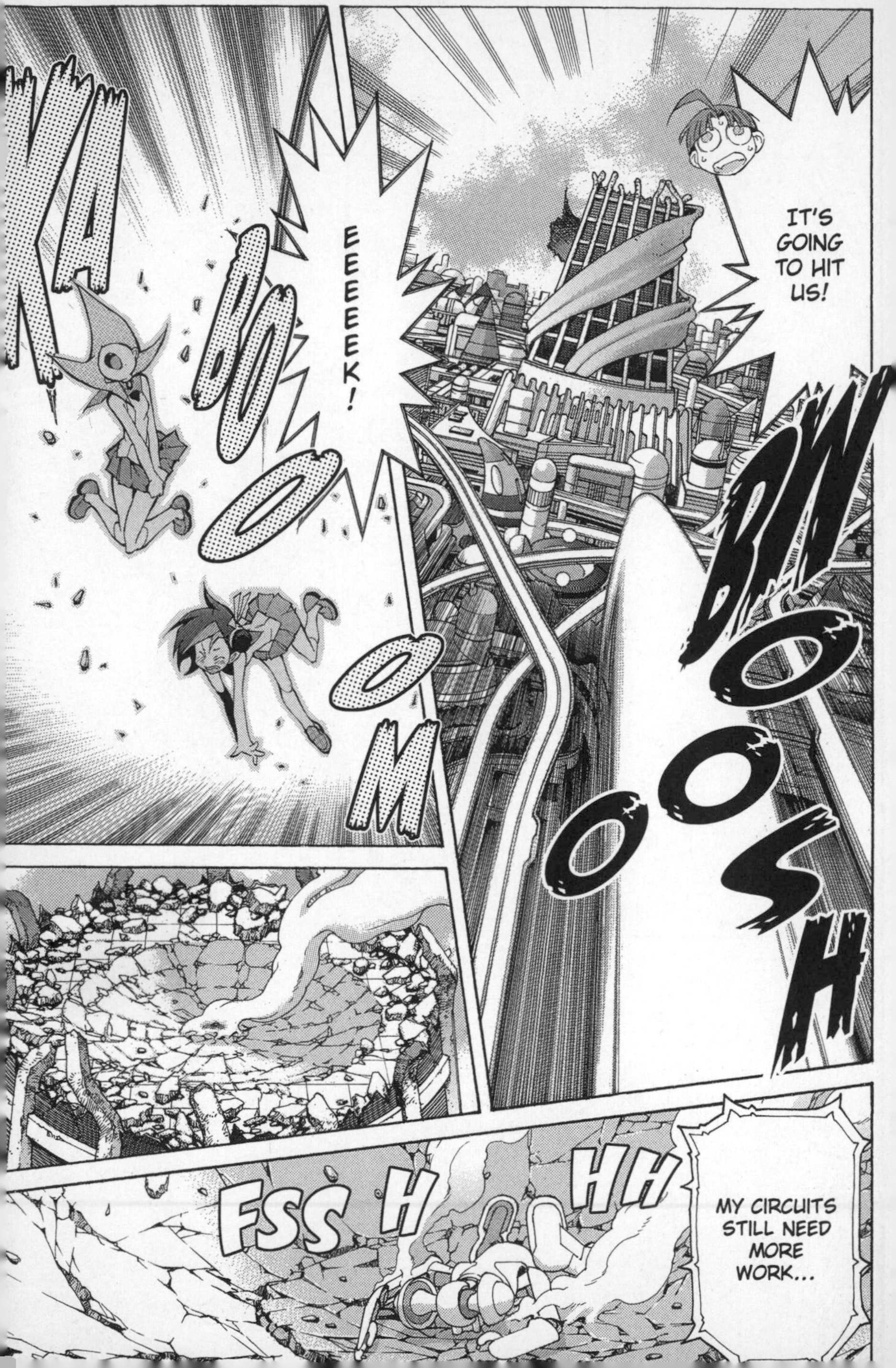
IT'S GOING TO HIT US!
BAWOOOSH
EEEEEEK!
KABOOOOM
FSSHHH
MY CIRCUITS STILL NEED MORE WORK...

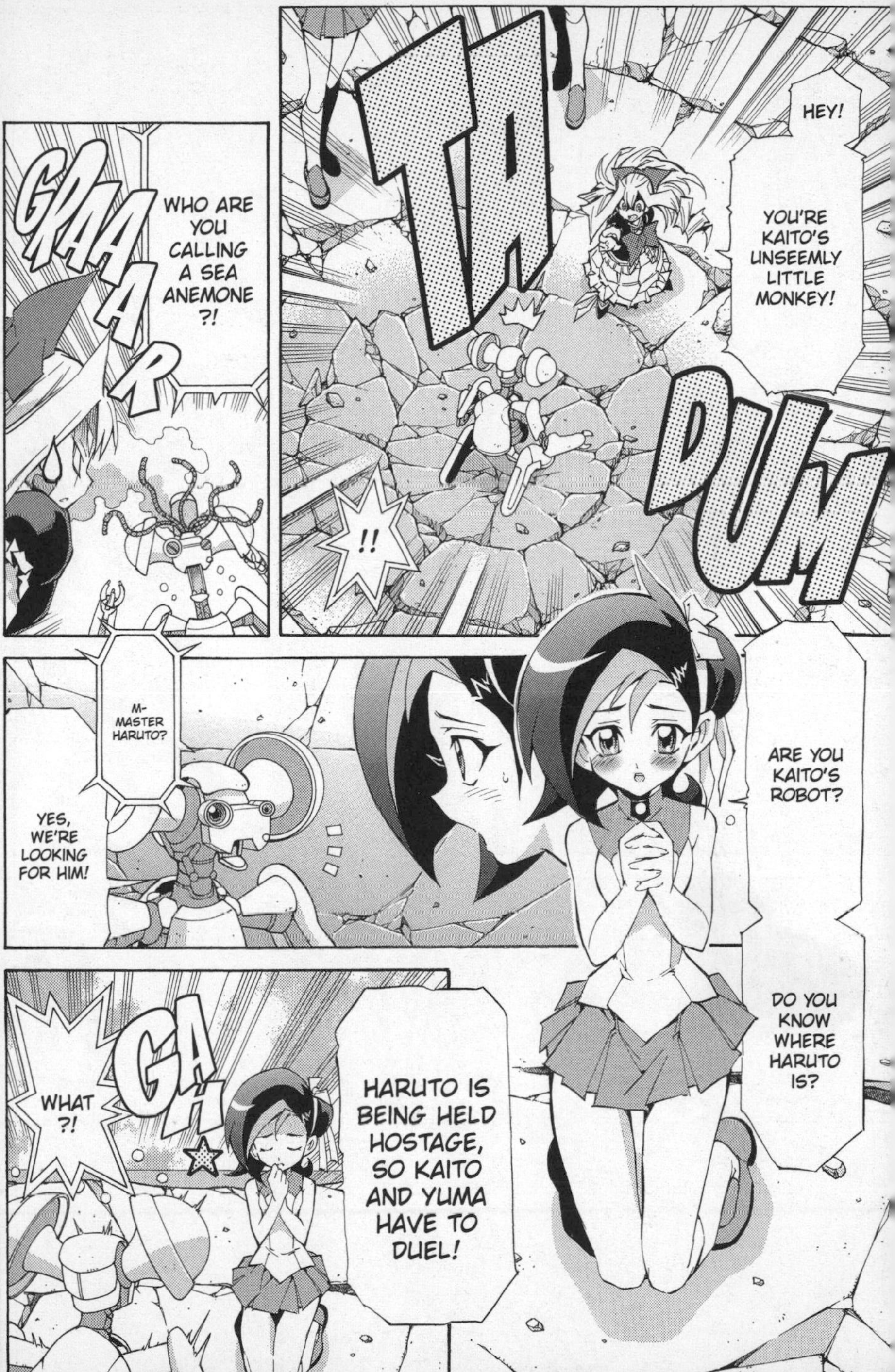
HEY!
YOU'RE KAITO'S UNSEEMLY LITTLE MONKEY!
TA
DUM
!!
GRAAAAR
WHO ARE YOU CALLING A SEA ANEMONE ?!
ARE YOU KAITO'S ROBOT?
DO YOU KNOW WHERE HARUTO IS?
M-MASTER HARUTO?
YES, WE'RE LOOKING FOR HIM!
HARUTO IS BEING HELD HOSTAGE, SO KAITO AND YUMA HAVE TO DUEL!
GAH
WHAT ?!

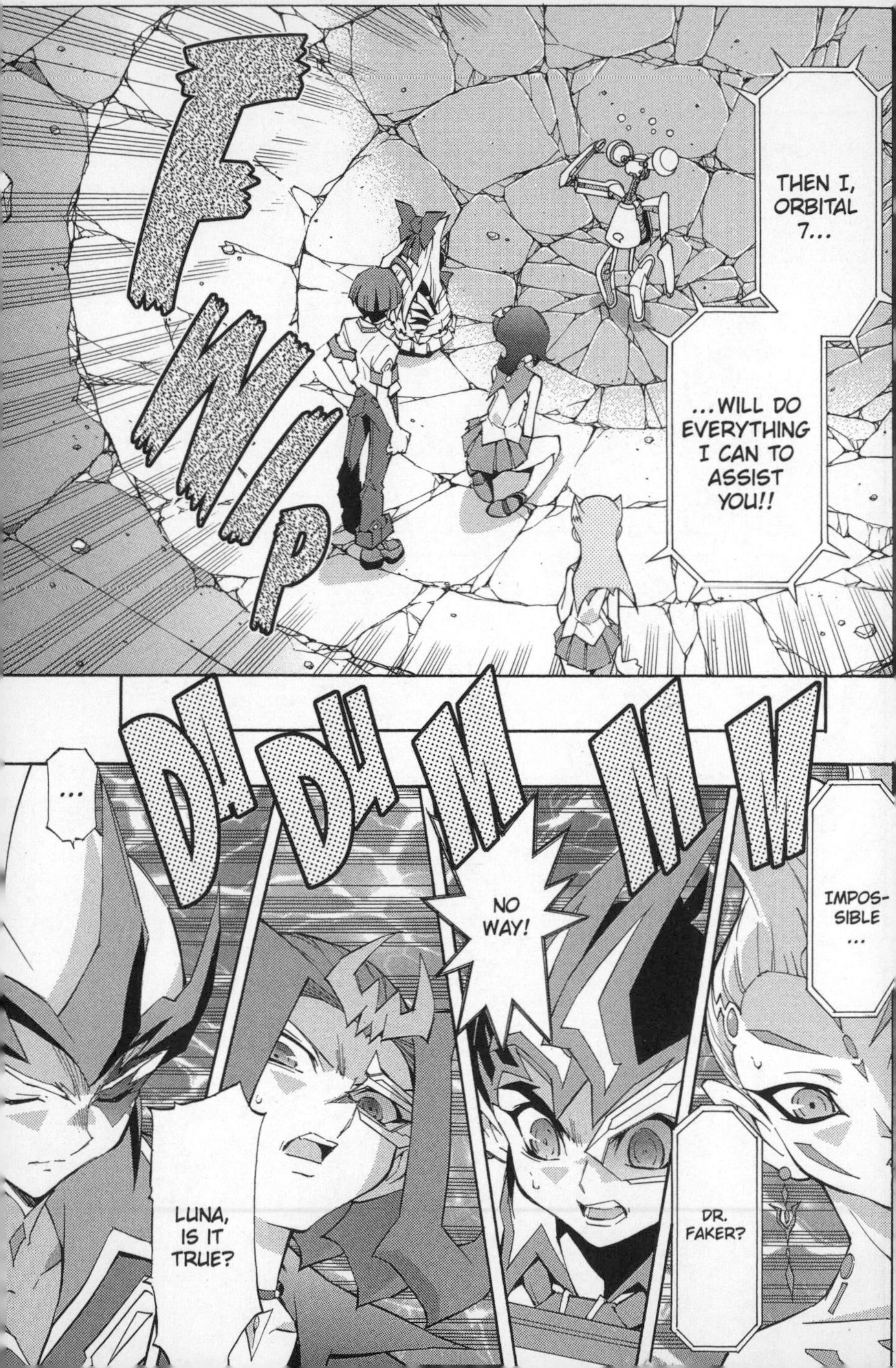
FWIP
THEN I, ORBITAL 7…
…WILL DO EVERYTHING I CAN TO ASSIST YOU!!
DADUMMM
IMPOS-SIBLE…
DR. FAKER?
NO WAY!
LUNA, IS IT TRUE?
…

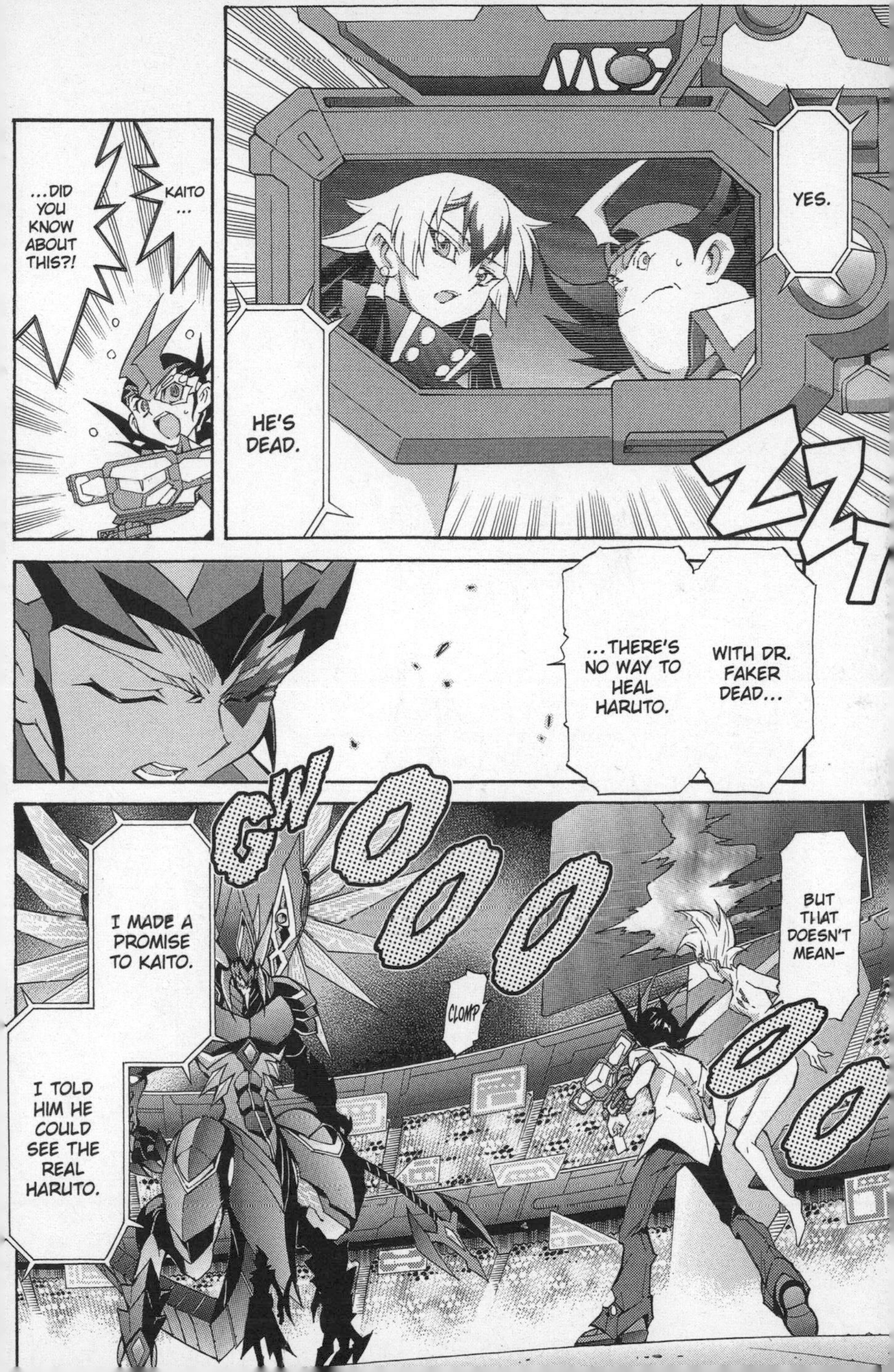
YES.
HE'S DEAD.
ZZT
KAITO...
...DID YOU KNOW ABOUT THIS?!
WITH DR. FAKER DEAD...
...THERE'S NO WAY TO HEAL HARUTO.
G'OOOOOOO
BUT THAT DOESN'T MEAN-
CLOMP
I MADE A PROMISE TO KAITO.
I TOLD HIM HE COULD SEE THE REAL HARUTO.

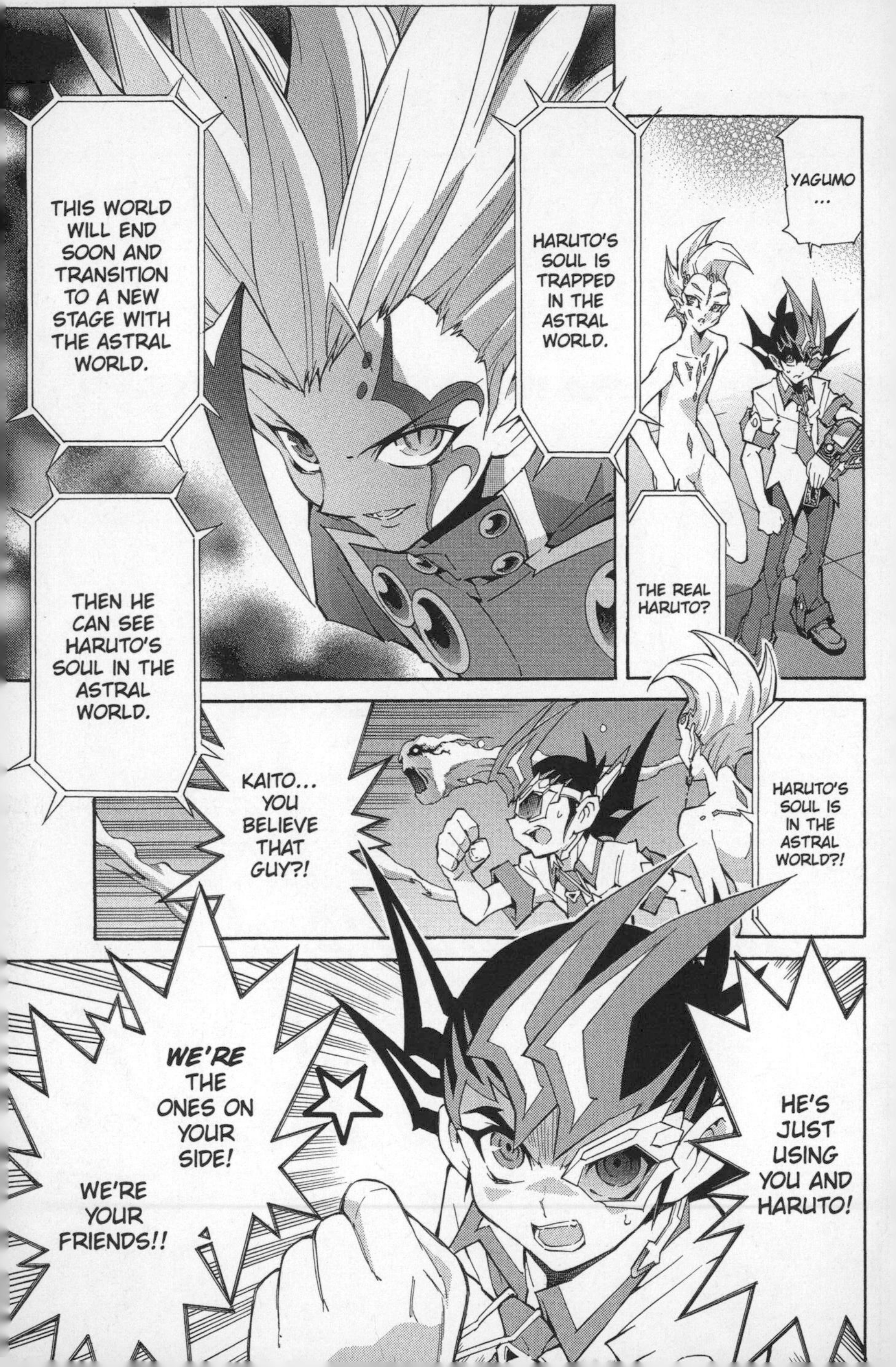
YAGUMO …
THE REAL HARUTO?
HARUTO'S SOUL IS TRAPPED IN THE ASTRAL WORLD.
THIS WORLD WILL END SOON AND TRANSITION TO A NEW STAGE WITH THE ASTRAL WORLD.
THEN HE CAN SEE HARUTO'S SOUL IN THE ASTRAL WORLD.
HARUTO'S SOUL IS IN THE ASTRAL WORLD?!
KAITO… YOU BELIEVE THAT GUY?!
HE'S JUST USING YOU AND HARUTO!
WE'RE THE ONES ON YOUR SIDE!
WE'RE YOUR FRIENDS!!

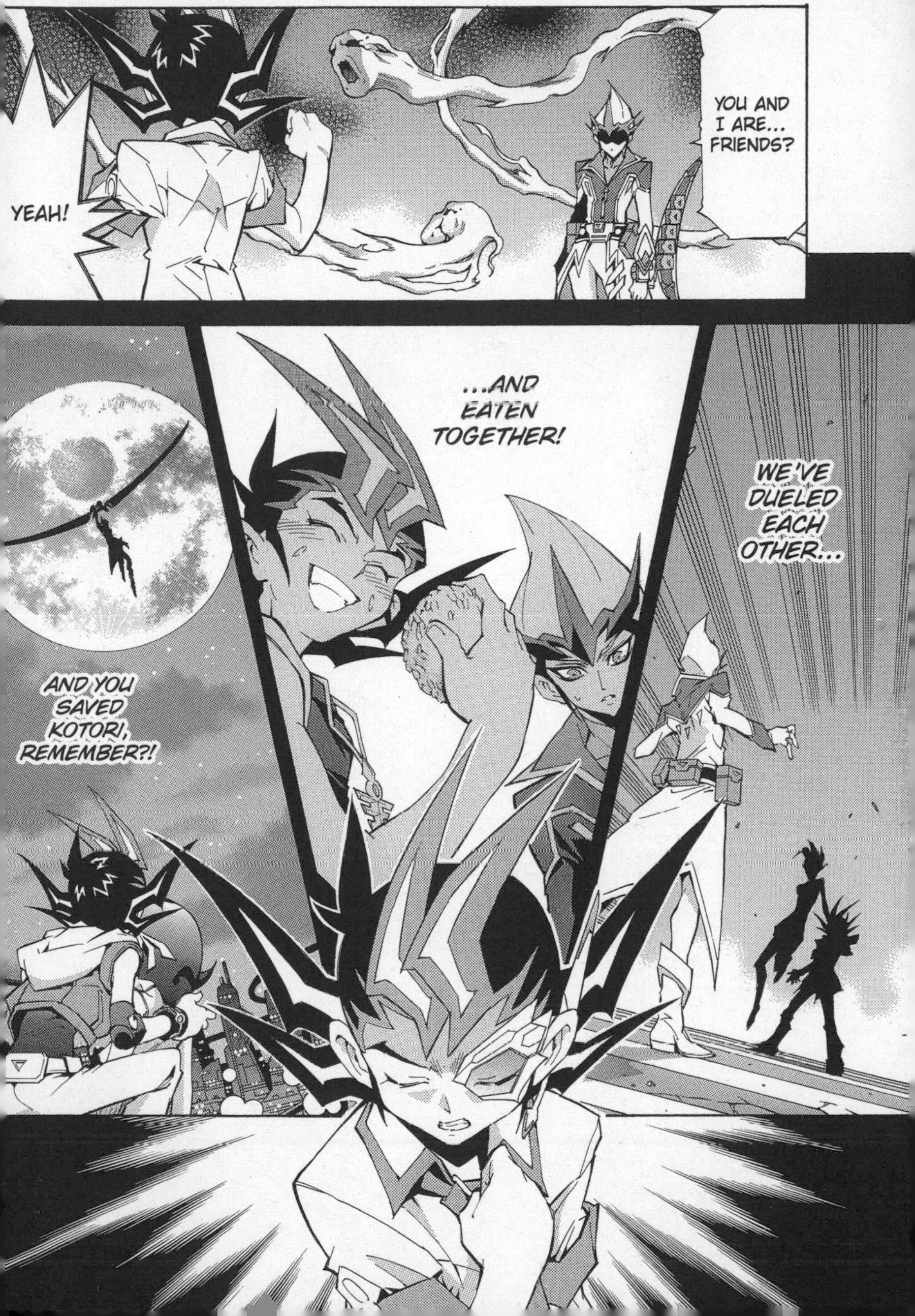
YOU AND I ARE... FRIENDS?
YEAH!
WE'VE DUELED EACH OTHER...
...AND EATEN TOGETHER!
AND YOU SAVED KOTORI, REMEMBER?!

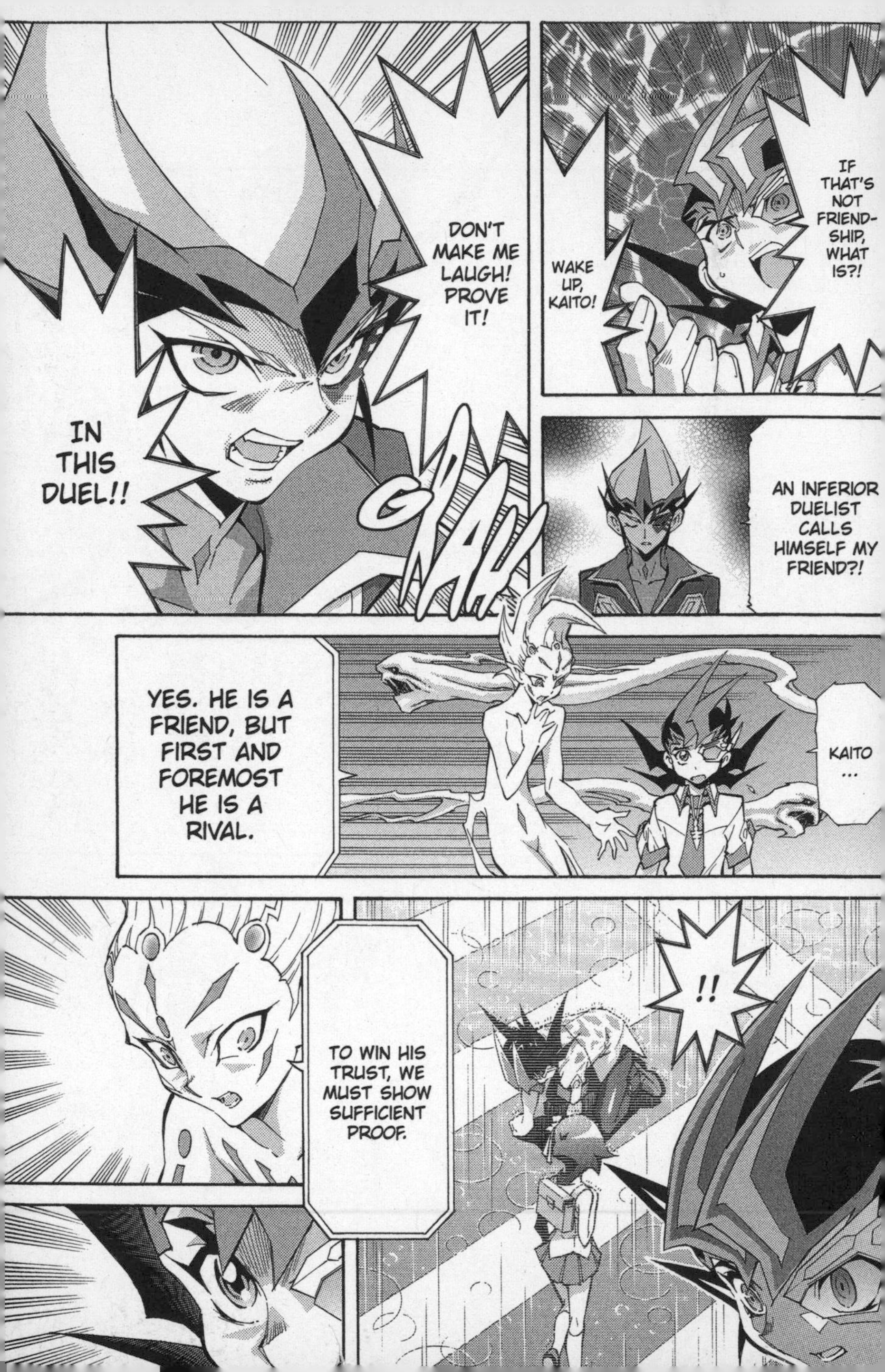
IF THAT'S NOT FRIEND-SHIP, WHAT IS?!
WAKE UP, KAITO!
AN INFERIOR DUELIST CALLS HIMSELF MY FRIEND?!
DON'T MAKE ME LAUGH! PROVE IT!
G'AH!!
IN THIS DUEL!!
KAITO...
YES. HE IS A FRIEND, BUT FIRST AND FOREMOST HE IS A RIVAL.
!!
TO WIN HIS TRUST, WE MUST SHOW SUFFICIENT PROOF.

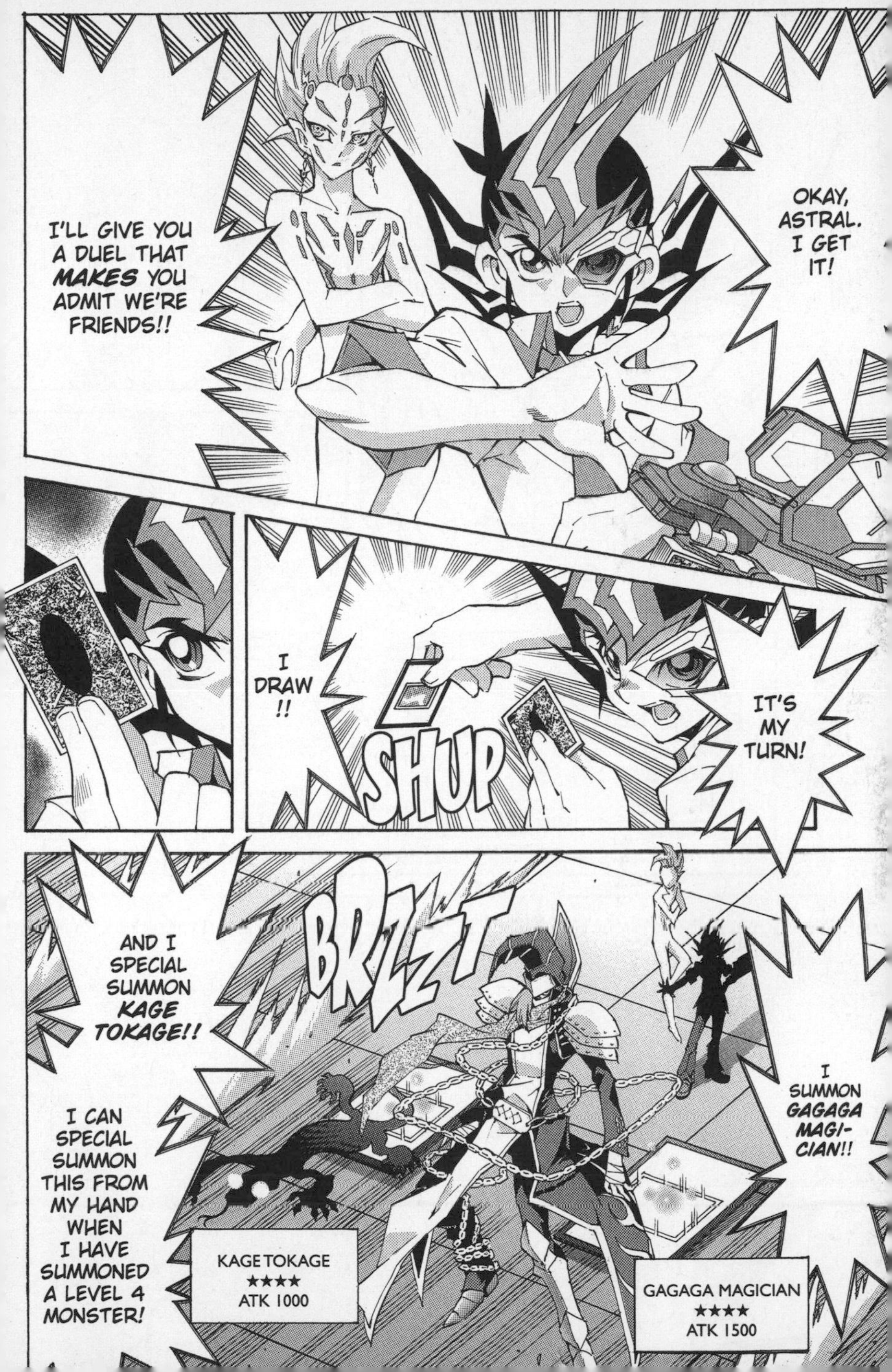
OKAY, ASTRAL. I GET IT!
I'LL GIVE YOU A DUEL THAT *MAKES* YOU ADMIT WE'RE FRIENDS!!
IT'S MY TURN!
I DRAW!!
SHUP
I SUMMON *GAGAGA MAGICIAN*!!
GAGAGA MAGICIAN ★★★★ ATK 1500
BRZZT
AND I SPECIAL SUMMON *KAGE TOKAGE*!!
I CAN SPECIAL SUMMON THIS FROM MY HAND WHEN I HAVE SUMMONED A LEVEL 4 MONSTER!
KAGE TOKAGE ★★★★ ATK 1000

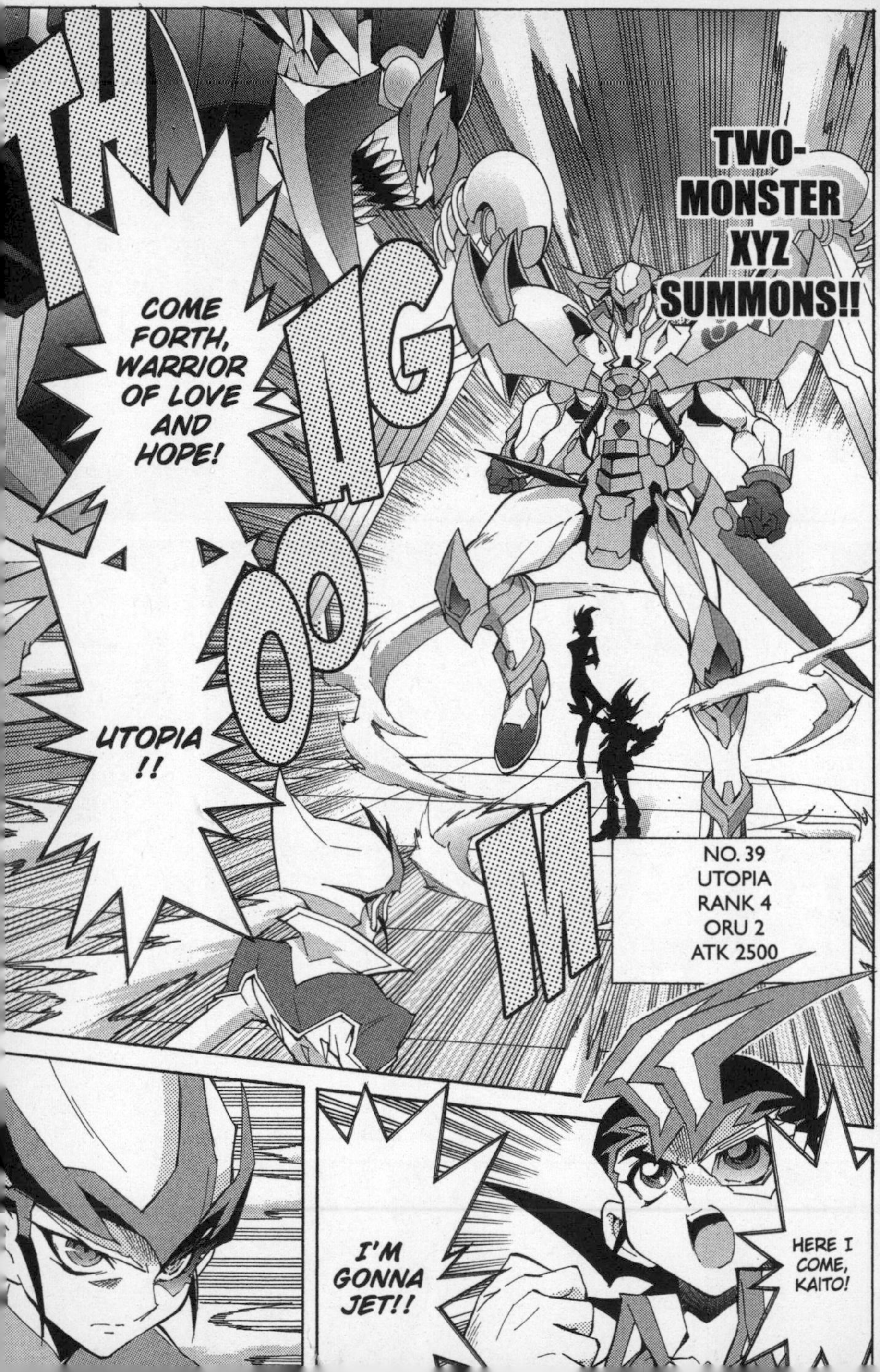
TWO-MONSTER XYZ SUMMONS!!
COME FORTH, WARRIOR OF LOVE AND HOPE!
UTOPIA!!
NO. 39 UTOPIA RANK 4 ORU 2 ATK 2500
HERE I COME, KAITO!
I'M GONNA JET!!

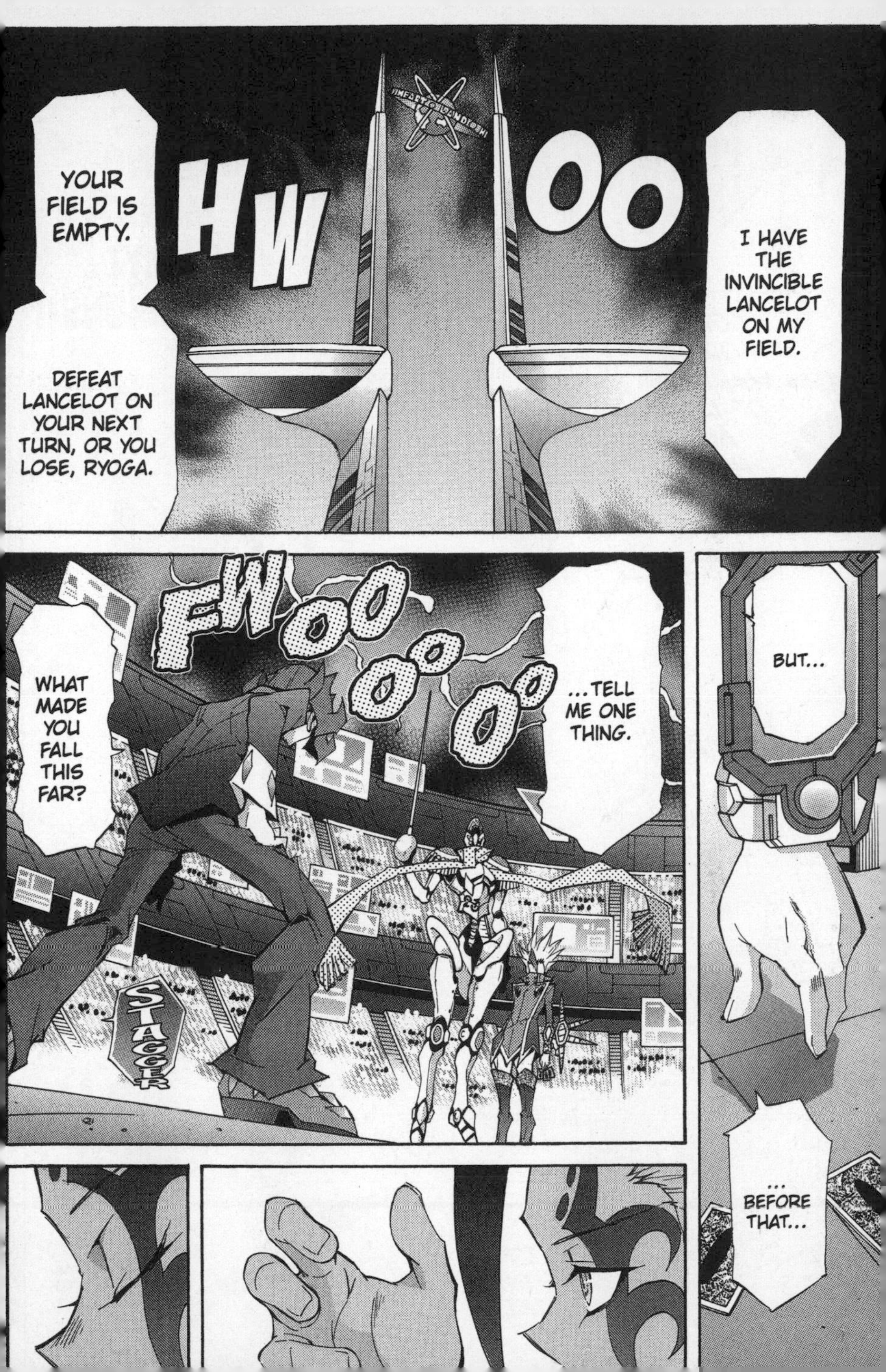
I HAVE THE INVINCIBLE LANCELOT ON MY FIELD.
HWOO
YOUR FIELD IS EMPTY.
DEFEAT LANCELOT ON YOUR NEXT TURN, OR YOU LOSE, RYOGA.
BUT...
...TELL ME ONE THING.
FWOOOOO
WHAT MADE YOU FALL THIS FAR?
STAGGER
... BEFORE THAT...

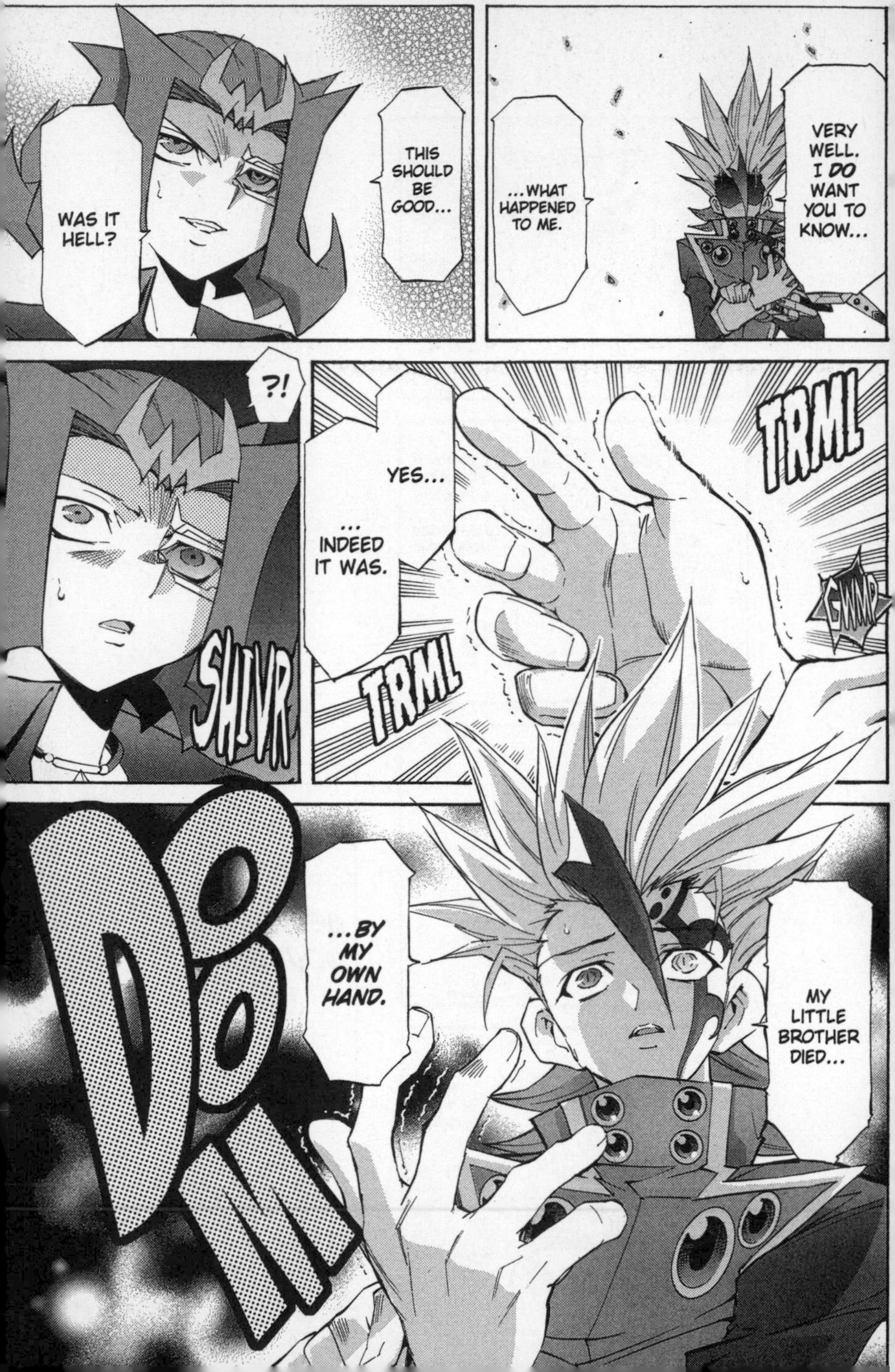
VERY WELL. I *DO* WANT YOU TO KNOW...
...WHAT HAPPENED TO ME.
THIS SHOULD BE GOOD...
WAS IT HELL?
TRML
GWMP
YES...
... INDEED IT WAS.
TRML
?!
SHIVR
MY LITTLE BROTHER DIED...
...BY MY OWN HAND.
DOOM

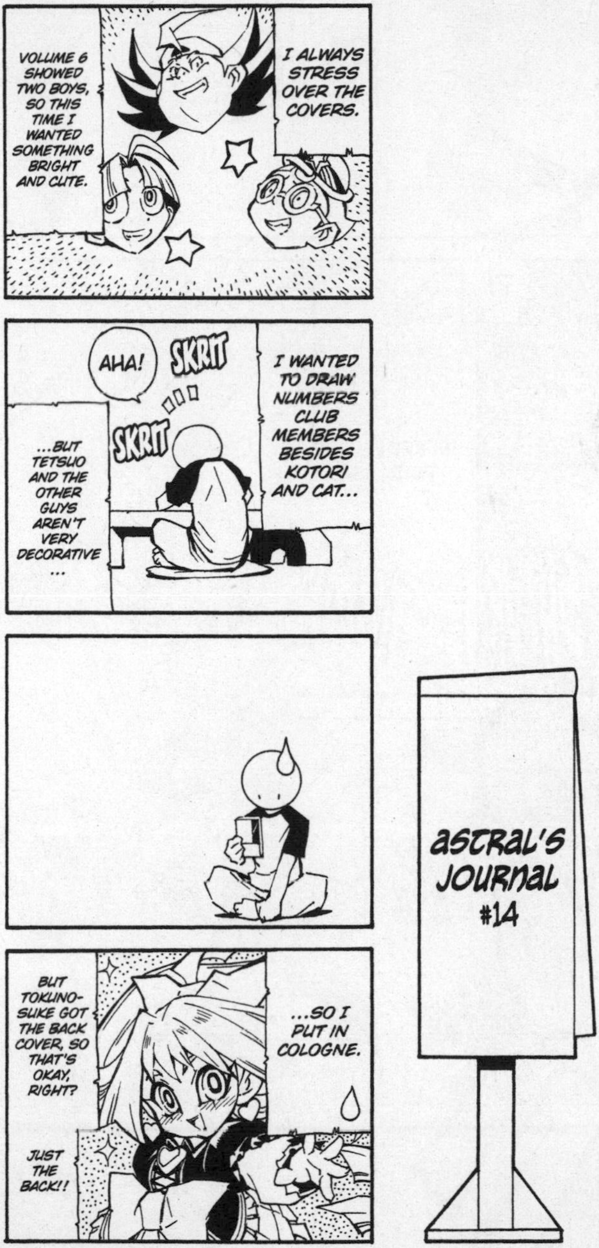
ASTRAL'S JOURNAL #14
I ALWAYS STRESS OVER THE COVERS.
VOLUME 6 SHOWED TWO BOYS, SO THIS TIME I WANTED SOMETHING BRIGHT AND CUTE.
I WANTED TO DRAW NUMBERS CLUB MEMBERS BESIDES KOTORI AND CAT...
AHA!
SKRIT
SKRIT
...BUT TETSUO AND THE OTHER GUYS AREN'T VERY DECORATIVE...
...SO I PUT IN COLOGNE.
BUT TOKUNOSUKE GOT THE BACK COVER, SO THAT'S OKAY, RIGHT?
JUST THE BACK!!

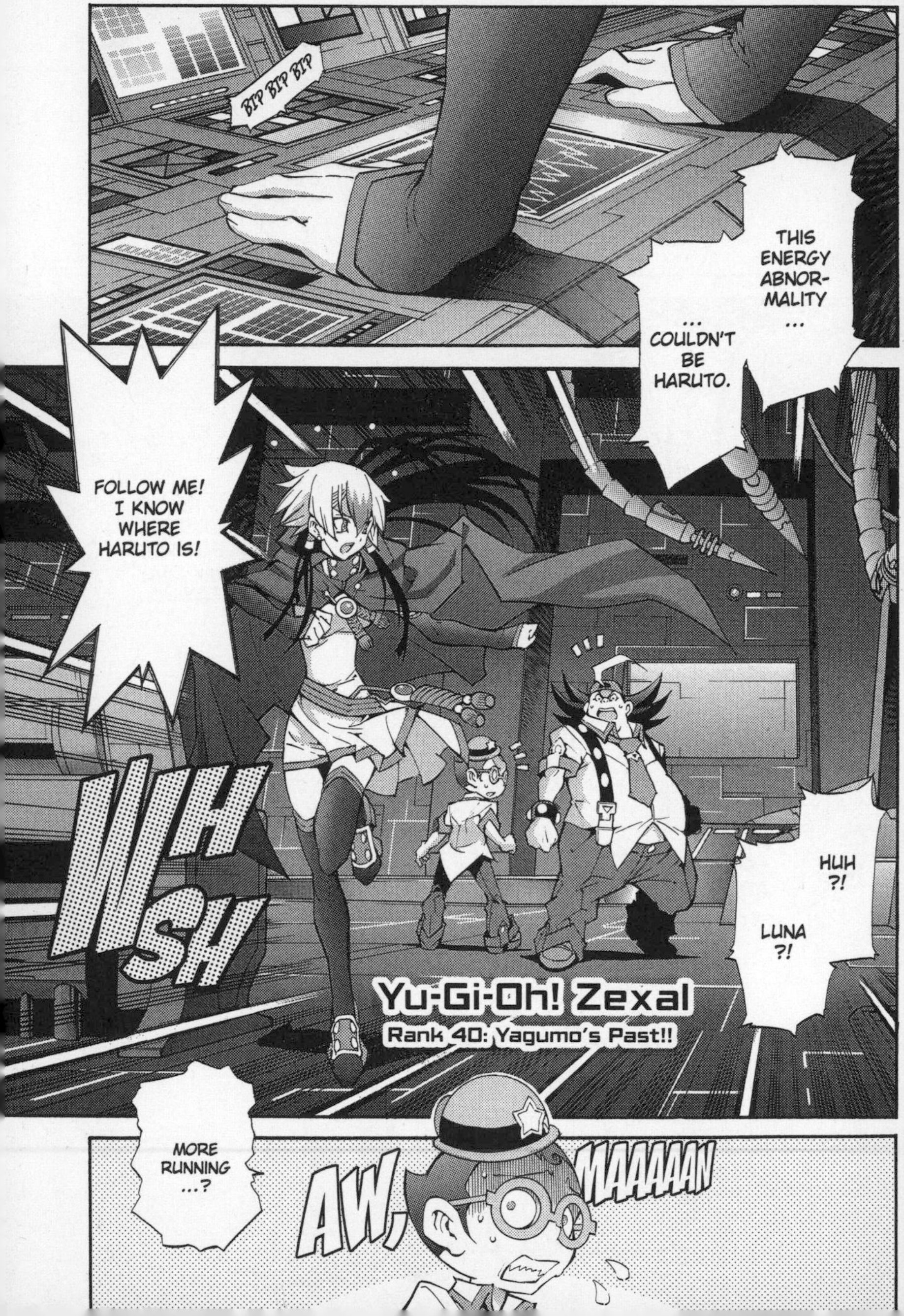
BIP BIP BIP
THIS ENERGY ABNORMALITY ...
... COULDN'T BE HARUTO.
FOLLOW ME! I KNOW WHERE HARUTO IS!
WHISH
HUH ?!
LUNA ?!
Yu-Gi-Oh! Zexal
Rank 40: Yagumo's Past!!
AW, MAAAAAN
MORE RUNNING ...?

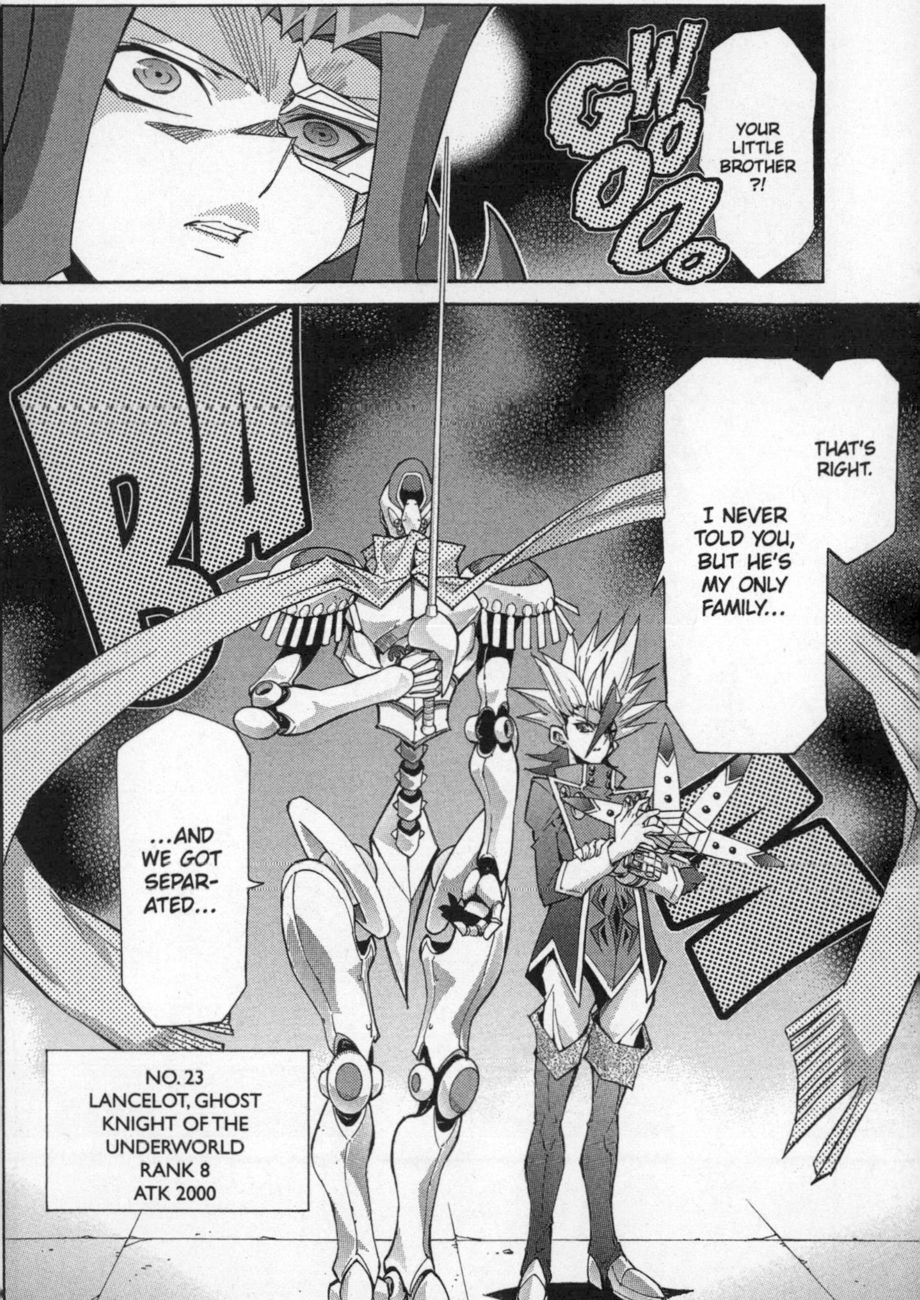
YOUR LITTLE BROTHER ?!
THAT'S RIGHT.
I NEVER TOLD YOU, BUT HE'S MY ONLY FAMILY...
...AND WE GOT SEPAR-ATED...
NO. 23 LANCELOT, GHOST KNIGHT OF THE UNDERWORLD RANK 8 ATK 2000

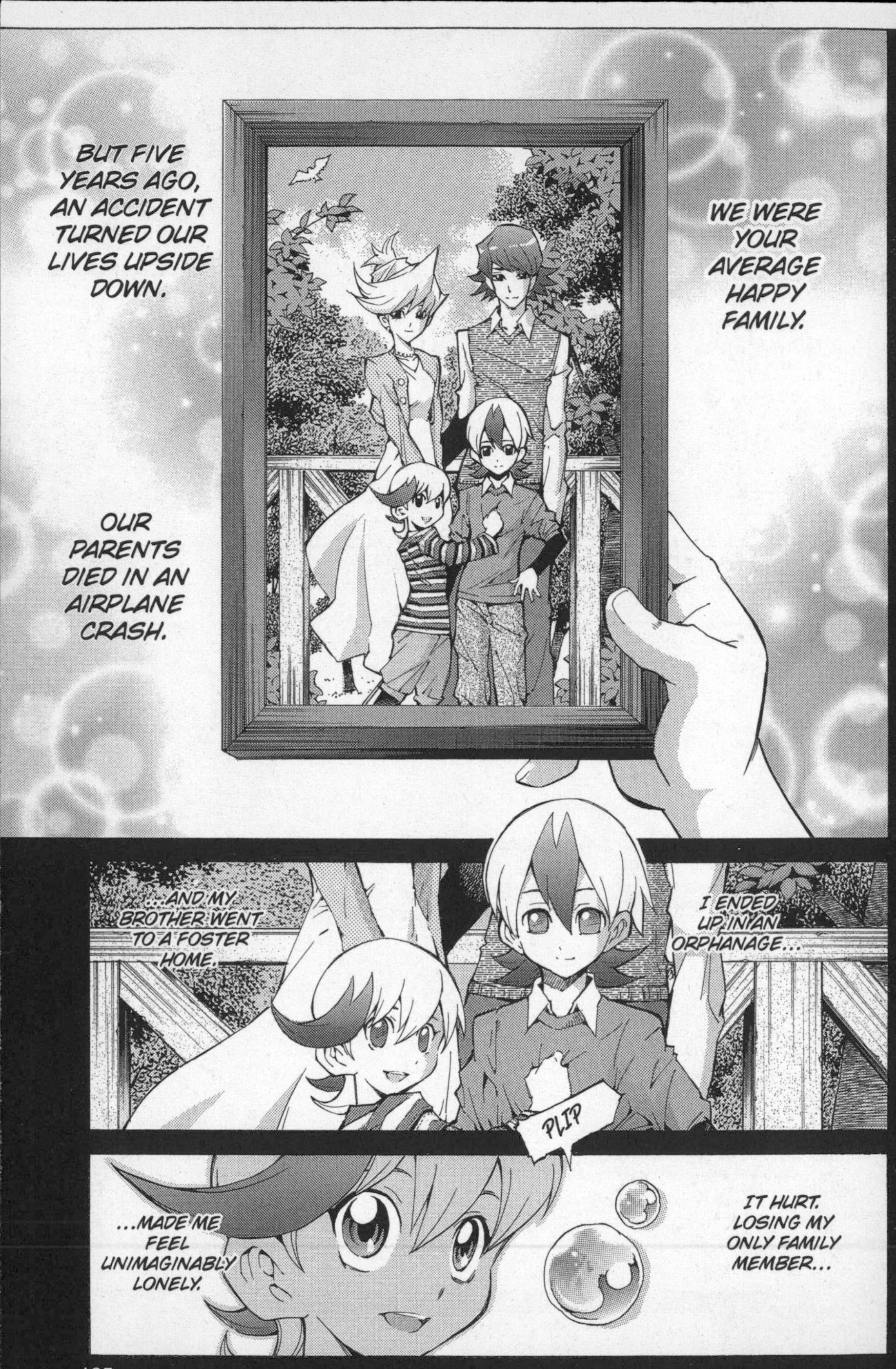
WE WERE YOUR AVERAGE HAPPY FAMILY.
BUT FIVE YEARS AGO, AN ACCIDENT TURNED OUR LIVES UPSIDE DOWN.
OUR PARENTS DIED IN AN AIRPLANE CRASH.
I ENDED UP IN AN ORPHANAGE...
...AND MY BROTHER WENT TO A FOSTER HOME.
PLIP
IT HURT. LOSING MY ONLY FAMILY MEMBER...
...MADE ME FEEL UNIMAGINABLY LONELY.

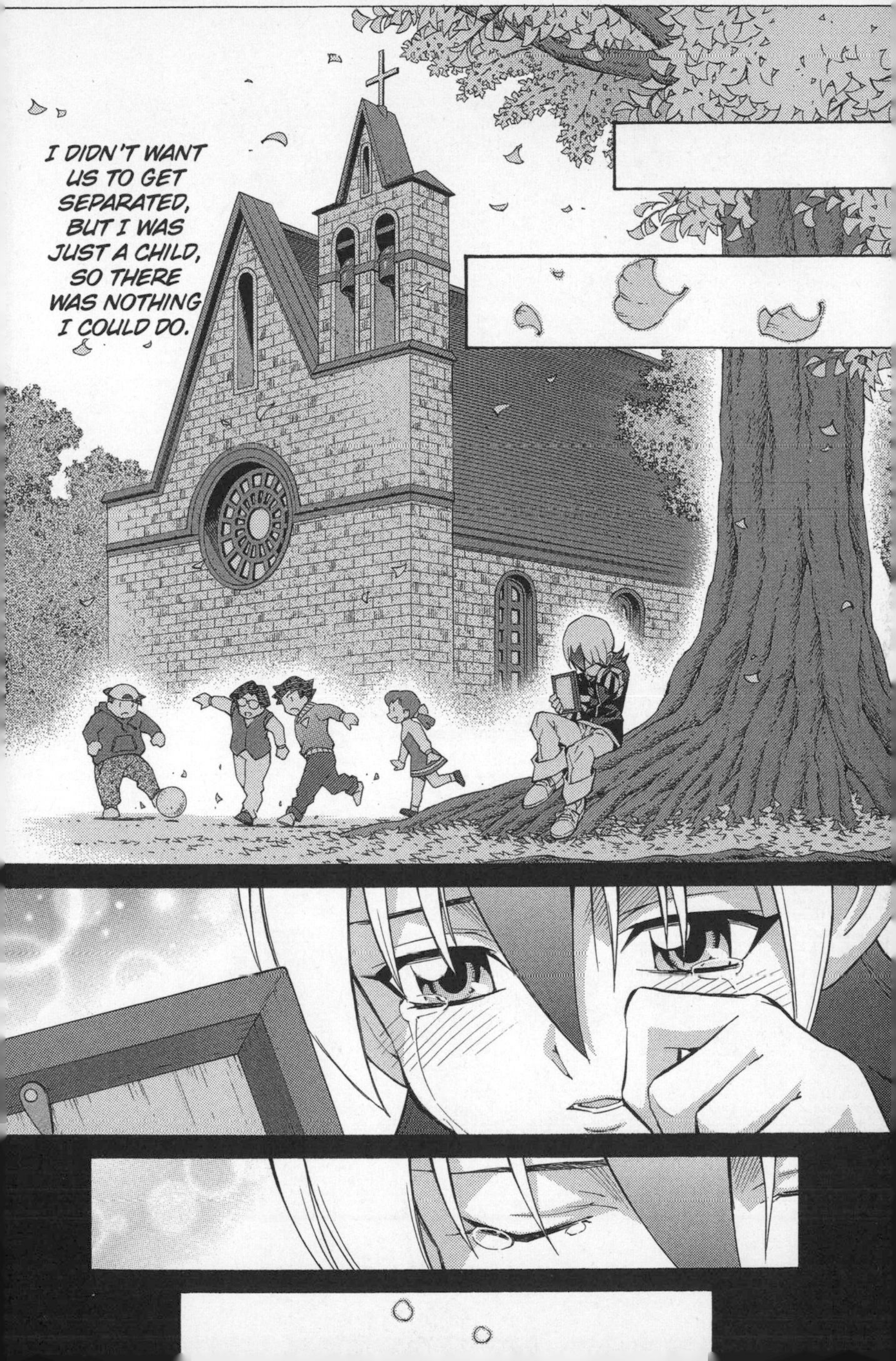
I DIDN'T WANT US TO GET SEPARATED, BUT I WAS JUST A CHILD, SO THERE WAS NOTHING I COULD DO.

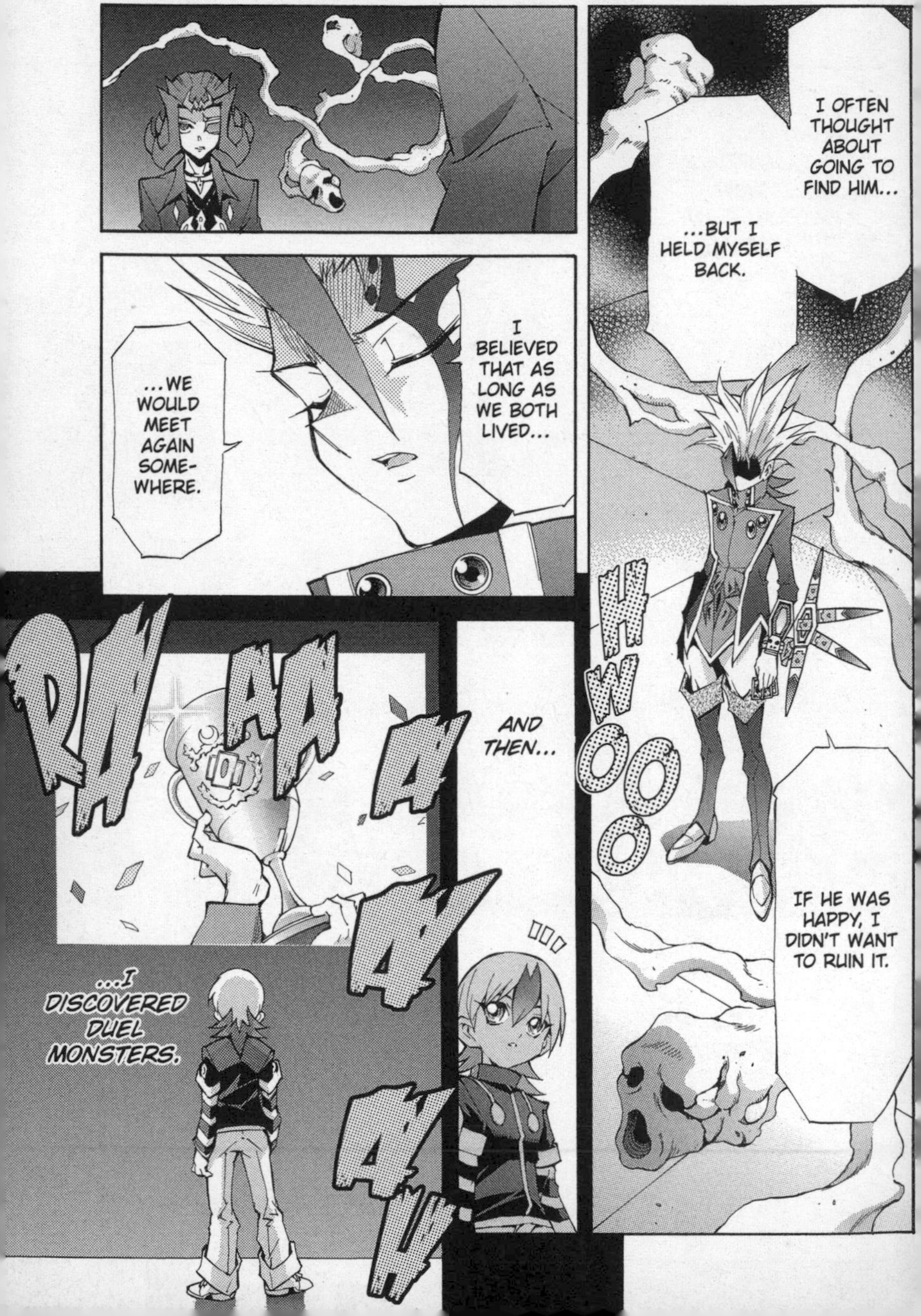
I OFTEN THOUGHT ABOUT GOING TO FIND HIM...
...BUT I HELD MYSELF BACK.
IF HE WAS HAPPY, I DIDN'T WANT TO RUIN IT.
I BELIEVED THAT AS LONG AS WE BOTH LIVED...
...WE WOULD MEET AGAIN SOME-WHERE.
AND THEN...
...I DISCOVERED DUEL MONSTERS.

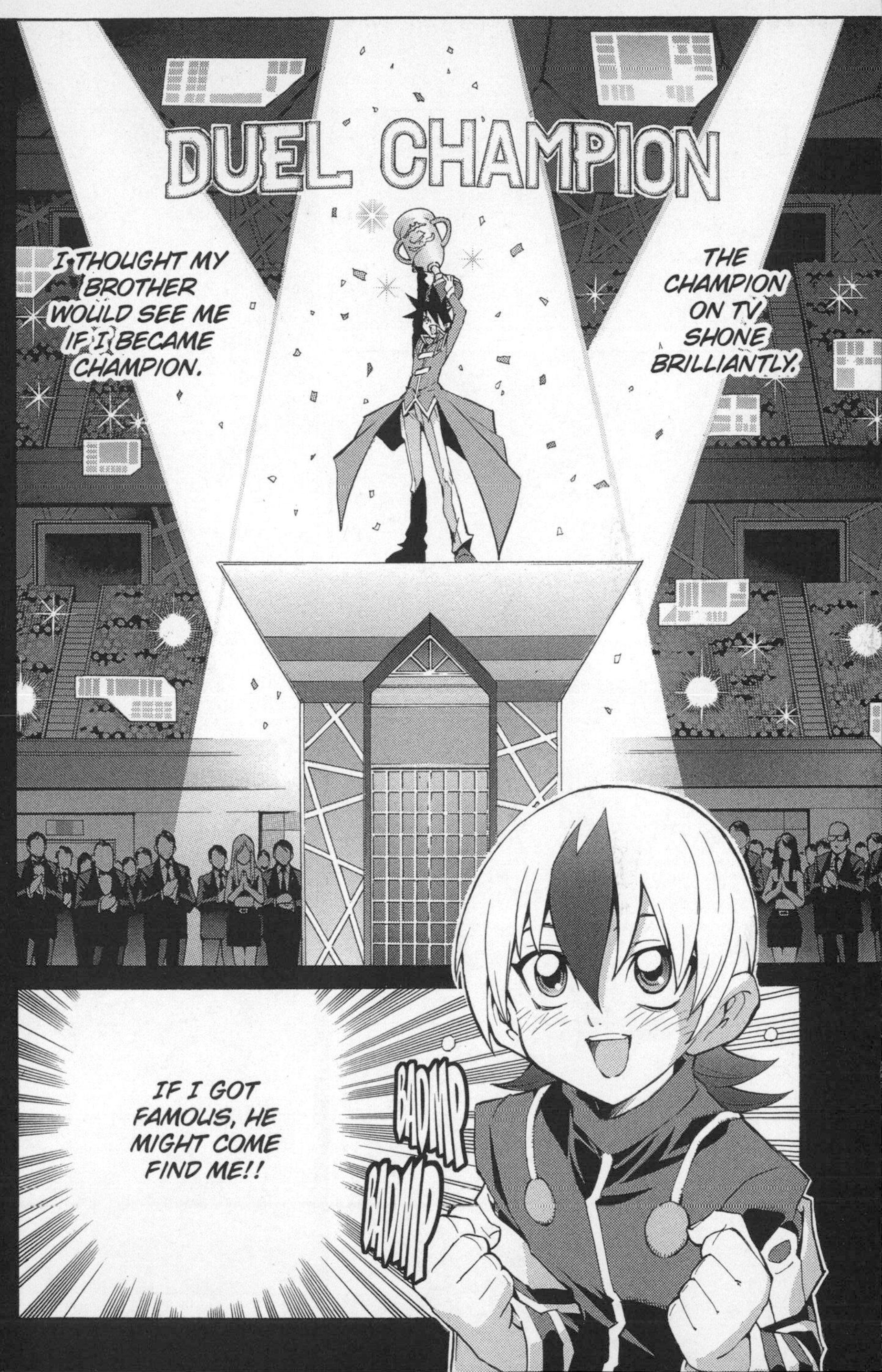
DUEL CHAMPION
THE CHAMPION ON TV SHONE BRILLIANTLY.
I THOUGHT MY BROTHER WOULD SEE ME IF I BECAME CHAMPION.
BADMP
BADMP
IF I GOT FAMOUS, HE MIGHT COME FIND ME!!

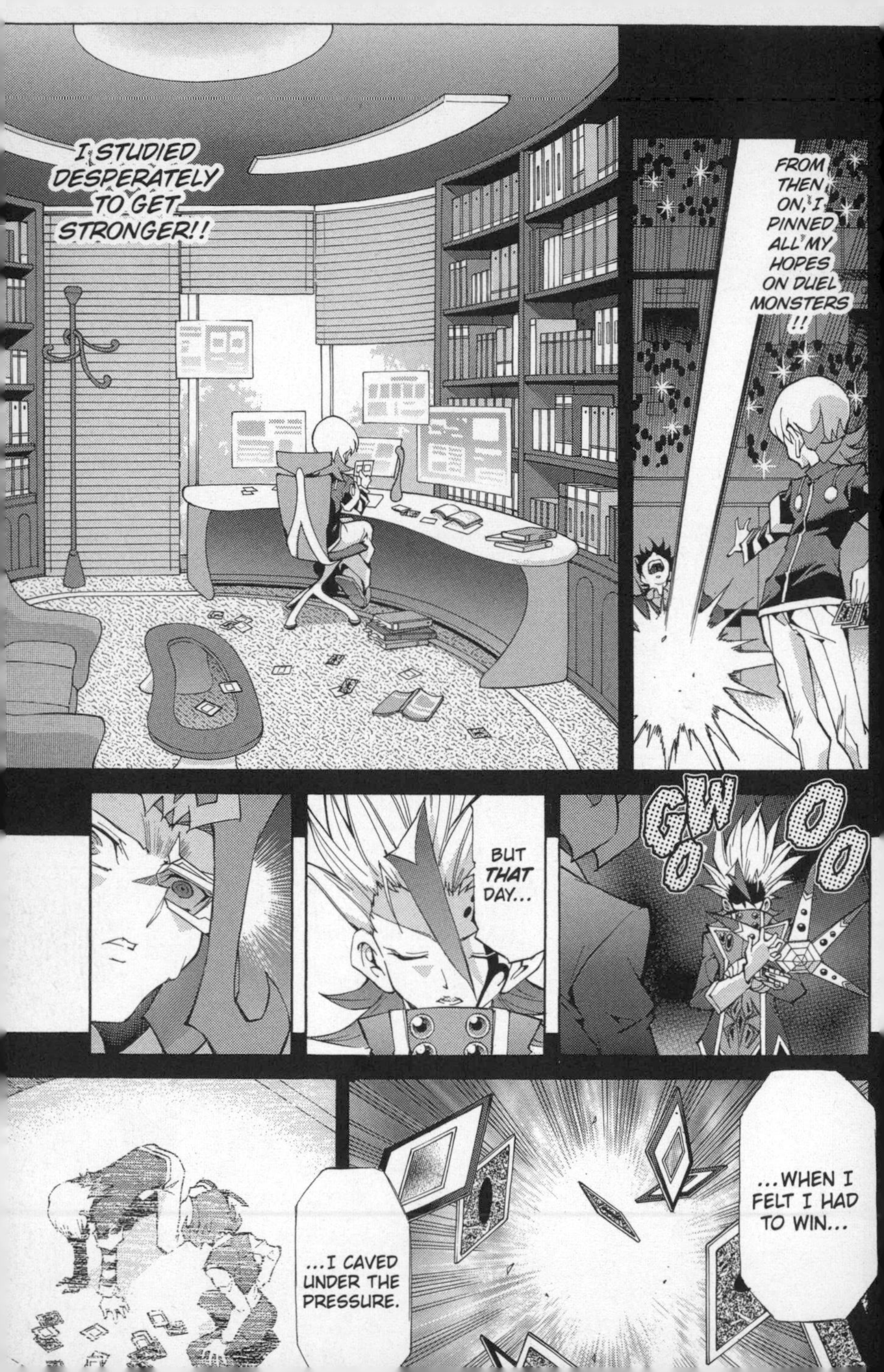
FROM THEN ON, I PINNED ALL MY HOPES ON DUEL MONSTERS!!
I STUDIED DESPERATELY TO GET STRONGER!!
GWOOOO
BUT *THAT* DAY...
...WHEN I FELT I HAD TO WIN...
...I CAVED UNDER THE PRESSURE.

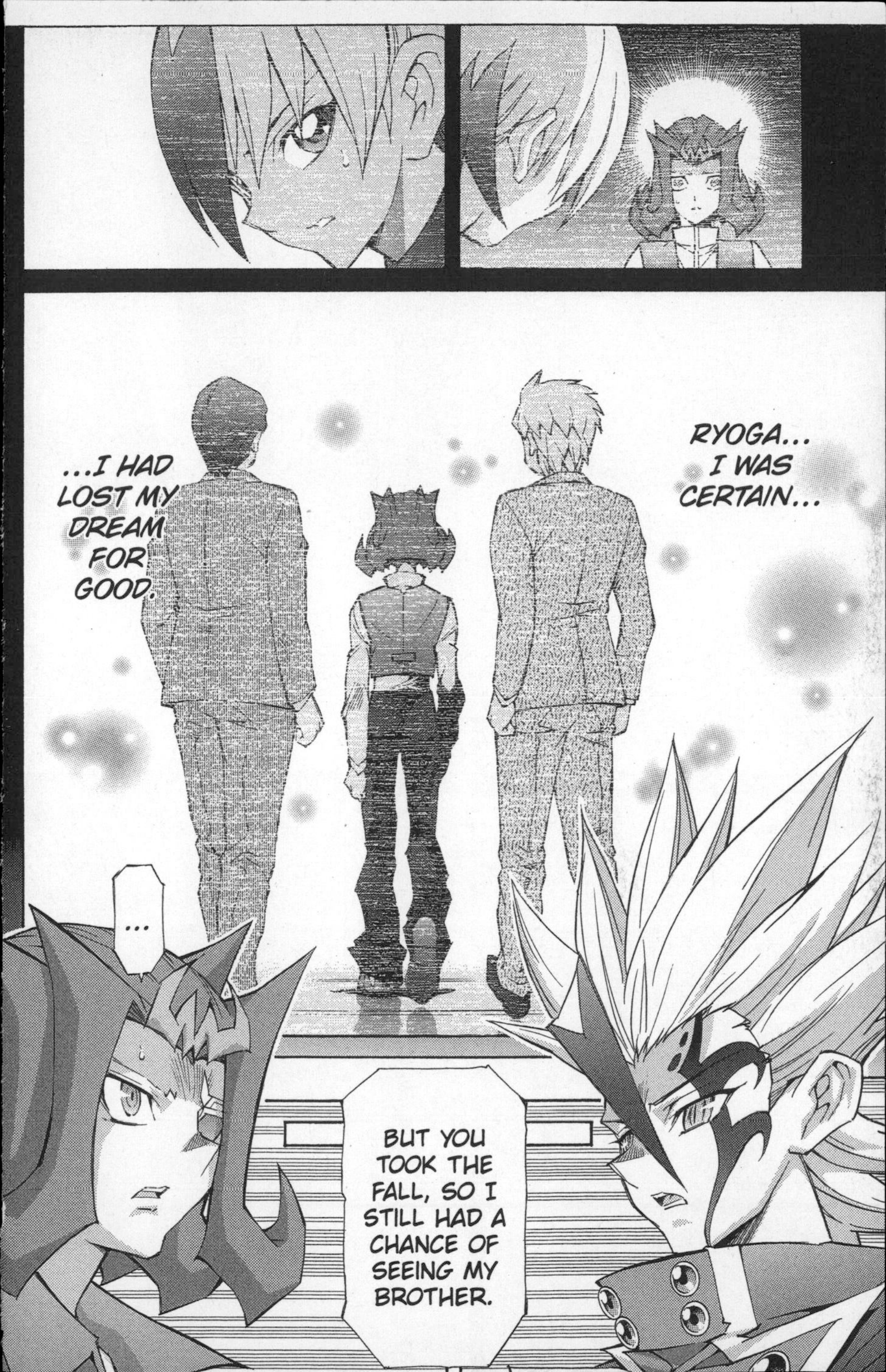
RYOGA... I WAS CERTAIN...
...I HAD LOST MY DREAM FOR GOOD.
...
BUT YOU TOOK THE FALL, SO I STILL HAD A CHANCE OF SEEING MY BROTHER.

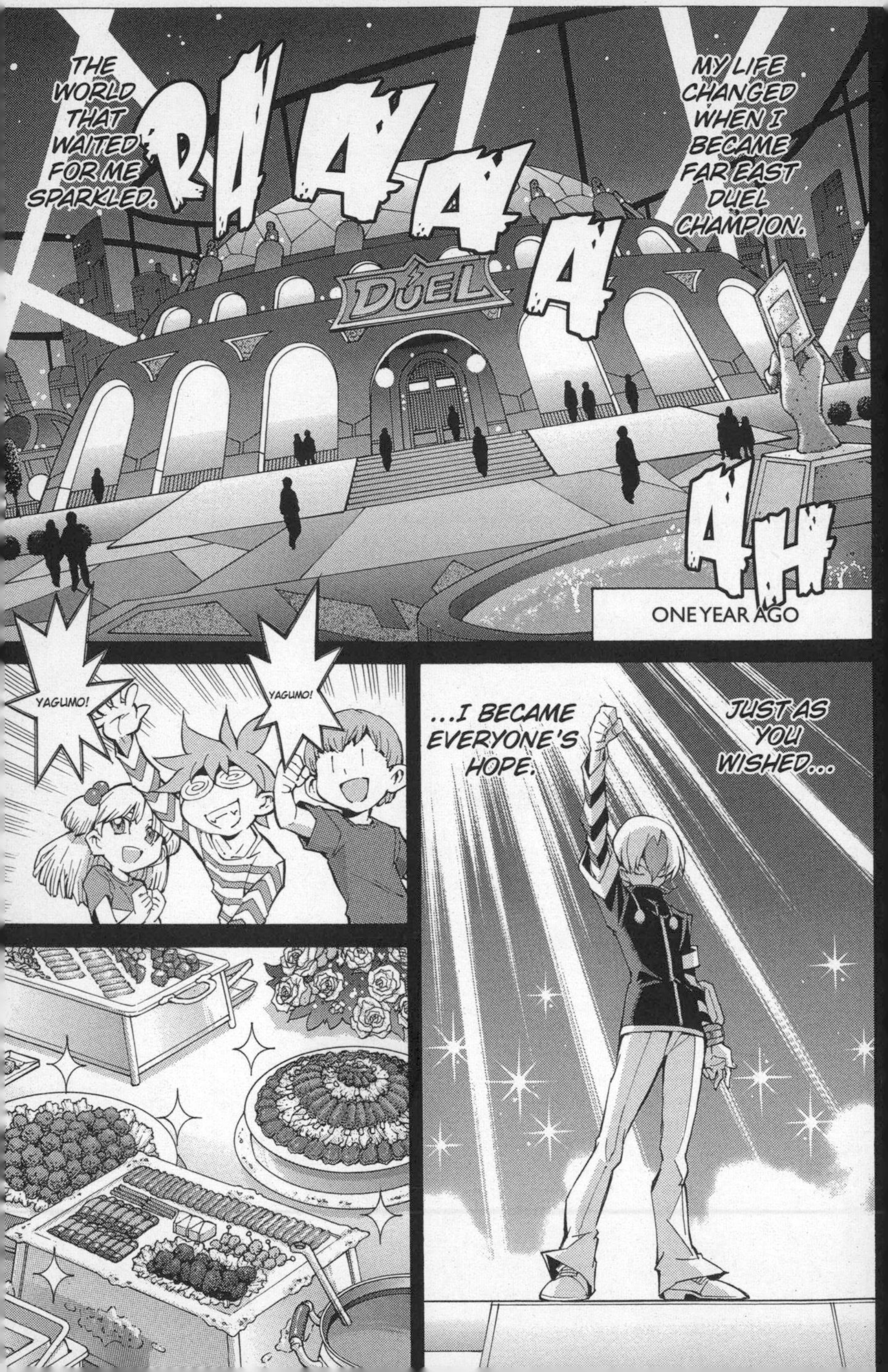
MY LIFE CHANGED WHEN I BECAME FAR EAST DUEL CHAMPION.
THE WORLD THAT WAITED FOR ME SPARKLED.
RAAAA
DUEL
AH
ONE YEAR AGO
JUST AS YOU WISHED...
...I BECAME EVERYONE'S HOPE.
YAGUMO!
YAGUMO!

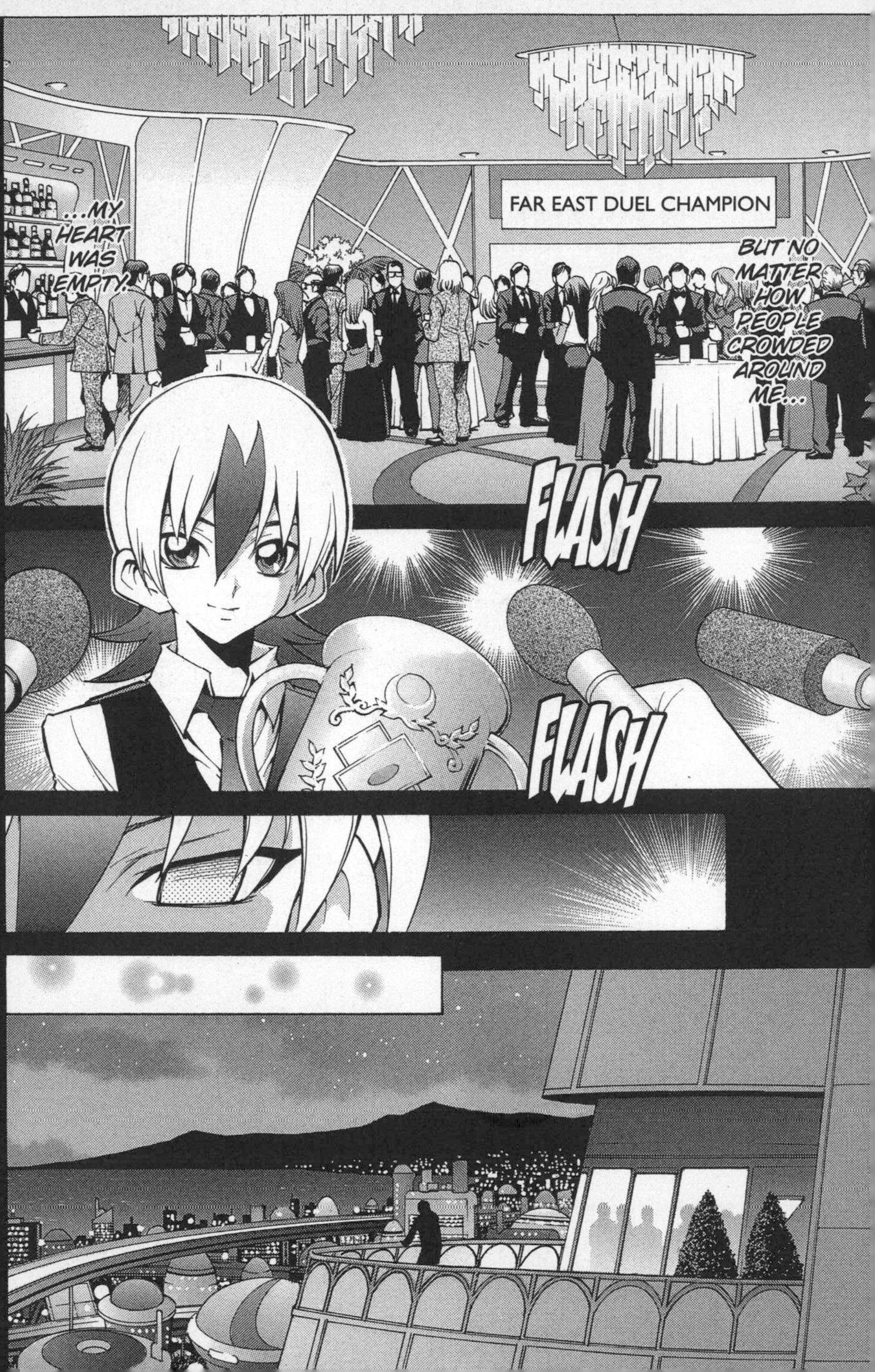
FAR EAST DUEL CHAMPION
BUT NO MATTER HOW PEOPLE CROWDED AROUND ME...
...MY HEART WAS EMPTY.
FLASH
FLASH

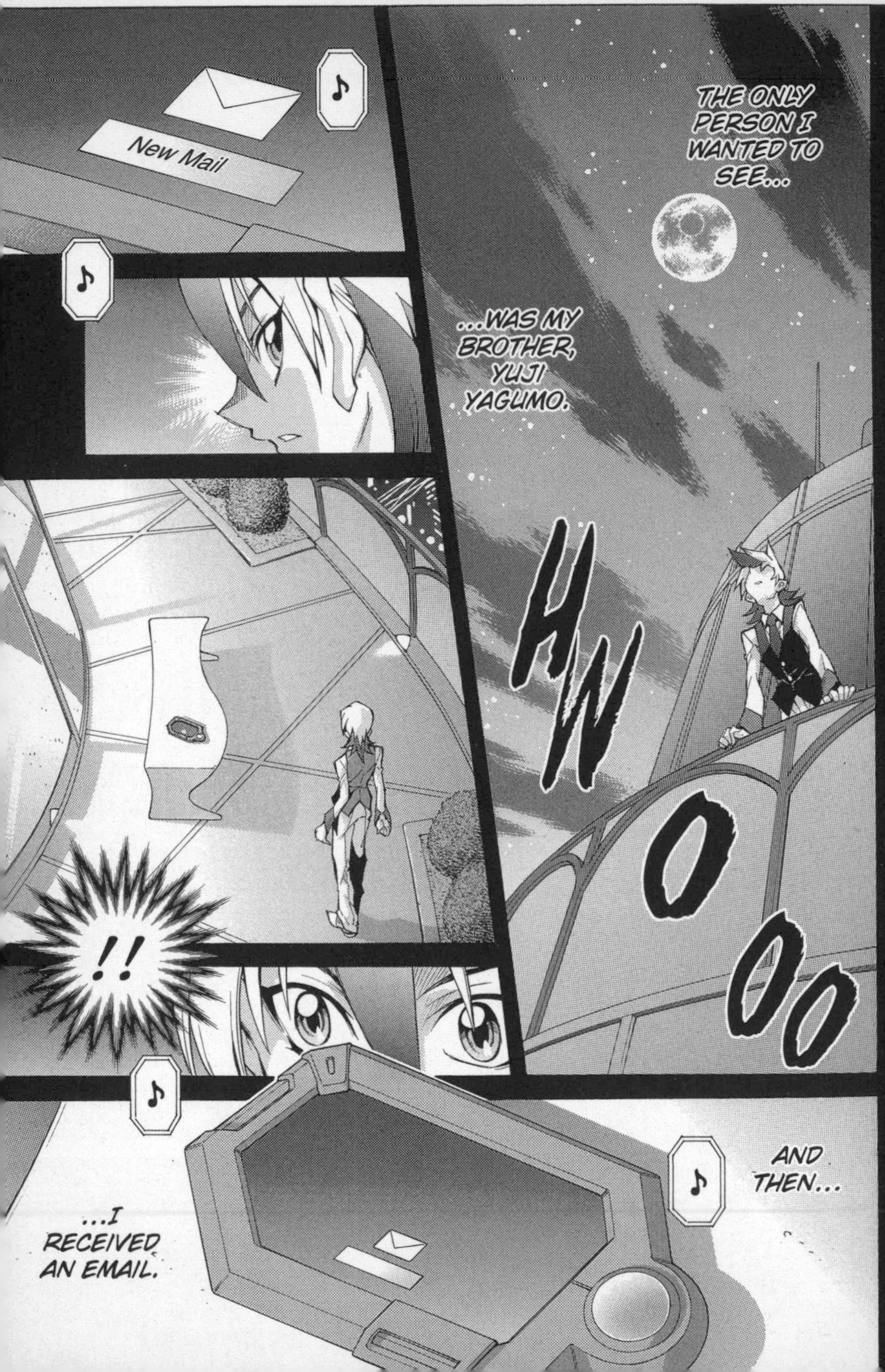
THE ONLY PERSON I WANTED TO SEE...
...WAS MY BROTHER, YUJI YAGUMO.
HWOOO
♪
New Mail
♪
!!
♪
AND THEN...
♪
...I RECEIVED AN EMAIL.

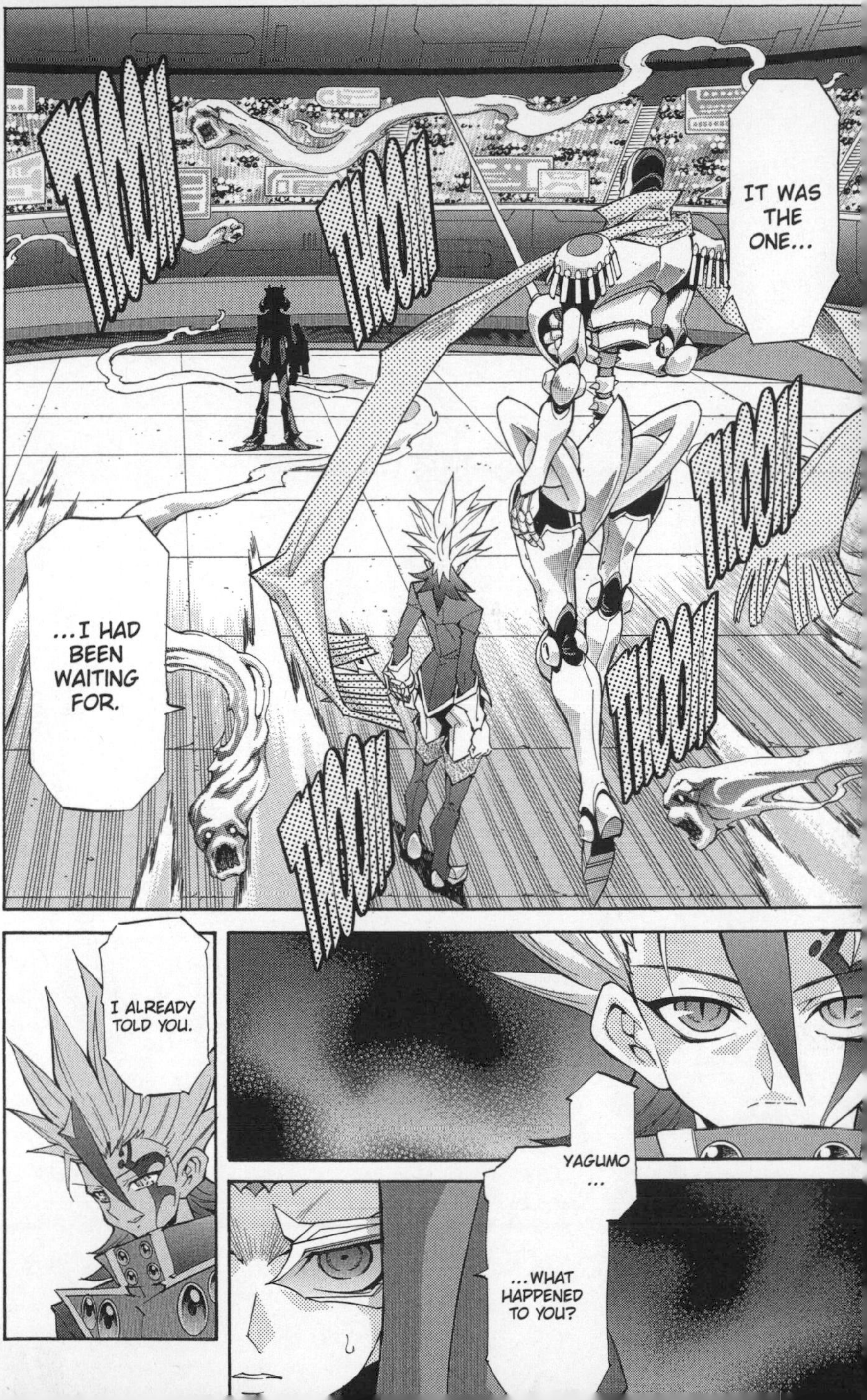
IT WAS THE ONE...
THOOM
THOOM
THOOM
THOOM
THOOM
...I HAD BEEN WAITING FOR.
YAGUMO ...
...WHAT HAPPENED TO YOU?
I ALREADY TOLD YOU.

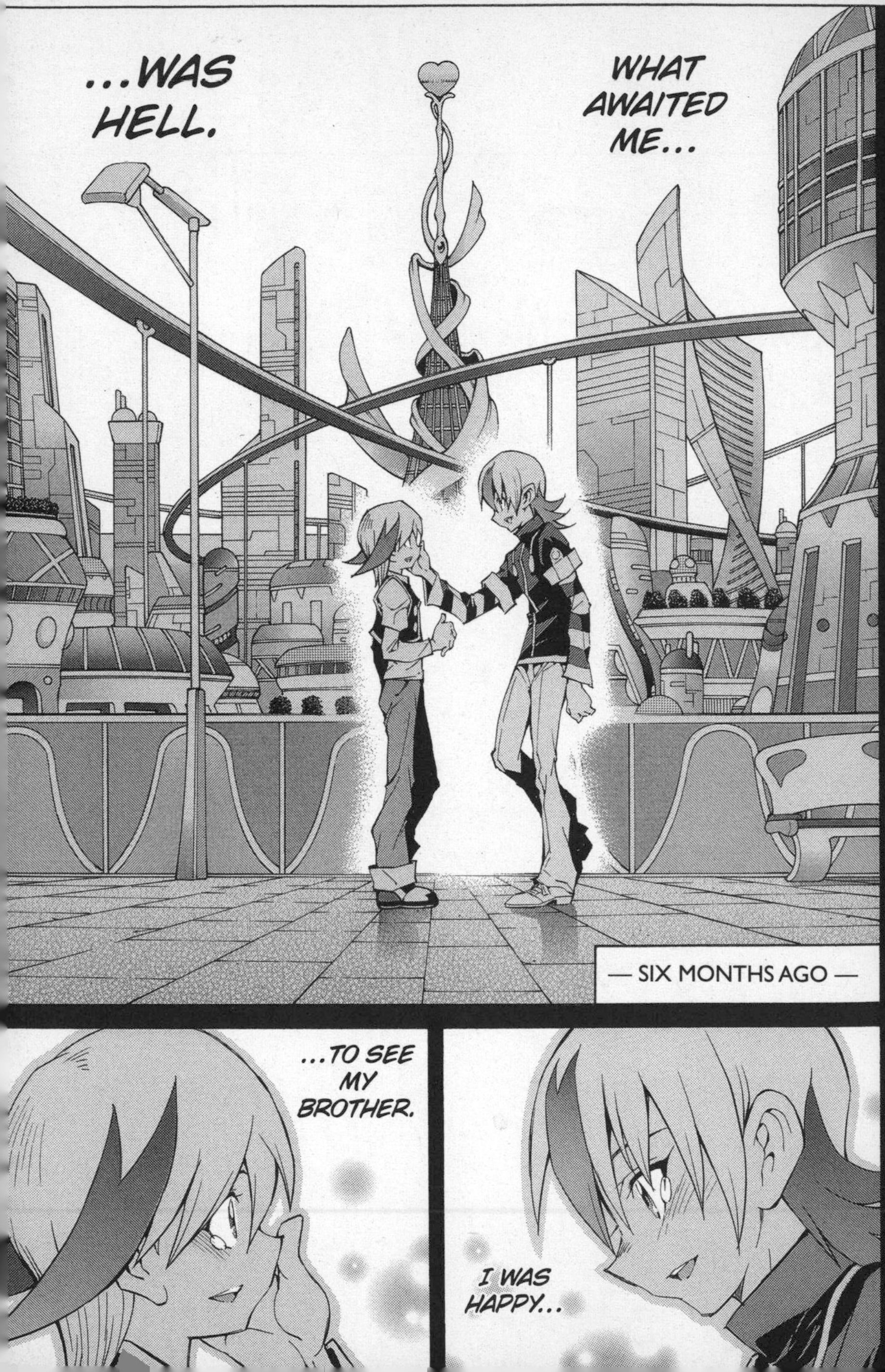
WHAT AWAITED ME...
...WAS HELL.
— SIX MONTHS AGO —
I WAS HAPPY...
...TO SEE MY BROTHER.

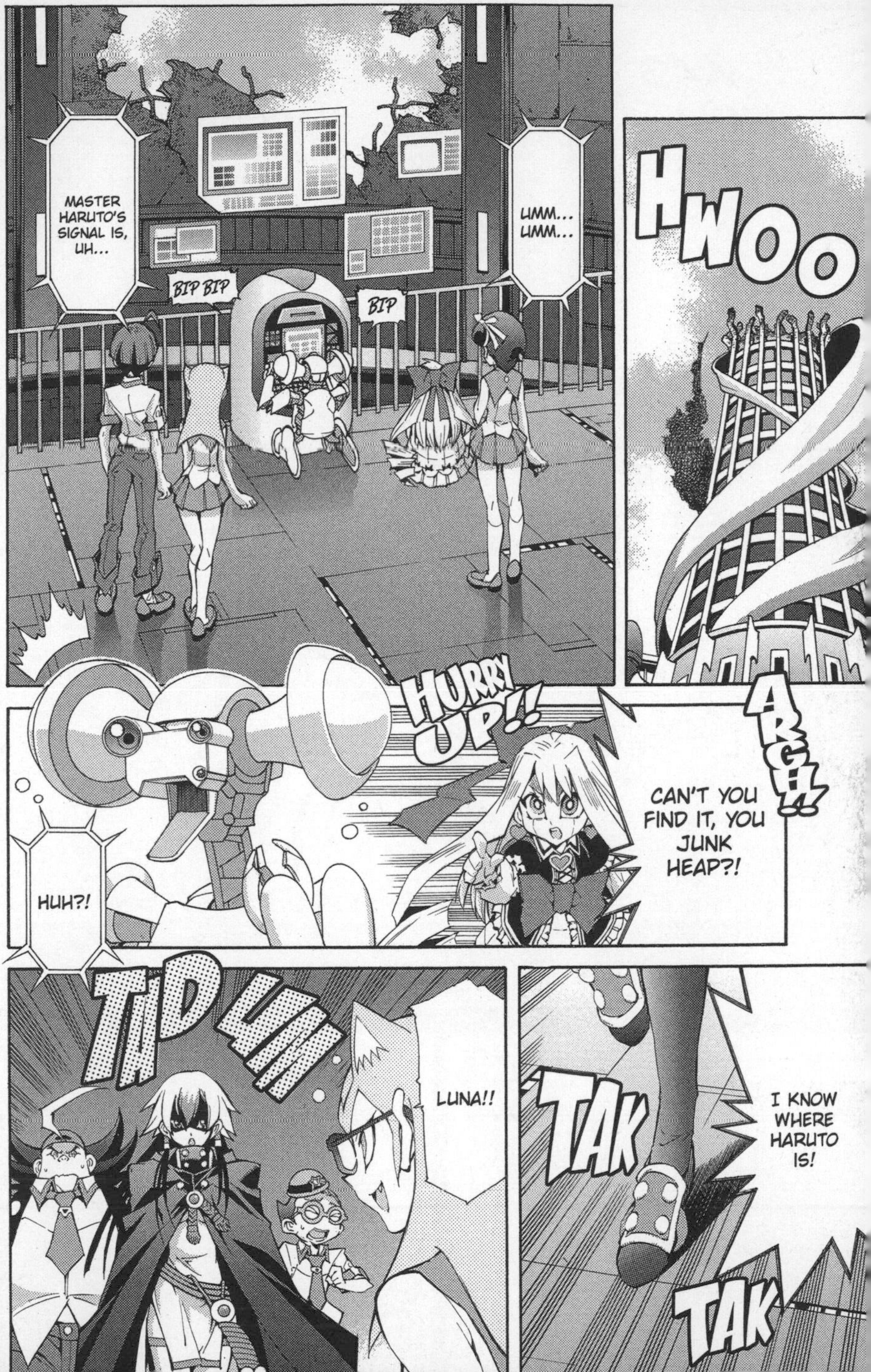
HWOOO
UMM... UMM...
BIP
BIP BIP
MASTER HARUTO'S SIGNAL IS, UH...
ARGH!!
CAN'T YOU FIND IT, YOU JUNK HEAP?!
HURRY UP!!
HUH?!
I KNOW WHERE HARUTO IS!
TAK
TAK
LUNA!!
TADUM

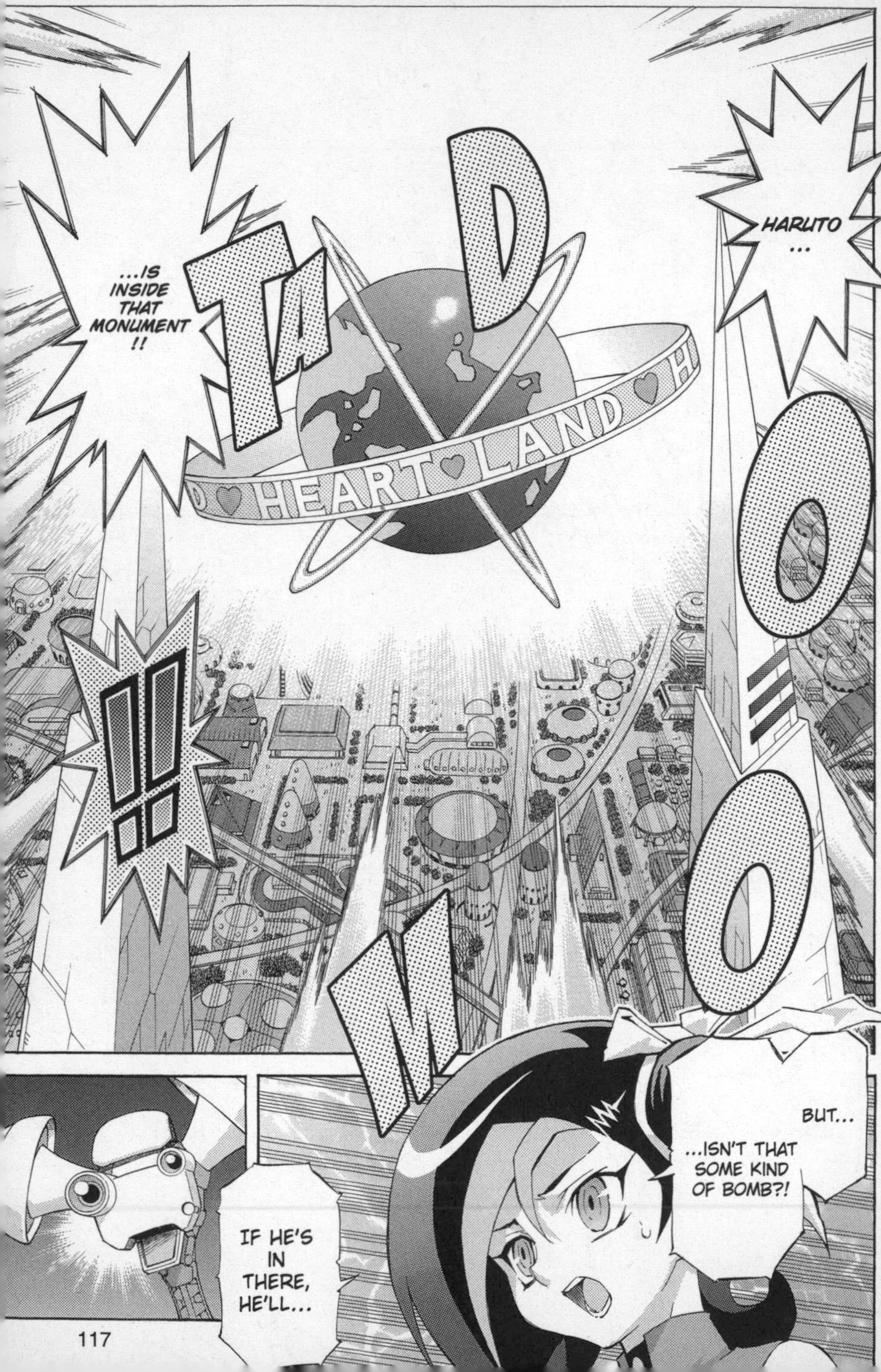

HARUTO...
...IS INSIDE THAT MONUMENT!!
TA
D
HEART♥LAND
O
O
M
!!
BUT...
...ISN'T THAT SOME KIND OF BOMB?!
IF HE'S IN THERE, HE'LL...

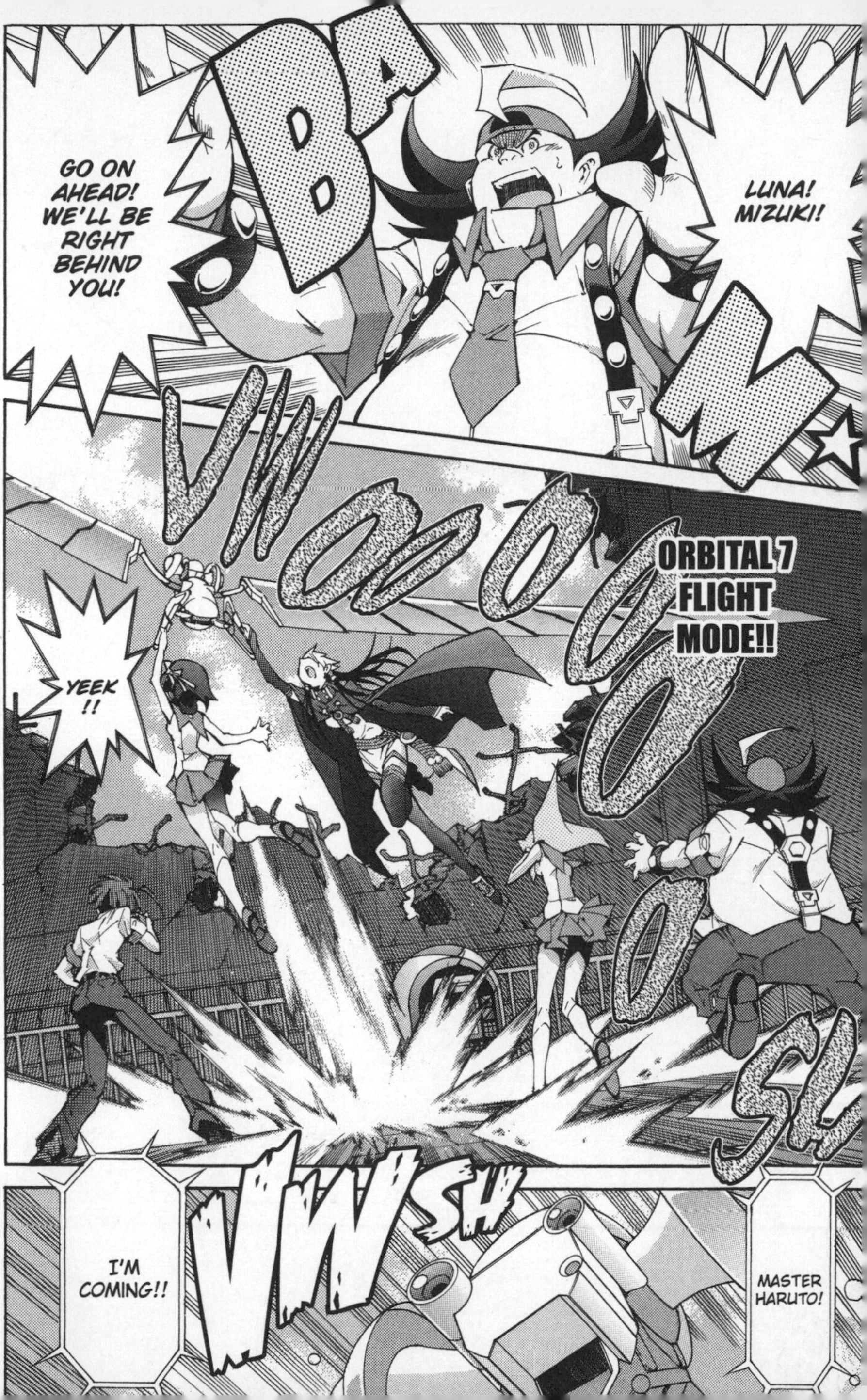
LUNA! MIZUKI!
BAM☆
GO ON AHEAD! WE'LL BE RIGHT BEHIND YOU!
ORBITAL 7 FLIGHT MODE!!
VWOOOOOOSH
YEEK!!
MASTER HARUTO!
VWSH
I'M COMING!!

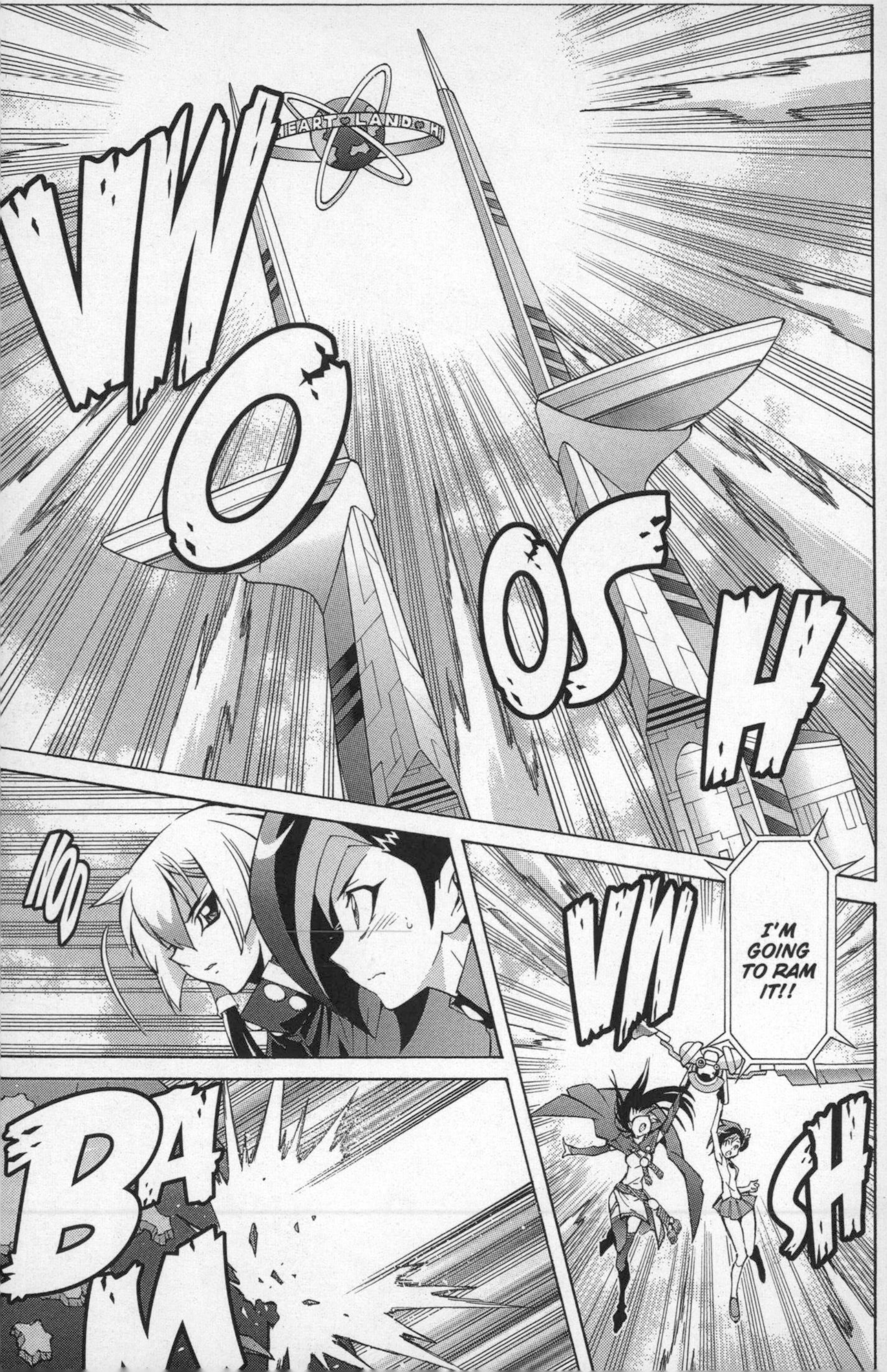
HEART LAND
VWOOSH
I'M GOING TO RAM IT!!
VWSH
NOD
BAM

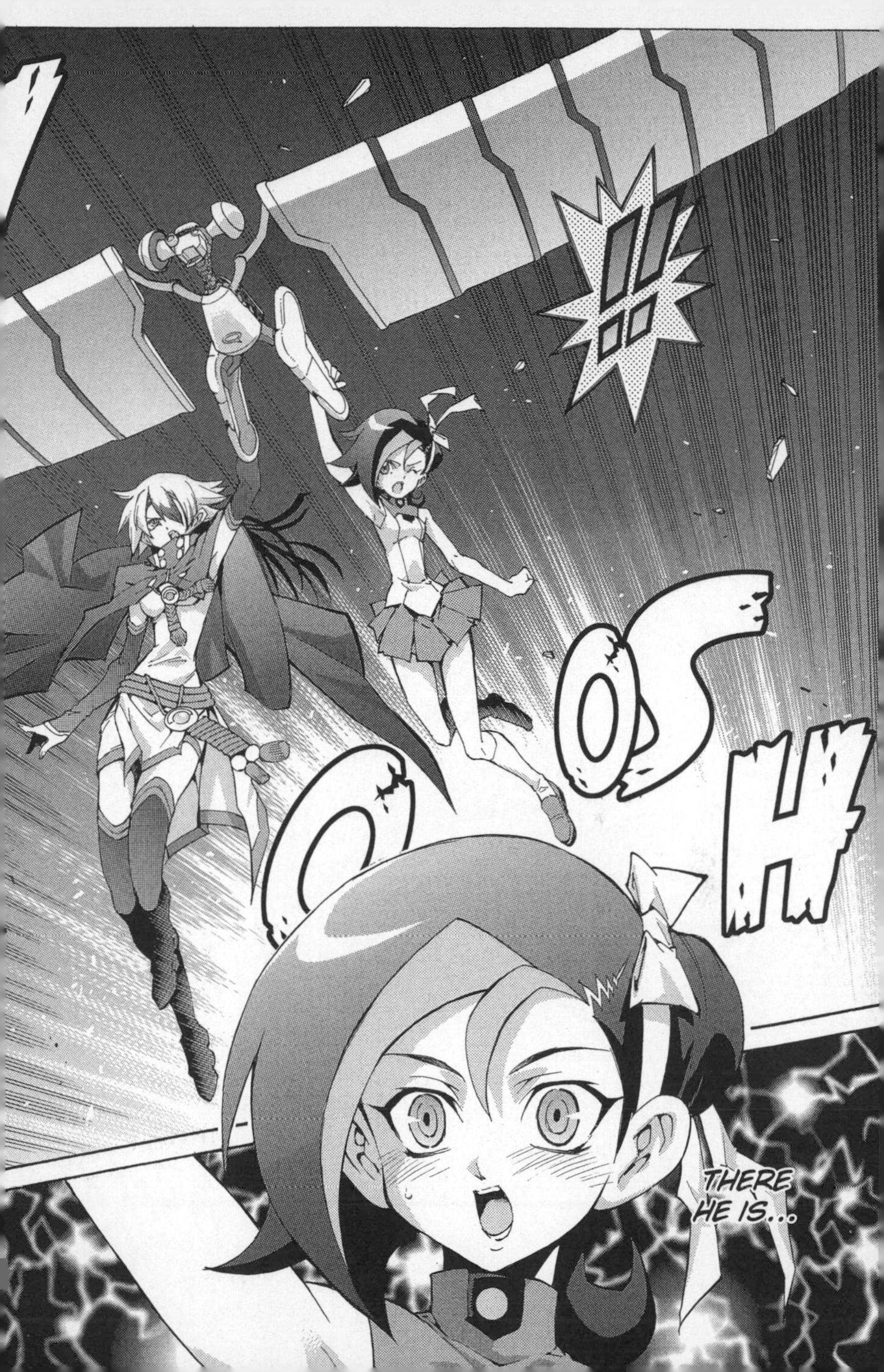
!!
!!
WOOSH
THERE HE IS...

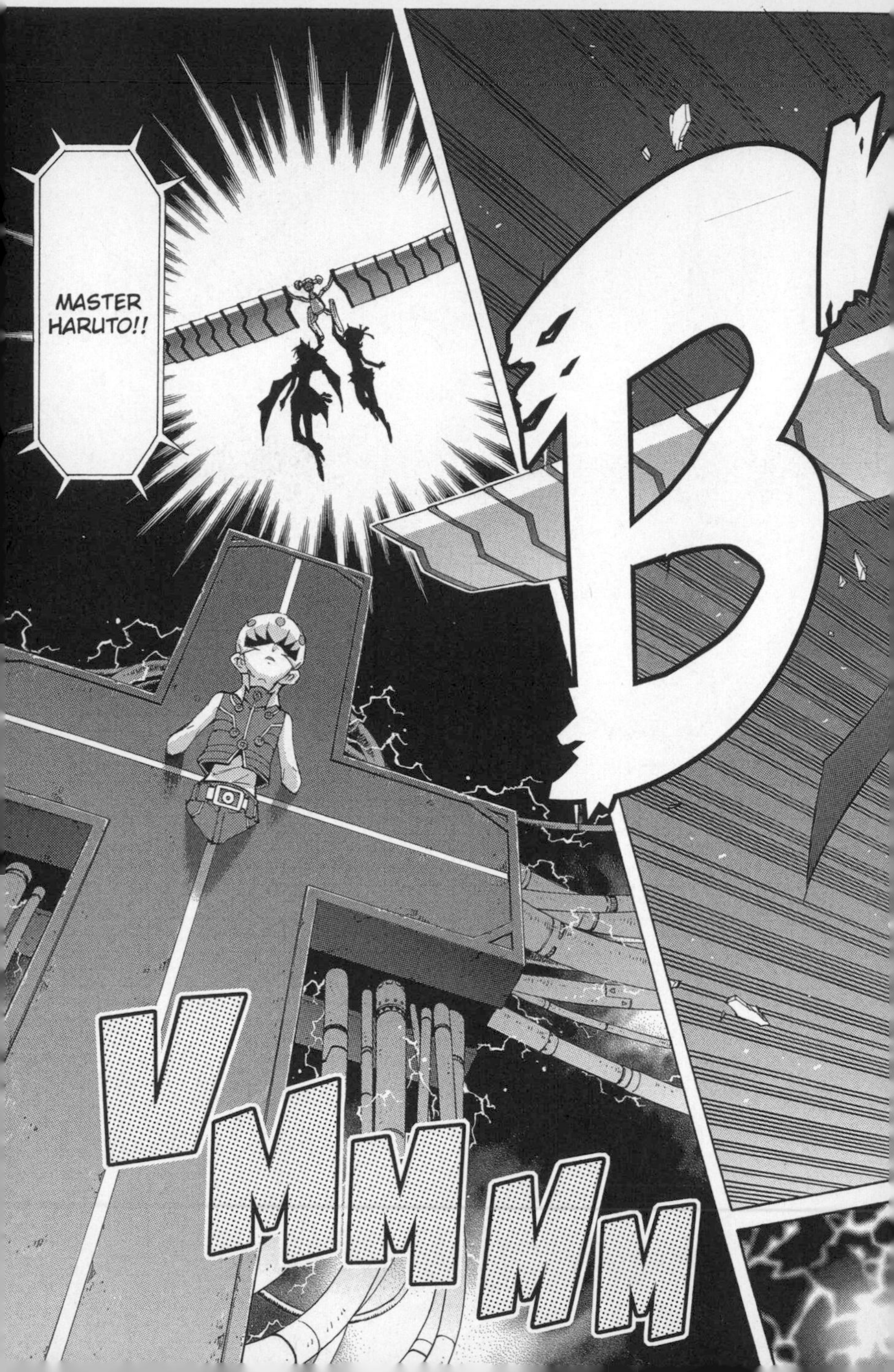
B
MASTER HARUTO!!
VMMMMMM

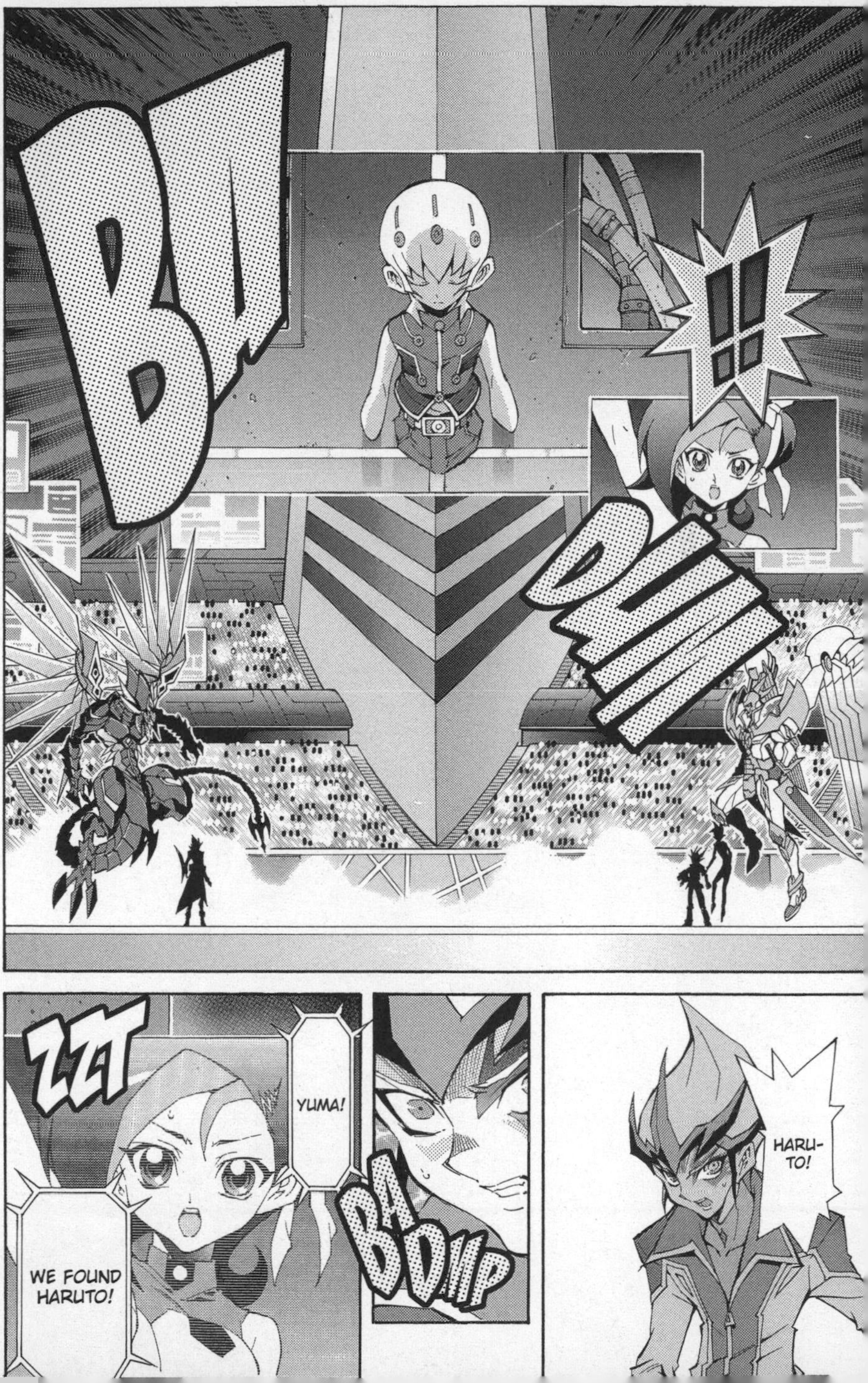
!!
BA
DUM
HARU-
TO!
BADUMP
YUMA!
ZZT
WE FOUND HARUTO!

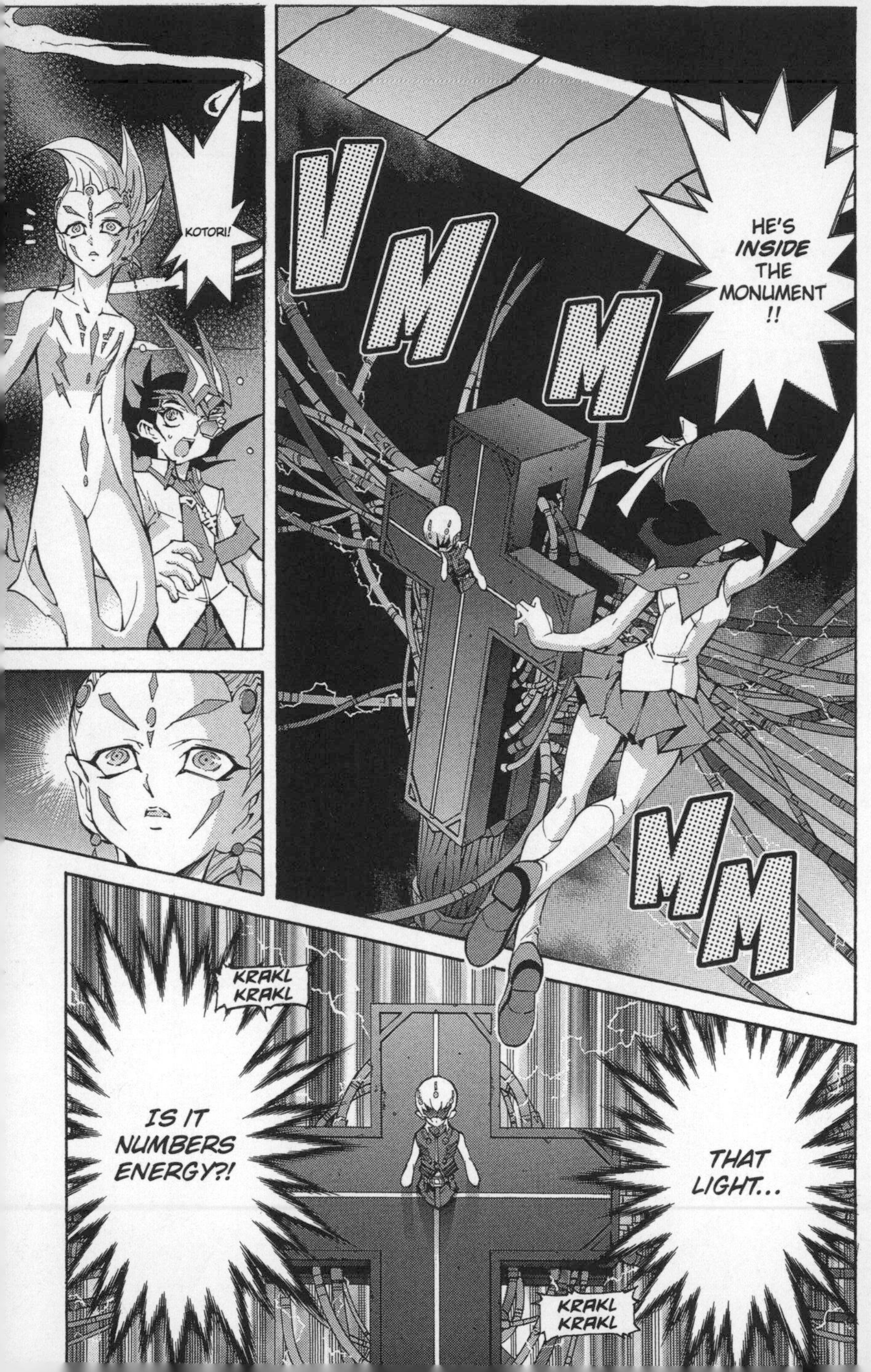
HE'S *INSIDE* THE MONUMENT !!
VMM
M
MM
KOTORI!
THAT LIGHT...
KRAKL KRAKL
IS IT NUMBERS ENERGY?!
KRAKL KRAKL

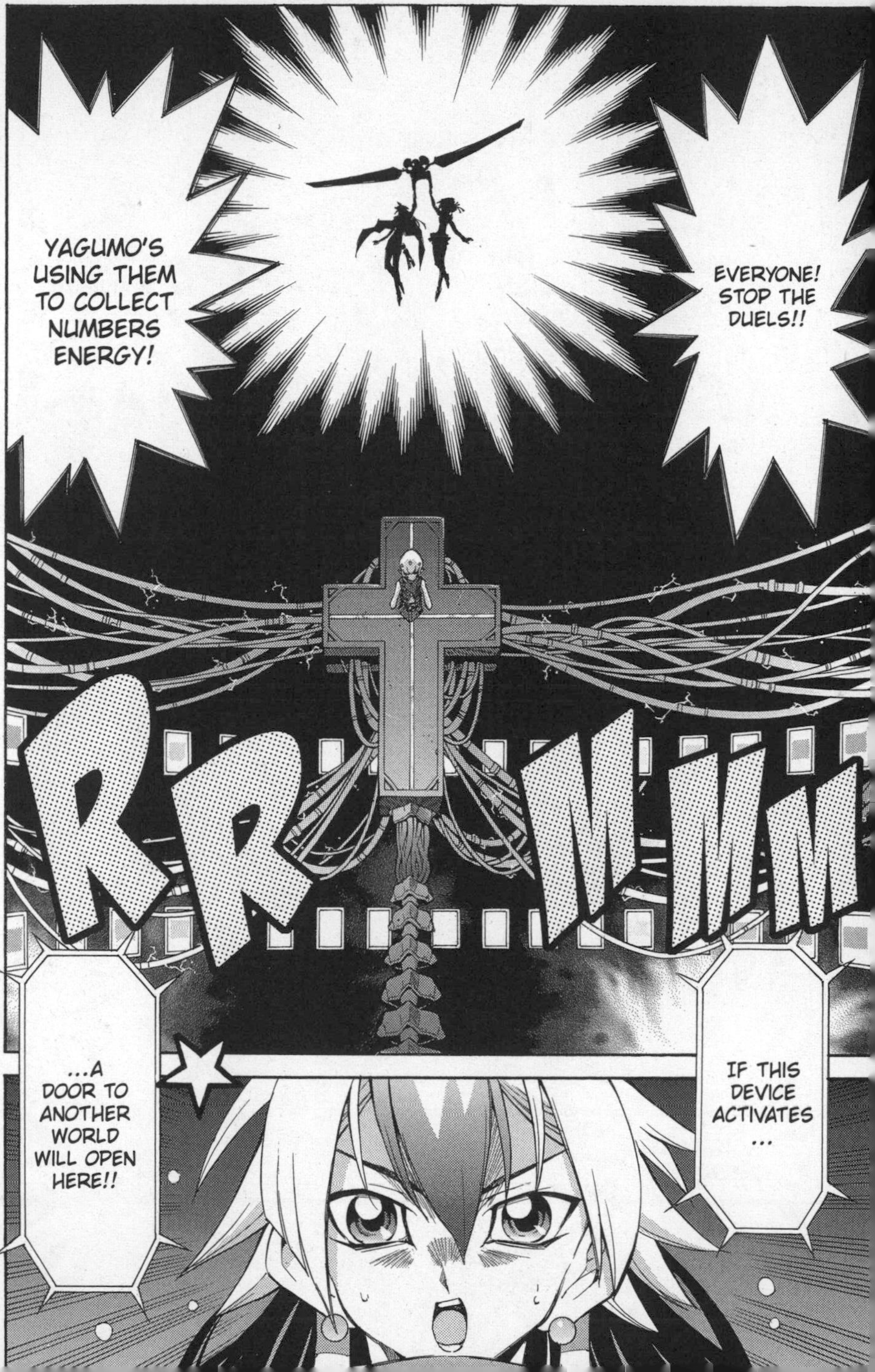
EVERYONE! STOP THE DUELS!!
YAGUMO'S USING THEM TO COLLECT NUMBERS ENERGY!
RRMMM
IF THIS DEVICE ACTIVATES...
...A DOOR TO ANOTHER WORLD WILL OPEN HERE!!

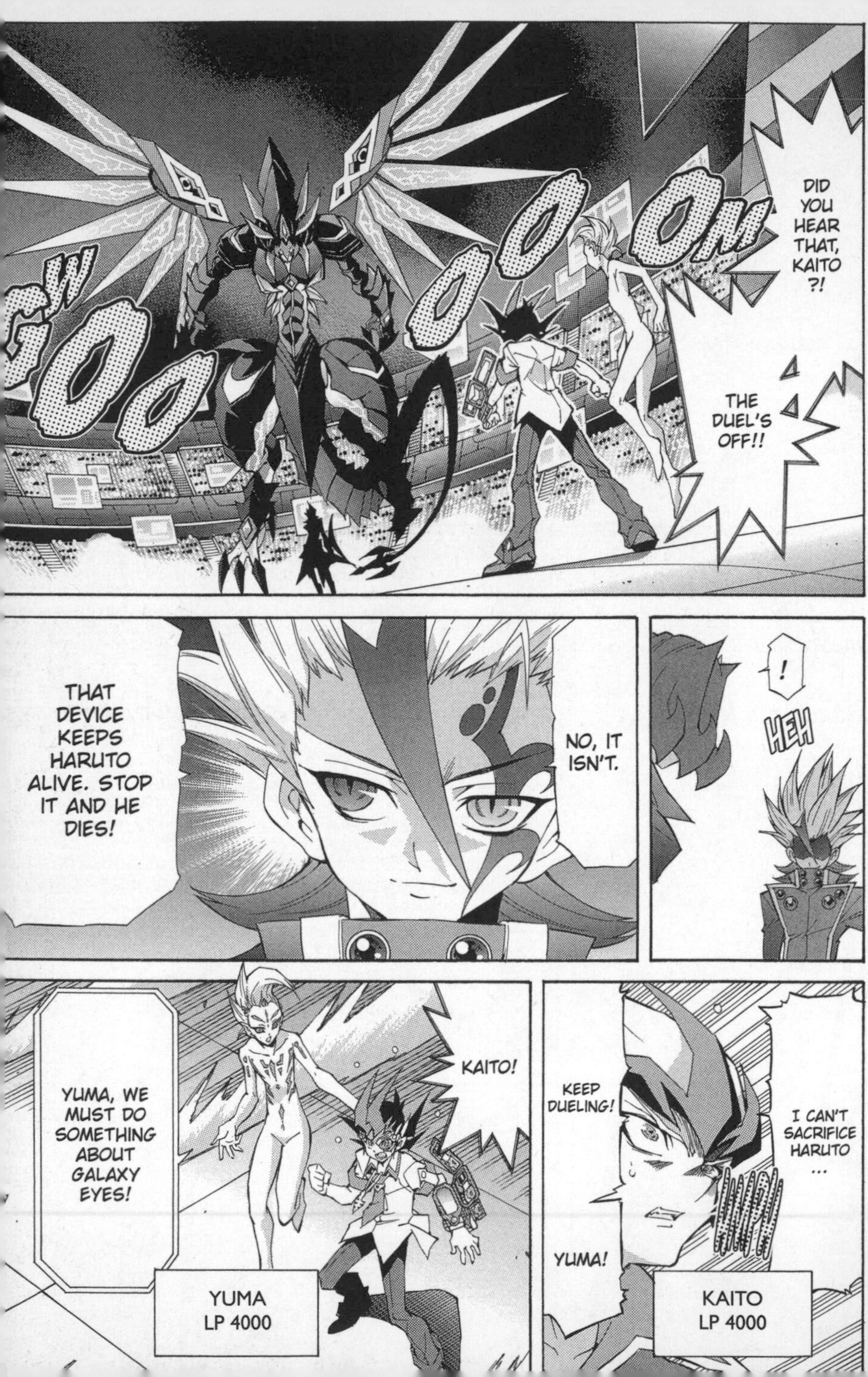
DID YOU HEAR THAT, KAITO?!
THE DUEL'S OFF!!
!
HEH
NO, IT ISN'T.
THAT DEVICE KEEPS HARUTO ALIVE. STOP IT AND HE DIES!
I CAN'T SACRIFICE HARUTO ...
KEEP DUELING!
YUMA!
KAITO LP 4000
KAITO!
YUMA, WE MUST DO SOMETHING ABOUT GALAXY EYES!
YUMA LP 4000

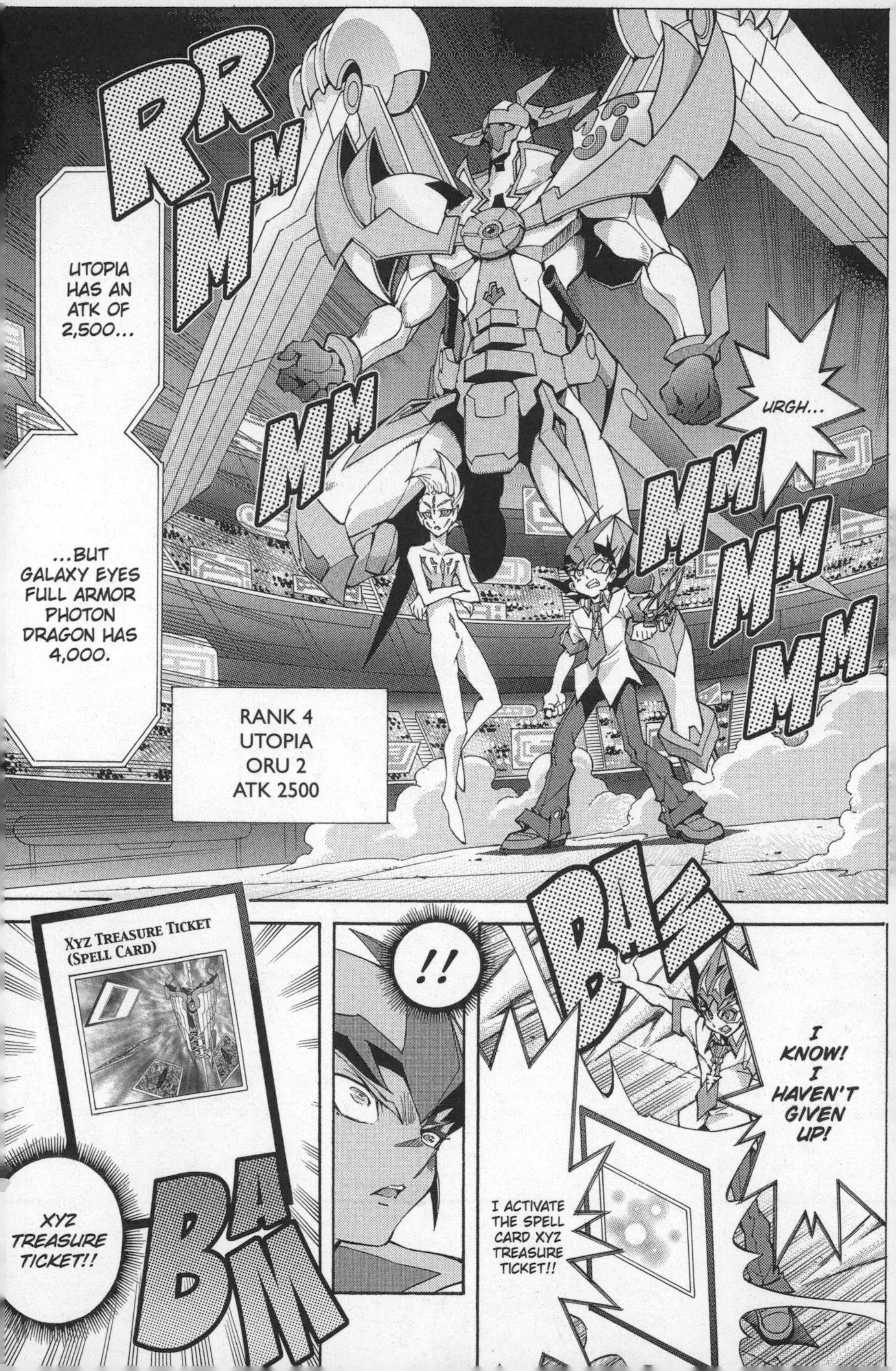
URGH...
MMM
MMM
MMM
RRMMM
MMM
UTOPIA HAS AN ATK OF 2,500...
RANK 4
UTOPIA
ORU 2
ATK 2500
...BUT GALAXY EYES FULL ARMOR PHOTON DRAGON HAS 4,000.
BAM
I KNOW! I HAVEN'T GIVEN UP!
I ACTIVATE THE SPELL CARD XYZ TREASURE TICKET!!
!!
Xyz Treasure Ticket
(Spell Card)
XYZ TREASURE TICKET!!
BAM

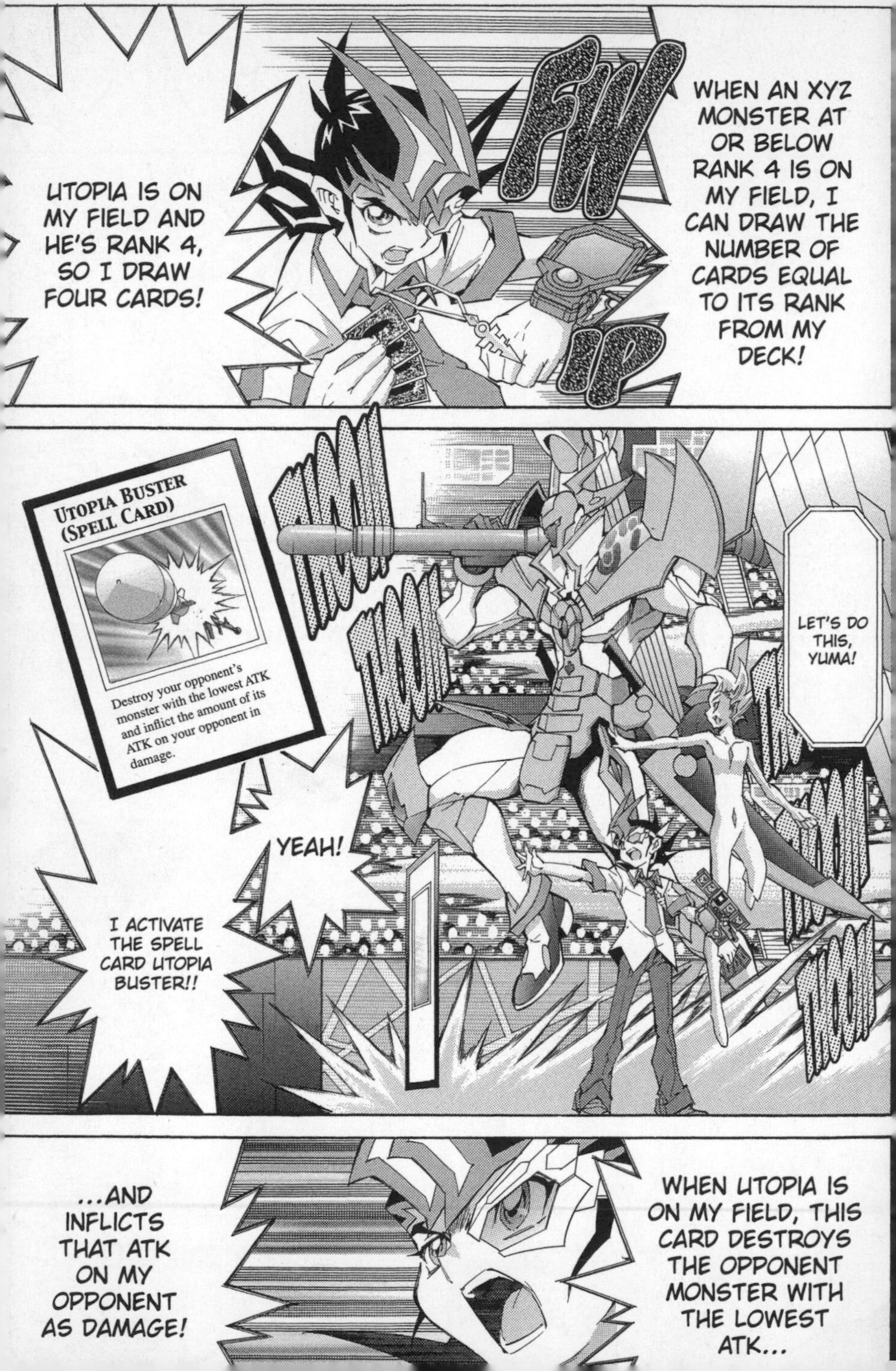
WHEN AN XYZ MONSTER AT OR BELOW RANK 4 IS ON MY FIELD, I CAN DRAW THE NUMBER OF CARDS EQUAL TO ITS RANK FROM MY DECK!
FWIP
UTOPIA IS ON MY FIELD AND HE'S RANK 4, SO I DRAW FOUR CARDS!
LET'S DO THIS, YUMA!
THOOM THOOM THOOM
UTOPIA BUSTER (SPELL CARD)
Destroy your opponent's monster with the lowest ATK and inflict the amount of its ATK on your opponent in damage.
YEAH!
I ACTIVATE THE SPELL CARD UTOPIA BUSTER!!
WHEN UTOPIA IS ON MY FIELD, THIS CARD DESTROYS THE OPPONENT MONSTER WITH THE LOWEST ATK...
...AND INFLICTS THAT ATK ON MY OPPONENT AS DAMAGE!

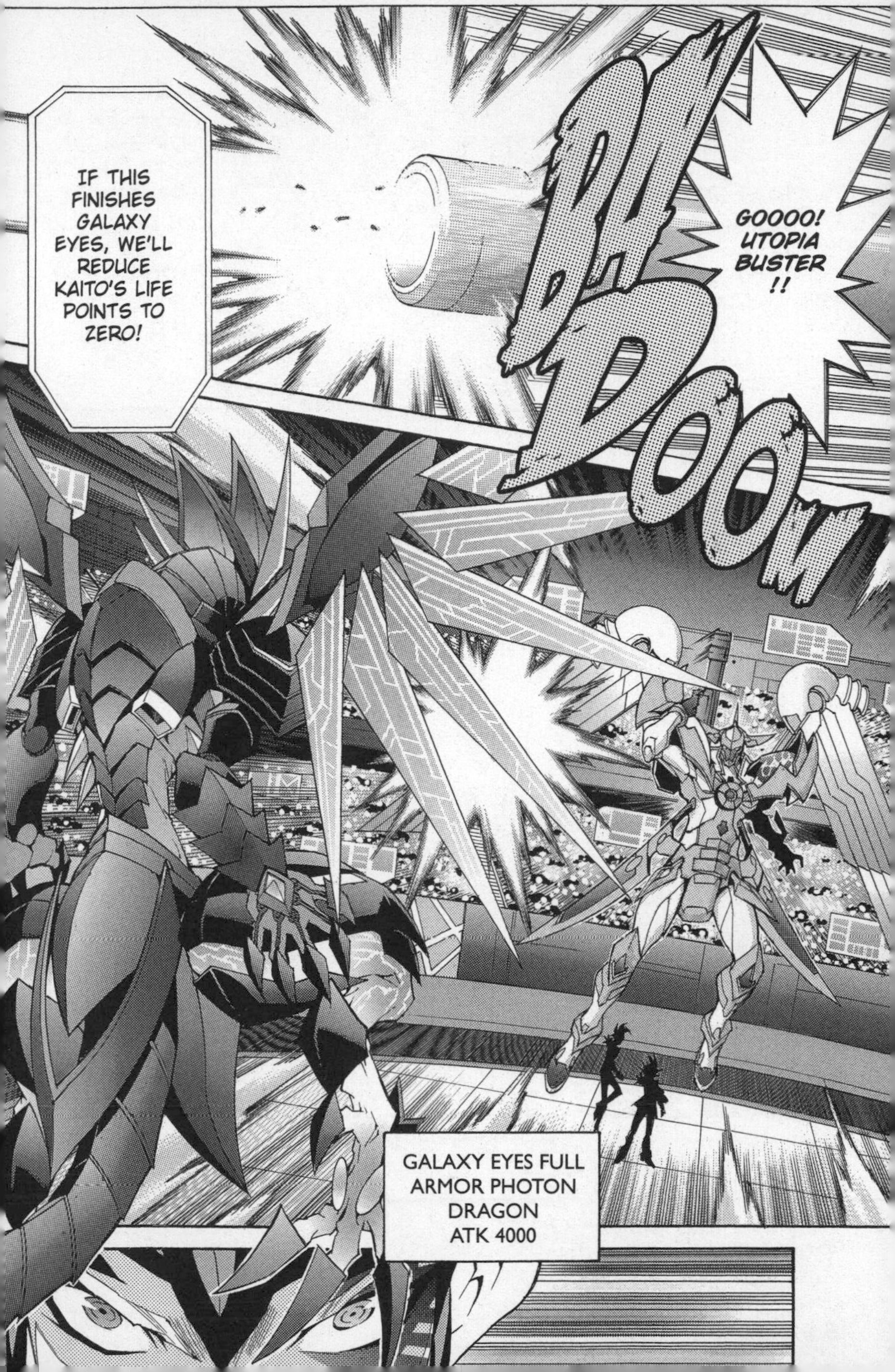
GOOOO! UTOPIA BUSTER !!
BADOOOM
IF THIS FINISHES GALAXY EYES, WE'LL REDUCE KAITO'S LIFE POINTS TO ZERO!
GALAXY EYES FULL ARMOR PHOTON DRAGON ATK 4000

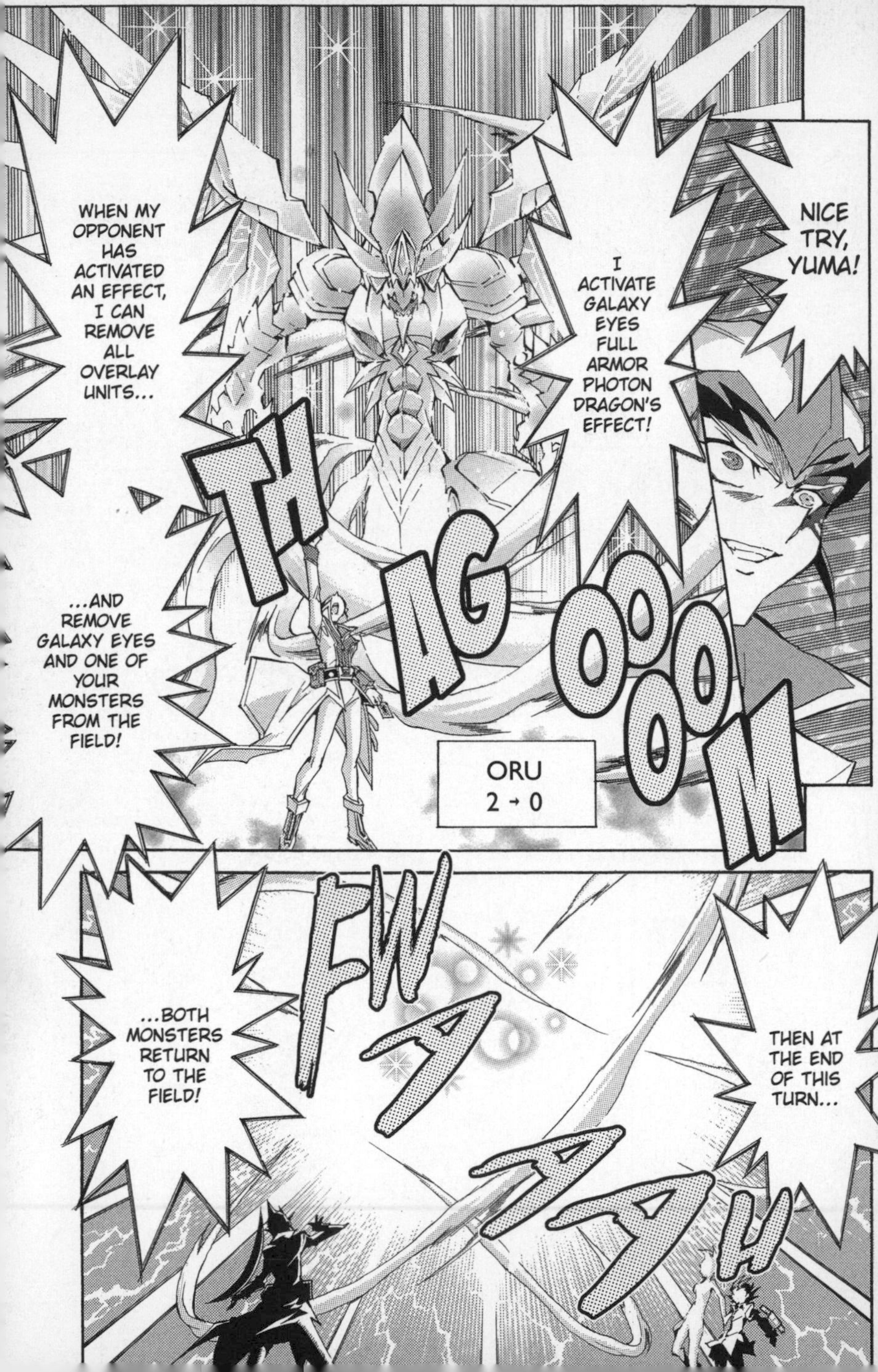
NICE TRY, YUMA!
I ACTIVATE GALAXY EYES FULL ARMOR PHOTON DRAGON'S EFFECT!
WHEN MY OPPONENT HAS ACTIVATED AN EFFECT, I CAN REMOVE ALL OVERLAY UNITS...
...AND REMOVE GALAXY EYES AND ONE OF YOUR MONSTERS FROM THE FIELD!
THAGOOOOOM
ORU
2 → 0
THEN AT THE END OF THIS TURN...
...BOTH MONSTERS RETURN TO THE FIELD!
FWAAAH

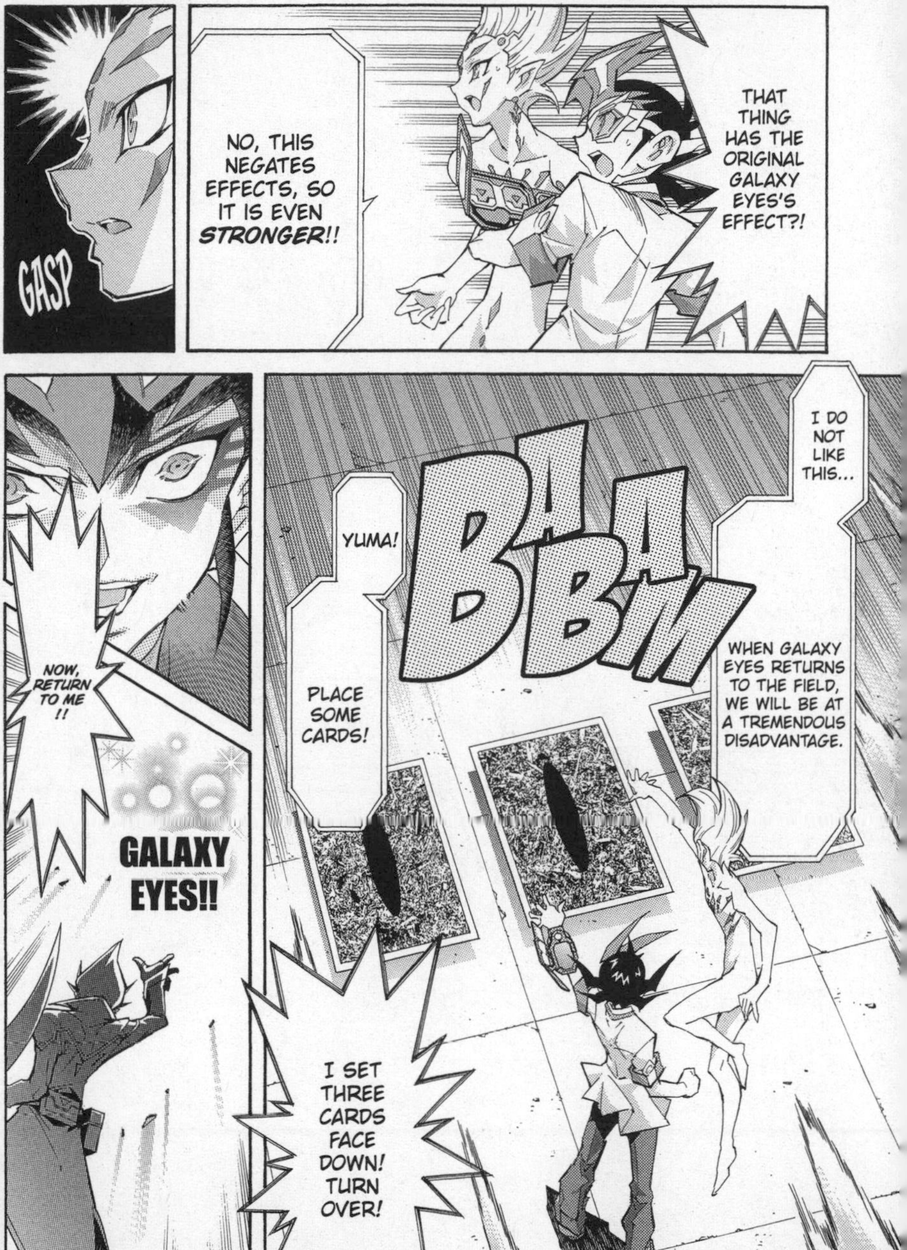
THAT THING HAS THE ORIGINAL GALAXY EYES'S EFFECT?!
NO, THIS NEGATES EFFECTS, SO IT IS EVEN STRONGER!!
GASP
I DO NOT LIKE THIS...
WHEN GALAXY EYES RETURNS TO THE FIELD, WE WILL BE AT A TREMENDOUS DISADVANTAGE.
BABAM
YUMA!
PLACE SOME CARDS!
I SET THREE CARDS FACE DOWN! TURN OVER!
NOW, RETURN TO ME!!
GALAXY EYES!!

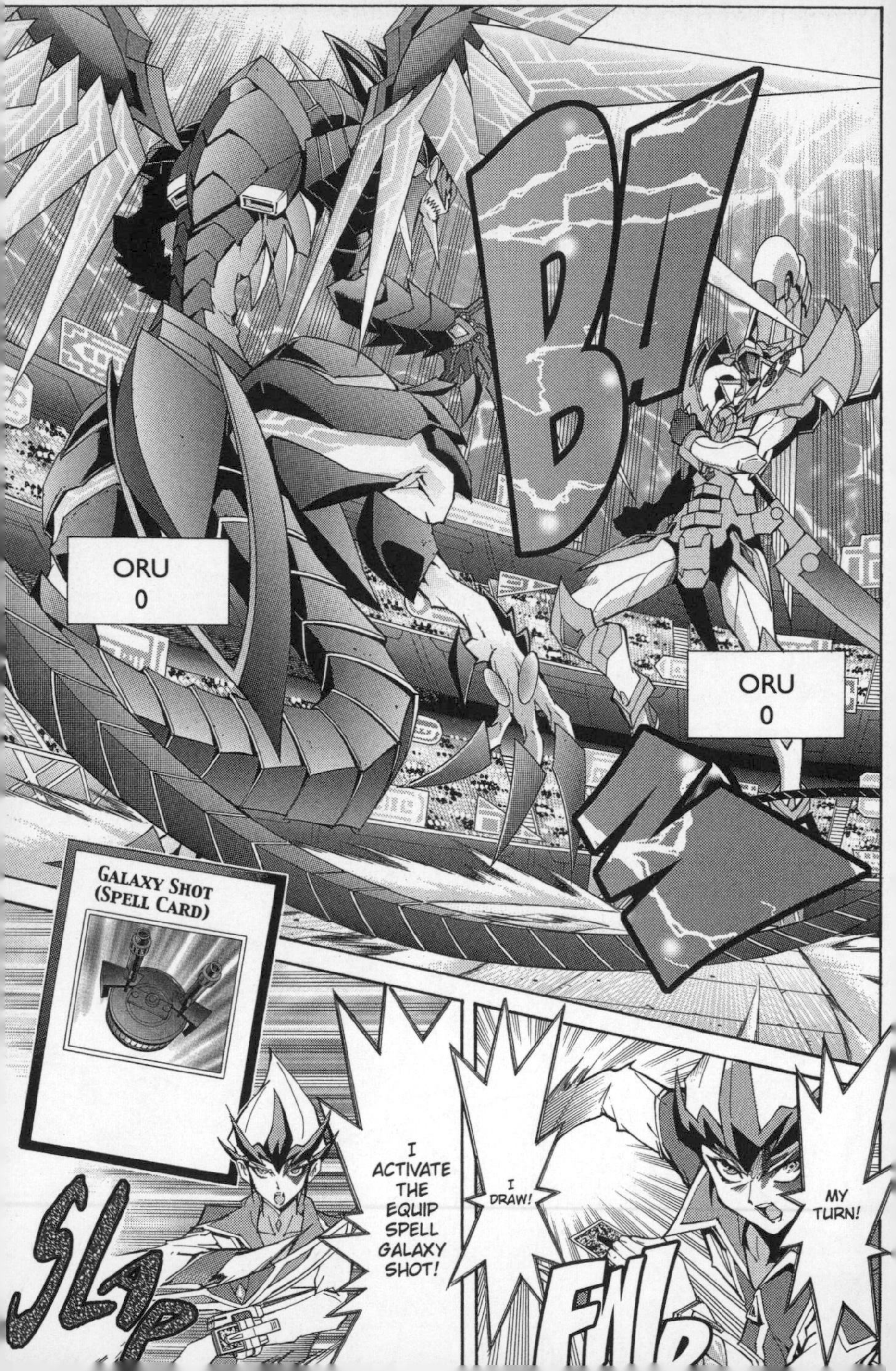
ORU
0
ORU
0
GALAXY SHOT
(SPELL CARD)
MY TURN!
I DRAW!
I ACTIVATE THE EQUIP SPELL GALAXY SHOT!
SLAP

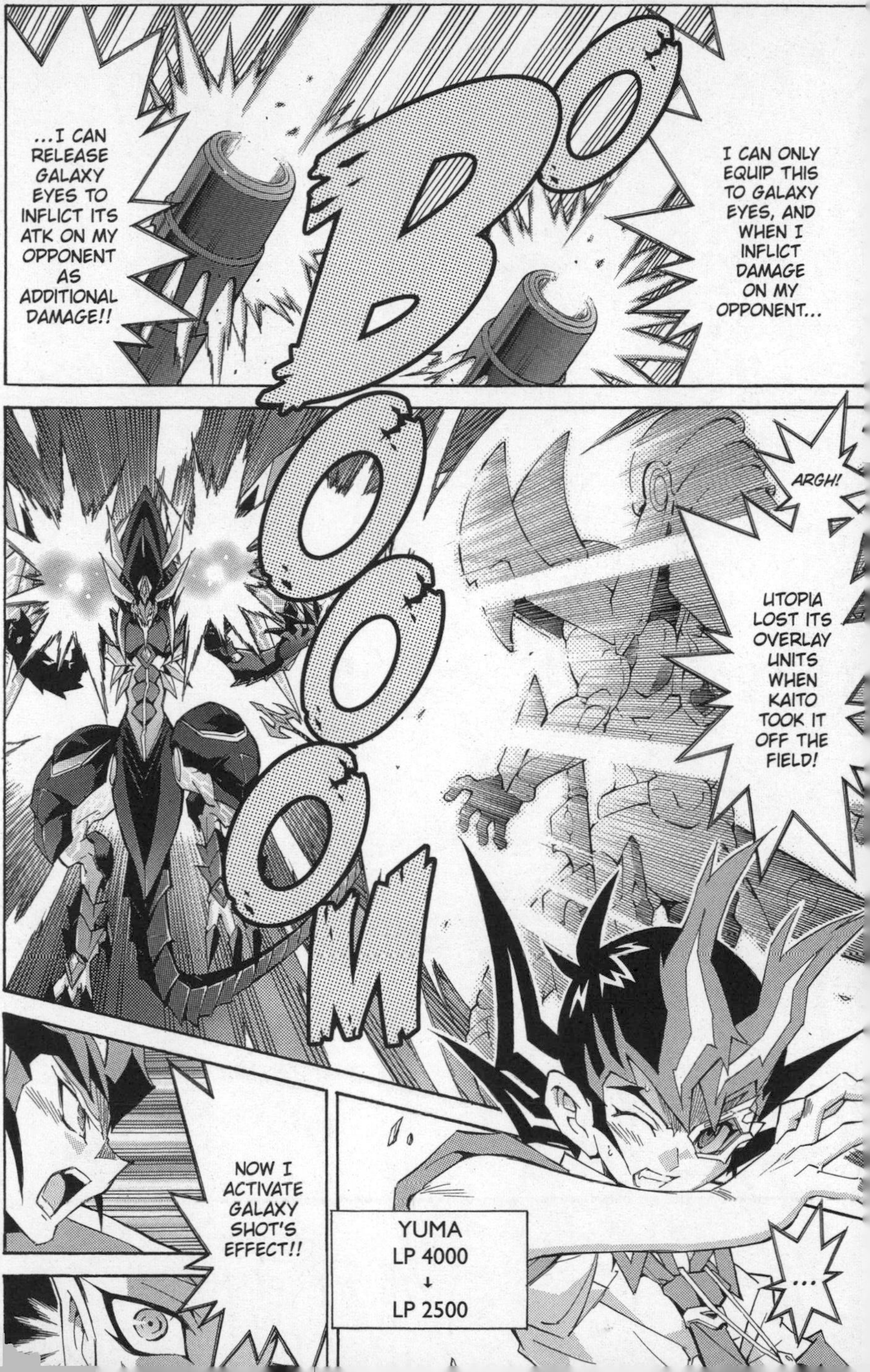
I CAN ONLY EQUIP THIS TO GALAXY EYES, AND WHEN I INFLICT DAMAGE ON MY OPPONENT...
...I CAN RELEASE GALAXY EYES TO INFLICT ITS ATK ON MY OPPONENT AS ADDITIONAL DAMAGE!!
BOOOOOM
ARGH!
UTOPIA LOST ITS OVERLAY UNITS WHEN KAITO TOOK IT OFF THE FIELD!
YUMA LP 4000 ↓ LP 2500
...
NOW I ACTIVATE GALAXY SHOT'S EFFECT!!

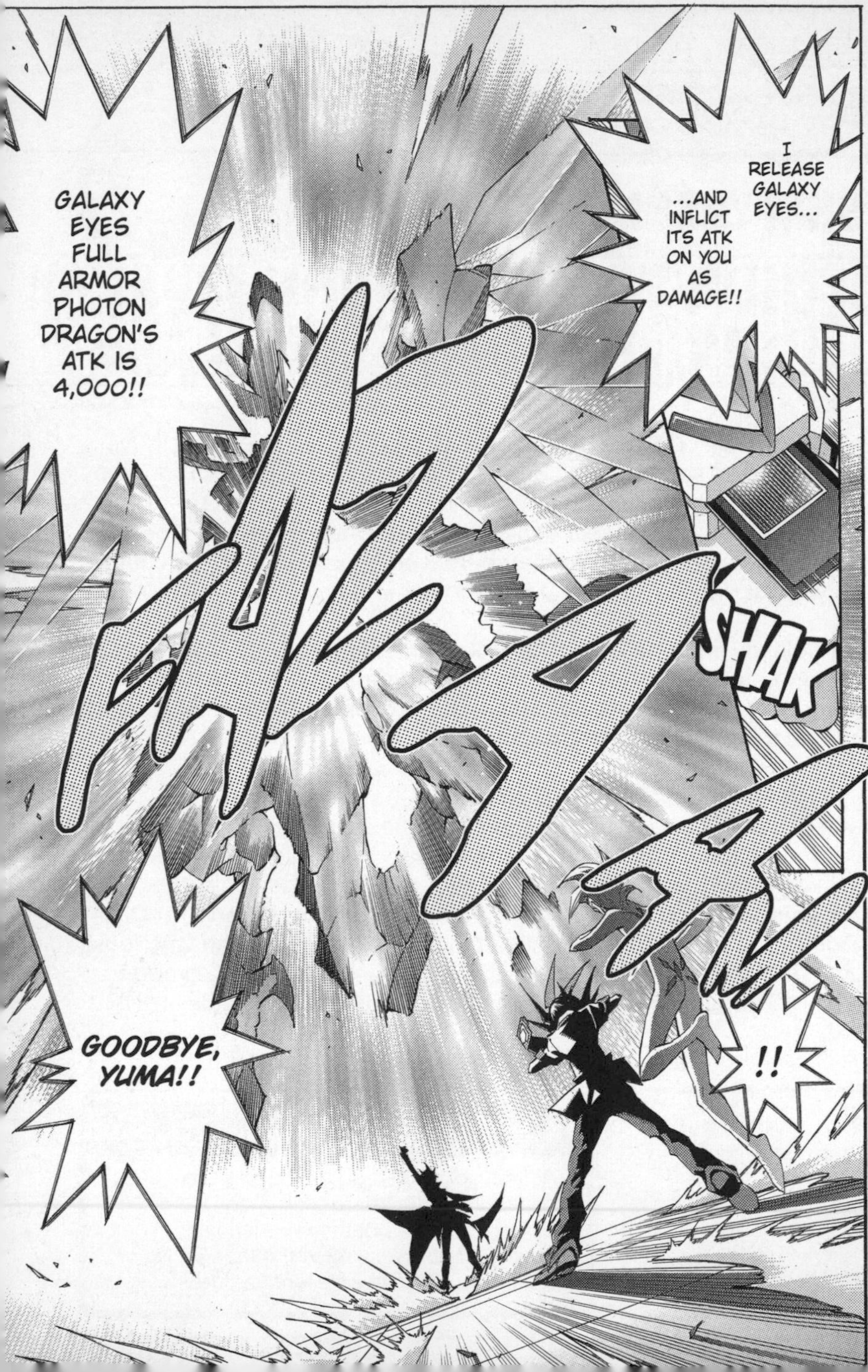
I RELEASE GALAXY EYES...
...AND INFLICT ITS ATK ON YOU AS DAMAGE!!
GALAXY EYES FULL ARMOR PHOTON DRAGON'S ATK IS 4,000!!
SHAK
!!
GOODBYE, YUMA!!

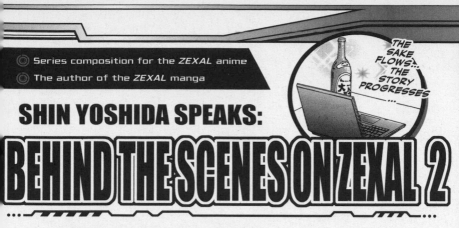

Series composition for the *ZEXAL* anime

The author of the *ZEXAL* manga

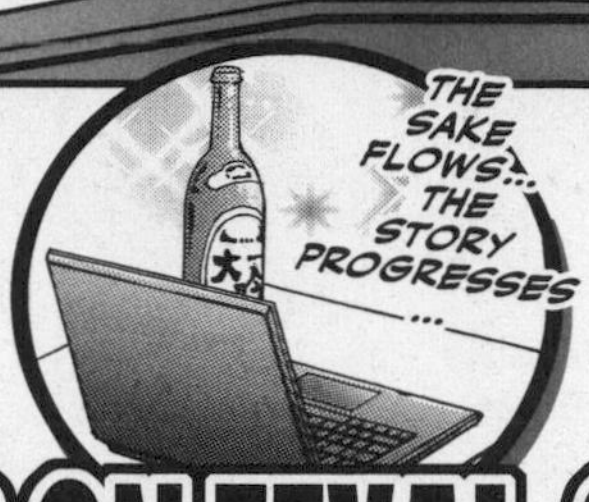
THE SAKE FLOWS... THE STORY PROGRESSES...

SHIN YOSHIDA SPEAKS:

BEHIND THE SCENES ON ZEXAL 2

*** THE ORIGIN OF LUNA'S CHARACTER**

Yuma and Astral are the central protagonists of *ZEXAL*. From the very beginning, I intended to group their central opponents—Kaito and Shark—into pairs as well. That's because when comparing the two teams, the side with fewer members would look weaker. So I came up with Haruto for Kaito and Luna for Shark.

I originally imagined Luna as a guy, but Miyoshi-san said he would prefer a girl. (I'd completely forgotten about that until Miyoshi-san reminded me the other day!) It's true that, left to my own devices, my stories have few female characters… (Oops…)

*** THE ORIGIN OF LUNA'S NAME**

As you may have guessed, Luna's name comes from the moon. When you hear "Shark," you think "ocean." I imagined a full moon shining down upon and watching over a quiet nighttime sea. Speaking of the moon, there's a Pink Floyd album called *The Dark Side of the Moon*. In the lyrics of one of the songs, a man who looks up at the moon is a lunatic. (In English, the word means someone crazy.) That's how Luna got her name. (Talk about complicated!)

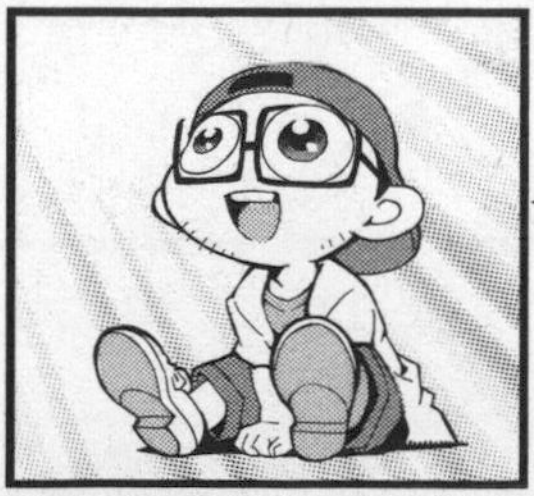

A Message from Miyoshi Sensei!

At first, you talked about making Luna a handsome bodyguard! (lol) A boy would have been fine, but there weren't any scenes of girls dueling in the manga. Now she's one of those rare female duelists!

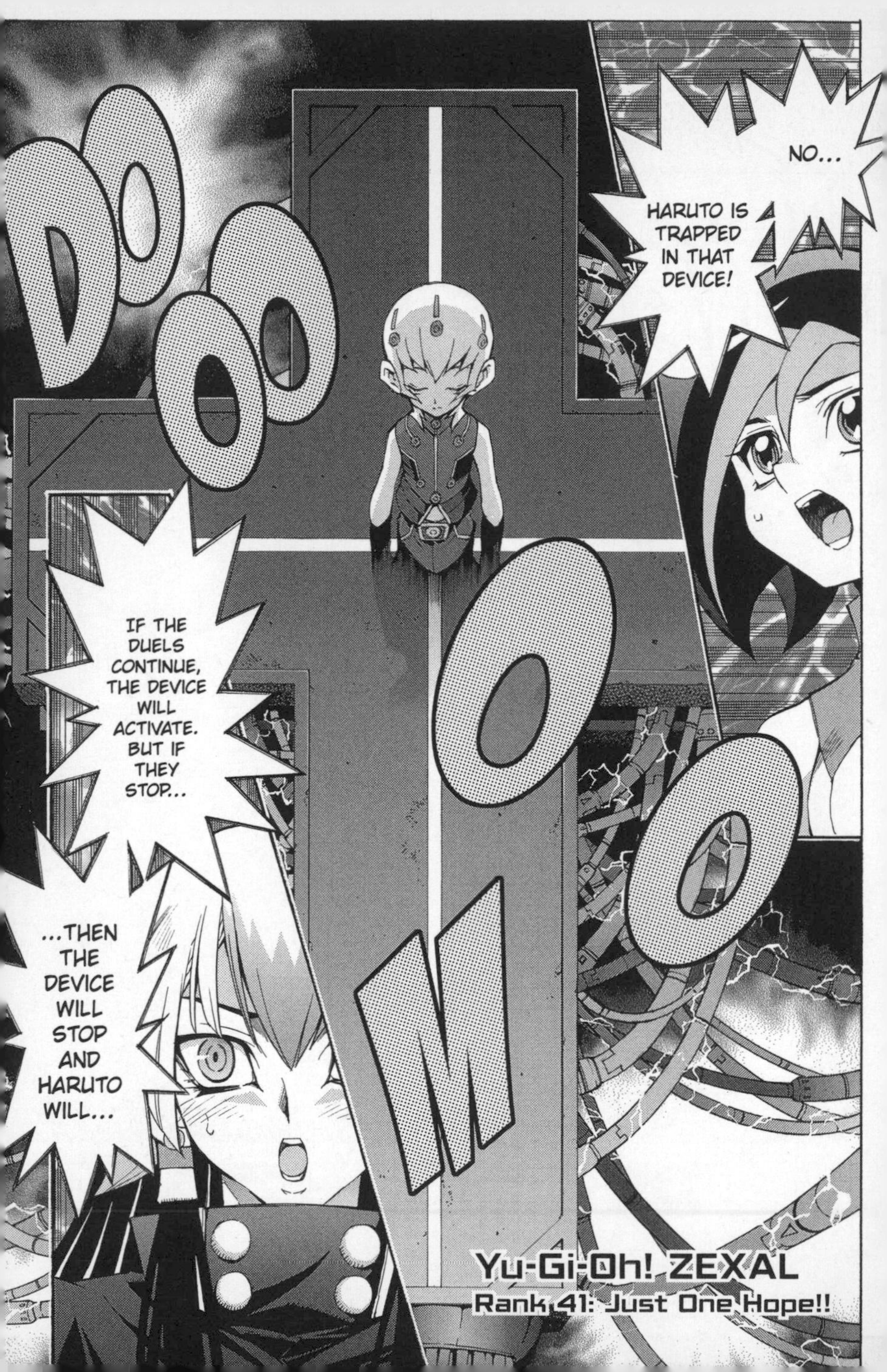
NO... HARUTO IS TRAPPED IN THAT DEVICE!
DOOOOOM
IF THE DUELS CONTINUE, THE DEVICE WILL ACTIVATE. BUT IF THEY STOP...
...THEN THE DEVICE WILL STOP AND HARUTO WILL...
Yu-Gi-Oh! ZEXAL
Rank 41: Just One Hope!!

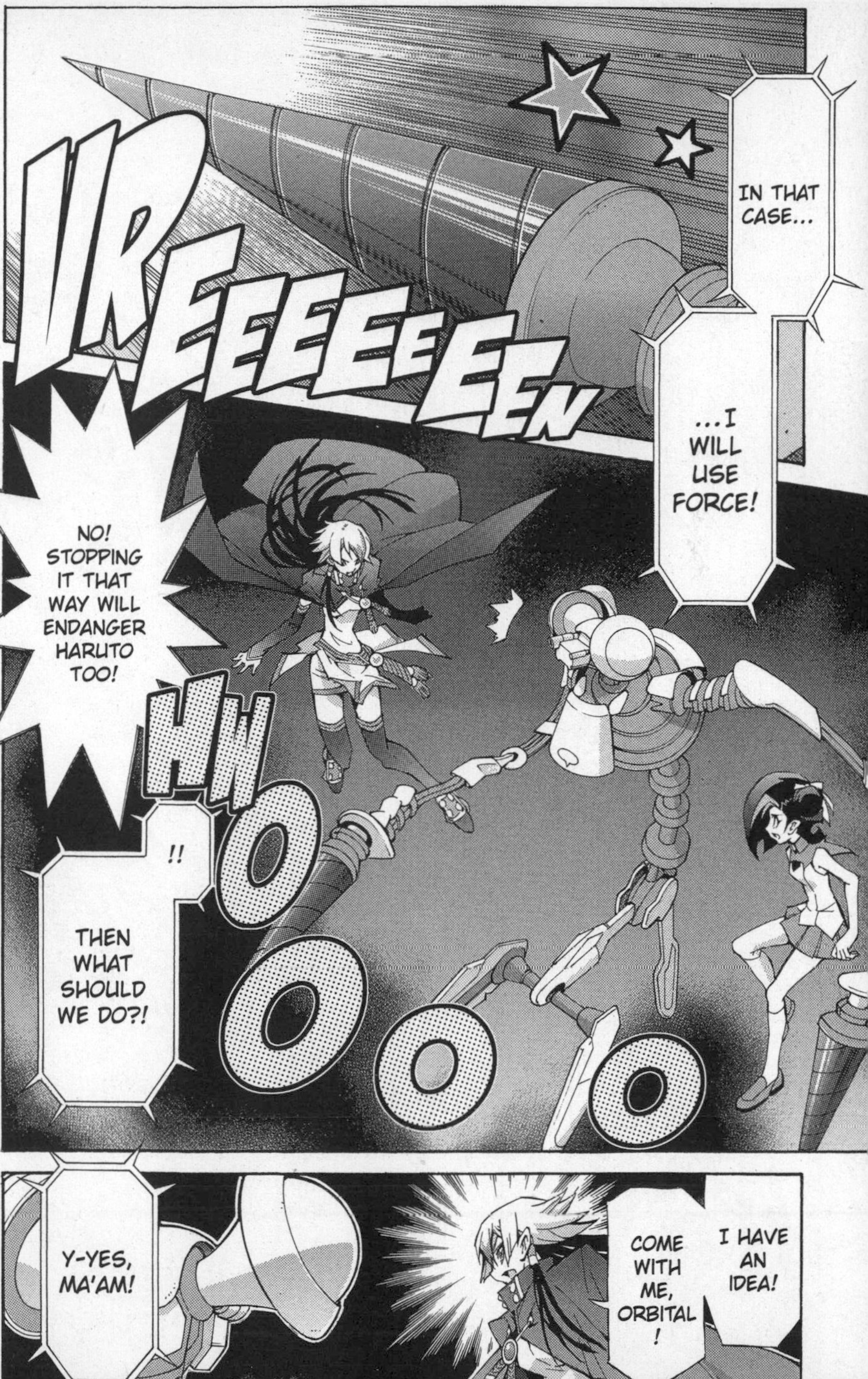
IN THAT CASE...
...I WILL USE FORCE!
VREEEEEEEN
NO! STOPPING IT THAT WAY WILL ENDANGER HARUTO TOO!
HWOOOO
!!
THEN WHAT SHOULD WE DO?!
I HAVE AN IDEA!
COME WITH ME, ORBITAL!
Y-YES, MA'AM!

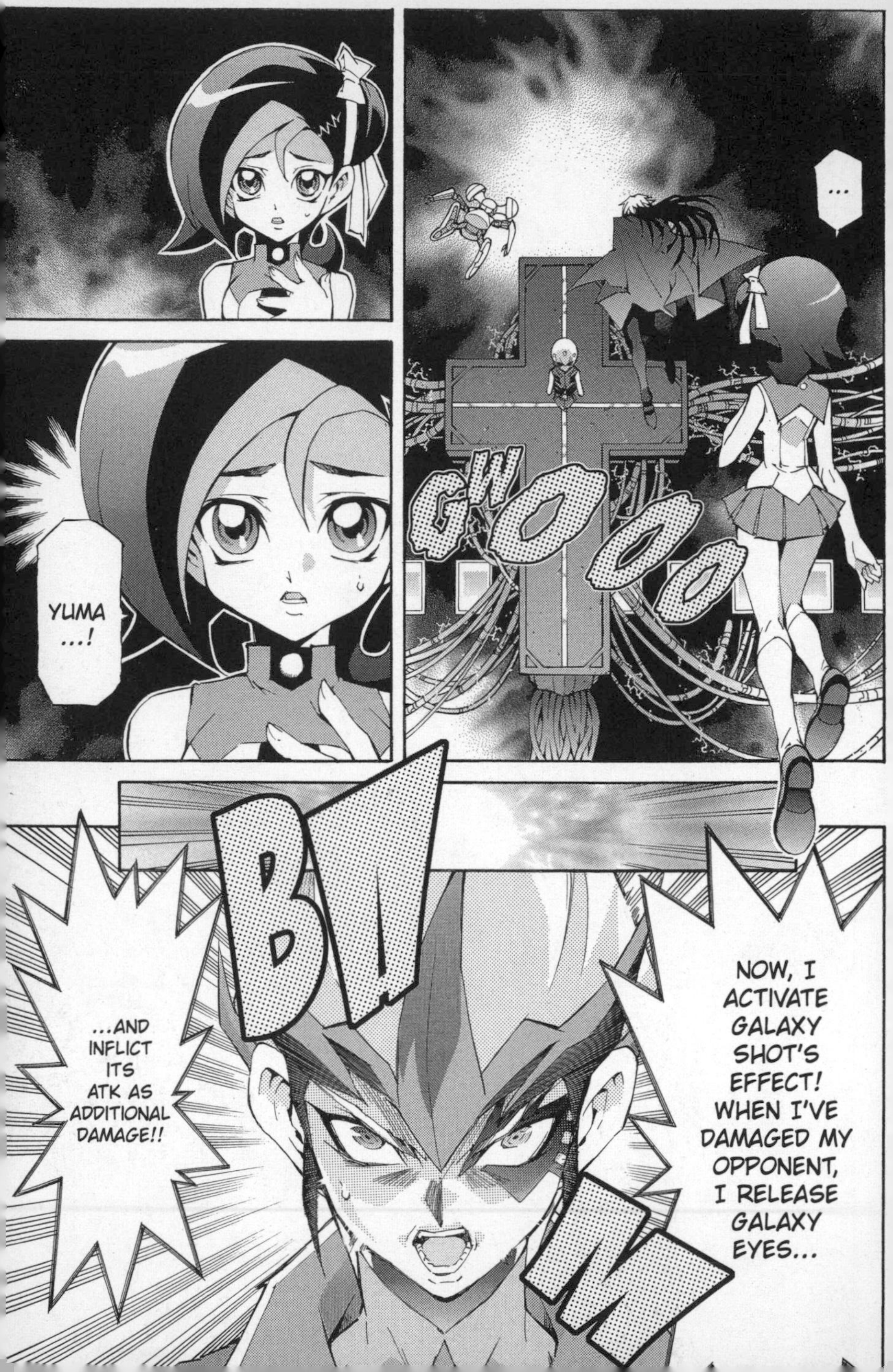
...
GWOOOO
YUMA ...!
NOW, I ACTIVATE GALAXY SHOT'S EFFECT! WHEN I'VE DAMAGED MY OPPONENT, I RELEASE GALAXY EYES...
BAM
...AND INFLICT ITS ATK AS ADDITIONAL DAMAGE!!

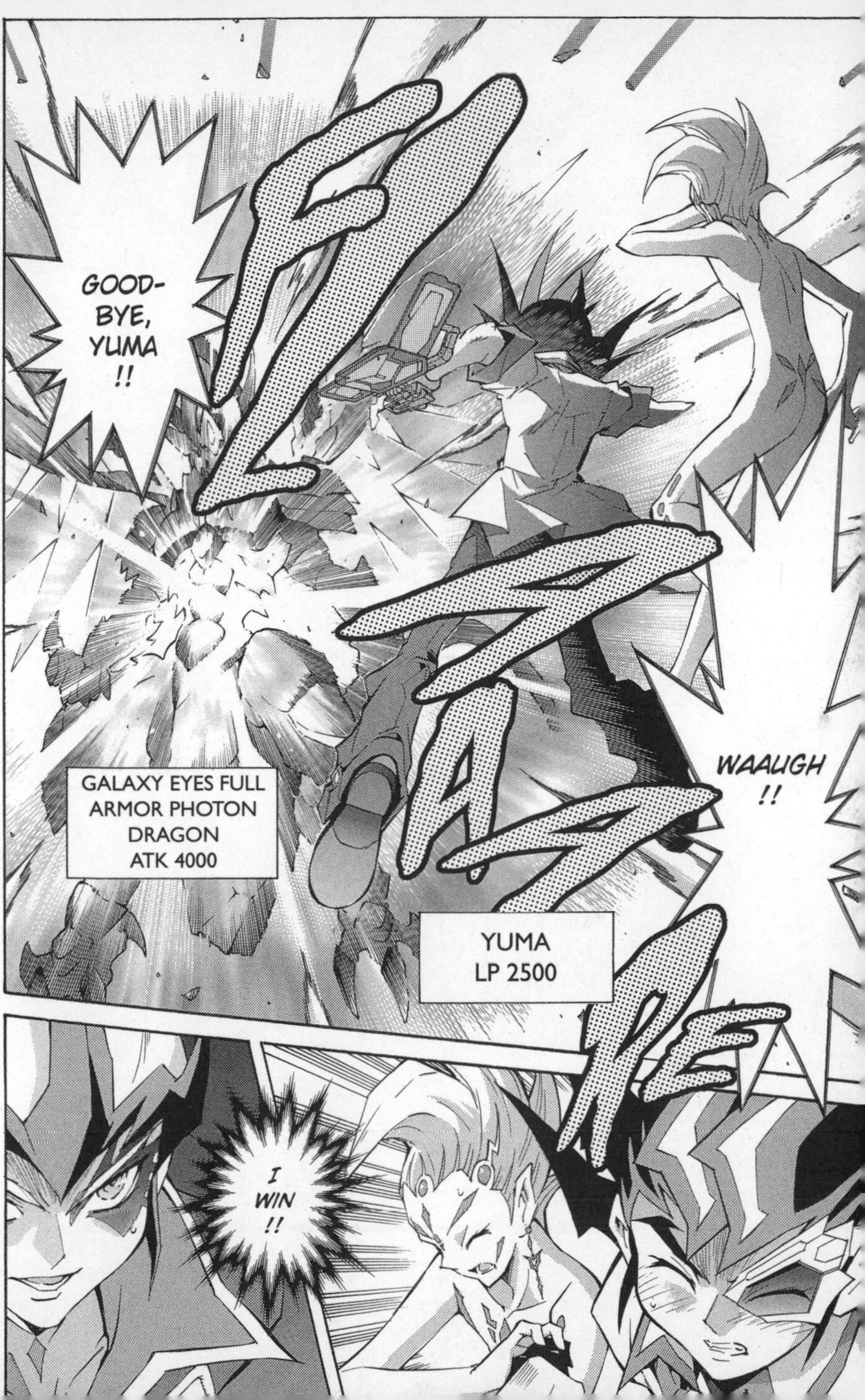
GOOD-BYE, YUMA!!
WAAUGH!!
GALAXY EYES FULL ARMOR PHOTON DRAGON ATK 4000
YUMA LP 2500
I WIN!!

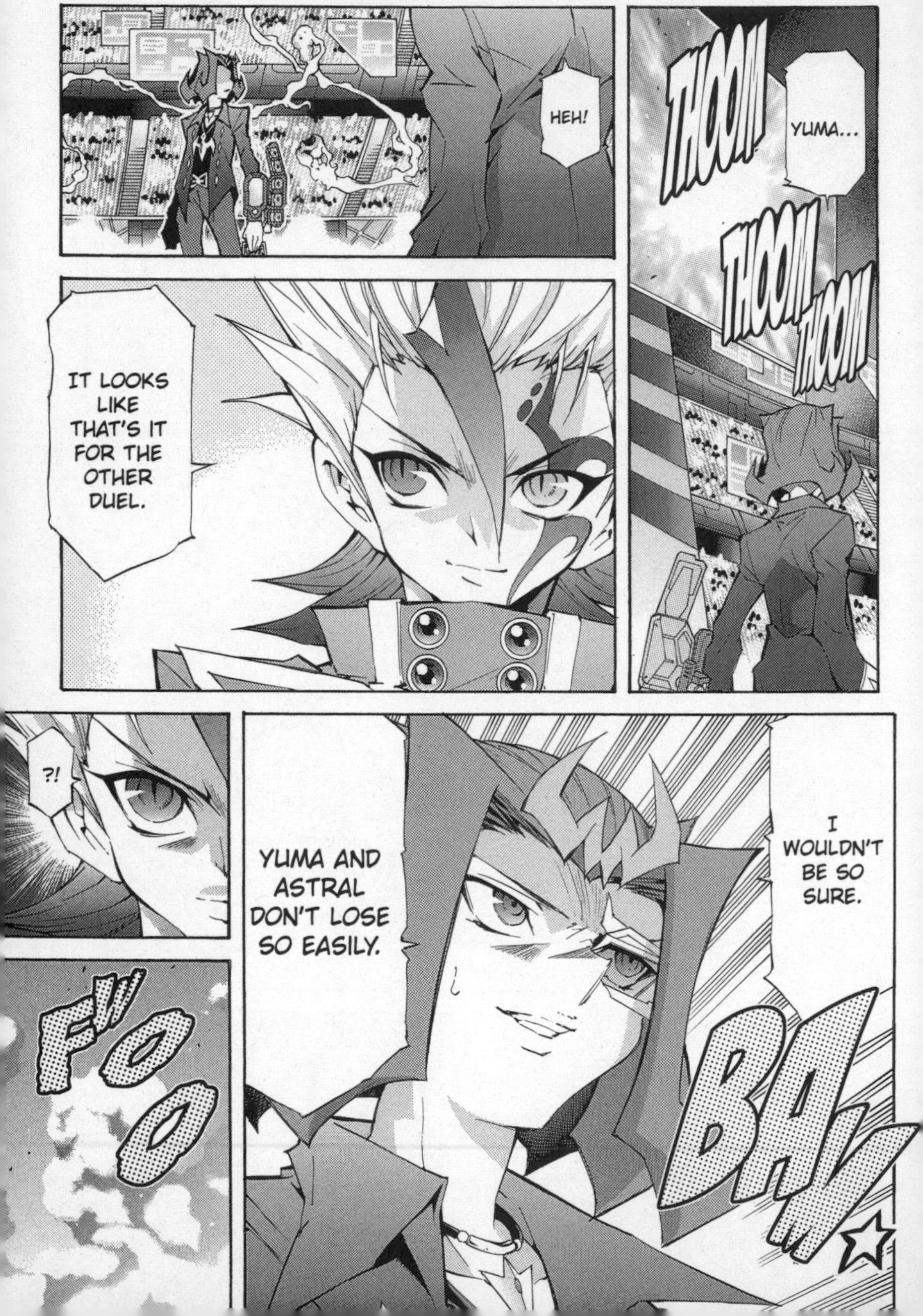
THOOM
YUMA...
THOOM
THOOM
HEH!
IT LOOKS LIKE THAT'S IT FOR THE OTHER DUEL.
I WOULDN'T BE SO SURE.
YUMA AND ASTRAL DON'T LOSE SO EASILY.
BA!
?!
F'OO

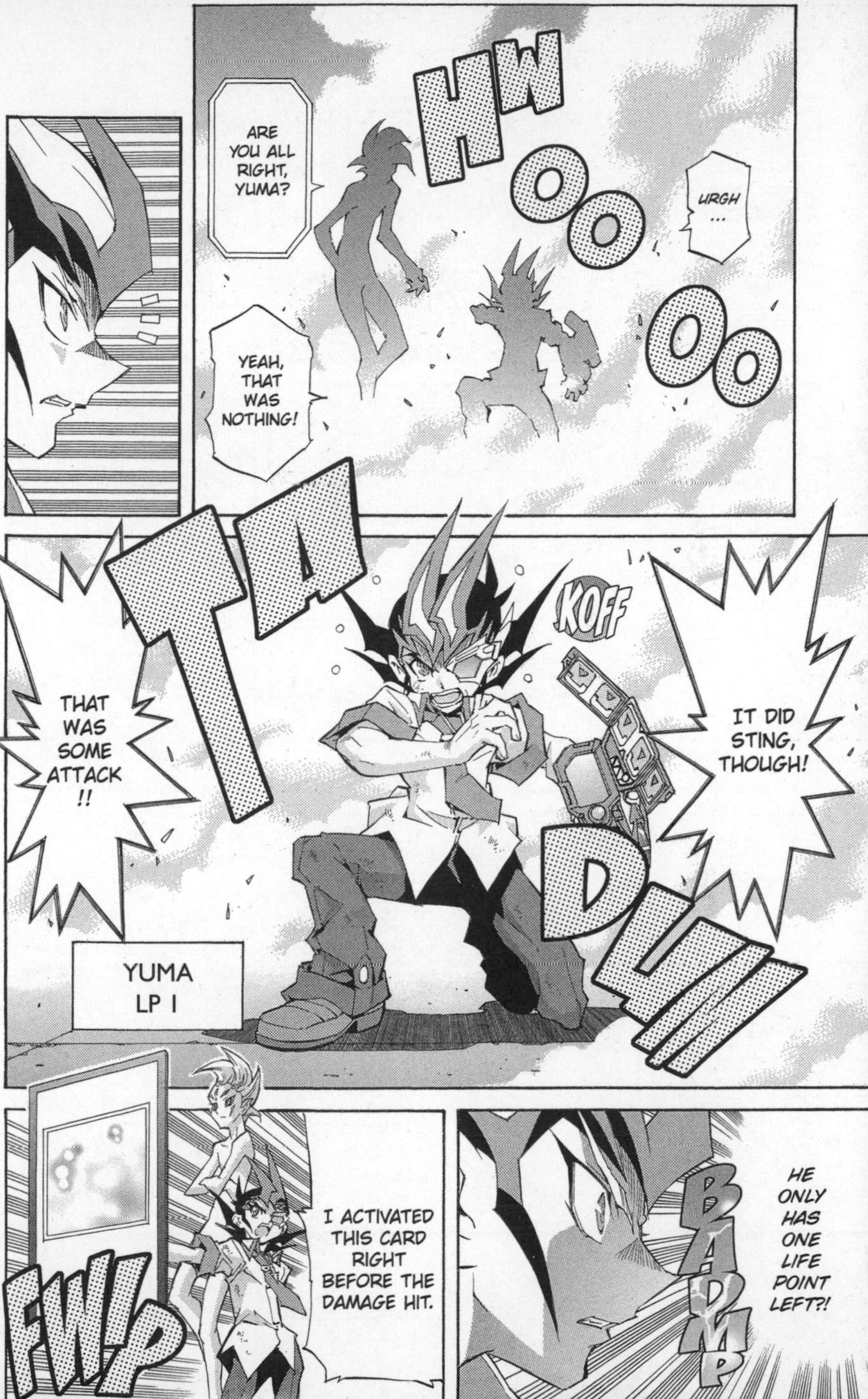
HWOOOOOO
URGH ...
ARE YOU ALL RIGHT, YUMA?
YEAH, THAT WAS NOTHING!
TA
KOFF
IT DID STING, THOUGH!
THAT WAS SOME ATTACK!!
DUMMM
YUMA LP 1
BADUMP
HE ONLY HAS ONE LIFE POINT LEFT?!
I ACTIVATED THIS CARD RIGHT BEFORE THE DAMAGE HIT.
FWIP

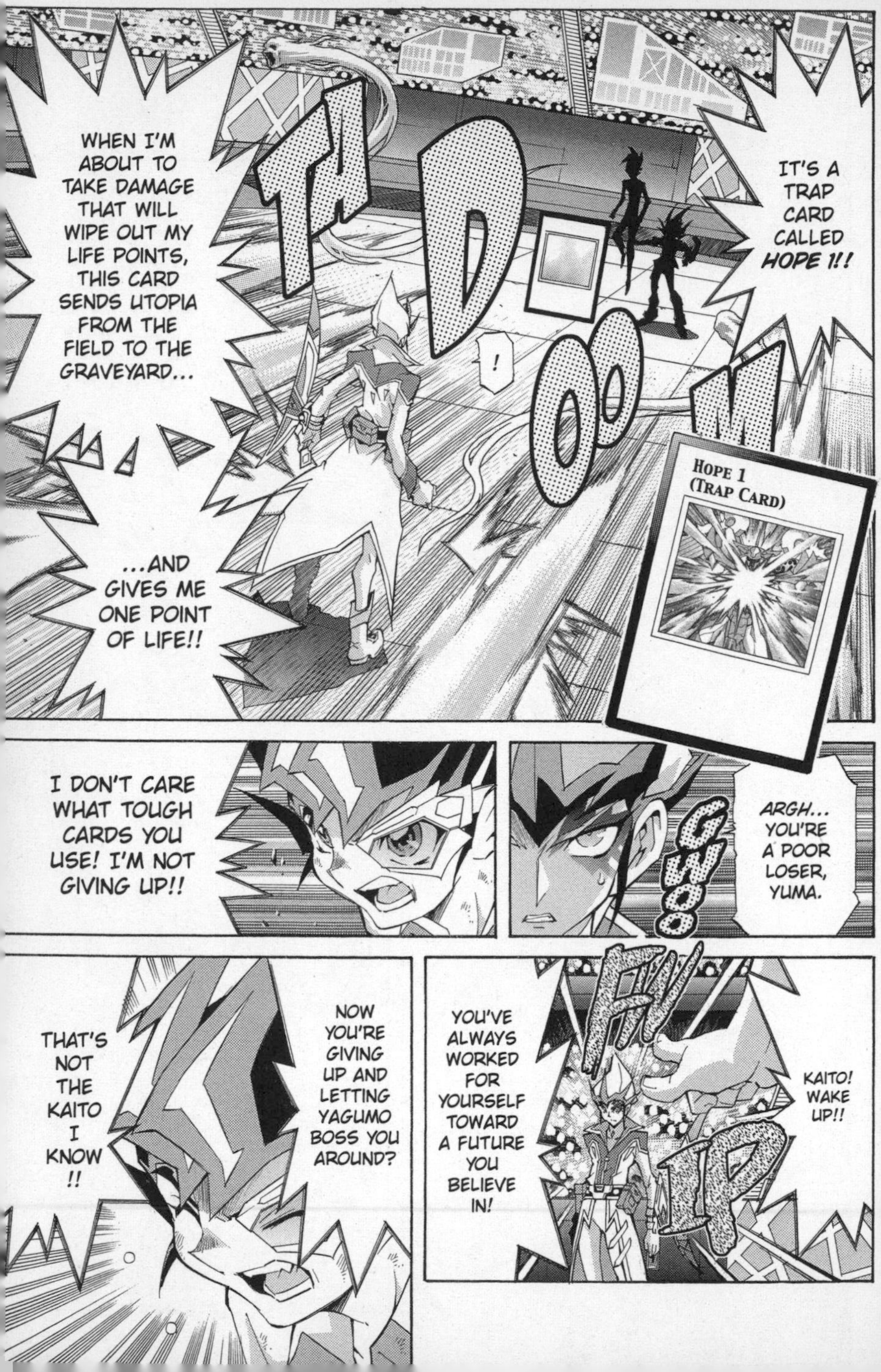
IT'S A TRAP CARD CALLED *HOPE 1*!!
THOOOM
!
HOPE 1 (TRAP CARD)
WHEN I'M ABOUT TO TAKE DAMAGE THAT WILL WIPE OUT MY LIFE POINTS, THIS CARD SENDS UTOPIA FROM THE FIELD TO THE GRAVEYARD...
...AND GIVES ME ONE POINT OF LIFE!!
ARGH... YOU'RE A POOR LOSER, YUMA.
I DON'T CARE WHAT TOUGH CARDS YOU USE! I'M NOT GIVING UP!!
KAITO! WAKE UP!!
YOU'VE ALWAYS WORKED FOR YOURSELF TOWARD A FUTURE YOU BELIEVE IN!
NOW YOU'RE GIVING UP AND LETTING YAGUMO BOSS YOU AROUND?
THAT'S NOT THE KAITO I KNOW!!

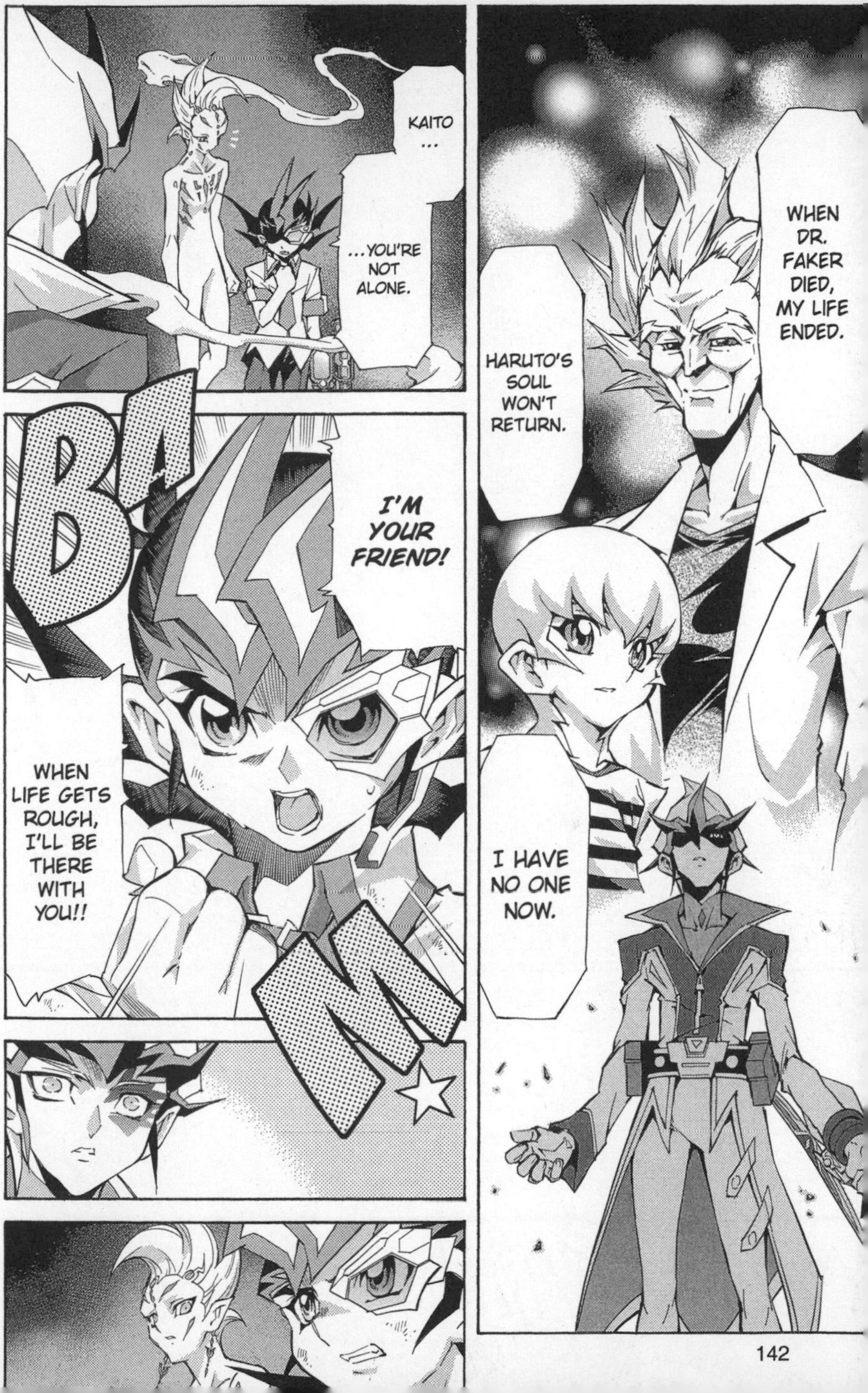
WHEN DR. FAKER DIED, MY LIFE ENDED.
HARUTO'S SOUL WON'T RETURN.
I HAVE NO ONE NOW.
KAITO ...
...YOU'RE NOT ALONE.
BAM
I'M YOUR FRIEND!
WHEN LIFE GETS ROUGH, I'LL BE THERE WITH YOU!!

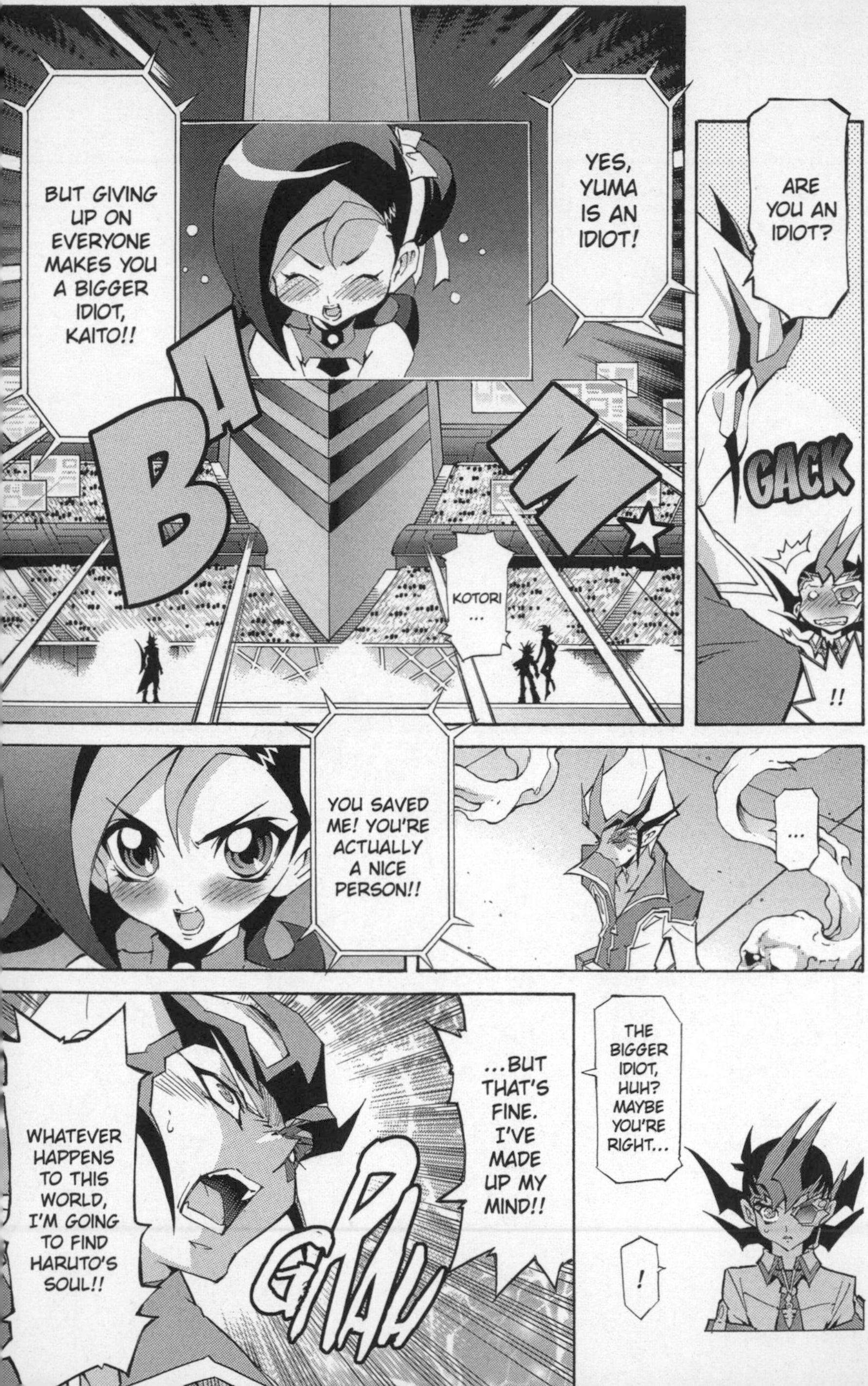
ARE YOU AN IDIOT?
GACK
!!
YES, YUMA IS AN IDIOT!
BUT GIVING UP ON EVERYONE MAKES YOU A BIGGER IDIOT, KAITO!!
BAM☆
KOTORI ...
...
YOU SAVED ME! YOU'RE ACTUALLY A NICE PERSON!!
THE BIGGER IDIOT, HUH? MAYBE YOU'RE RIGHT...
!
...BUT THAT'S FINE. I'VE MADE UP MY MIND!!
WHATEVER HAPPENS TO THIS WORLD, I'M GOING TO FIND HARUTO'S SOUL!!
GRAH

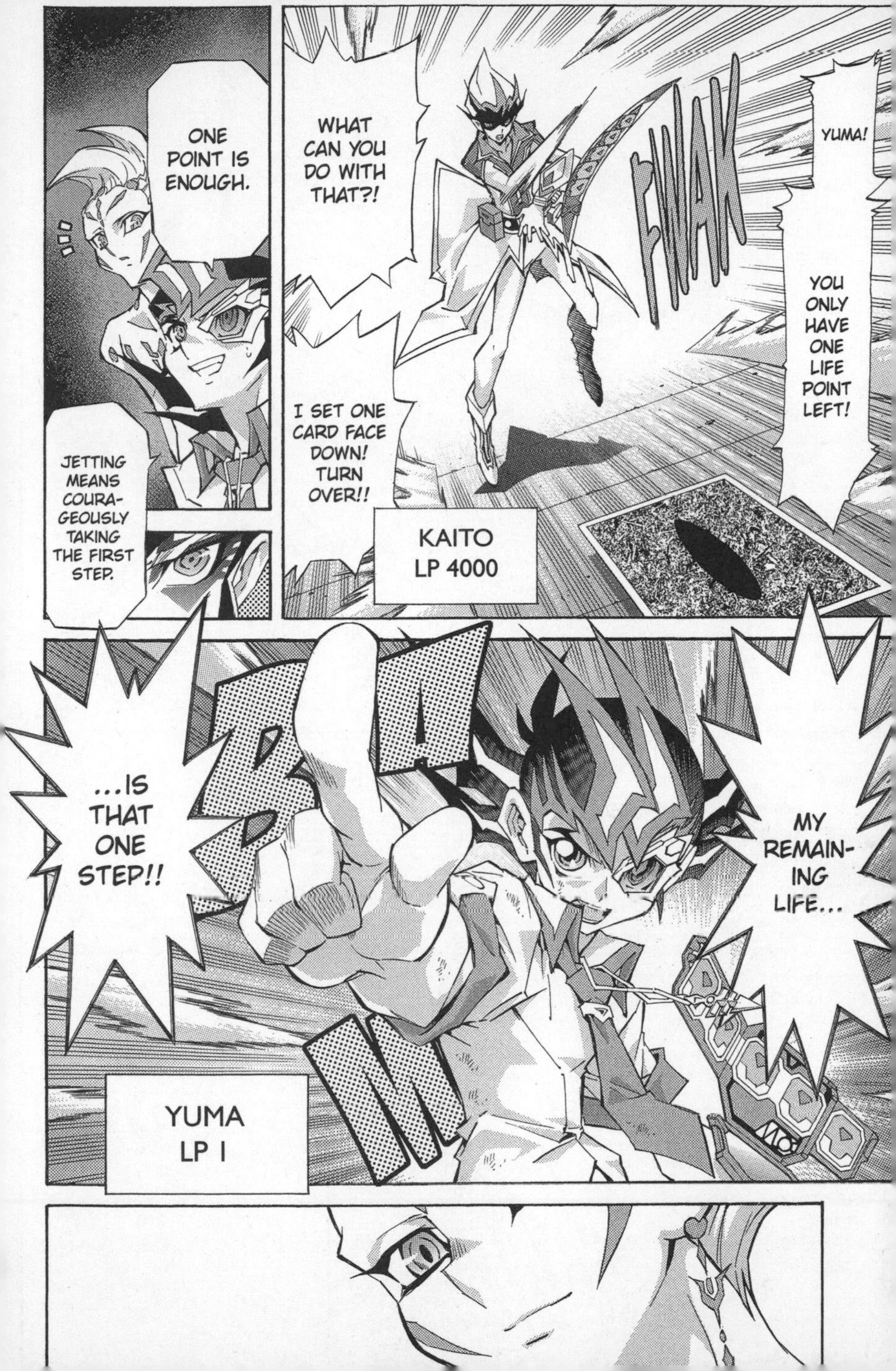
YUMA!
YOU ONLY HAVE ONE LIFE POINT LEFT!
FWAK
WHAT CAN YOU DO WITH THAT?!
I SET ONE CARD FACE DOWN! TURN OVER!!
KAITO LP 4000
ONE POINT IS ENOUGH.
JETTING MEANS COURAGEOUSLY TAKING THE FIRST STEP.
MY REMAINING LIFE...
BAM
...IS THAT ONE STEP!!
YUMA LP 1

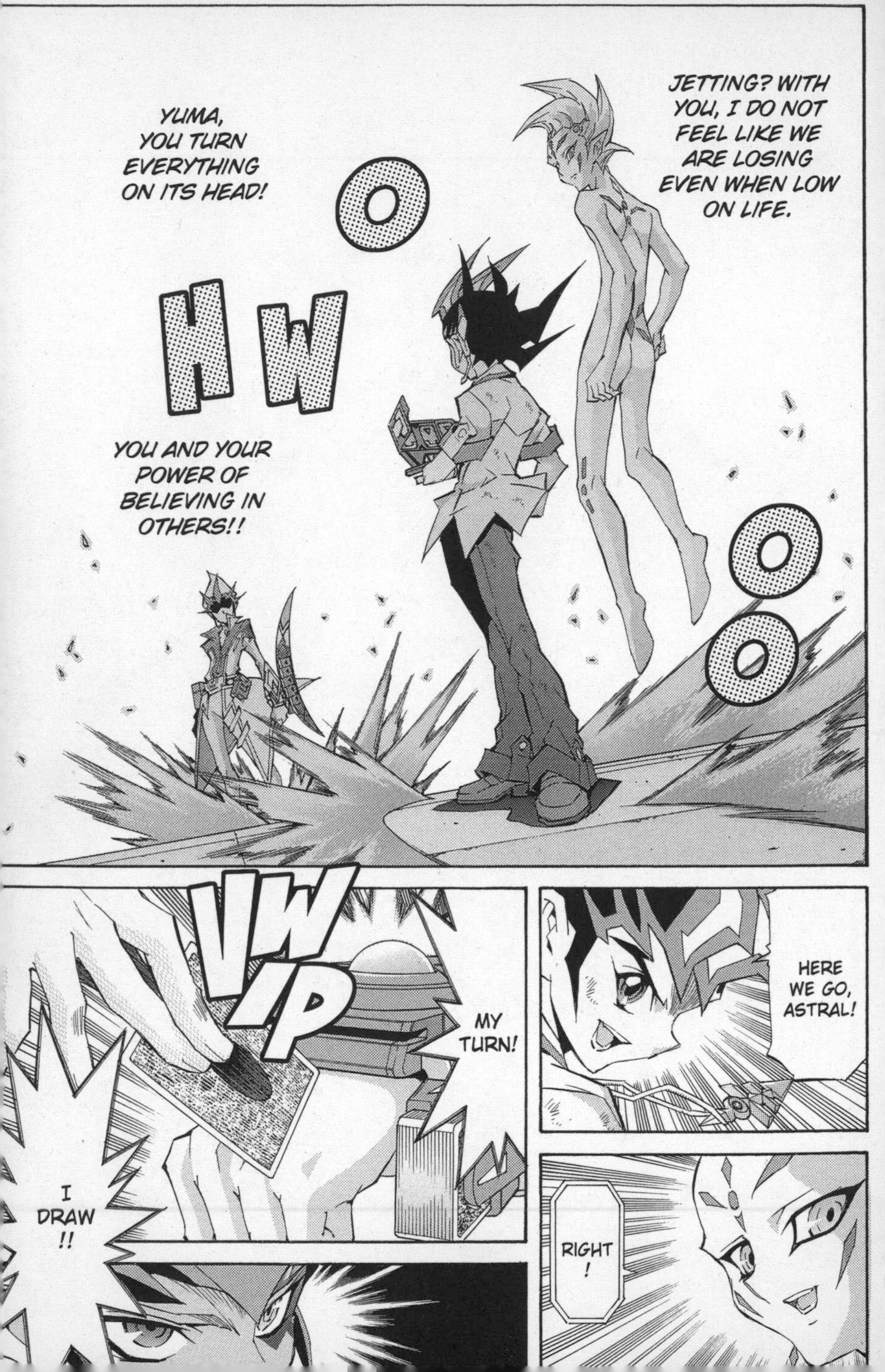
JETTING? WITH YOU, I DO NOT FEEL LIKE WE ARE LOSING EVEN WHEN LOW ON LIFE.
YUMA, YOU TURN EVERYTHING ON ITS HEAD!
WHOOOO
YOU AND YOUR POWER OF BELIEVING IN OTHERS!!
HERE WE GO, ASTRAL!
RIGHT!
WHIP
MY TURN!
I DRAW!!

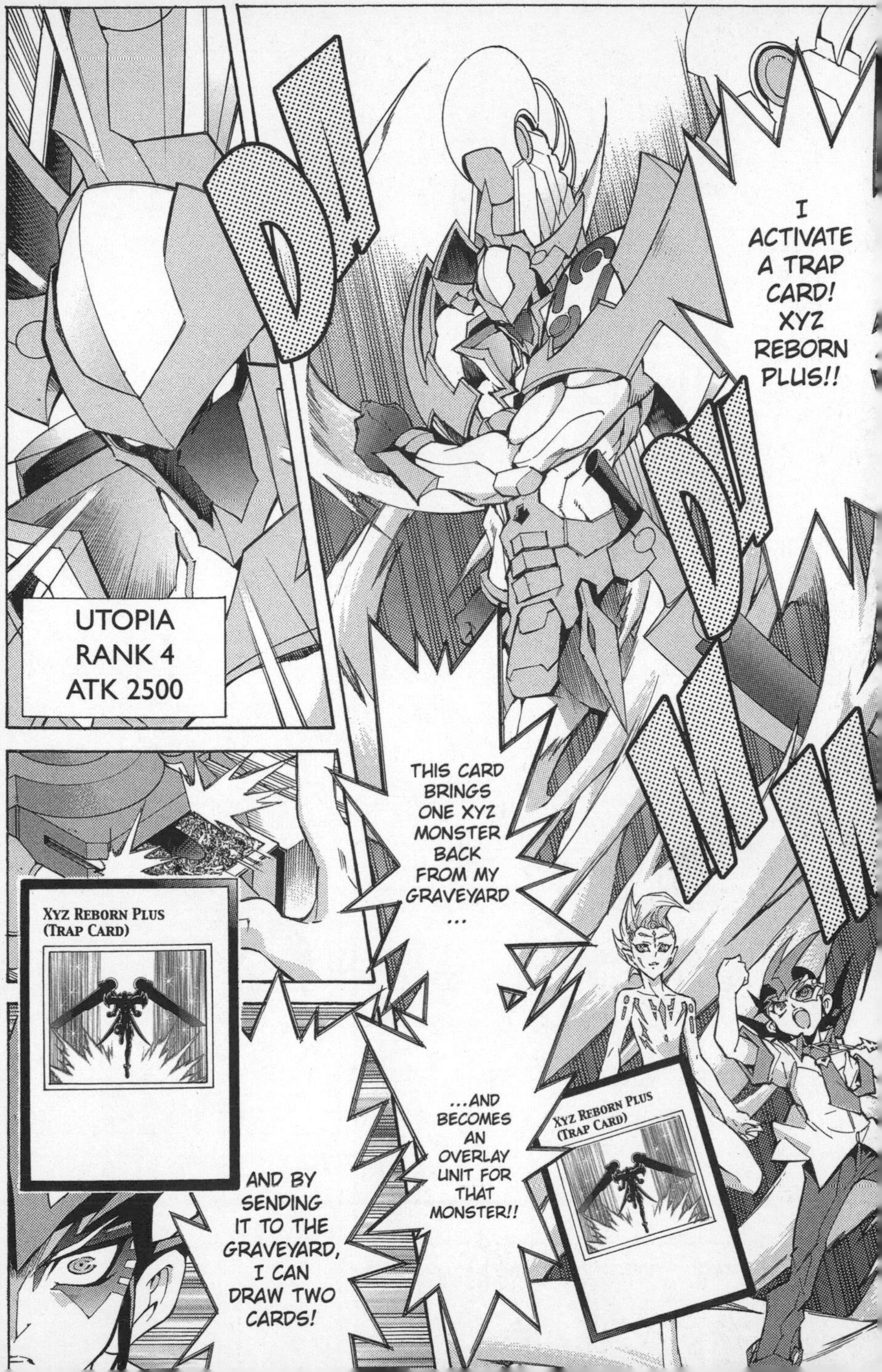
I ACTIVATE A TRAP CARD! XYZ REBORN PLUS!!
UTOPIA RANK 4 ATK 2500
THIS CARD BRINGS ONE XYZ MONSTER BACK FROM MY GRAVEYARD...
...AND BECOMES AN OVERLAY UNIT FOR THAT MONSTER!!
XYZ REBORN PLUS (TRAP CARD)
XYZ REBORN PLUS (TRAP CARD)
AND BY SENDING IT TO THE GRAVEYARD, I CAN DRAW TWO CARDS!

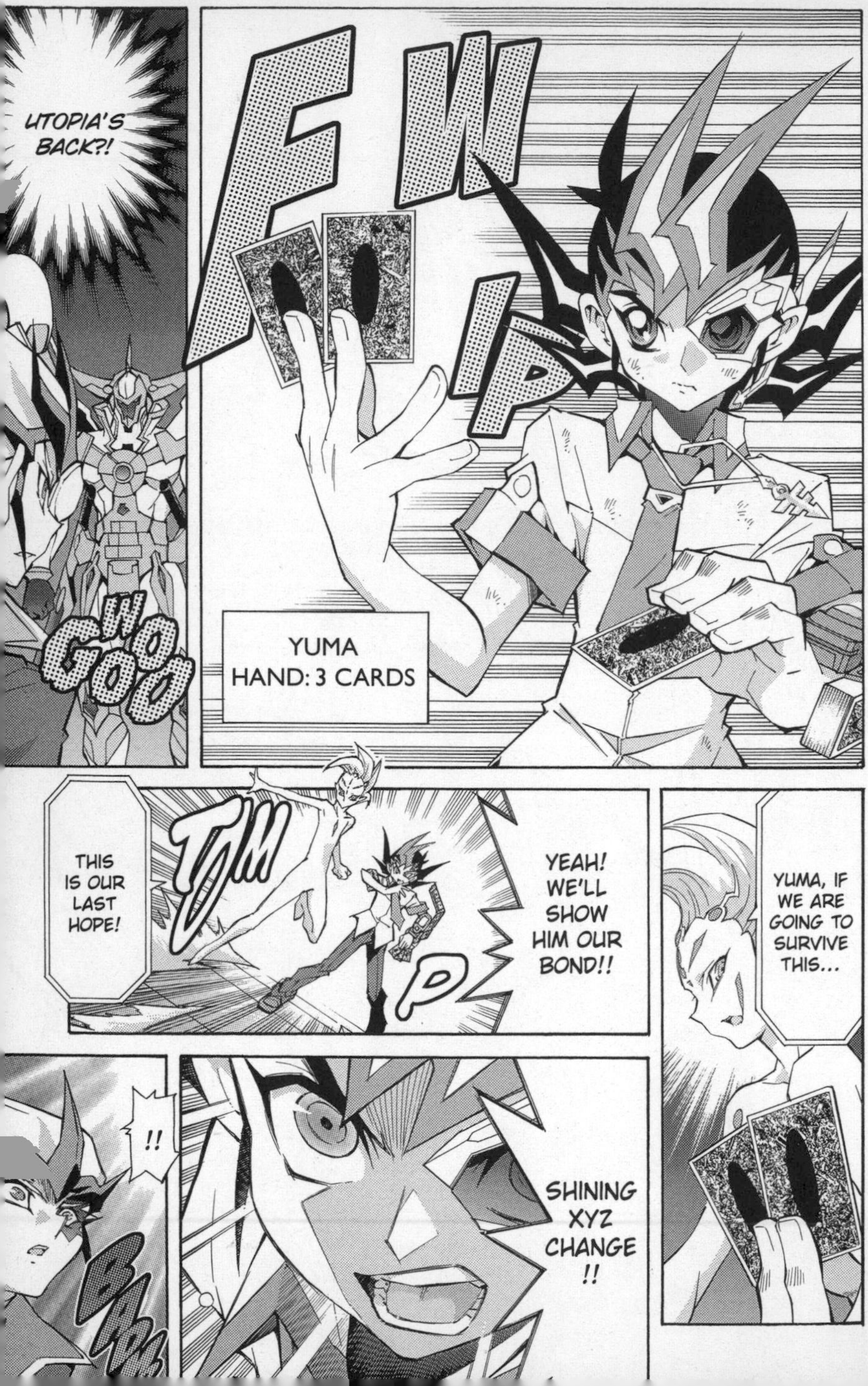
FWIP
YUMA
HAND: 3 CARDS
UTOPIA'S BACK?!
GWOOOO
YUMA, IF WE ARE GOING TO SURVIVE THIS...
YEAH! WE'LL SHOW HIM OUR BOND!!
TMP
THIS IS OUR LAST HOPE!
SHINING XYZ CHANGE !!
!!

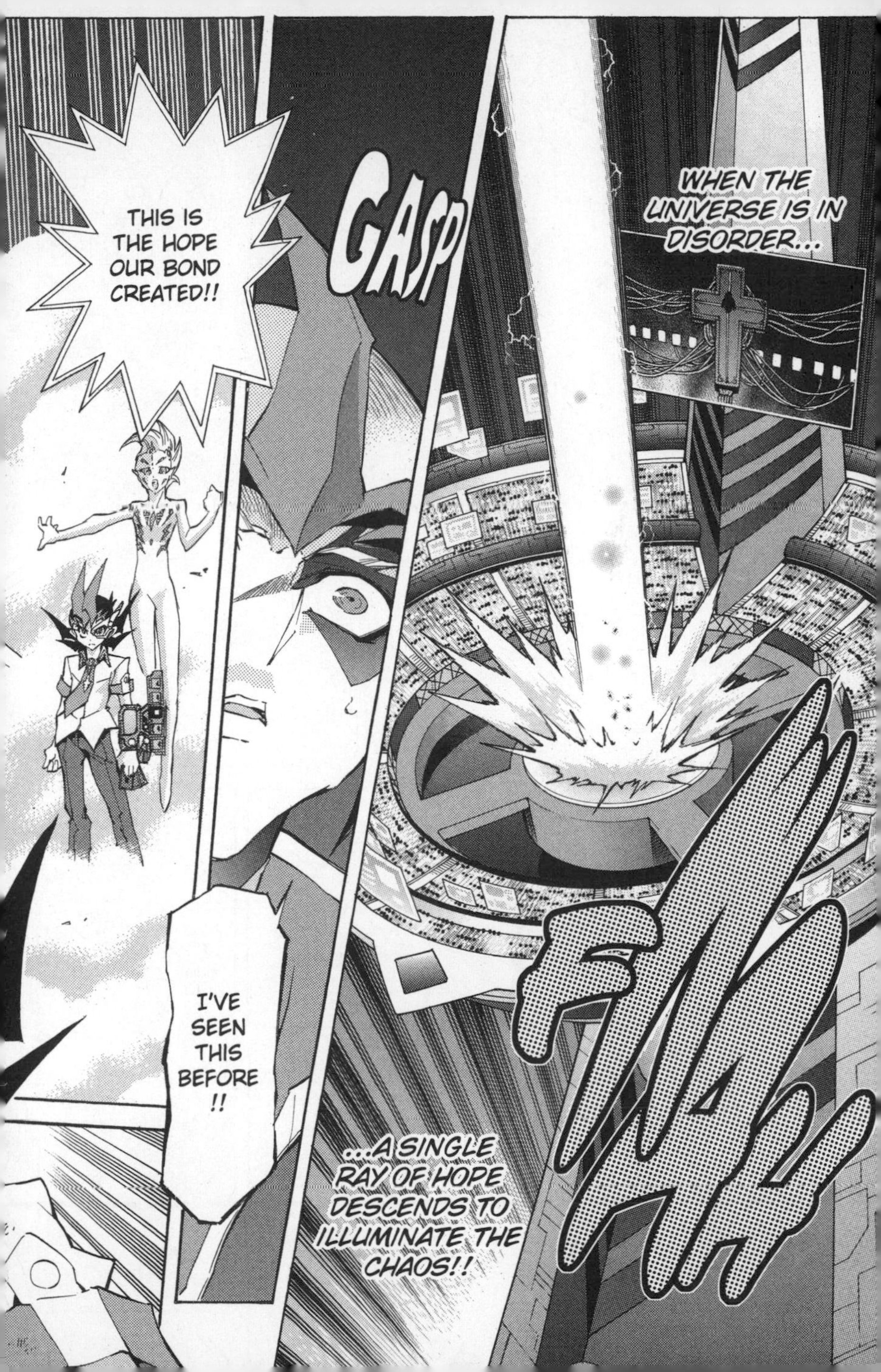
WHEN THE UNIVERSE IS IN DISORDER...
...A SINGLE RAY OF HOPE DESCENDS TO ILLUMINATE THE CHAOS!!
GASP
I'VE SEEN THIS BEFORE!!
THIS IS THE HOPE OUR BOND CREATED!!

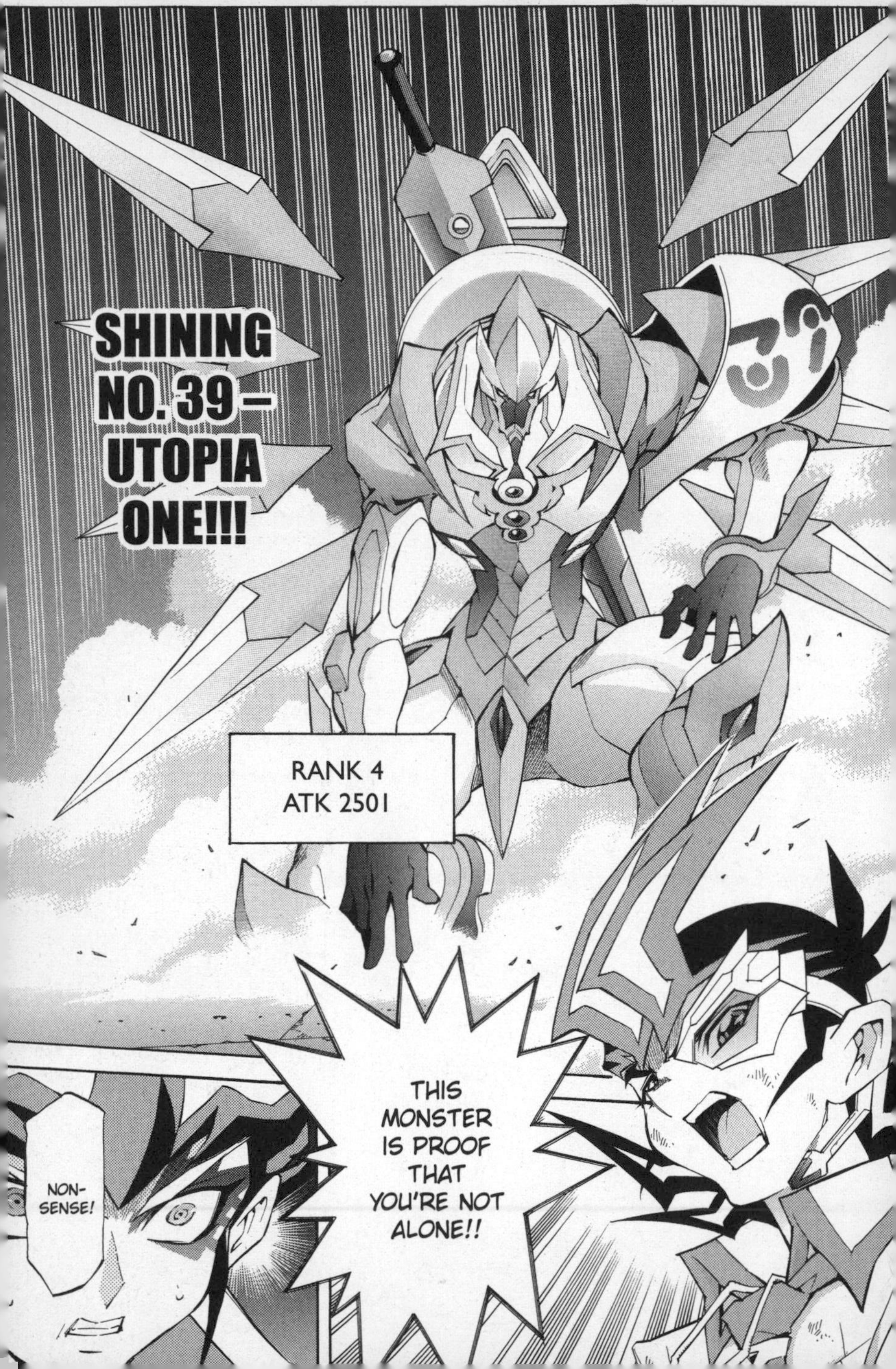
SHINING NO. 39 – UTOPIA ONE!!!
RANK 4 ATK 2501
THIS MONSTER IS PROOF THAT YOU'RE NOT ALONE!!
NON-SENSE!

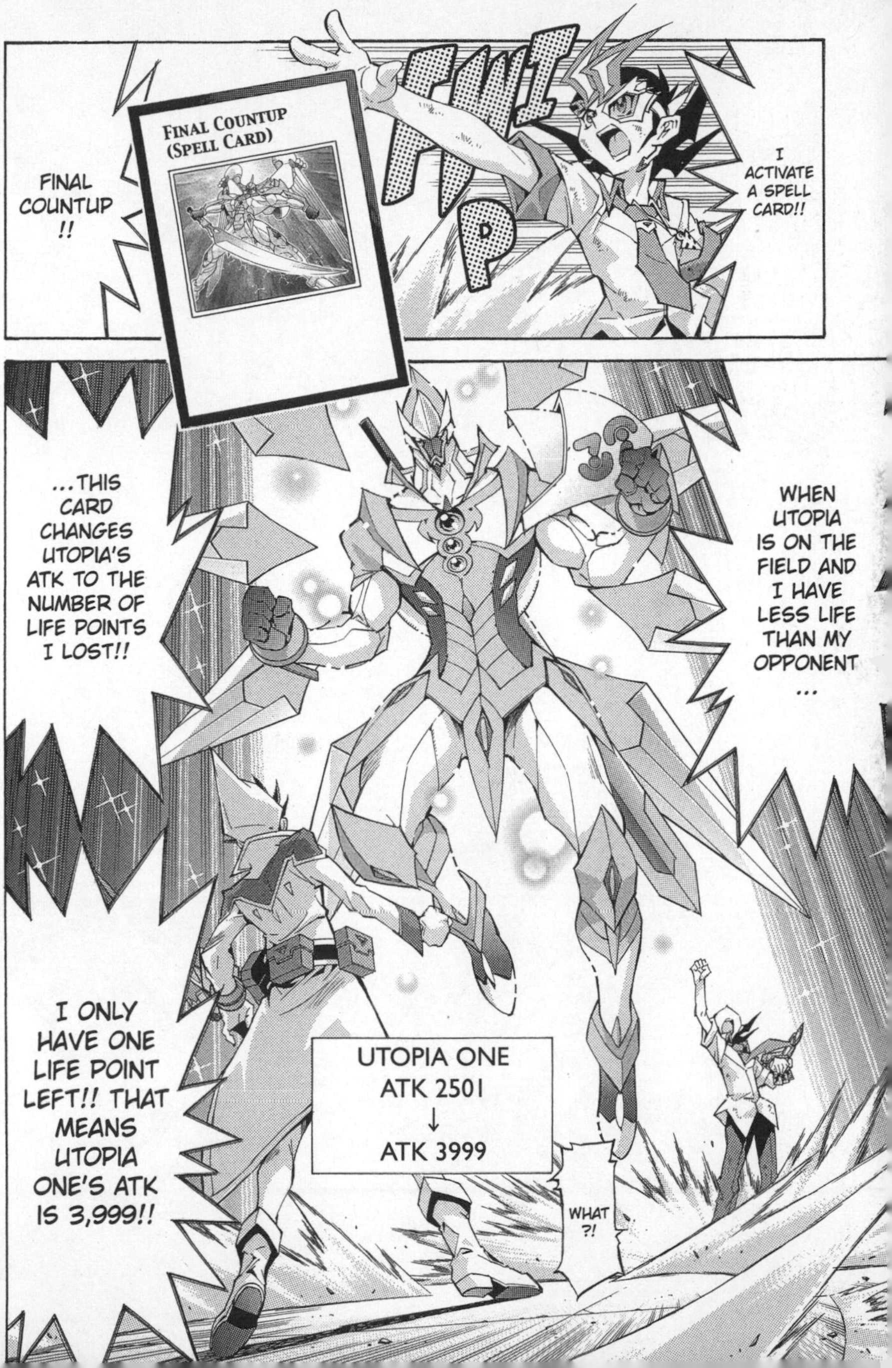
I ACTIVATE A SPELL CARD!!
FINAL COUNTUP (SPELL CARD)
FINAL COUNTUP!!
WHEN UTOPIA IS ON THE FIELD AND I HAVE LESS LIFE THAN MY OPPONENT...
...THIS CARD CHANGES UTOPIA'S ATK TO THE NUMBER OF LIFE POINTS I LOST!!
WHAT?!
UTOPIA ONE ATK 2501 ↓ ATK 3999
I ONLY HAVE ONE LIFE POINT LEFT!! THAT MEANS UTOPIA ONE'S ATK IS 3,999!!

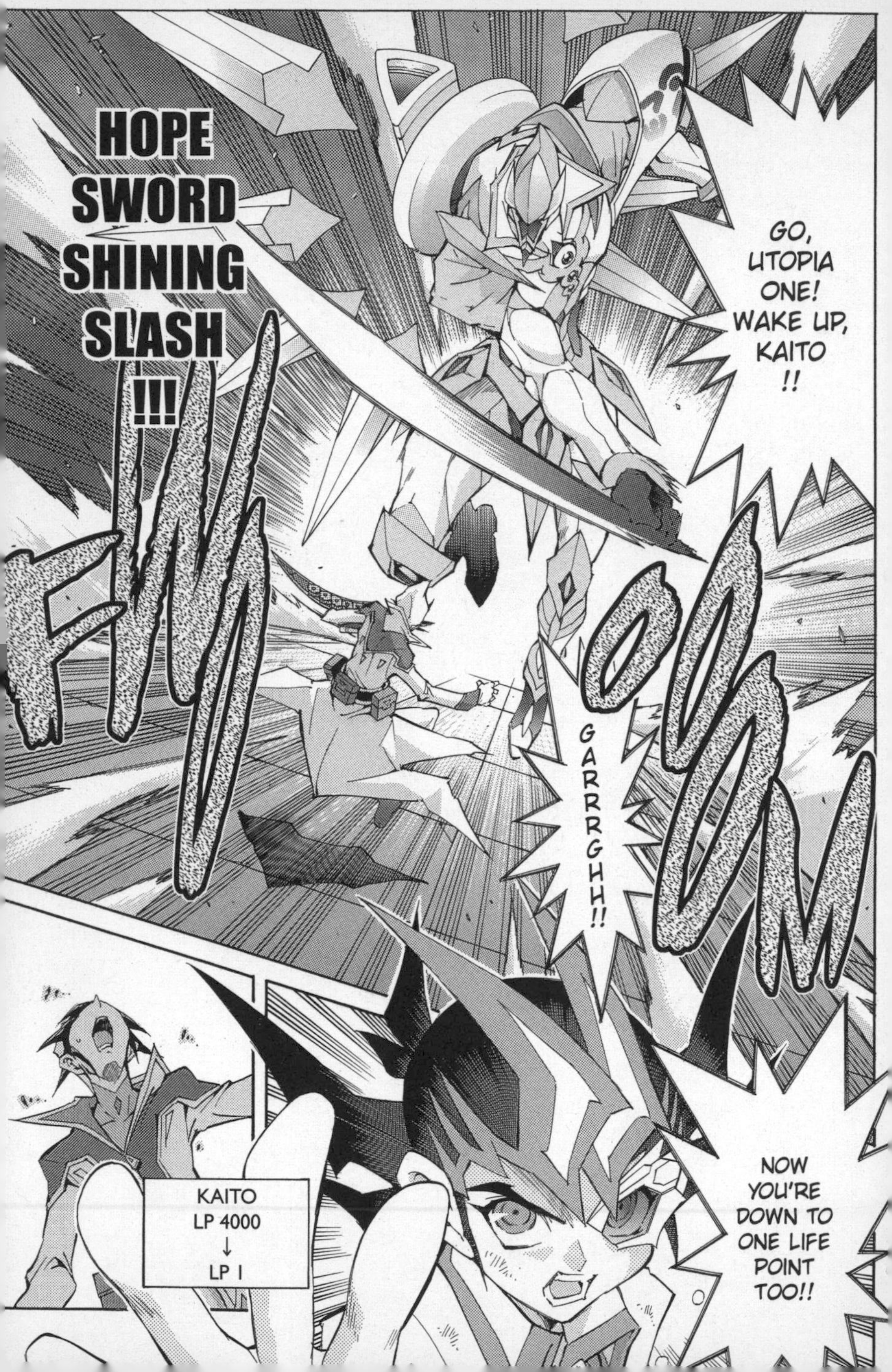
GO, UTOPIA ONE! WAKE UP, KAITO!!
HOPE SWORD SHINING SLASH!!!
GARRRGHH!!
NOW YOU'RE DOWN TO ONE LIFE POINT TOO!!
KAITO LP 4000 ↓ LP 1

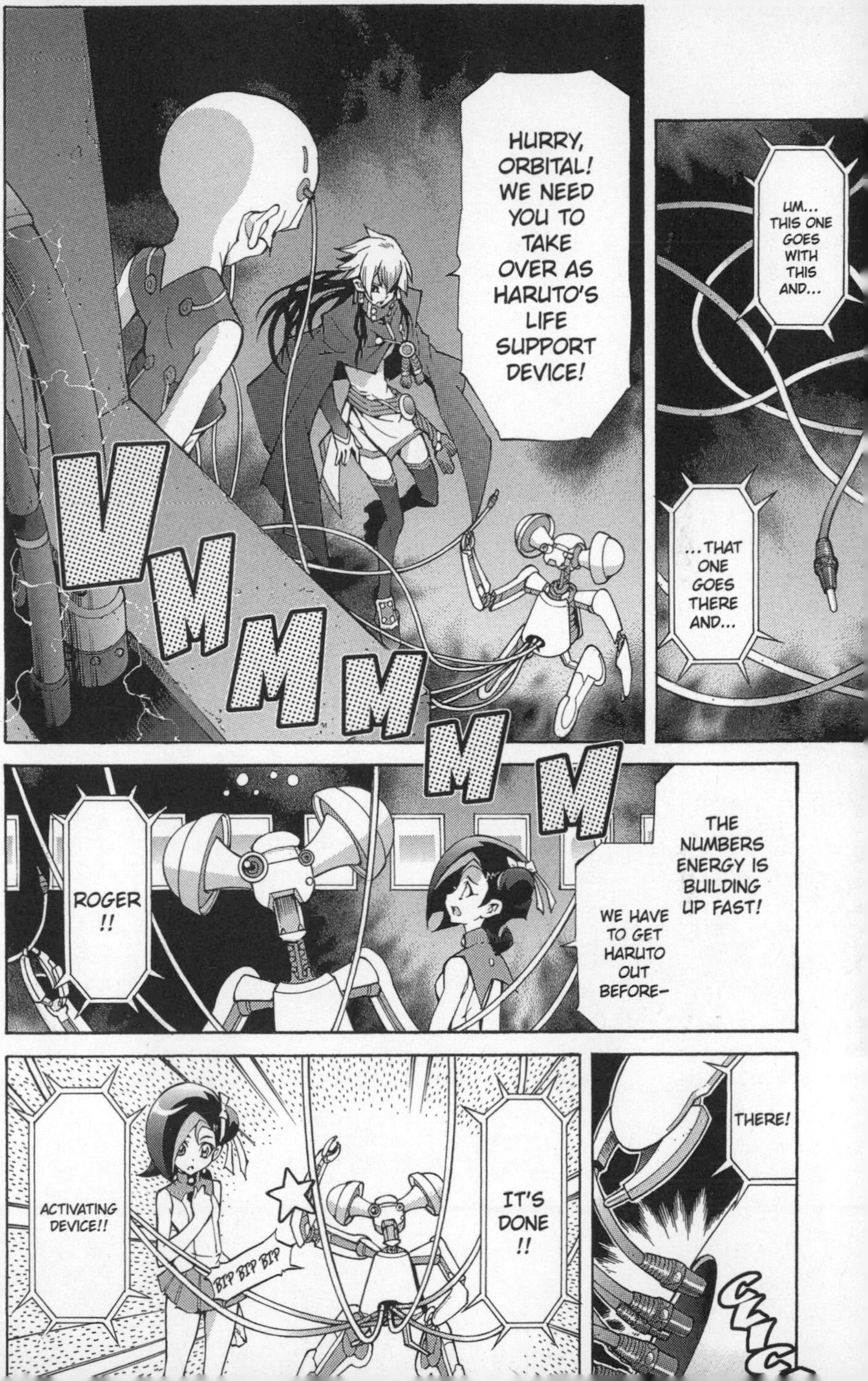
UM... THIS ONE GOES WITH THIS AND...
...THAT ONE GOES THERE AND...
HURRY, ORBITAL! WE NEED YOU TO TAKE OVER AS HARUTO'S LIFE SUPPORT DEVICE!
VMMMMM
THE NUMBERS ENERGY IS BUILDING UP FAST!
WE HAVE TO GET HARUTO OUT BEFORE-
ROGER!!
THERE!
IT'S DONE!!
BIP BIP BIP
ACTIVATING DEVICE!!

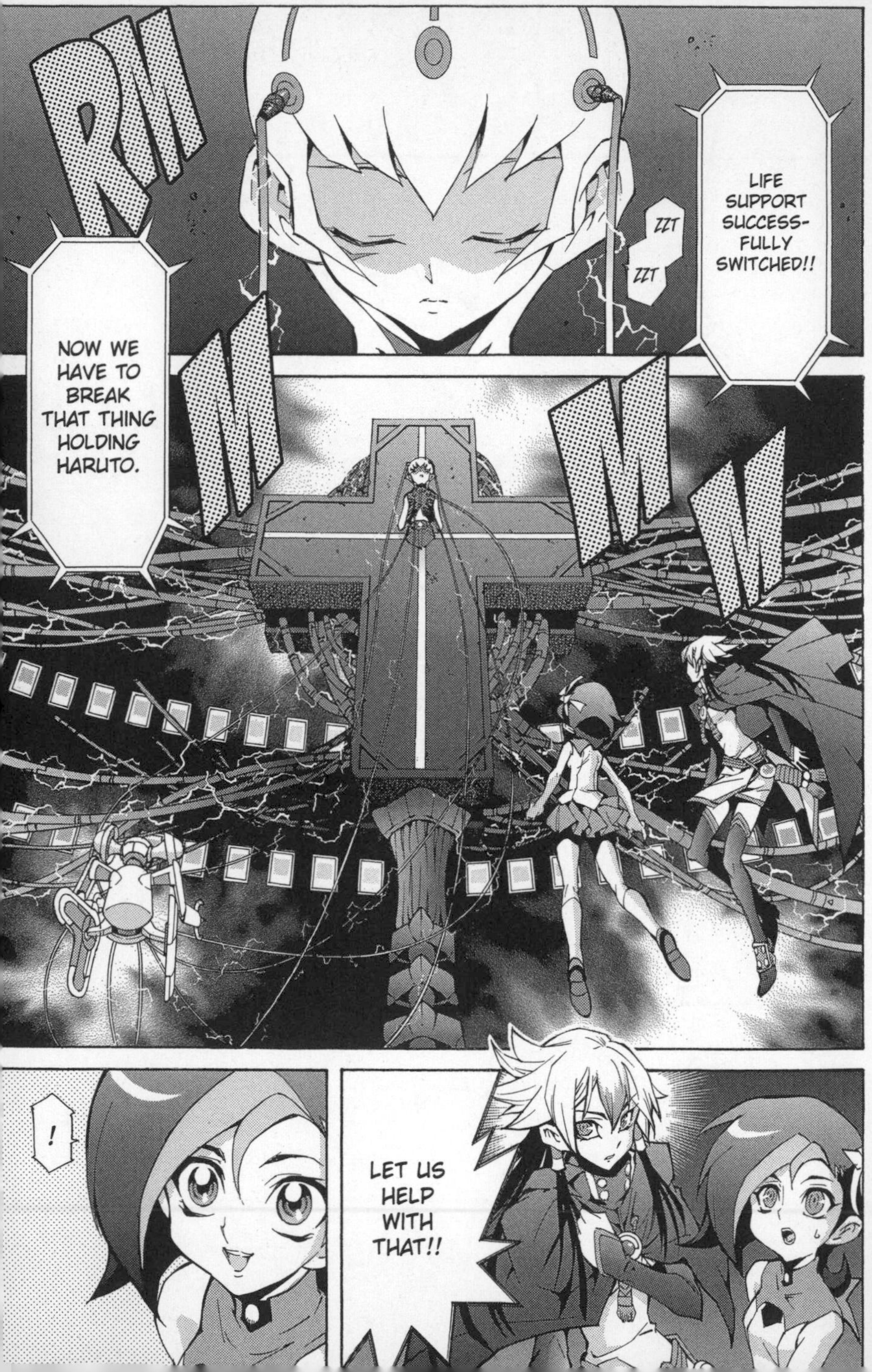
LIFE SUPPORT SUCCESS-FULLY SWITCHED!!
ZZT
ZZT
RMMMM
NOW WE HAVE TO BREAK THAT THING HOLDING HARUTO.
LET US HELP WITH THAT!!
!

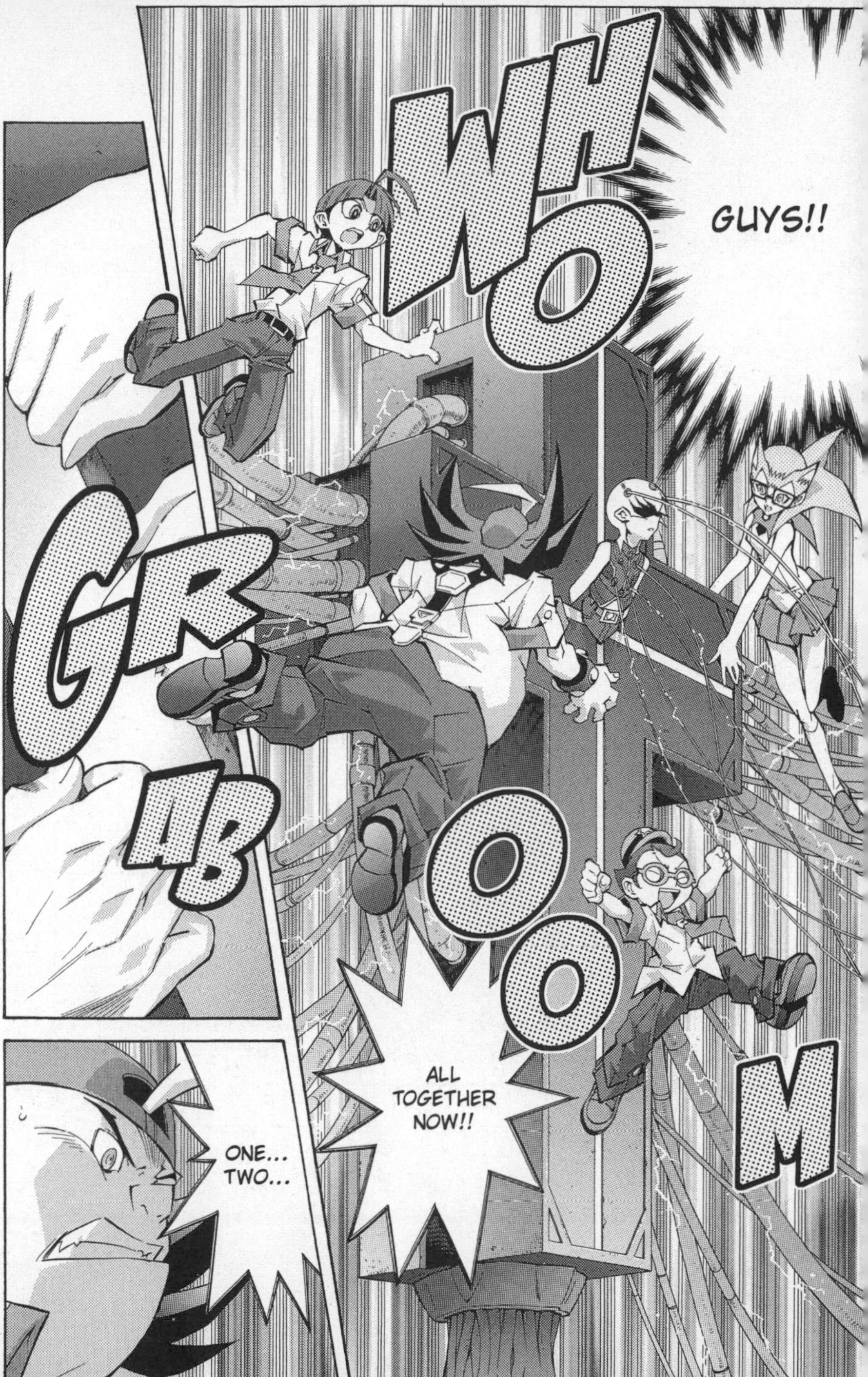
GUYS!!
WHWOOOM
ALL TOGETHER NOW!!
GRAB
ONE... TWO...

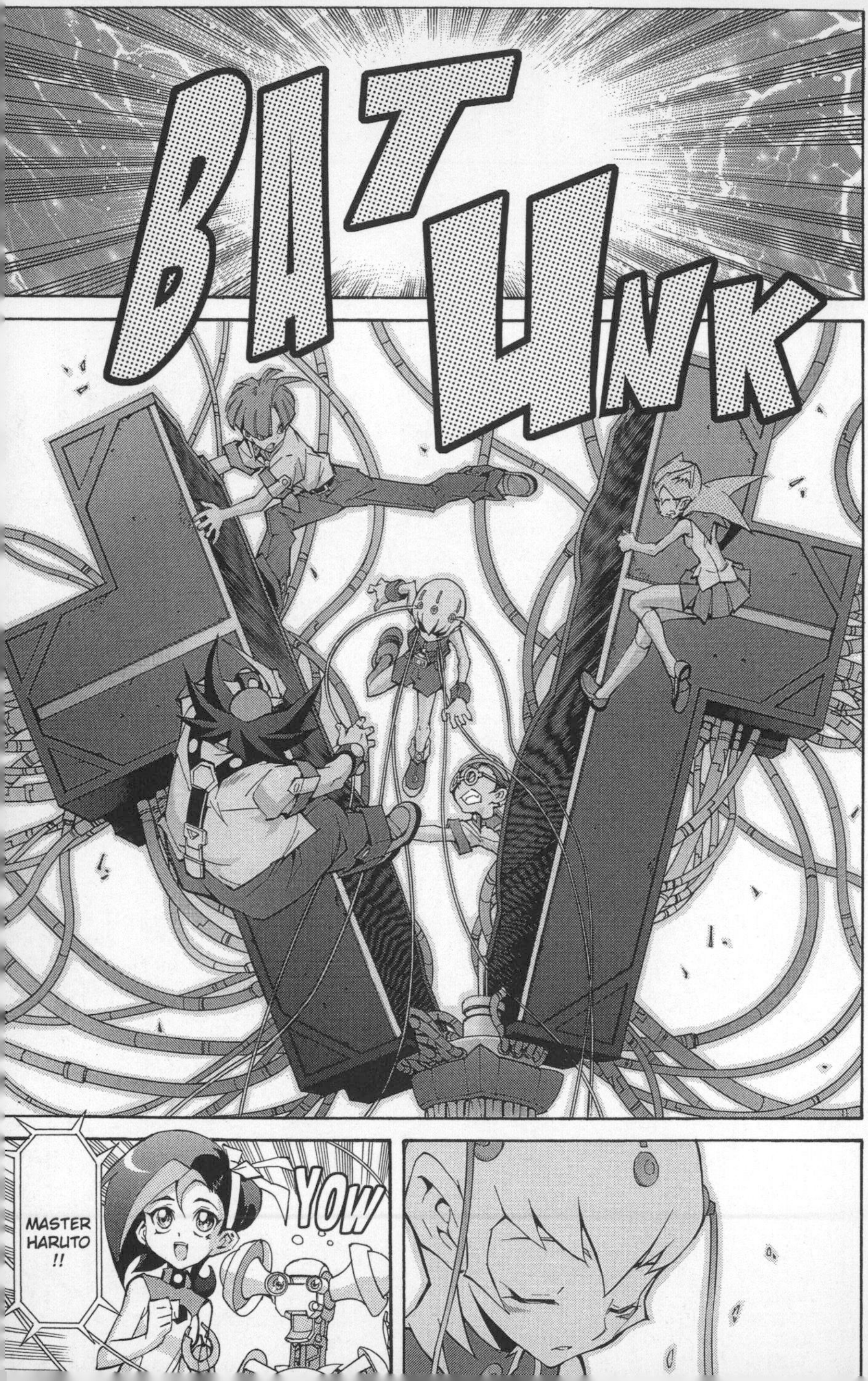
BATLINK
MASTER HARUTO!!
YOW

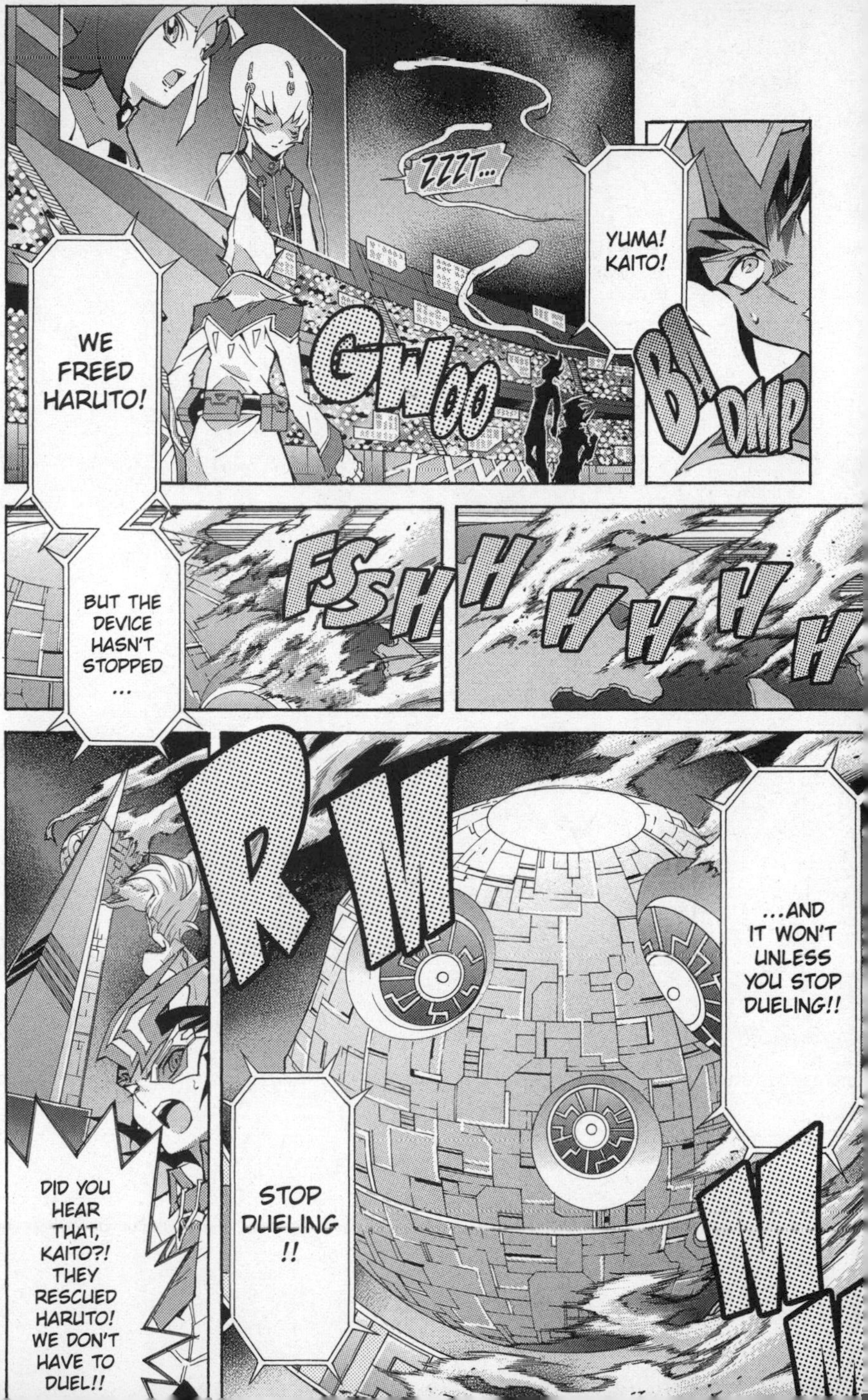
YUMA! KAITO!
BA-DOMP
ZZZT...
GWOO
WE FREED HARUTO!
FSHHHHHHH
BUT THE DEVICE HASN'T STOPPED ...
...AND IT WON'T UNLESS YOU STOP DUELING!!
RMMM
STOP DUELING !!
DID YOU HEAR THAT, KAITO?! THEY RESCUED HARUTO! WE DON'T HAVE TO DUEL!!

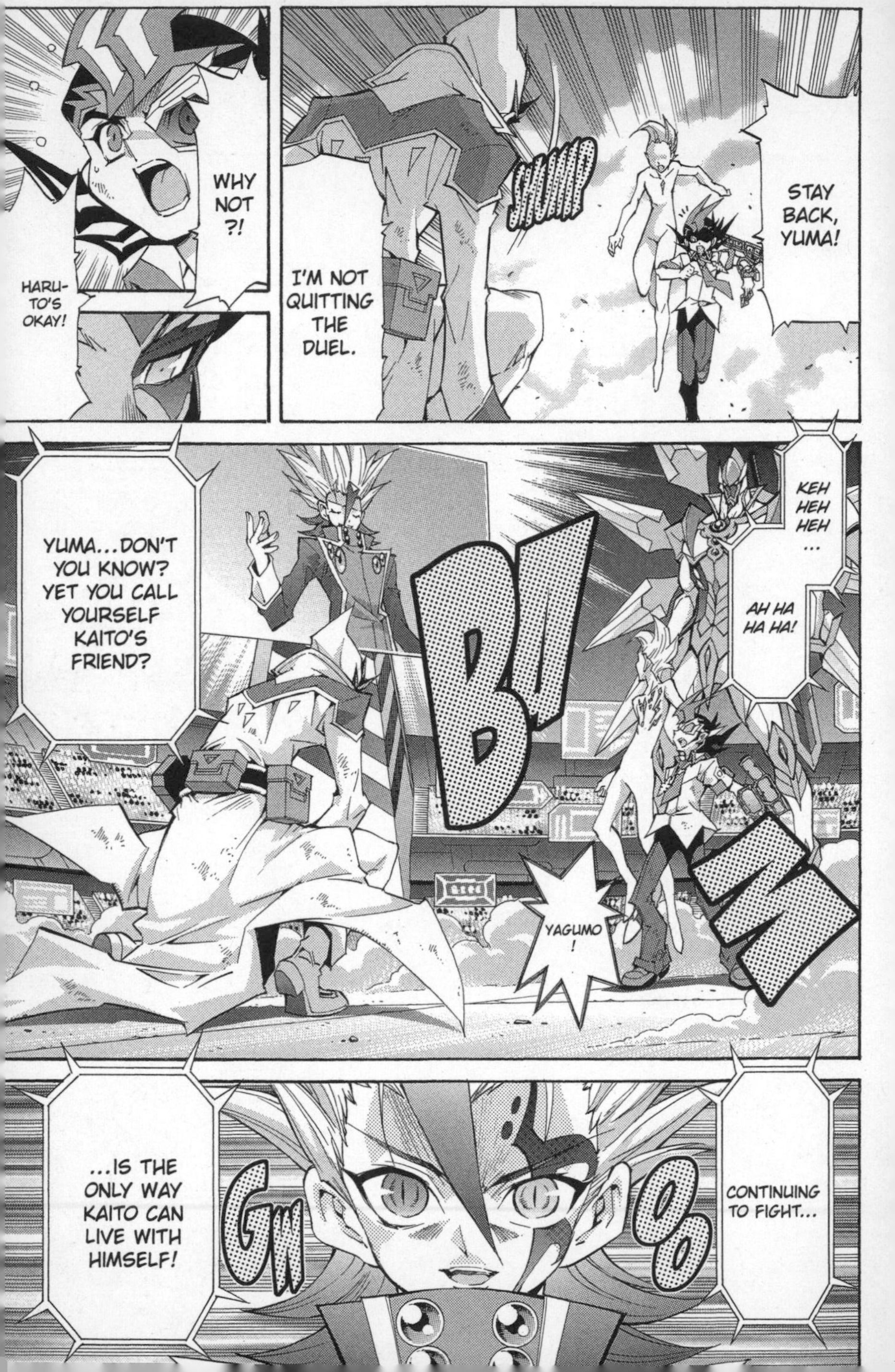
STAY BACK, YUMA!
I'M NOT QUITTING THE DUEL.
WHY NOT ?!
HARU-TO'S OKAY!
KEH HEH HEH ...
AH HA HA HA!
YUMA...DON'T YOU KNOW? YET YOU CALL YOURSELF KAITO'S FRIEND?
YAGUMO !
CONTINUING TO FIGHT...
...IS THE ONLY WAY KAITO CAN LIVE WITH HIMSELF!

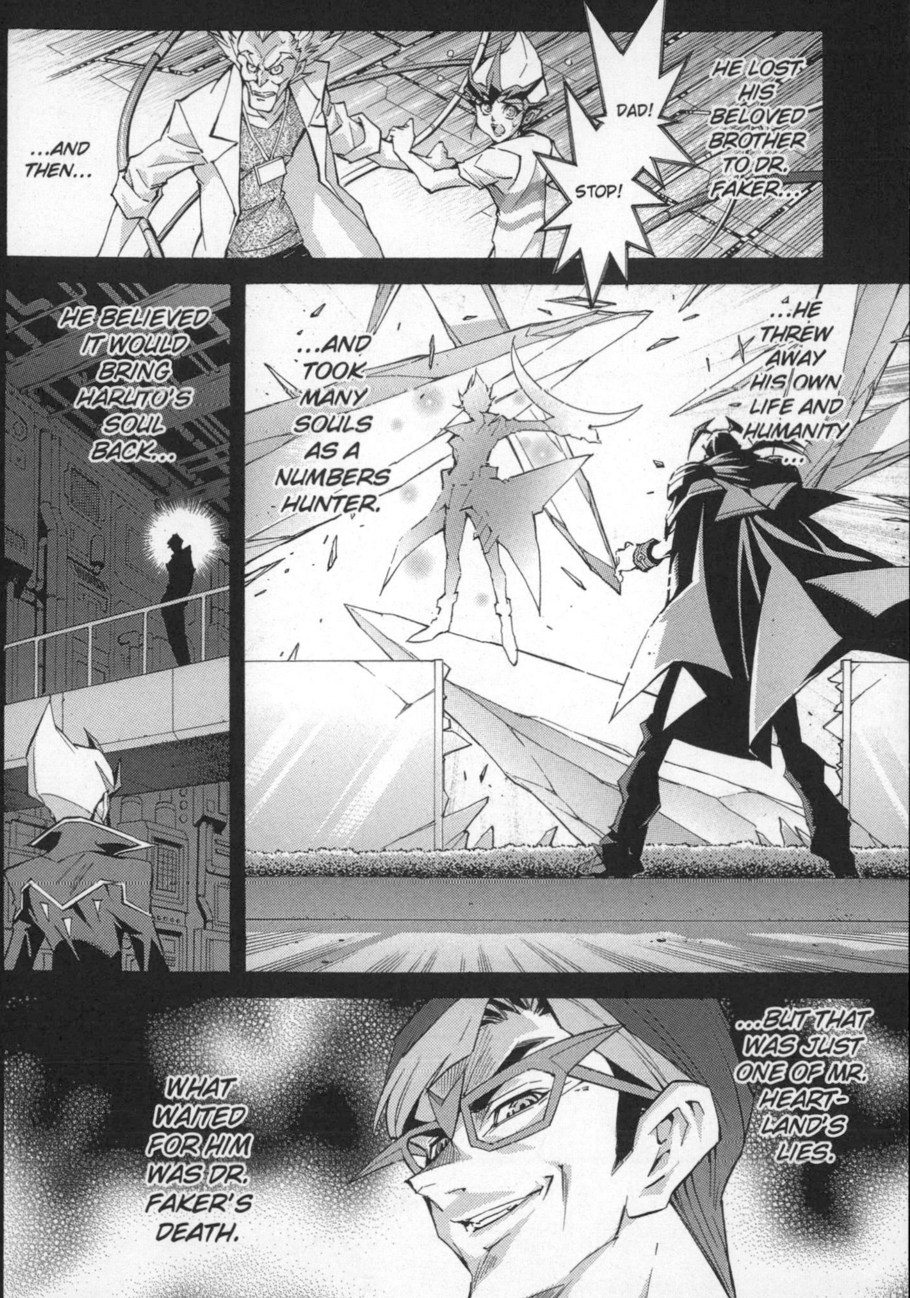
HE LOST HIS BELOVED BROTHER TO DR. FAKER...
DAD!
STOP!
...AND THEN...
...HE THREW AWAY HIS OWN LIFE AND HUMANITY...
...AND TOOK MANY SOULS AS A NUMBERS HUNTER.
HE BELIEVED IT WOULD BRING HARUTO'S SOUL BACK...
...BUT THAT WAS JUST ONE OF MR. HEART-LAND'S LIES.
WHAT WAITED FOR HIM WAS DR. FAKER'S DEATH.

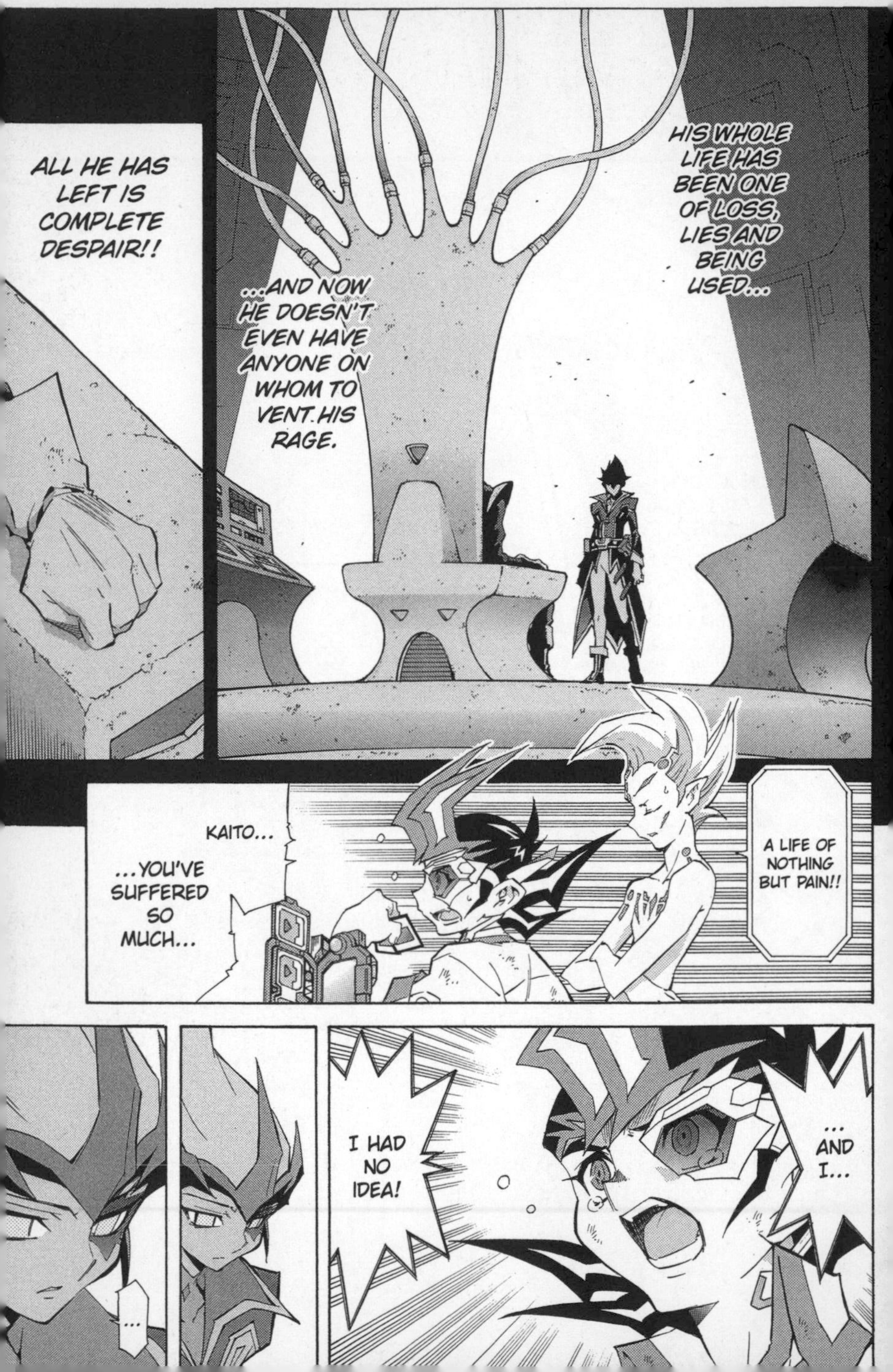
HIS WHOLE LIFE HAS BEEN ONE OF LOSS, LIES AND BEING USED...
...AND NOW HE DOESN'T EVEN HAVE ANYONE ON WHOM TO VENT HIS RAGE.
ALL HE HAS LEFT IS COMPLETE DESPAIR!!
A LIFE OF NOTHING BUT PAIN!!
KAITO...
...YOU'VE SUFFERED SO MUCH...
...AND I...
I HAD NO IDEA!
...

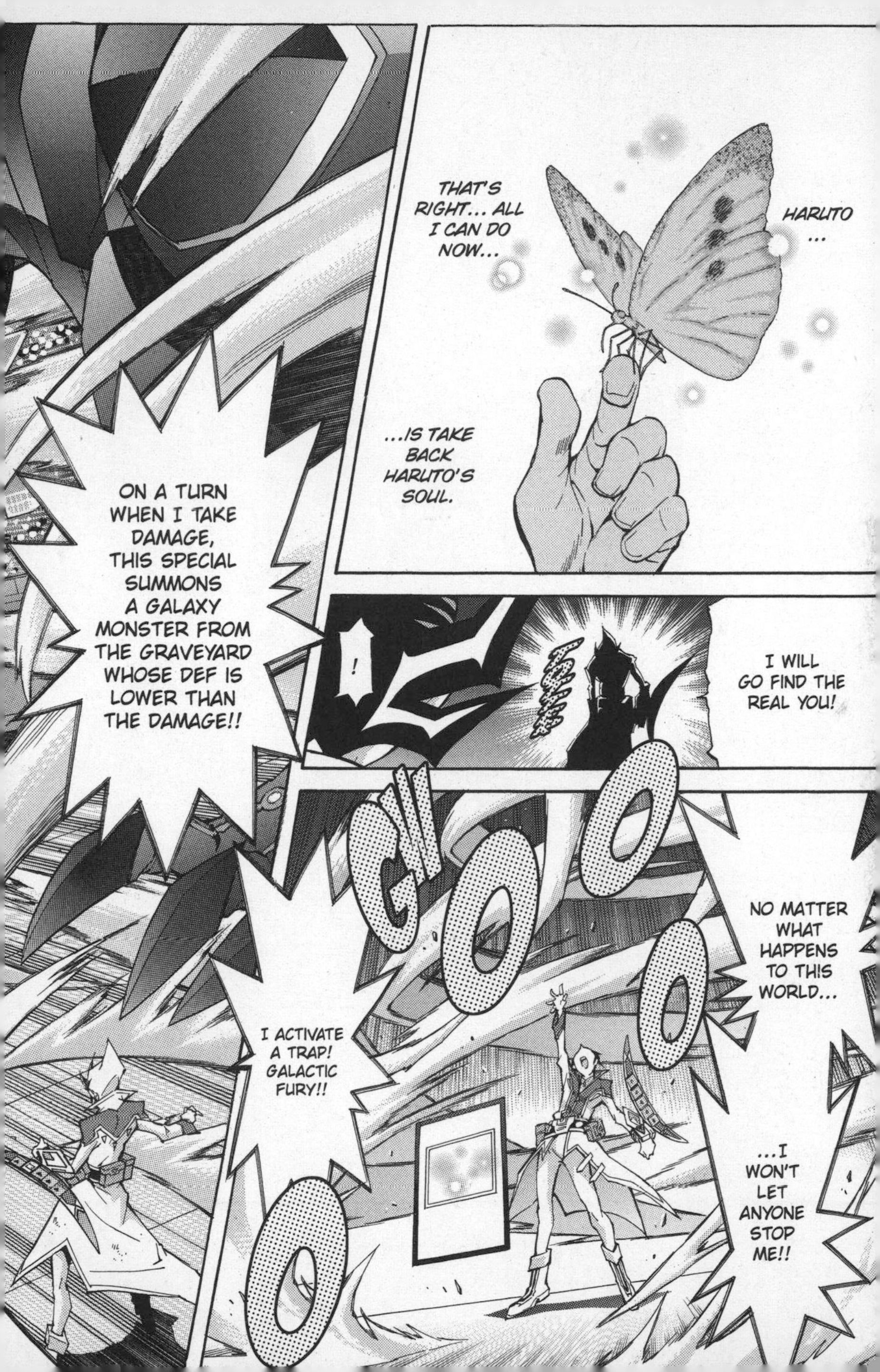
HARUTO ...
THAT'S RIGHT... ALL I CAN DO NOW...
...IS TAKE BACK HARUTO'S SOUL.
I WILL GO FIND THE REAL YOU!
!
ON A TURN WHEN I TAKE DAMAGE, THIS SPECIAL SUMMONS A GALAXY MONSTER FROM THE GRAVEYARD WHOSE DEF IS LOWER THAN THE DAMAGE!!
NO MATTER WHAT HAPPENS TO THIS WORLD...
...I WON'T LET ANYONE STOP ME!!
I ACTIVATE A TRAP! GALACTIC FURY!!

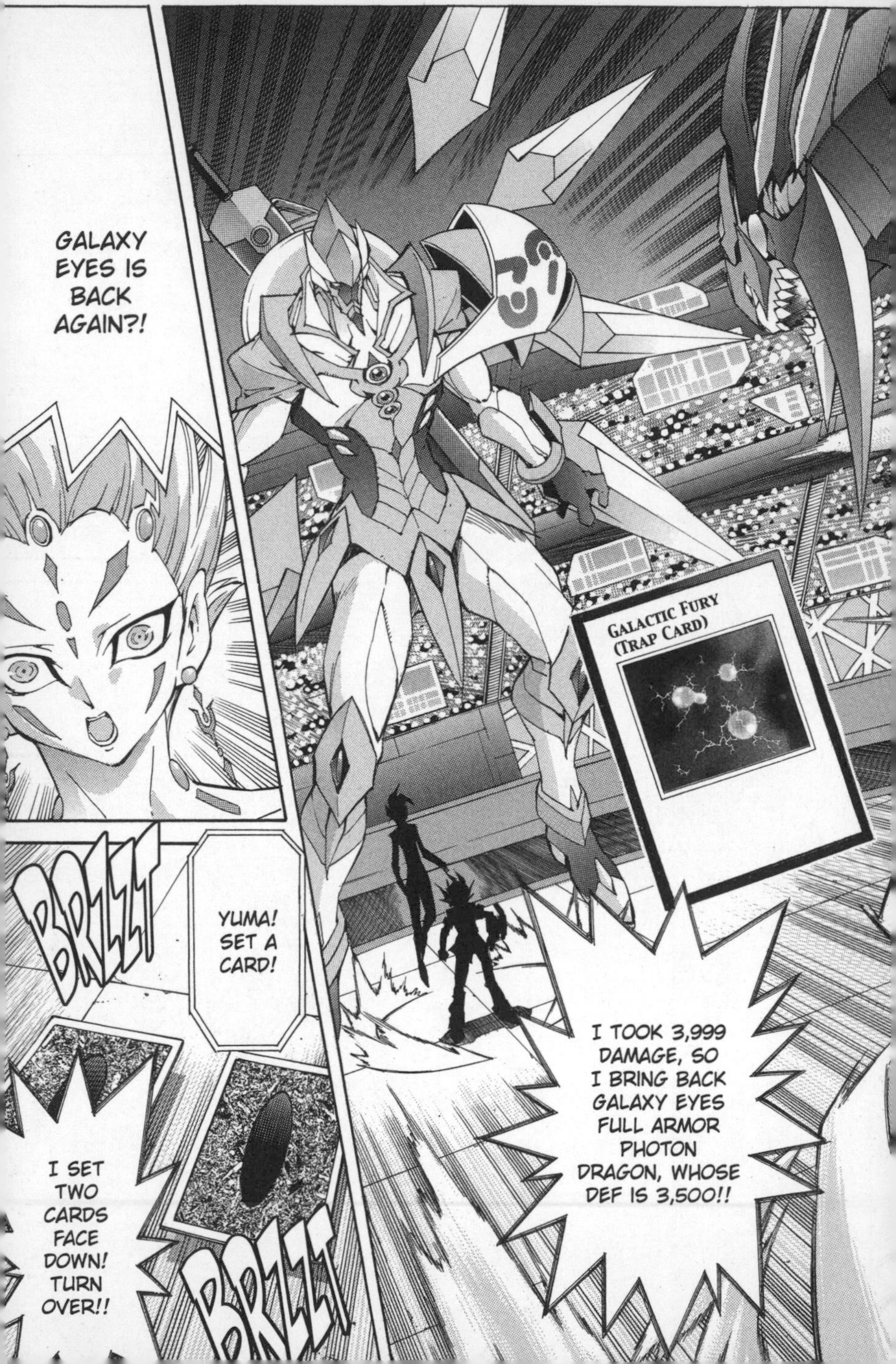
GALACTIC FURY (TRAP CARD)
I TOOK 3,999 DAMAGE, SO I BRING BACK GALAXY EYES FULL ARMOR PHOTON DRAGON, WHOSE DEF IS 3,500!!
GALAXY EYES IS BACK AGAIN?!
YUMA! SET A CARD!
BRZZT
I SET TWO CARDS FACE DOWN! TURN OVER!!
BRZZT

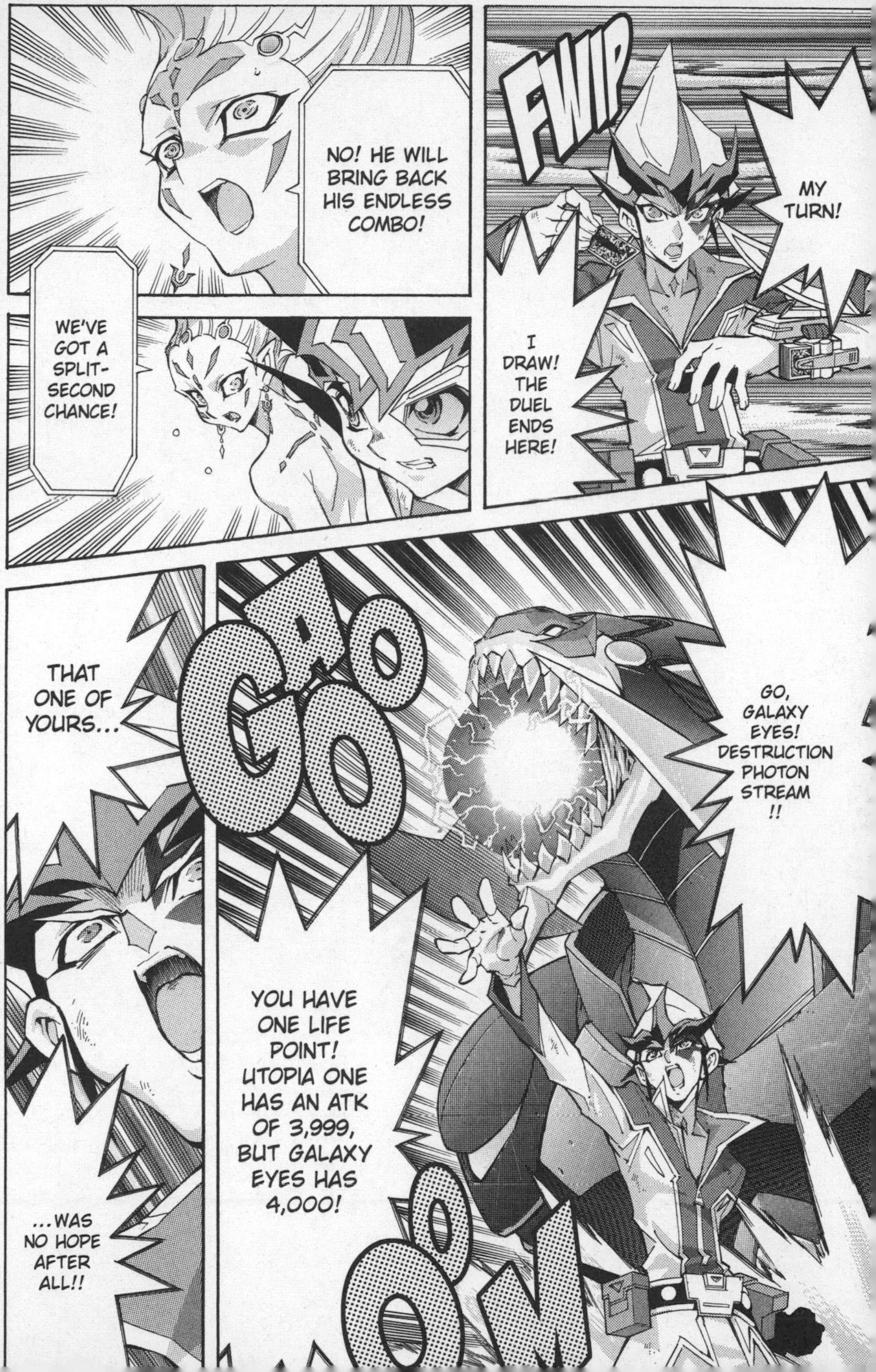
FWIP
MY TURN!
I DRAW! THE DUEL ENDS HERE!
NO! HE WILL BRING BACK HIS ENDLESS COMBO!
WE'VE GOT A SPLIT-SECOND CHANCE!
GO, GALAXY EYES! DESTRUCTION PHOTON STREAM !!
YOU HAVE ONE LIFE POINT! UTOPIA ONE HAS AN ATK OF 3,999, BUT GALAXY EYES HAS 4,000!
THAT ONE OF YOURS...
...WAS NO HOPE AFTER ALL!!

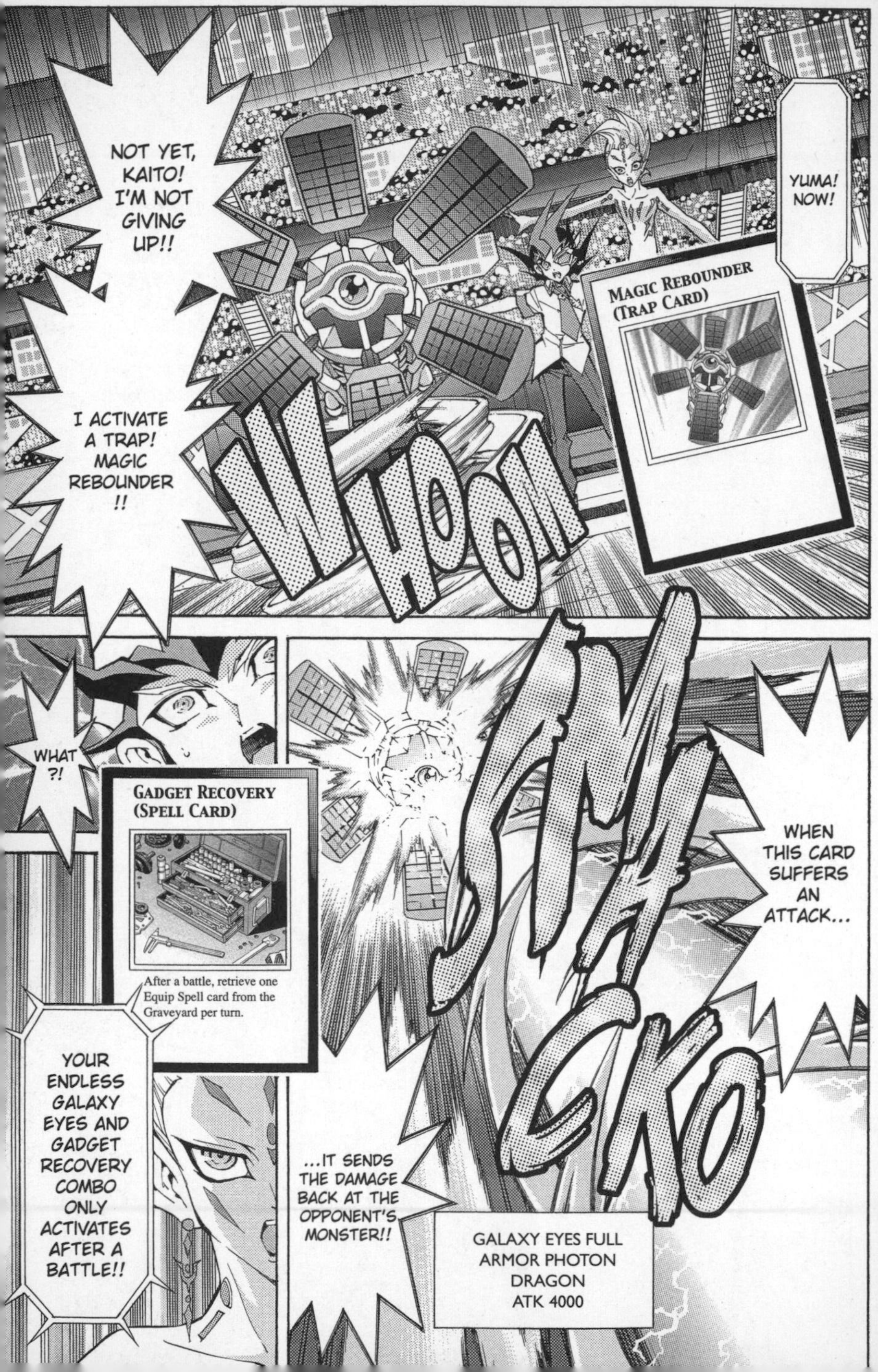
YUMA! NOW!
NOT YET, KAITO! I'M NOT GIVING UP!!
I ACTIVATE A TRAP! MAGIC REBOUNDER!!
MAGIC REBOUNDER (TRAP CARD)
WHOOM
WHEN THIS CARD SUFFERS AN ATTACK...
SMACKO
...IT SENDS THE DAMAGE BACK AT THE OPPONENT'S MONSTER!!
GALAXY EYES FULL ARMOR PHOTON DRAGON ATK 4000
WHAT?!
GADGET RECOVERY (SPELL CARD)
After a battle, retrieve one Equip Spell card from the Graveyard per turn.
YOUR ENDLESS GALAXY EYES AND GADGET RECOVERY COMBO ONLY ACTIVATES AFTER A BATTLE!!

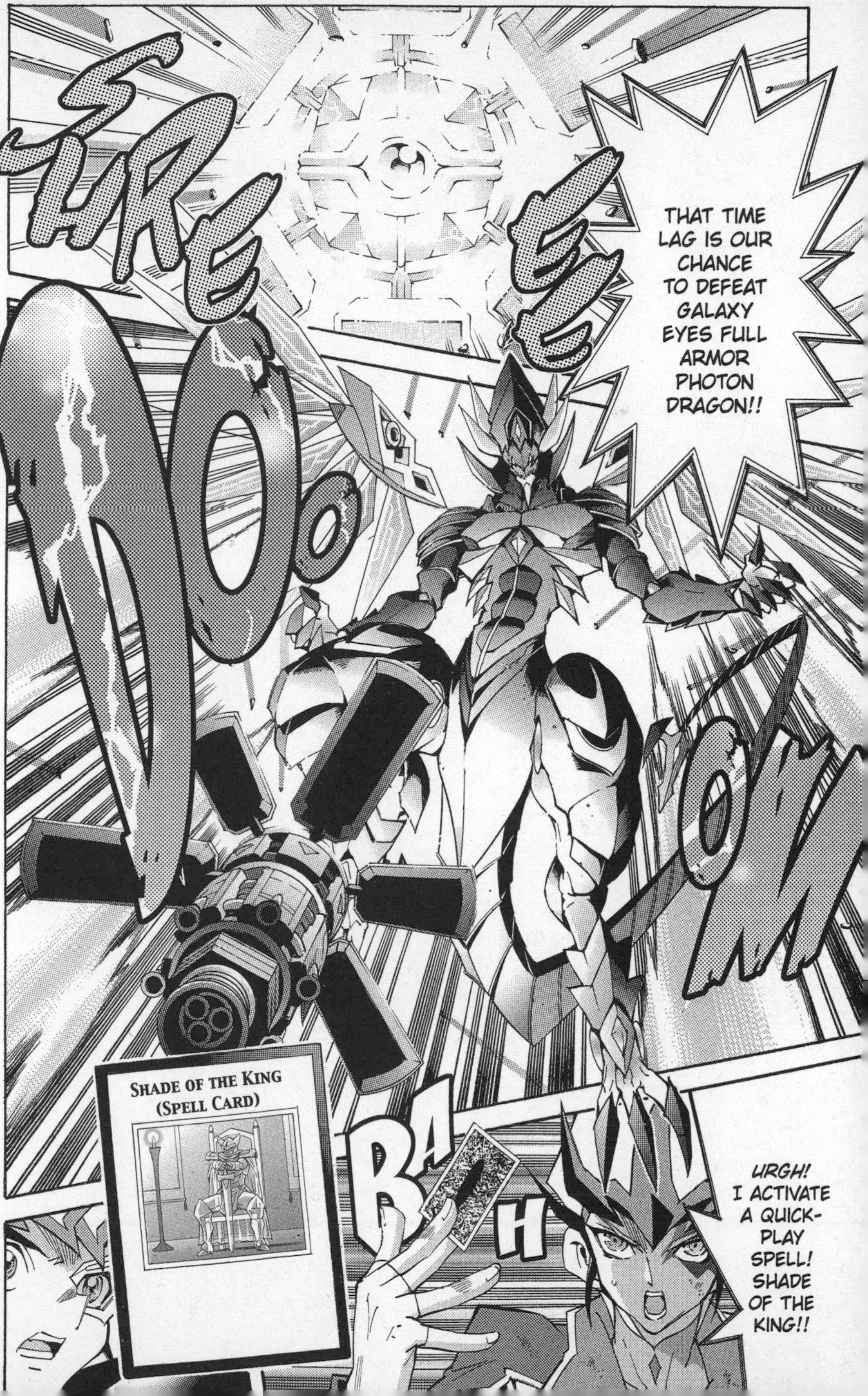
THAT TIME LAG IS OUR CHANCE TO DEFEAT GALAXY EYES FULL ARMOR PHOTON DRAGON!!
SHREEE
URGH! I ACTIVATE A QUICK-PLAY SPELL! SHADE OF THE KING!!
SHADE OF THE KING (SPELL CARD)

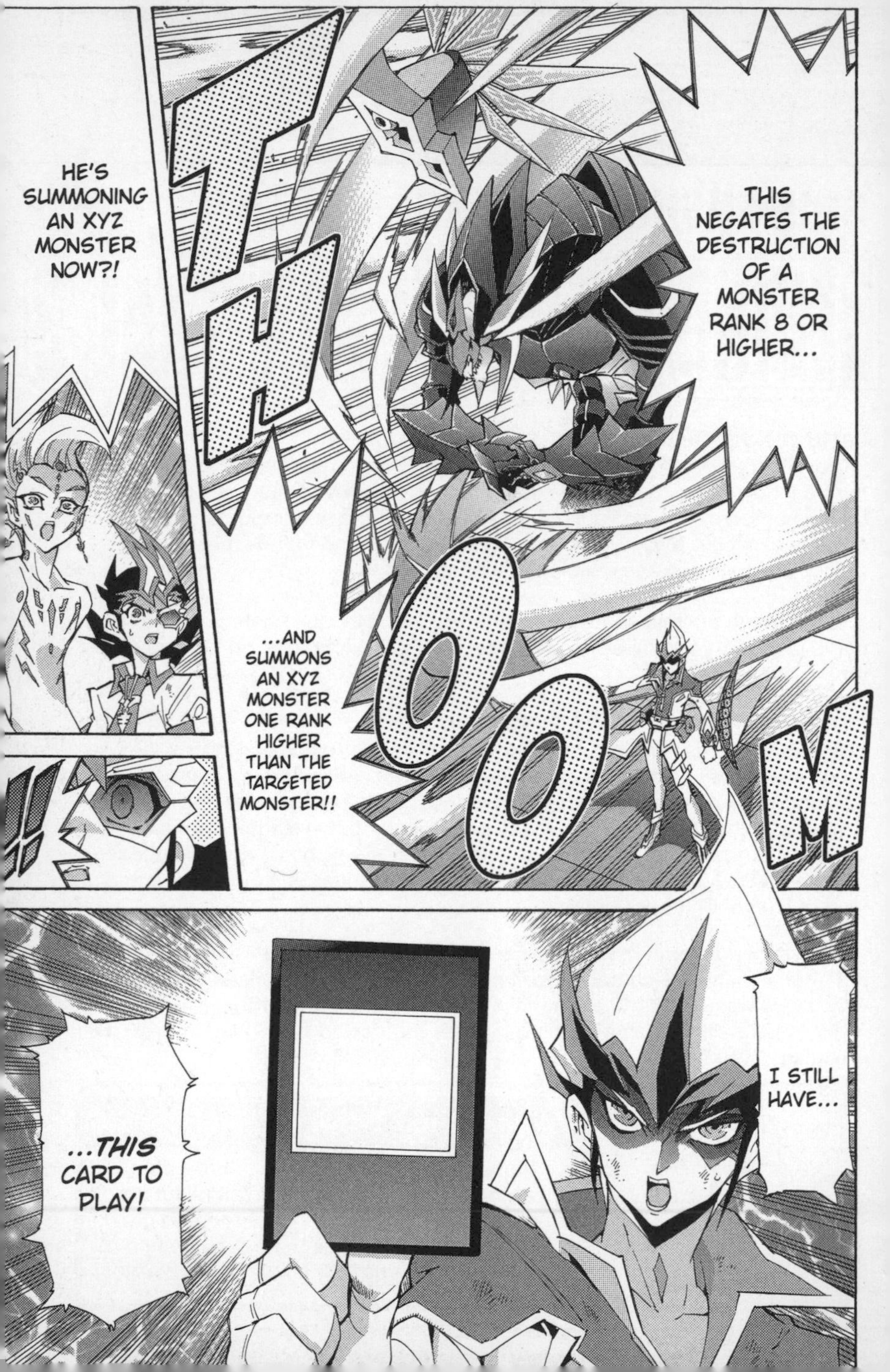
THWOOOM
THIS NEGATES THE DESTRUCTION OF A MONSTER RANK 8 OR HIGHER...
...AND SUMMONS AN XYZ MONSTER ONE RANK HIGHER THAN THE TARGETED MONSTER!!
HE'S SUMMONING AN XYZ MONSTER NOW?!
!!
I STILL HAVE...
...*THIS* CARD TO PLAY!

Series composition for the *ZEXAL* anime

The author of the *ZEXAL* manga

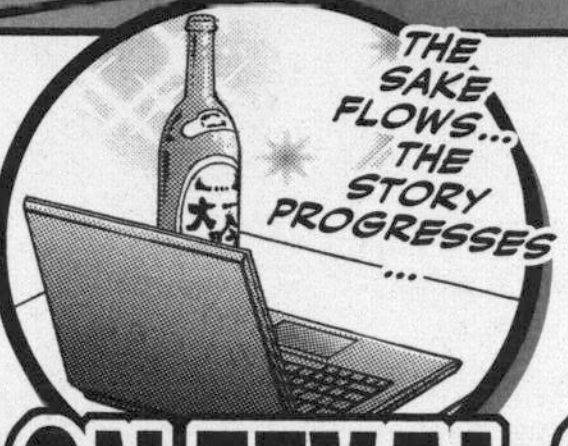
THE SAKE FLOWS... THE STORY PROGRESSES...

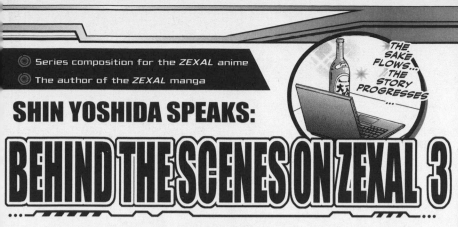

SHIN YOSHIDA SPEAKS:

BEHIND THE SCENES ON ZEXAL 3

*** THE ORIGIN OF KYOJI YAGUMO'S CHARACTER**

Kyoji Yagumo is the biggest enemy Yuma, Shark and Kaito face in this story. He's a lonely character. He has lots of underlings but no real friends. Judging by the numbers, you would think he's beating Yuma and the others, but he's actually all alone. Maybe Yuma and his group will find friends for him or maybe they will become his friends themselves.

He's a tough enemy, so I wanted to make him a unique character who has come unglued. Miyoshi-san's character design is incredible, so I think he has turned out well.

*** THE ORIGIN OF KYOJI YAGUMO'S NAME**

His name comes from the writer Koizumi Yakumo (Lafcadio Hearn). He's a tough enemy, so I wanted a name that had mystical and creepy connotations. Koizumi Yakumo is famous for ghost stories. Both Yakumo and Yagumo are written with the characters for "eight" and "cloud," but in Yagumo's case, I had in mind characters meaning "eight" and "spider"—which is a nice fit because spiders have eight legs! Also, the way Yagumo sounds is suggestive of the land of Izumo. So it was perfect!

The first character in "Kyoji" is written with the character for "entertainment," but I had in mind the character for "insane," which is pronounced the same way. I've always liked the sound *kyo*. In 5D's, even though Kiryu Kyosuke (Kalin Kessler) is written with the character for "capital city," I had in mind the meaning of "insane."

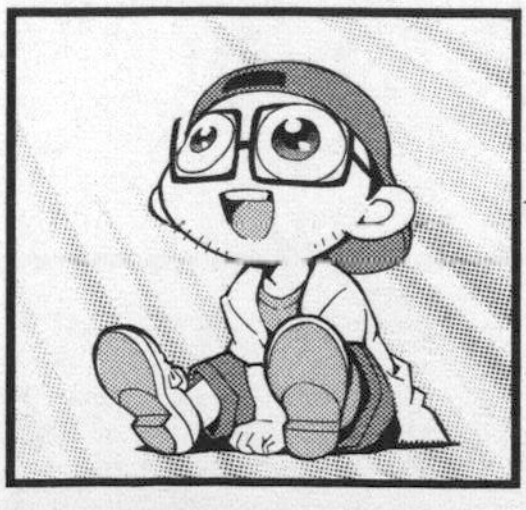

A Message from Miyoshi Sensei!

That was the first time I ever heard about Yagumo's background! (hah) I think he's a character who still has a lot of room to grow in Yoshida Sensei's mind. I'll draw both Yagumo and Luna to the best of my abilities!

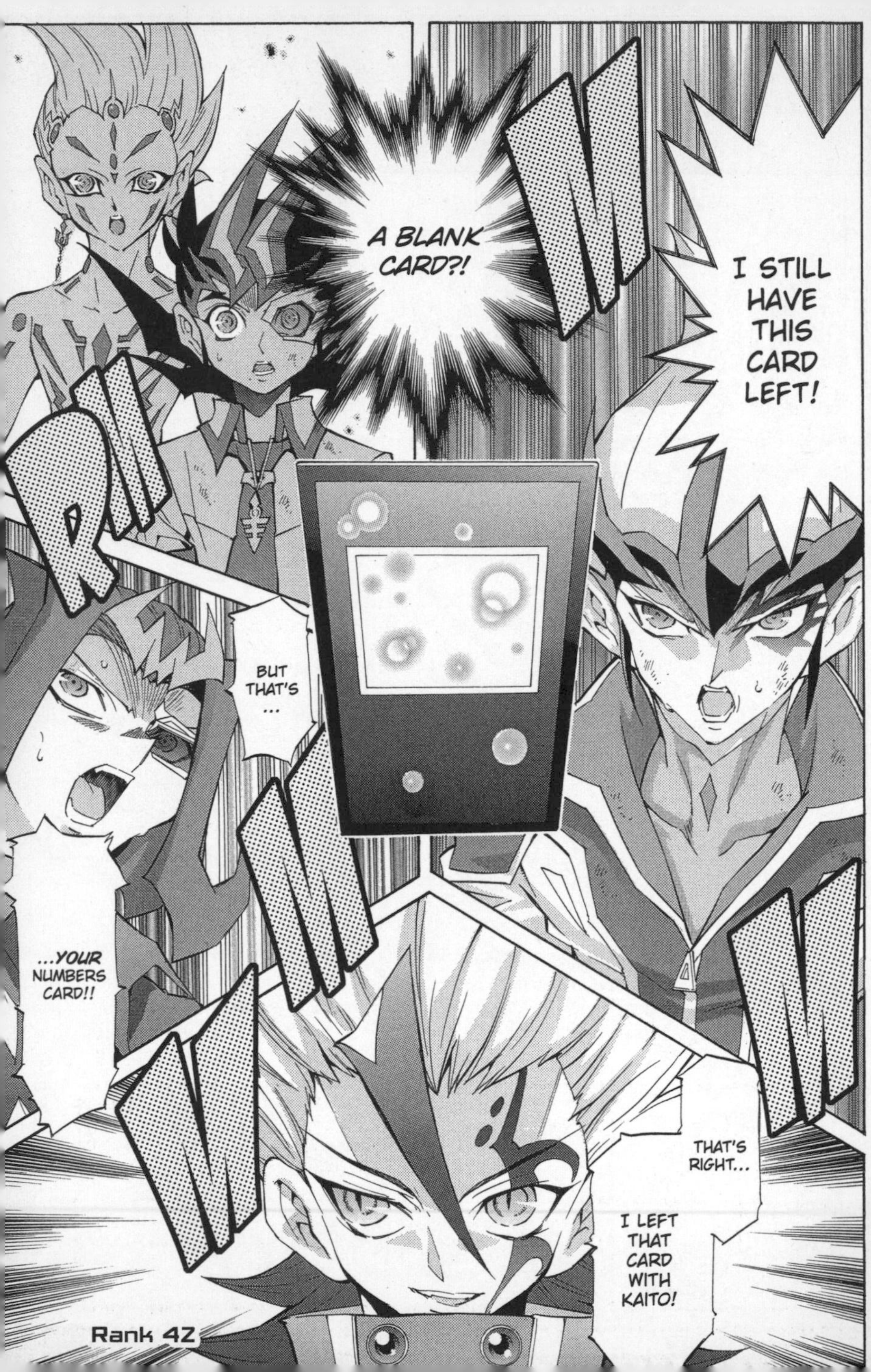
I STILL HAVE THIS CARD LEFT!
A BLANK CARD?!
BUT THAT'S...
...YOUR NUMBERS CARD!!
THAT'S RIGHT...
I LEFT THAT CARD WITH KAITO!

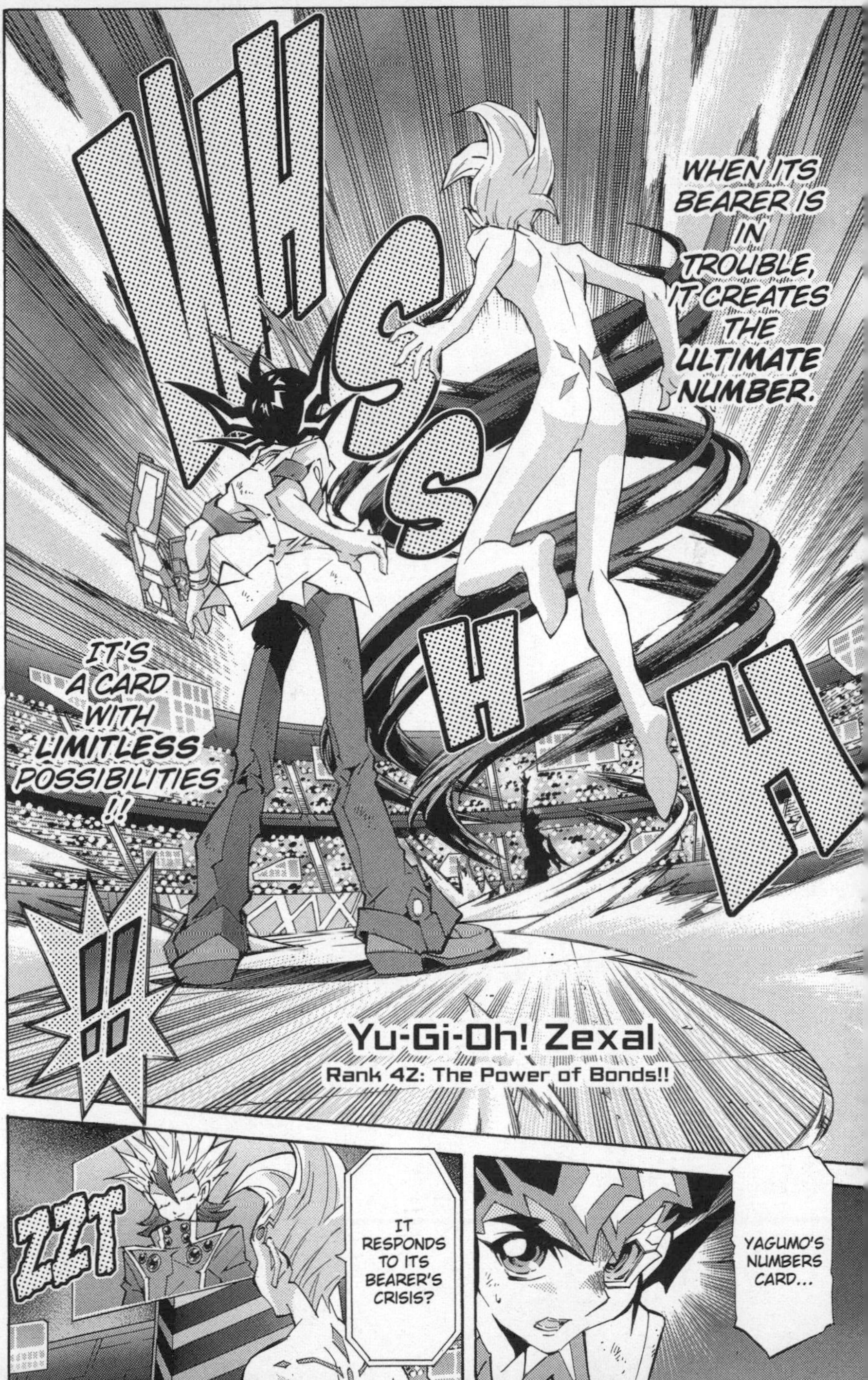
WHEN ITS BEARER IS IN TROUBLE, IT CREATES THE ULTIMATE NUMBER.
IT'S A CARD WITH LIMITLESS POSSIBILITIES!!
!!
Yu-Gi-Oh! Zexal
Rank 42: The Power of Bonds!!
YAGUMO'S NUMBERS CARD...
IT RESPONDS TO ITS BEARER'S CRISIS?
ZZT

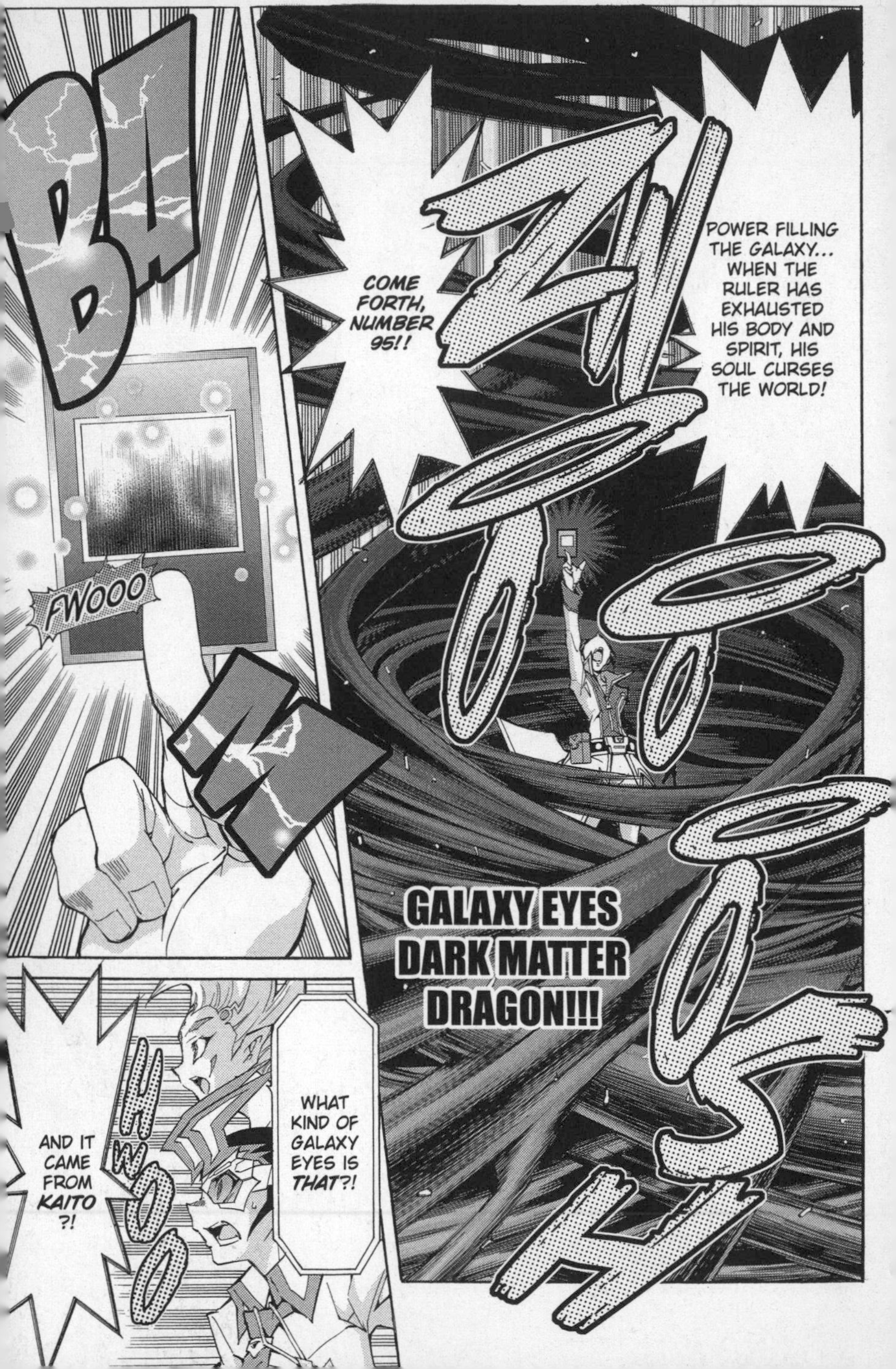
POWER FILLING THE GALAXY... WHEN THE RULER HAS EXHAUSTED HIS BODY AND SPIRIT, HIS SOUL CURSES THE WORLD!
COME FORTH, NUMBER 95!!
GALAXY EYES DARK MATTER DRAGON!!!
BA
FWOOO
WHAT KIND OF GALAXY EYES IS *THAT*?!
AND IT CAME FROM *KAITO*?!

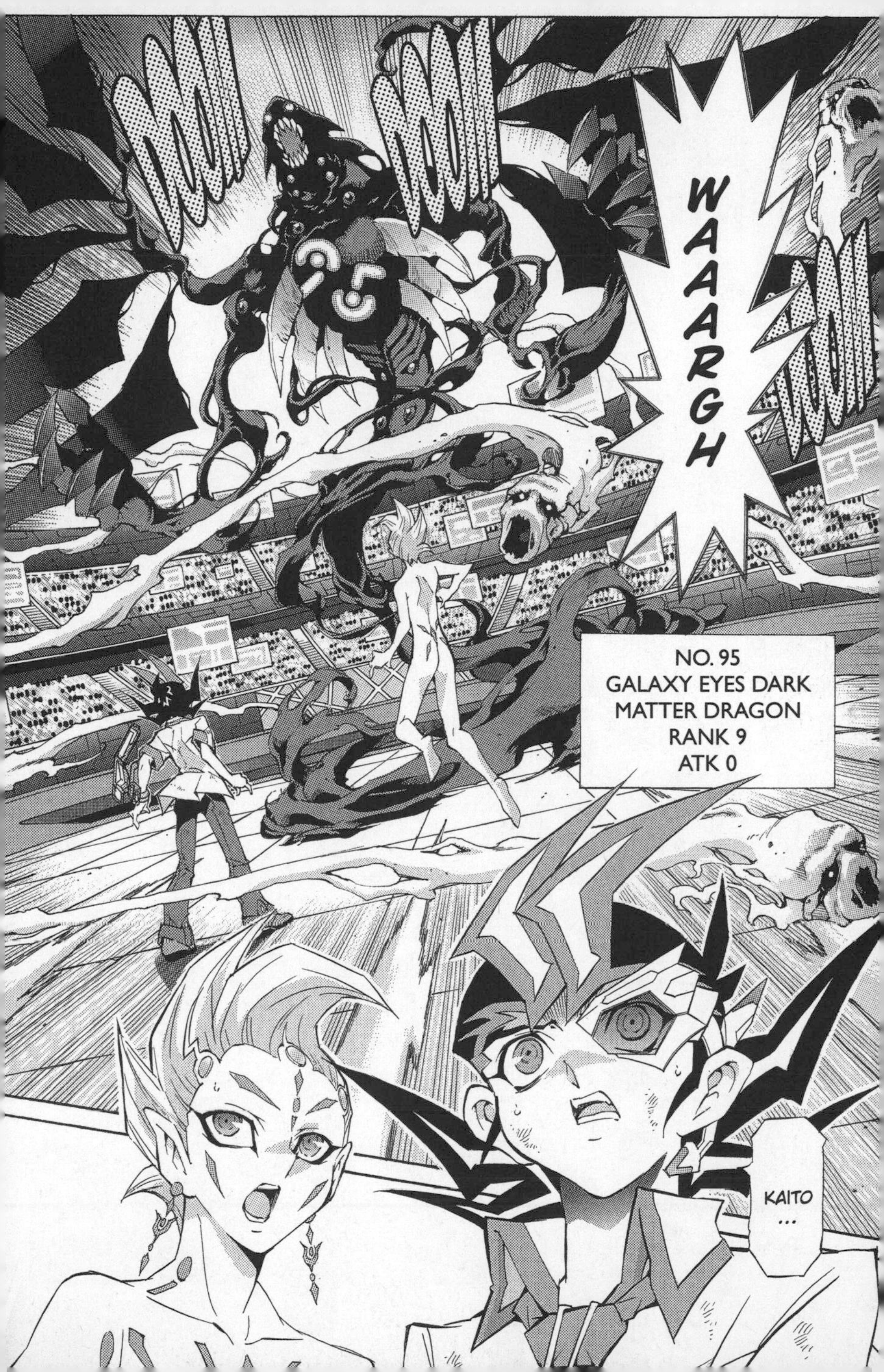
WAAARGH
NO. 95
GALAXY EYES DARK
MATTER DRAGON
RANK 9
ATK 0
KAITO
...

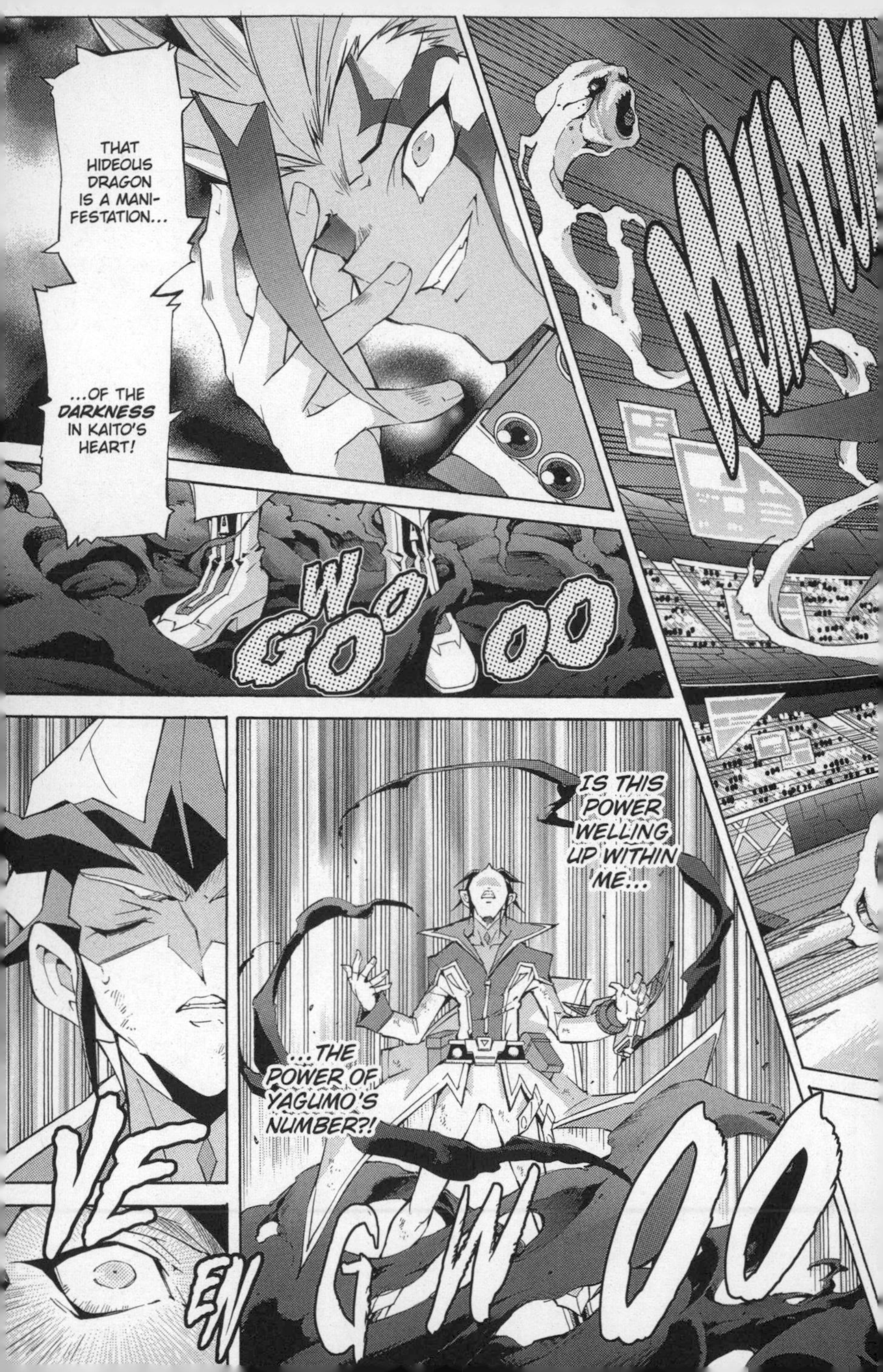
THAT HIDEOUS DRAGON IS A MANI-FESTATION...
...OF THE *DARKNESS* IN KAITO'S HEART!
IS THIS POWER WELLING UP WITHIN ME...
...THE POWER OF YAGUMO'S NUMBER?!

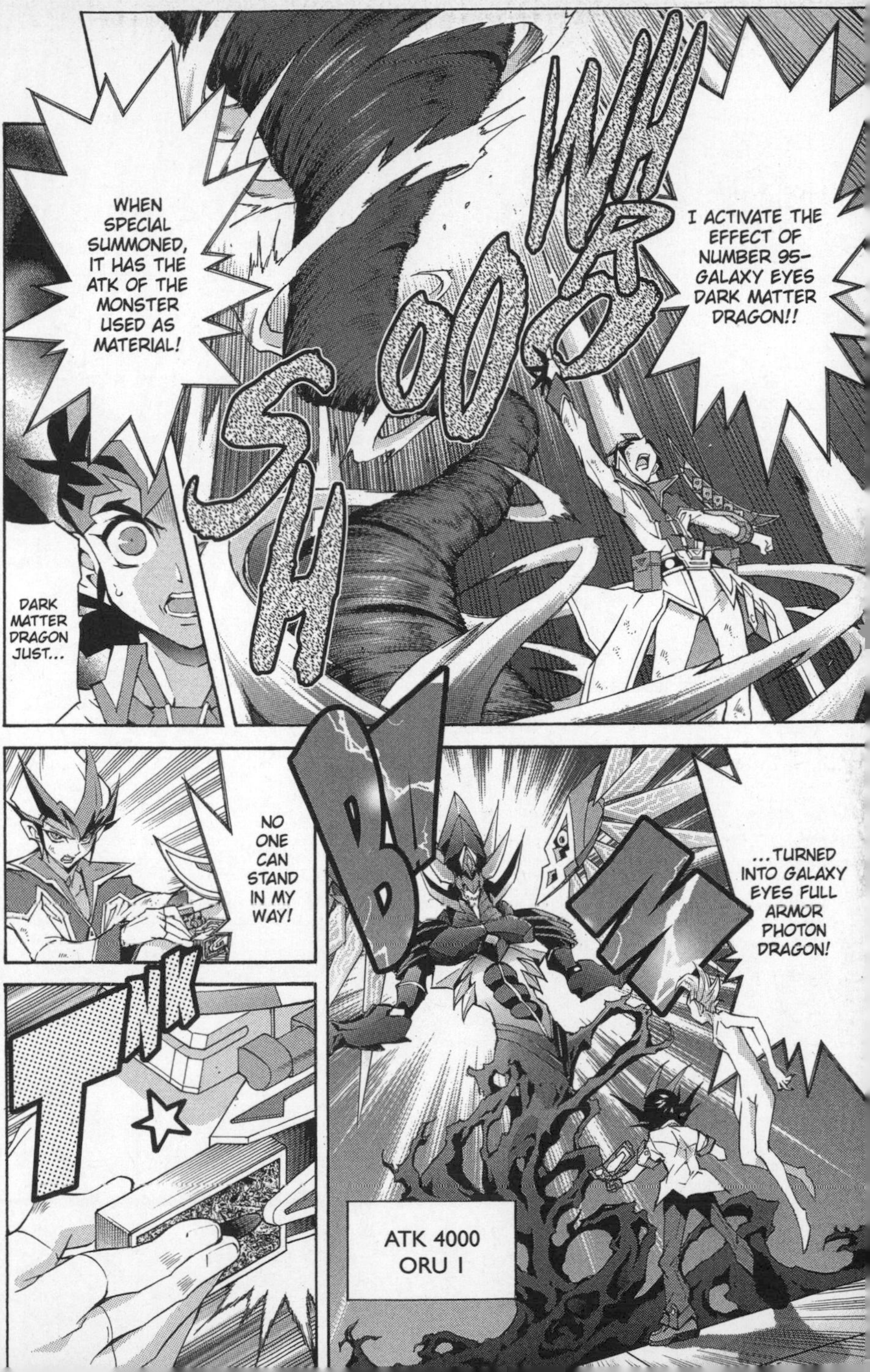
I ACTIVATE THE EFFECT OF NUMBER 95-GALAXY EYES DARK MATTER DRAGON!!
WHEN SPECIAL SUMMONED, IT HAS THE ATK OF THE MONSTER USED AS MATERIAL!
DARK MATTER DRAGON JUST...
...TURNED INTO GALAXY EYES FULL ARMOR PHOTON DRAGON!
ATK 4000
ORU 1
NO ONE CAN STAND IN MY WAY!
TINK

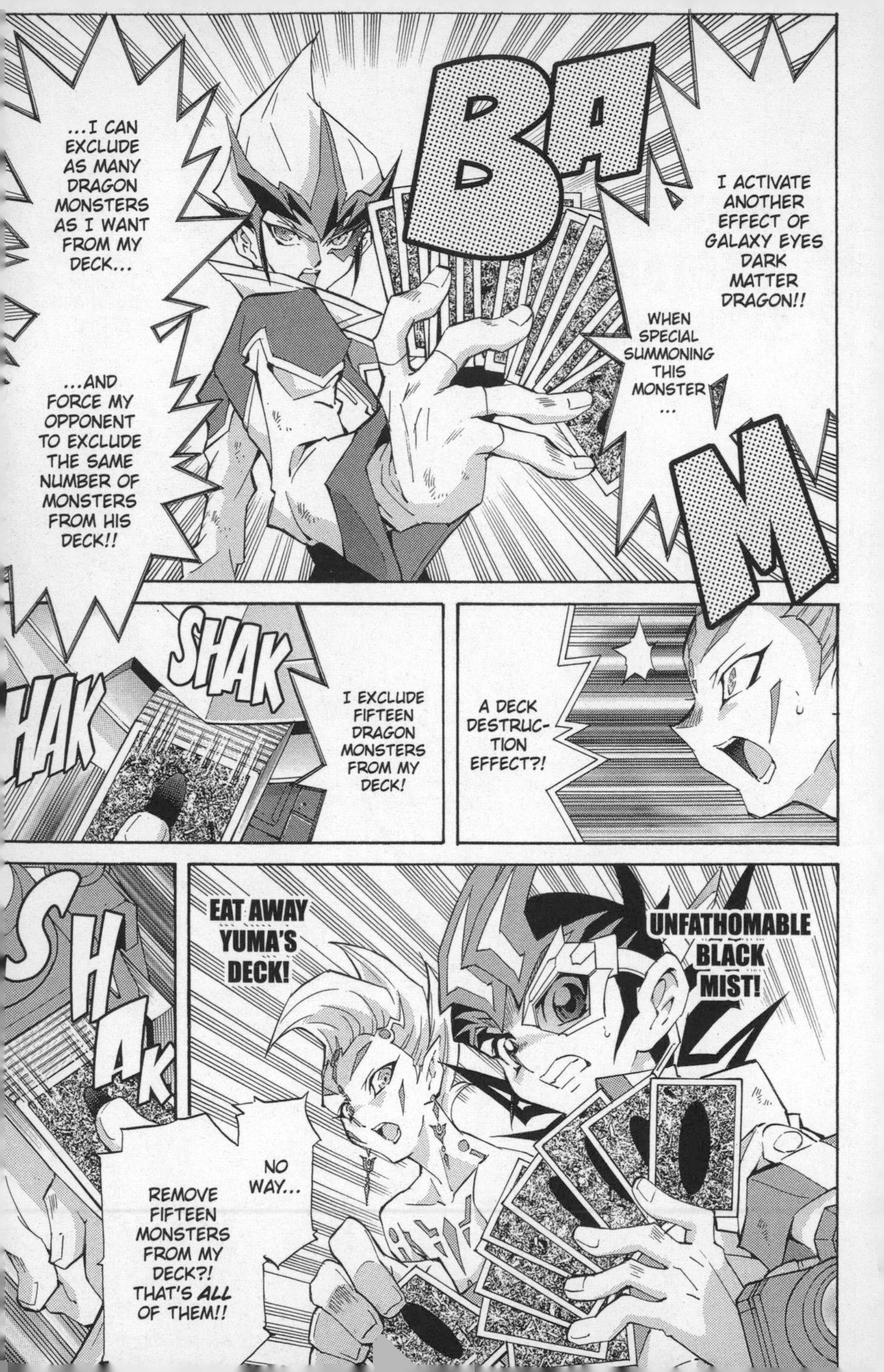
BAM
I ACTIVATE ANOTHER EFFECT OF GALAXY EYES DARK MATTER DRAGON!!
WHEN SPECIAL SUMMONING THIS MONSTER...
...I CAN EXCLUDE AS MANY DRAGON MONSTERS AS I WANT FROM MY DECK...
...AND FORCE MY OPPONENT TO EXCLUDE THE SAME NUMBER OF MONSTERS FROM HIS DECK!!
A DECK DESTRUCTION EFFECT?!
I EXCLUDE FIFTEEN DRAGON MONSTERS FROM MY DECK!
SHAK
HAK
UNFATHOMABLE BLACK MIST!
EAT AWAY YUMA'S DECK!
NO WAY...
REMOVE FIFTEEN MONSTERS FROM MY DECK?! THAT'S *ALL* OF THEM!!
SHAK

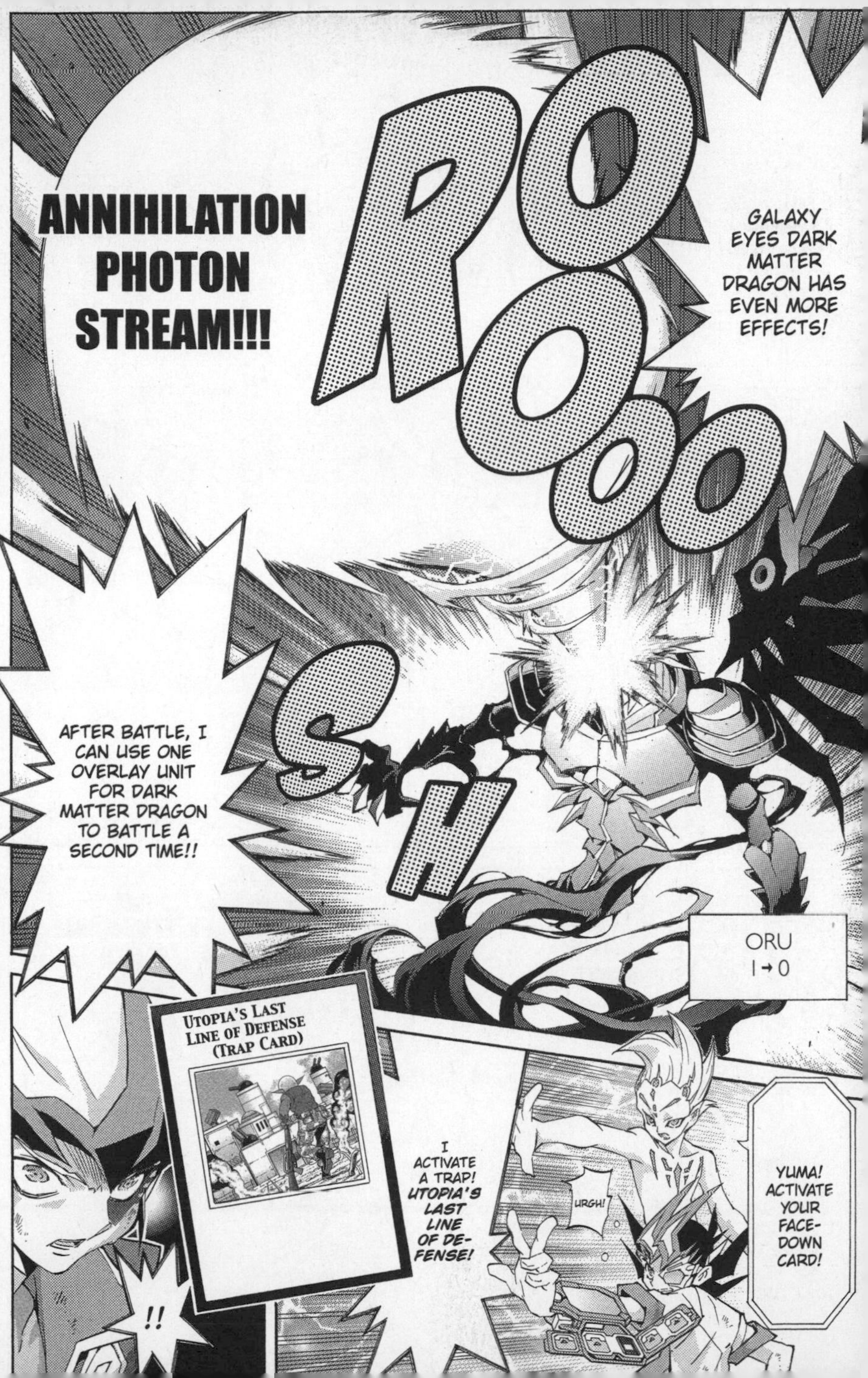
GALAXY EYES DARK MATTER DRAGON HAS EVEN MORE EFFECTS!
ROOOOO
ANNIHILATION PHOTON STREAM!!!
SH
AFTER BATTLE, I CAN USE ONE OVERLAY UNIT FOR DARK MATTER DRAGON TO BATTLE A SECOND TIME!!
ORU
1→0
YUMA! ACTIVATE YOUR FACE-DOWN CARD!
URGH!
I ACTIVATE A TRAP! UTOPIA'S LAST LINE OF DE-FENSE!
UTOPIA'S LAST LINE OF DEFENSE (TRAP CARD)
!!

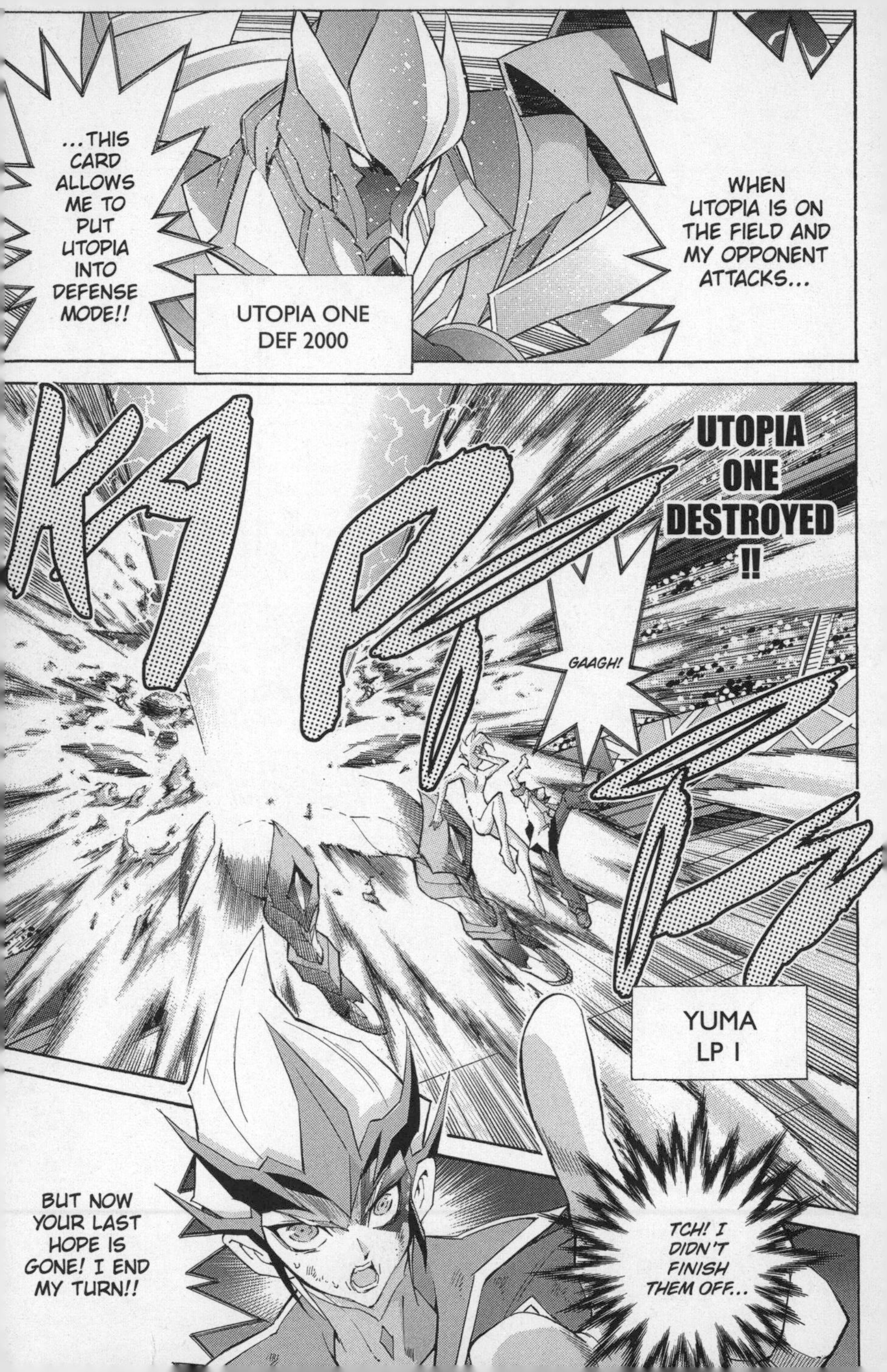
WHEN UTOPIA IS ON THE FIELD AND MY OPPONENT ATTACKS...
...THIS CARD ALLOWS ME TO PUT UTOPIA INTO DEFENSE MODE!!
UTOPIA ONE DEF 2000
UTOPIA ONE DESTROYED !!
KA
GAAGH!
YUMA LP 1
TCH! I DIDN'T FINISH THEM OFF...
BUT NOW YOUR LAST HOPE IS GONE! I END MY TURN!!

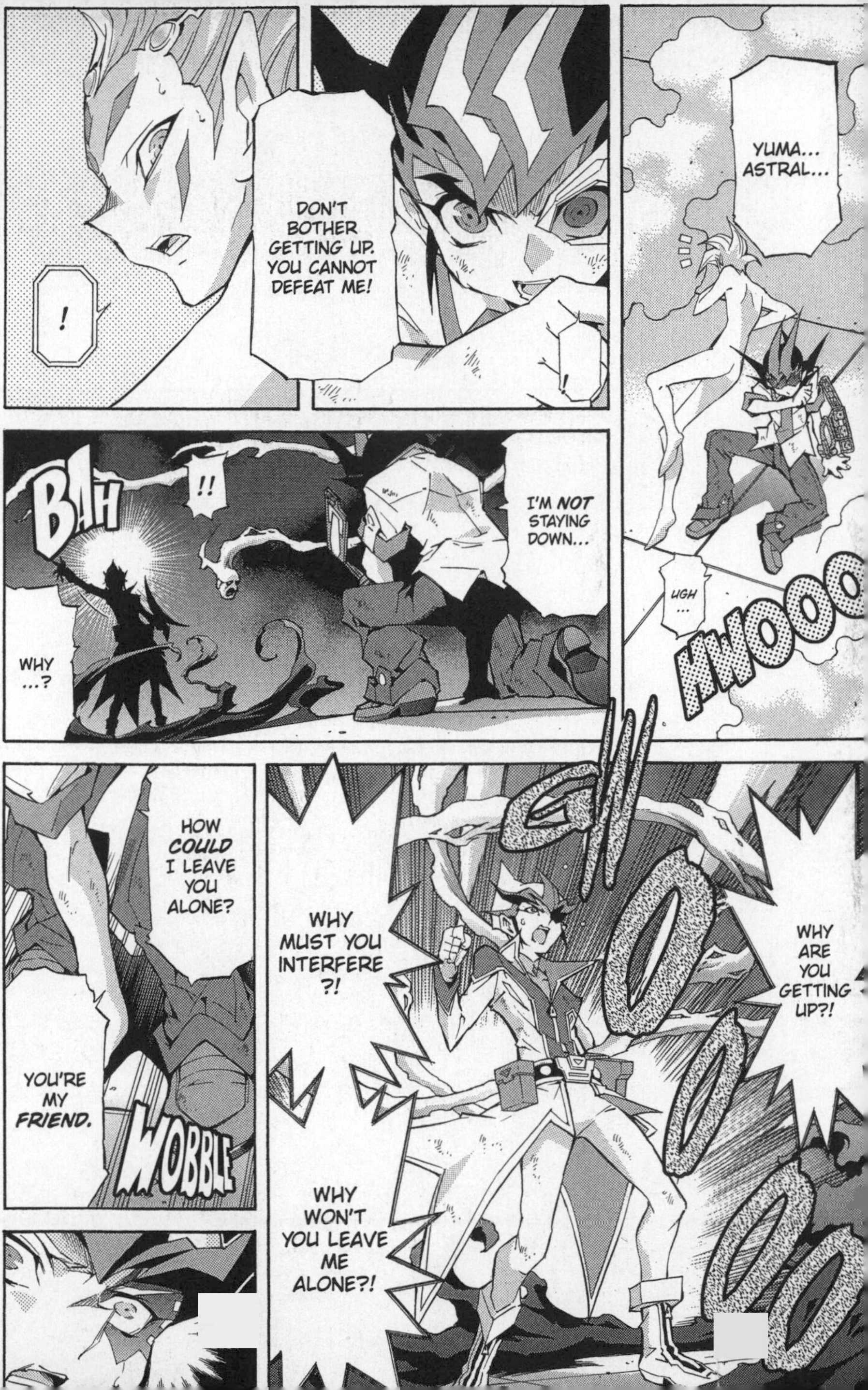
YUMA... ASTRAL...
UGH ...
HWOOOO
DON'T BOTHER GETTING UP. YOU CANNOT DEFEAT ME!
!
I'M NOT STAYING DOWN...
!!
BAH
WHY ...?
WHY ARE YOU GETTING UP?!
WHY MUST YOU INTERFERE ?!
GOOOOO
WHY WON'T YOU LEAVE ME ALONE?!
HOW COULD I LEAVE YOU ALONE?
YOU'RE MY FRIEND.
WOBBLE

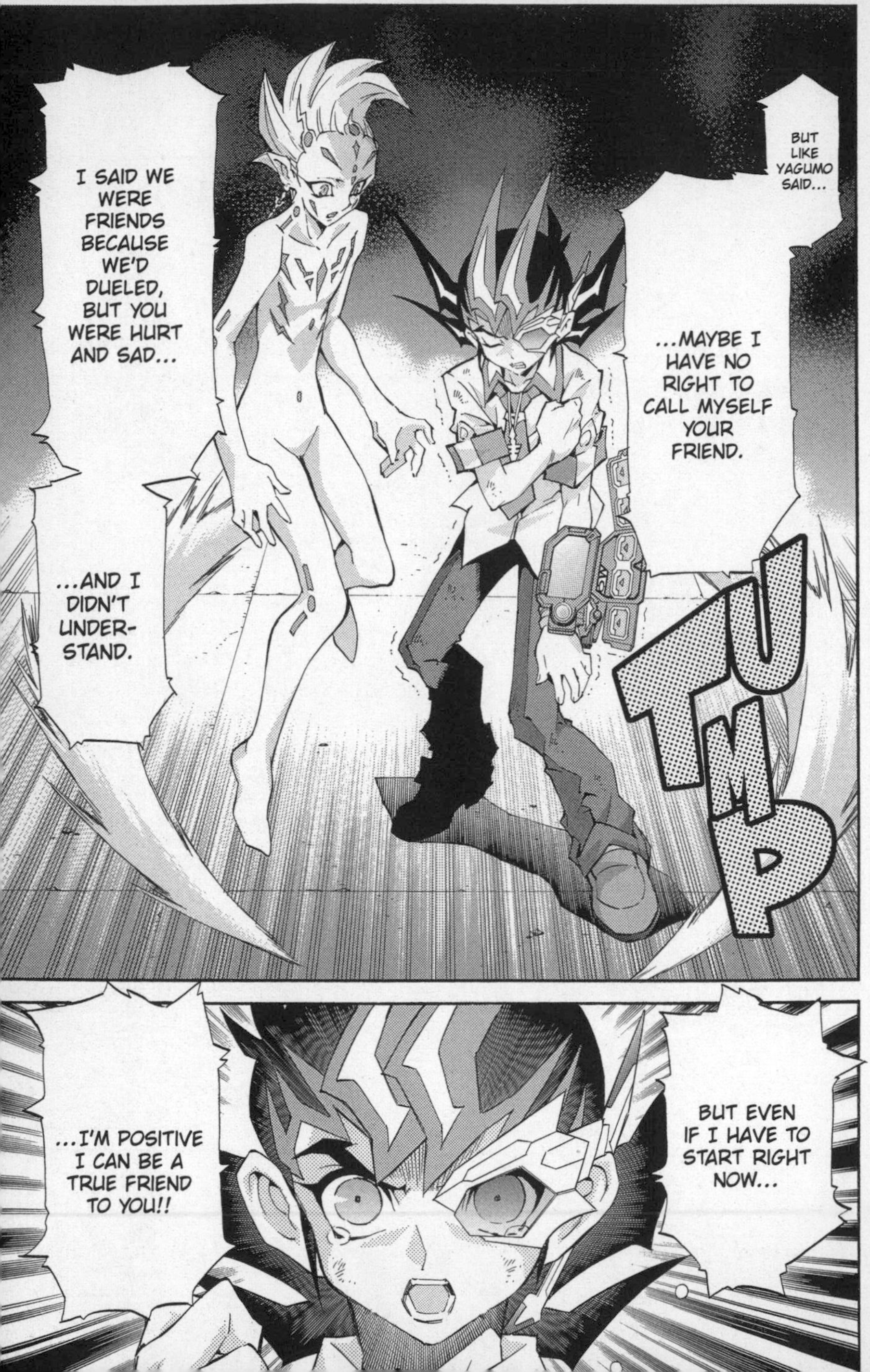
BUT LIKE YAGUMO SAID...
...MAYBE I HAVE NO RIGHT TO CALL MYSELF YOUR FRIEND.
I SAID WE WERE FRIENDS BECAUSE WE'D DUELED, BUT YOU WERE HURT AND SAD...
TUMP
...AND I DIDN'T UNDERSTAND.
BUT EVEN IF I HAVE TO START RIGHT NOW...
...I'M POSITIVE I CAN BE A TRUE FRIEND TO YOU!!

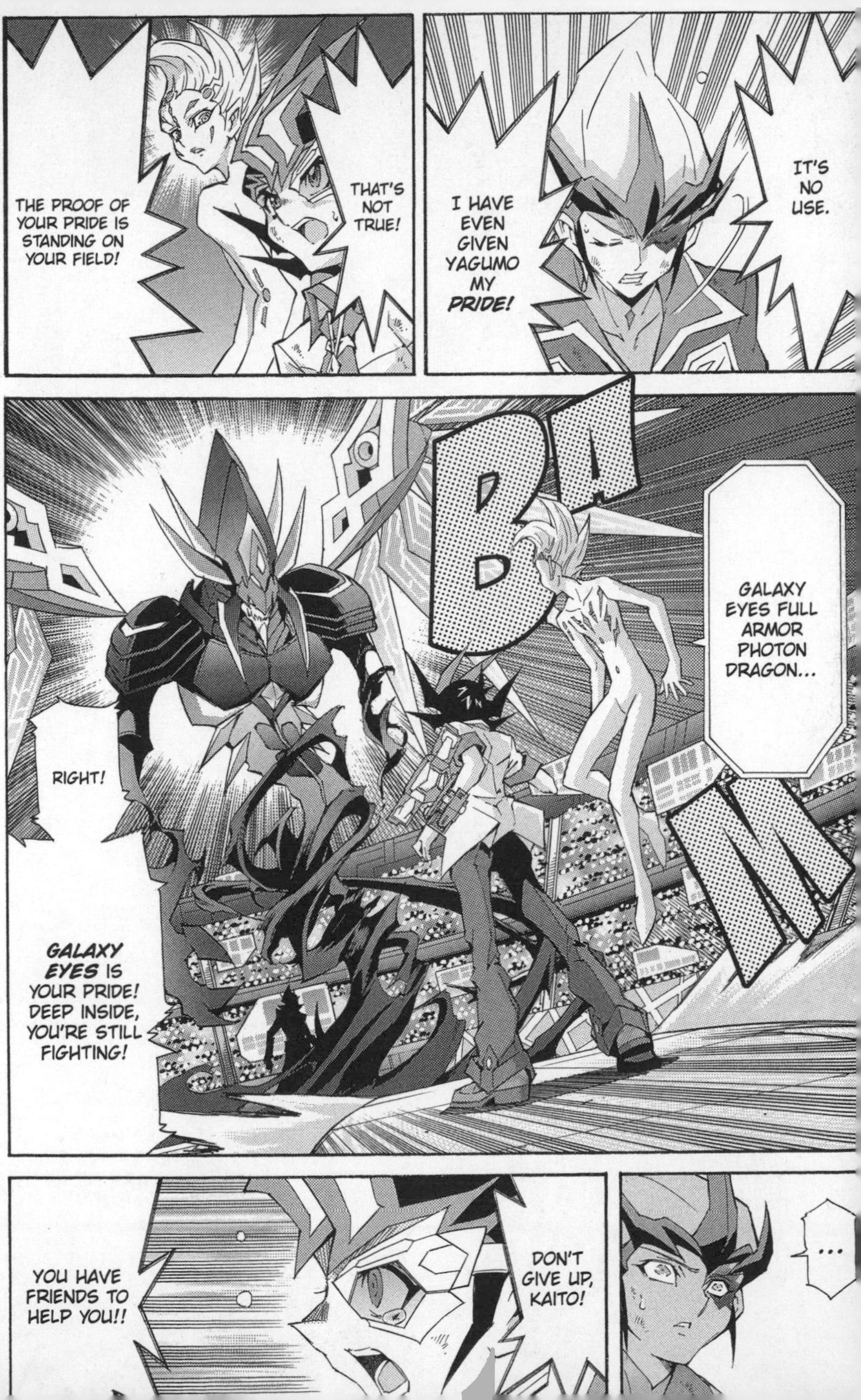
IT'S NO USE.
I HAVE EVEN GIVEN YAGUMO MY *PRIDE!*
THAT'S NOT TRUE!
THE PROOF OF YOUR PRIDE IS STANDING ON YOUR FIELD!
GALAXY EYES FULL ARMOR PHOTON DRAGON...
RIGHT!
GALAXY EYES IS YOUR PRIDE! DEEP INSIDE, YOU'RE STILL FIGHTING!
...
DON'T GIVE UP, KAITO!
YOU HAVE FRIENDS TO HELP YOU!!

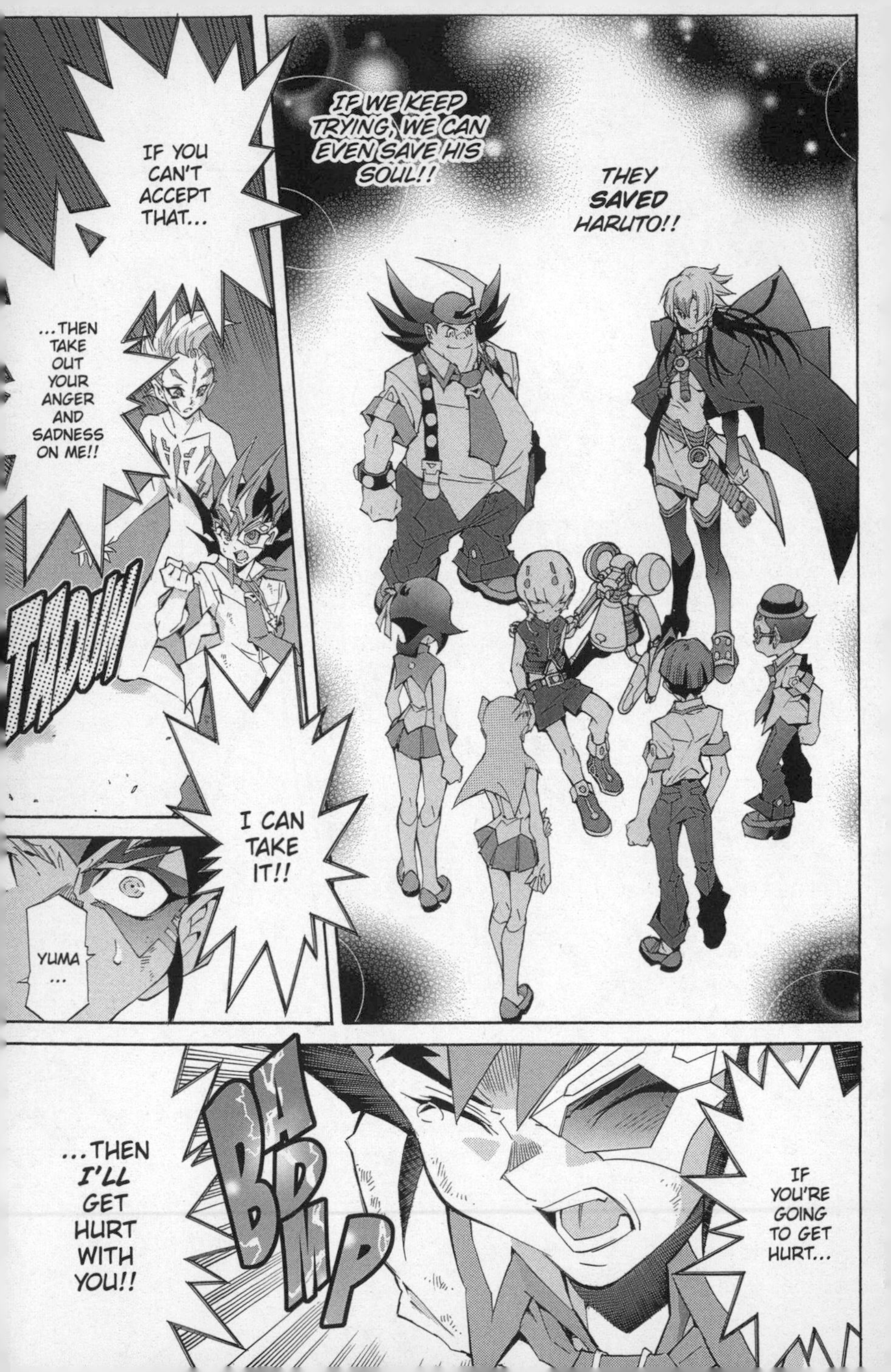
THEY SAVED HARUTO!!
IF WE KEEP TRYING, WE CAN EVEN SAVE HIS SOUL!!
IF YOU CAN'T ACCEPT THAT...
...THEN TAKE OUT YOUR ANGER AND SADNESS ON ME!!
THDUN
I CAN TAKE IT!!
YUMA...
IF YOU'RE GOING TO GET HURT...
BADMP
...THEN I'LL GET HURT WITH YOU!!

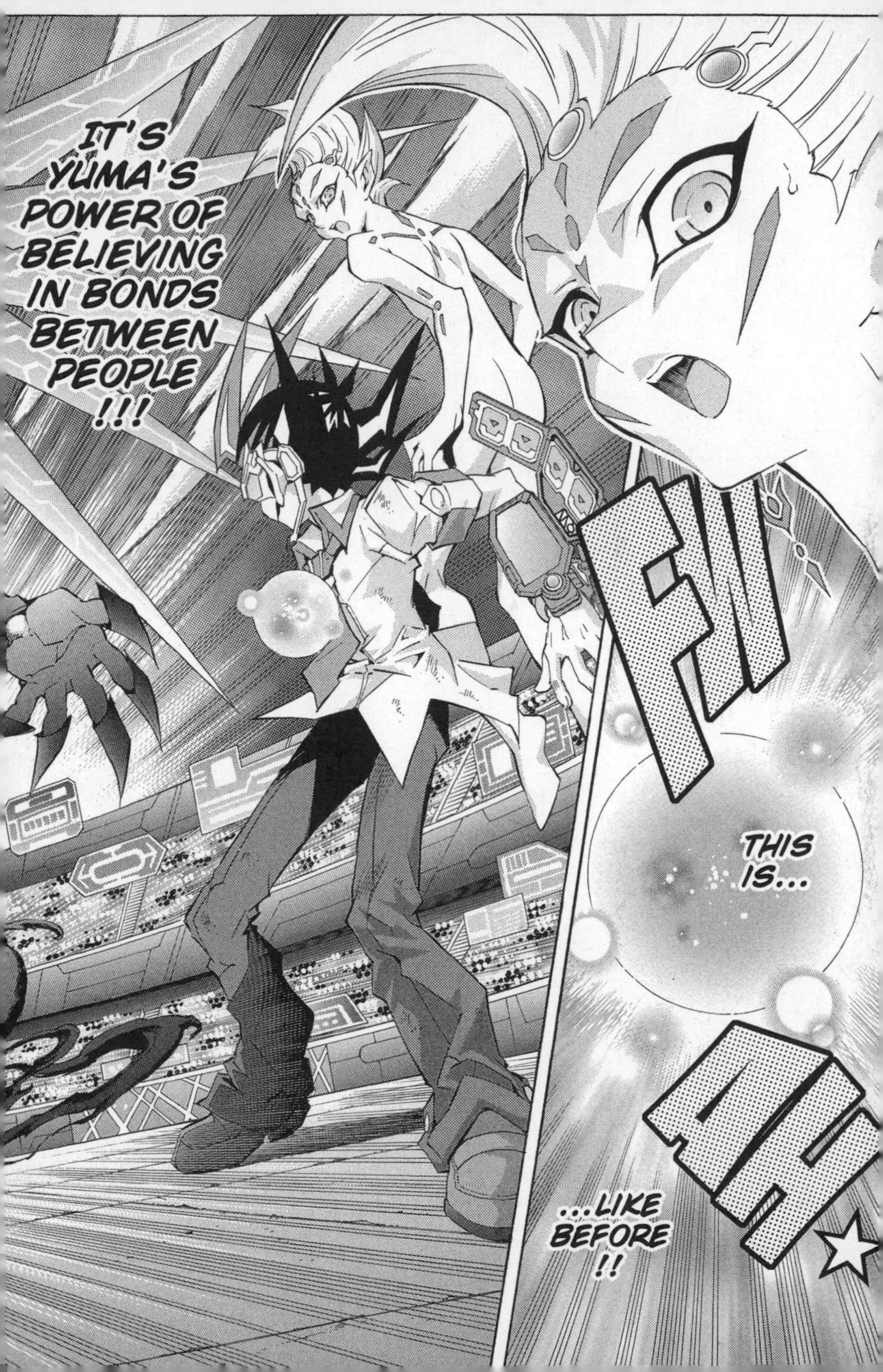
THIS IS...
...LIKE BEFORE !!
IT'S YUMA'S POWER OF BELIEVING IN BONDS BETWEEN PEOPLE !!!

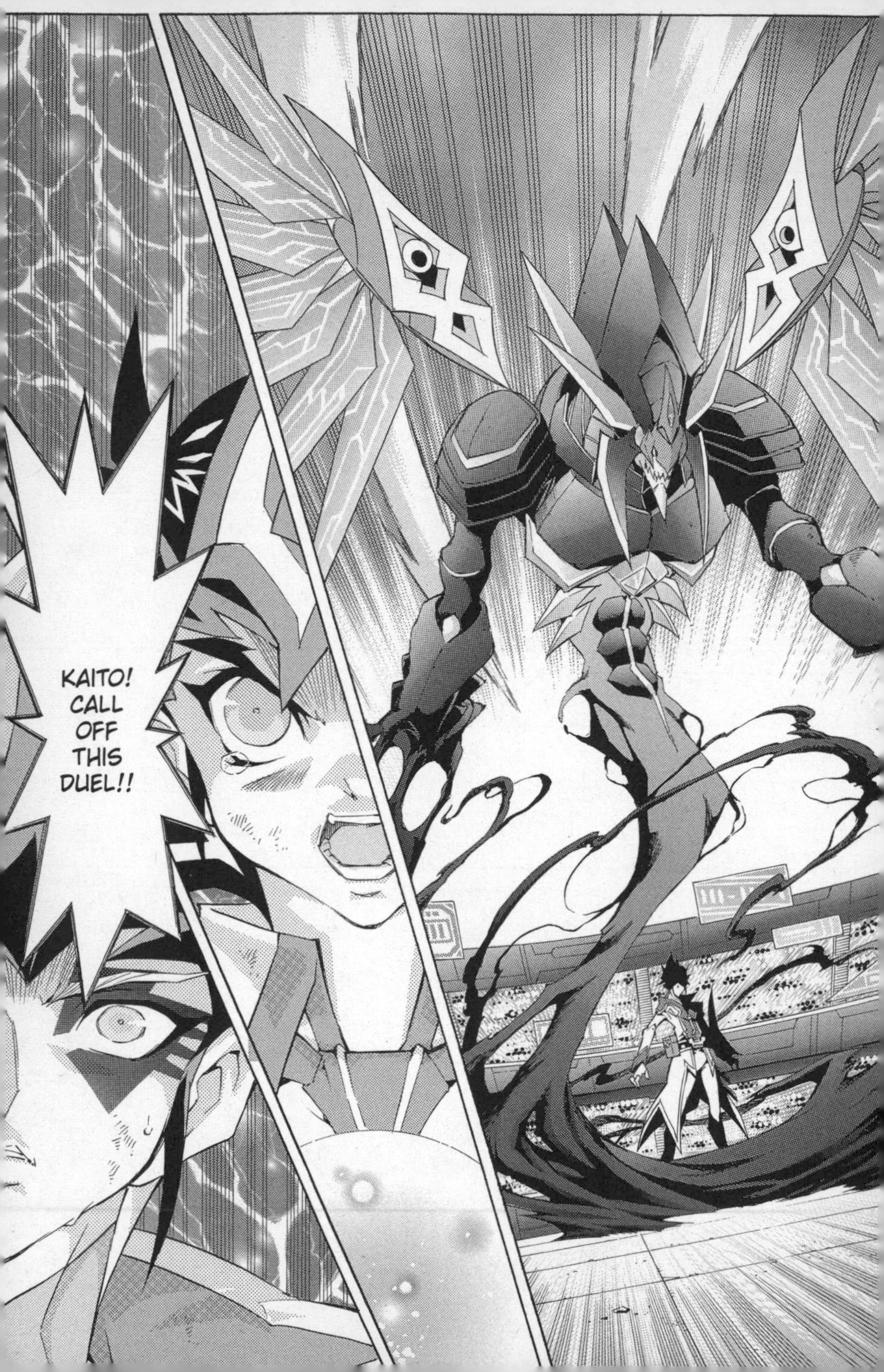
KAITO! CALL OFF THIS DUEL!!

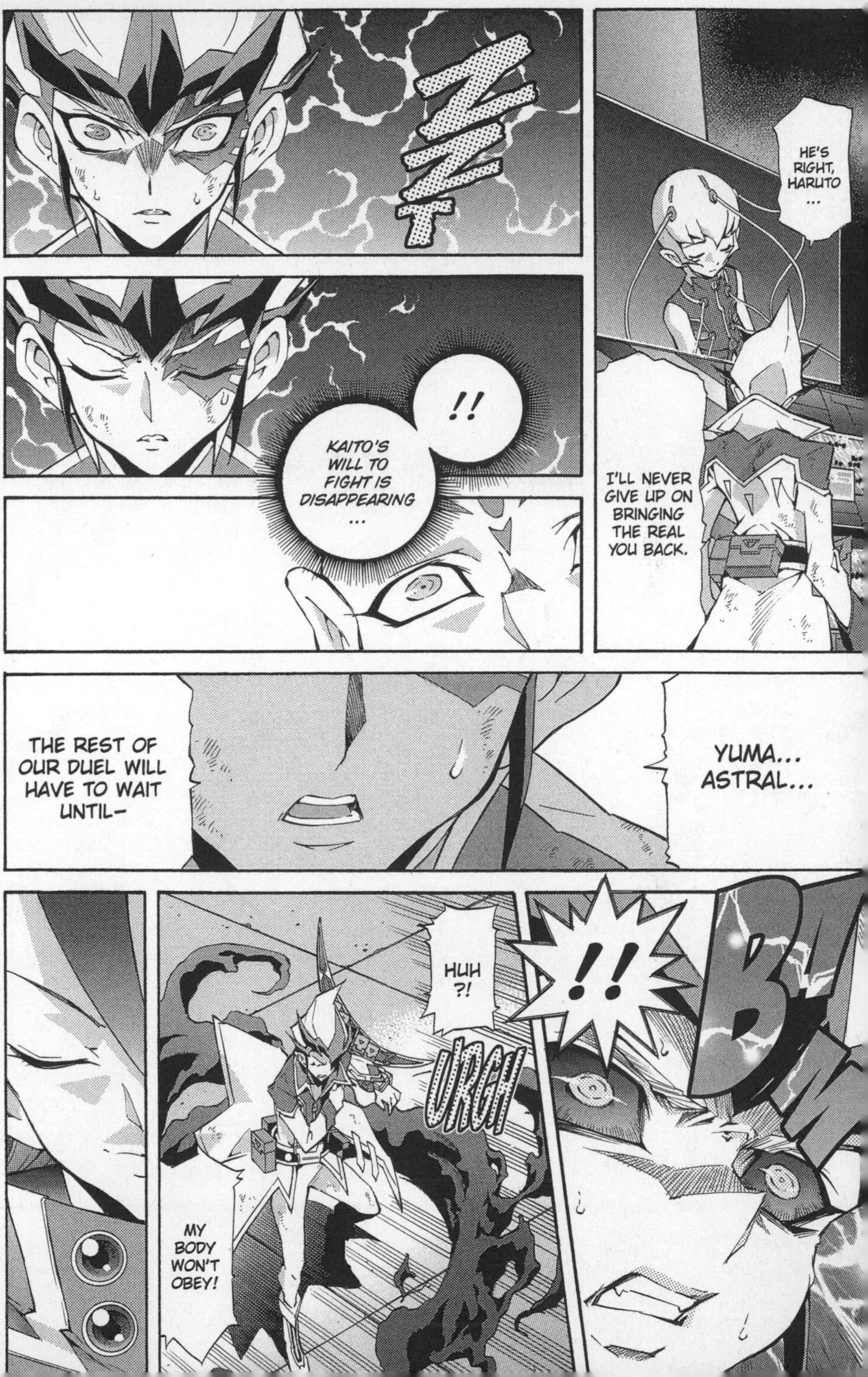
HE'S RIGHT, HARUTO ...
I'LL NEVER GIVE UP ON BRINGING THE REAL YOU BACK.
ZNNT
!!
KAITO'S WILL TO FIGHT IS DISAPPEARING ...
YUMA... ASTRAL...
THE REST OF OUR DUEL WILL HAVE TO WAIT UNTIL-
!!
HUH ?!
URGH
MY BODY WON'T OBEY!

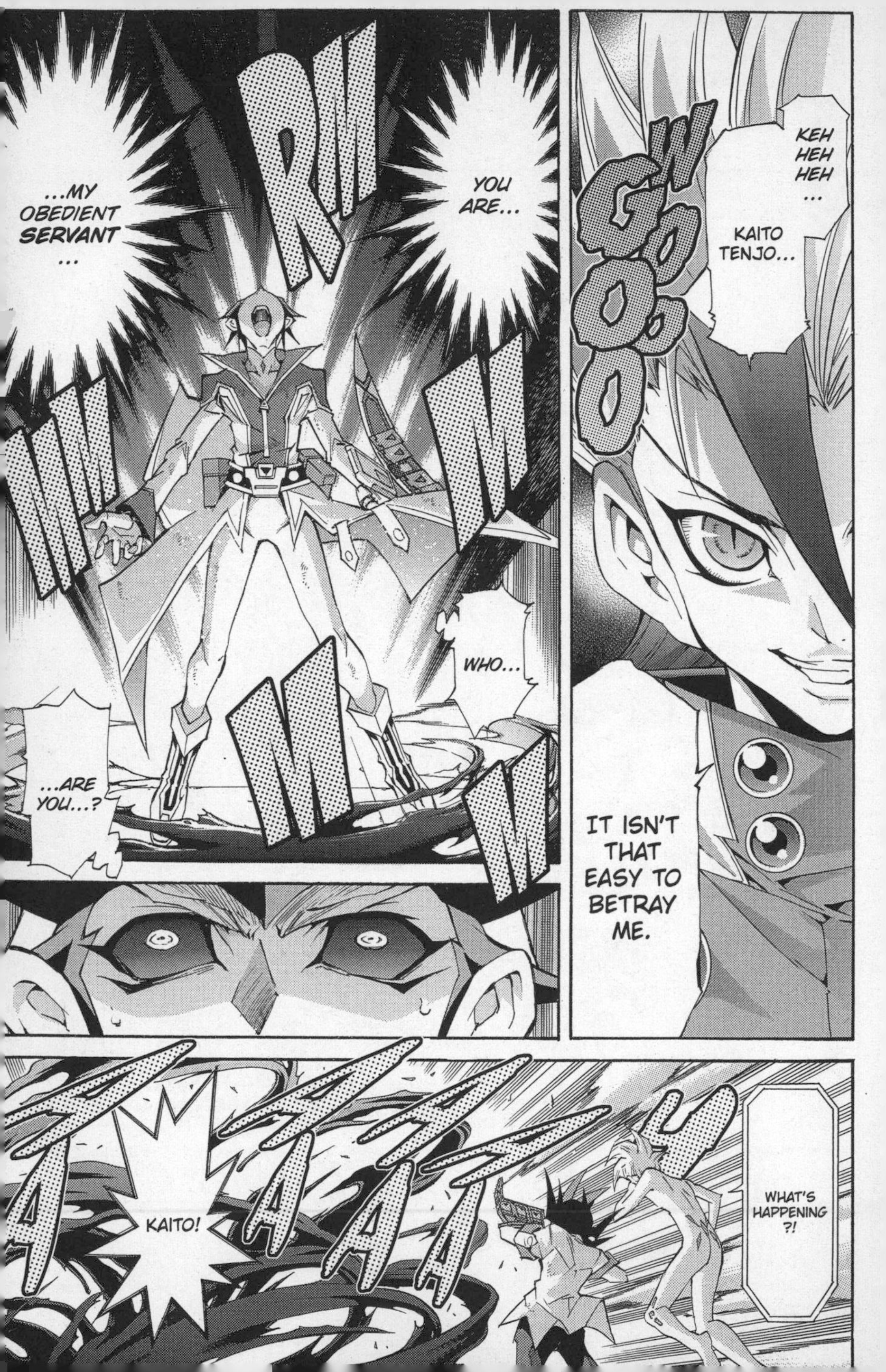
KEH HEH HEH...
KAITO TENJO...
GWOOOO
IT ISN'T THAT EASY TO BETRAY ME.
YOU ARE...
...MY OBEDIENT SERVANT...
WHO...
...ARE YOU...?
WHAT'S HAPPENING?!
KAITO!

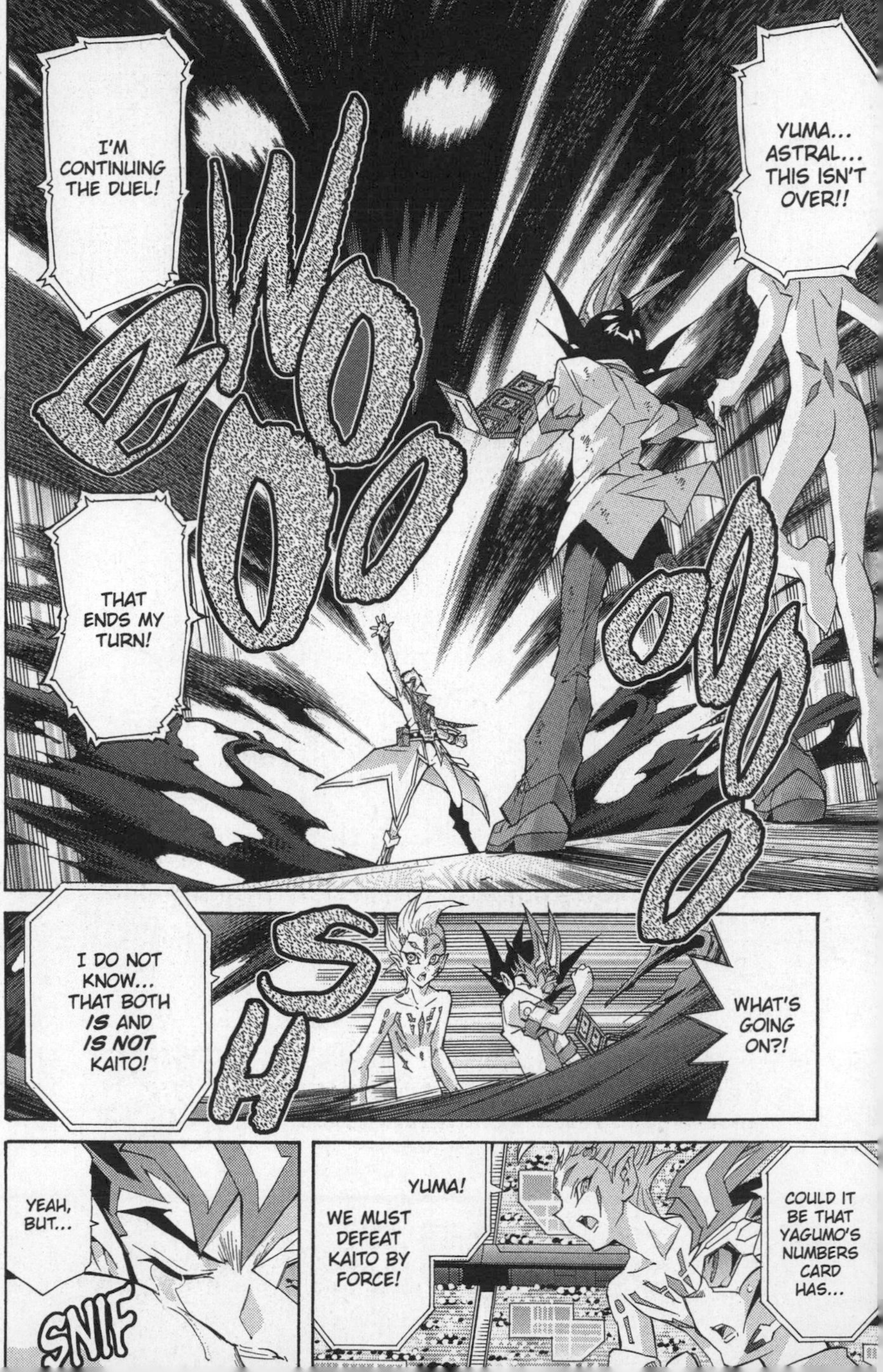
YUMA... ASTRAL... THIS ISN'T OVER!!
I'M CONTINUING THE DUEL!
THAT ENDS MY TURN!
WHAT'S GOING ON?!
I DO NOT KNOW... THAT BOTH *IS* AND *IS NOT* KAITO!
COULD IT BE THAT YAGUMO'S NUMBERS CARD HAS...
YUMA!
WE MUST DEFEAT KAITO BY FORCE!
YEAH, BUT...
SNIF

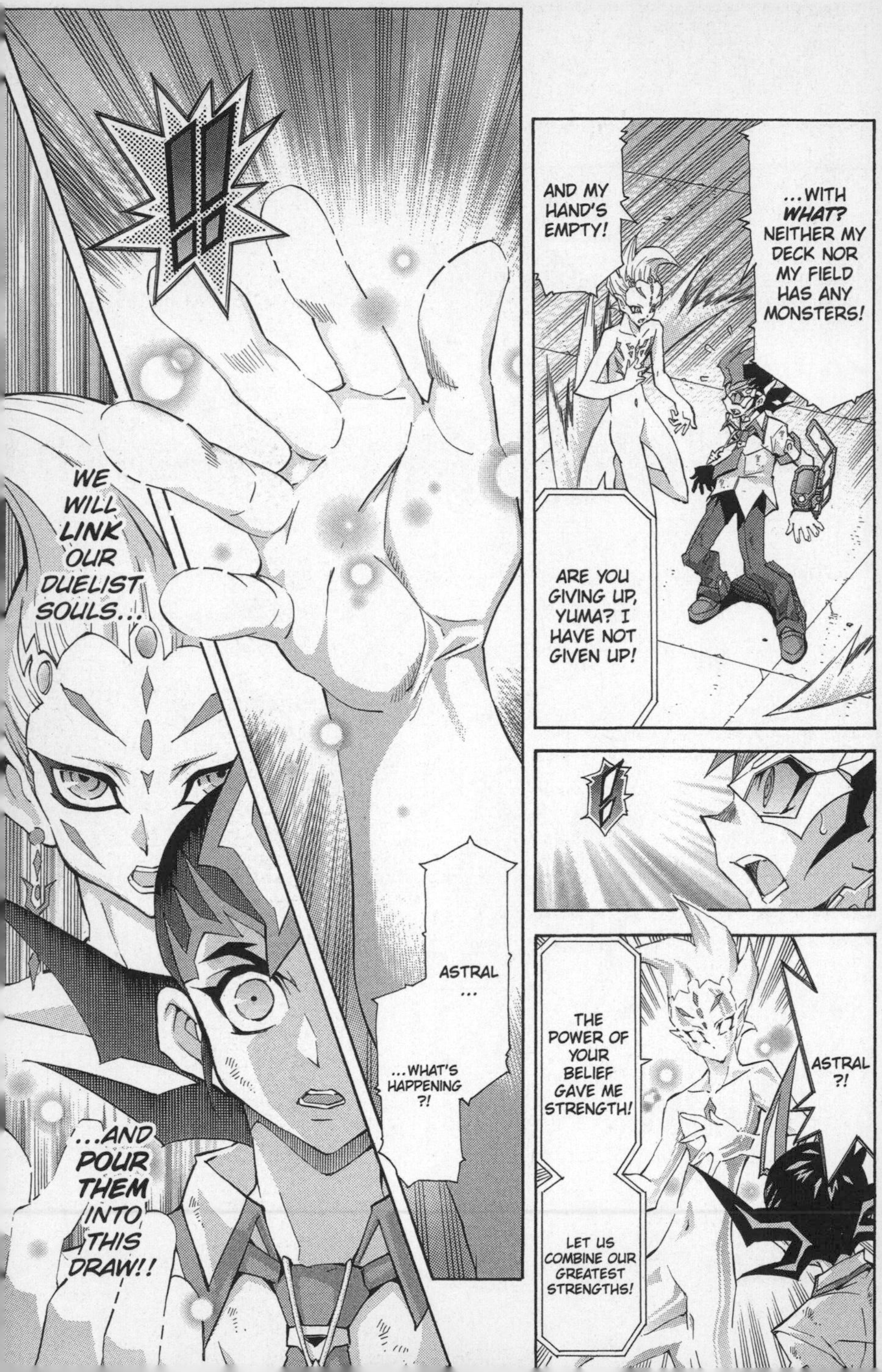
...WITH *WHAT?* NEITHER MY DECK NOR MY FIELD HAS ANY MONSTERS!
AND MY HAND'S EMPTY!
ARE YOU GIVING UP, YUMA? I HAVE NOT GIVEN UP!
!
ASTRAL ?!
THE POWER OF YOUR BELIEF GAVE ME STRENGTH!
LET US COMBINE OUR GREATEST STRENGTHS!
!!
WE WILL LINK OUR DUELIST SOULS...
ASTRAL ...
...WHAT'S HAPPENING ?!
...AND POUR THEM INTO THIS DRAW!!

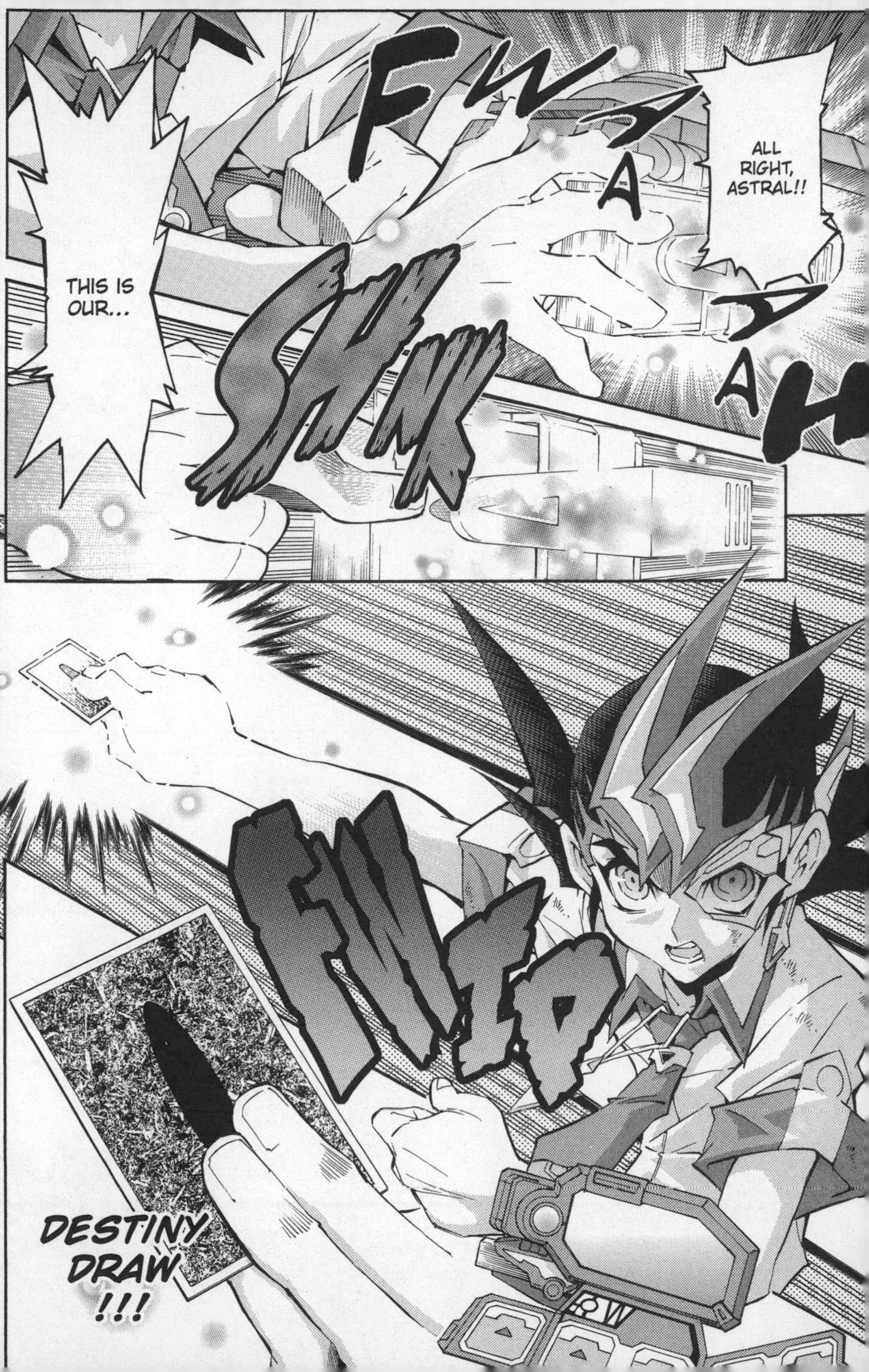
ALL RIGHT, ASTRAL!!
FWAAAAH
SHINK
THIS IS OUR...
FWIP
DESTINY DRAW!!!

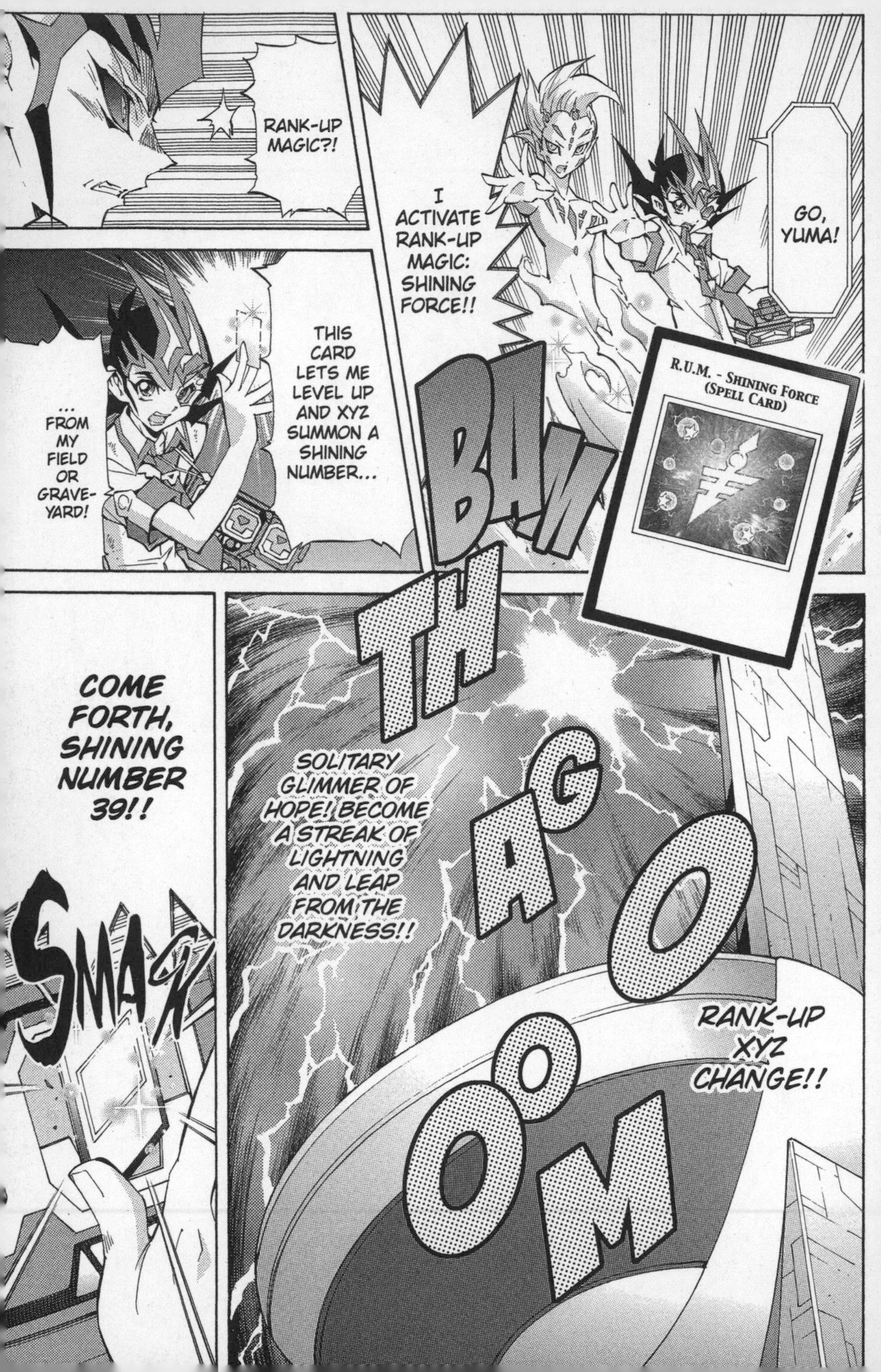
GO, YUMA!
I ACTIVATE RANK-UP MAGIC: SHINING FORCE!!
BAM
R.U.M. - SHINING FORCE (SPELL CARD)
RANK-UP MAGIC?!
THIS CARD LETS ME LEVEL UP AND XYZ SUMMON A SHINING NUMBER...
...FROM MY FIELD OR GRAVEYARD!
THAGOOOM
RANK-UP XYZ CHANGE!!
SOLITARY GLIMMER OF HOPE! BECOME A STREAK OF LIGHTNING AND LEAP FROM THE DARKNESS!!
COME FORTH, SHINING NUMBER 39!!
SMACK

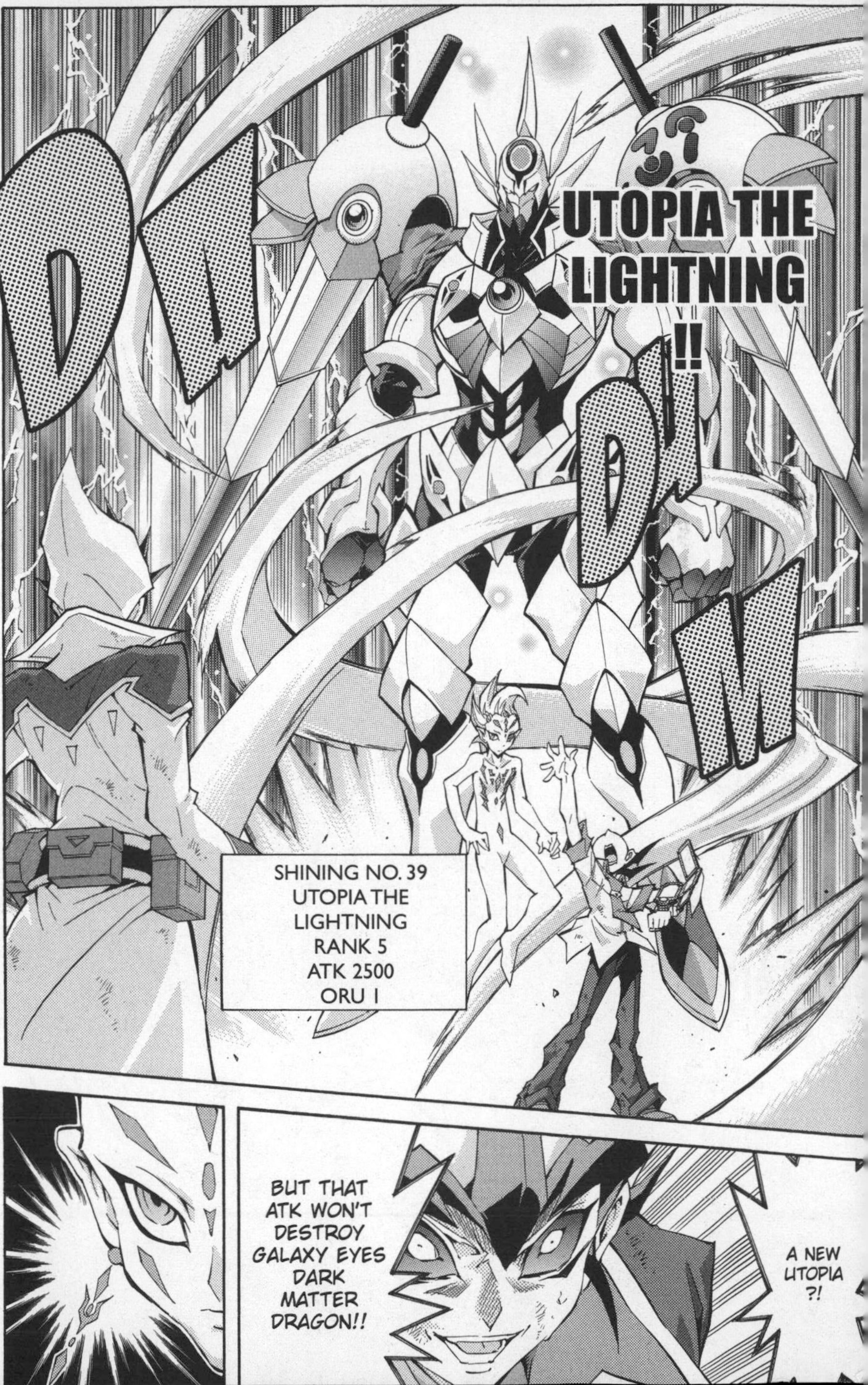
UTOPIA THE LIGHTNING!!
SHINING NO. 39
UTOPIA THE
LIGHTNING
RANK 5
ATK 2500
ORU 1
A NEW UTOPIA ?!
BUT THAT ATK WON'T DESTROY GALAXY EYES DARK MATTER DRAGON!!

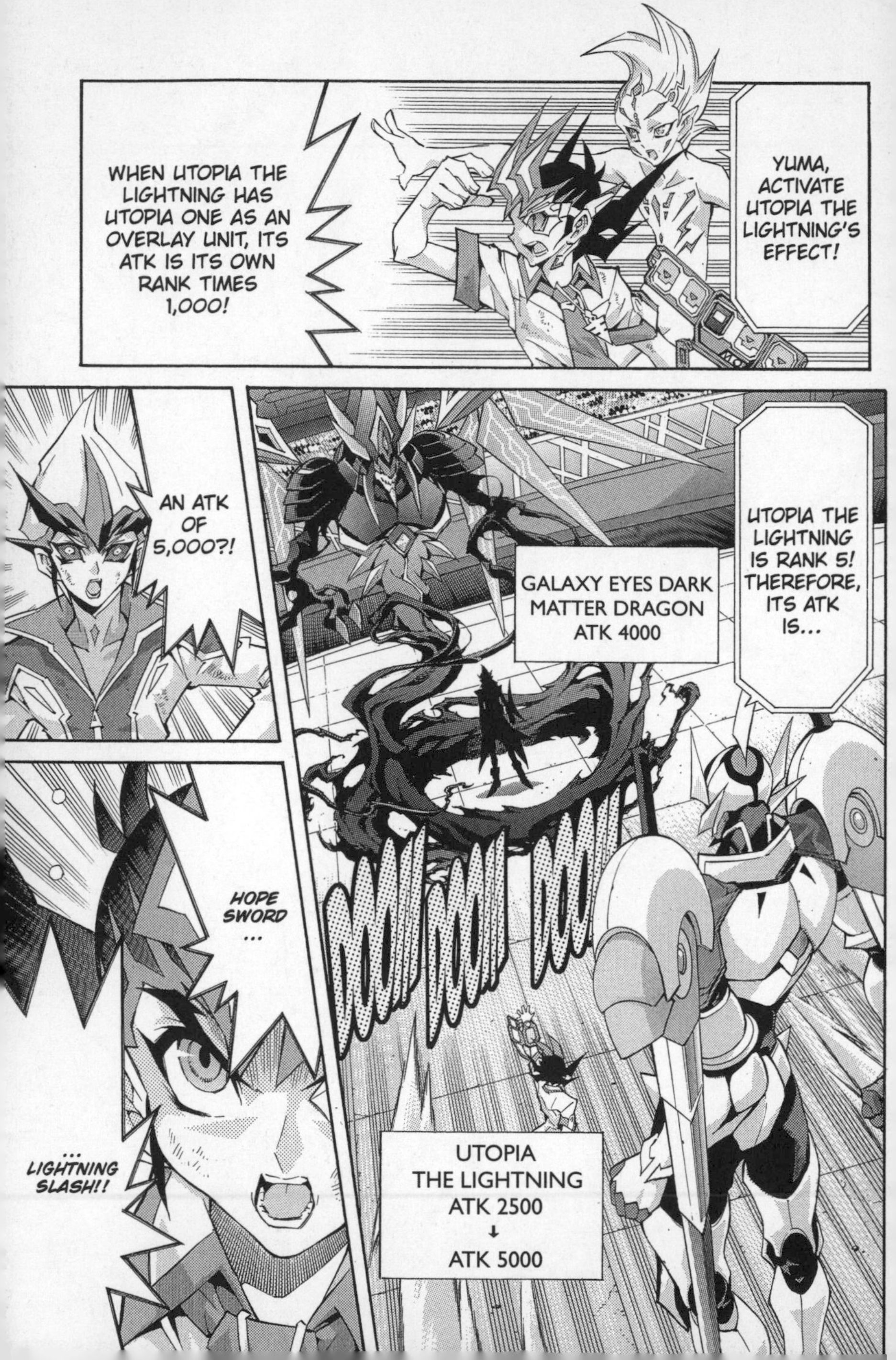
YUMA, ACTIVATE UTOPIA THE LIGHTNING'S EFFECT!
WHEN UTOPIA THE LIGHTNING HAS UTOPIA ONE AS AN OVERLAY UNIT, ITS ATK IS ITS OWN RANK TIMES 1,000!
UTOPIA THE LIGHTNING IS RANK 5! THEREFORE, ITS ATK IS...
GALAXY EYES DARK MATTER DRAGON ATK 4000
UTOPIA THE LIGHTNING ATK 2500 ↓ ATK 5000
AN ATK OF 5,000?!
HOPE SWORD ...
... LIGHTNING SLASH!!

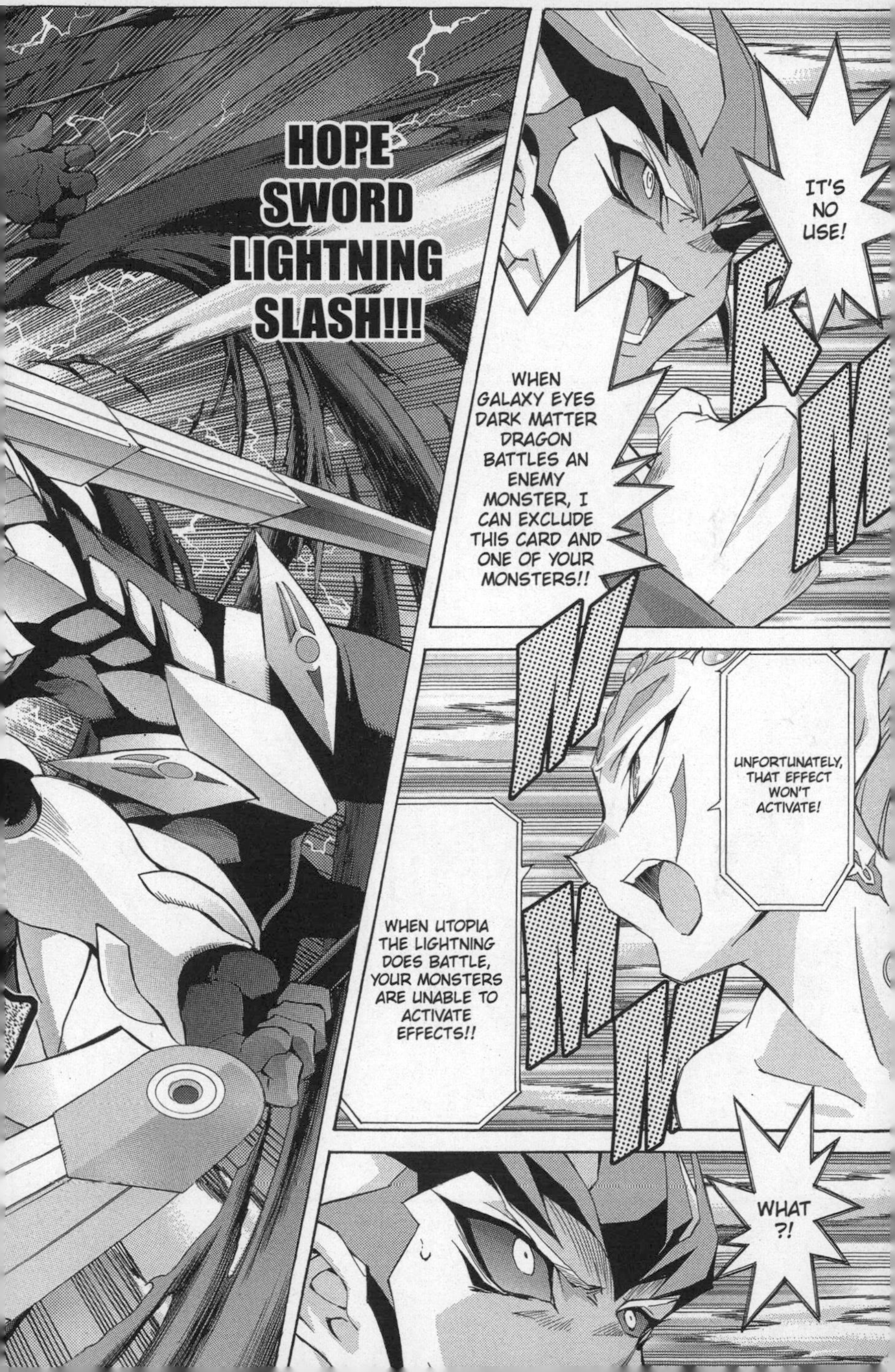

IT'S NO USE!
WHEN GALAXY EYES DARK MATTER DRAGON BATTLES AN ENEMY MONSTER, I CAN EXCLUDE THIS CARD AND ONE OF YOUR MONSTERS!!
UNFORTUNATELY, THAT EFFECT WON'T ACTIVATE!
WHEN UTOPIA THE LIGHTNING DOES BATTLE, YOUR MONSTERS ARE UNABLE TO ACTIVATE EFFECTS!!
WHAT?!
HOPE SWORD LIGHTNING SLASH!!!

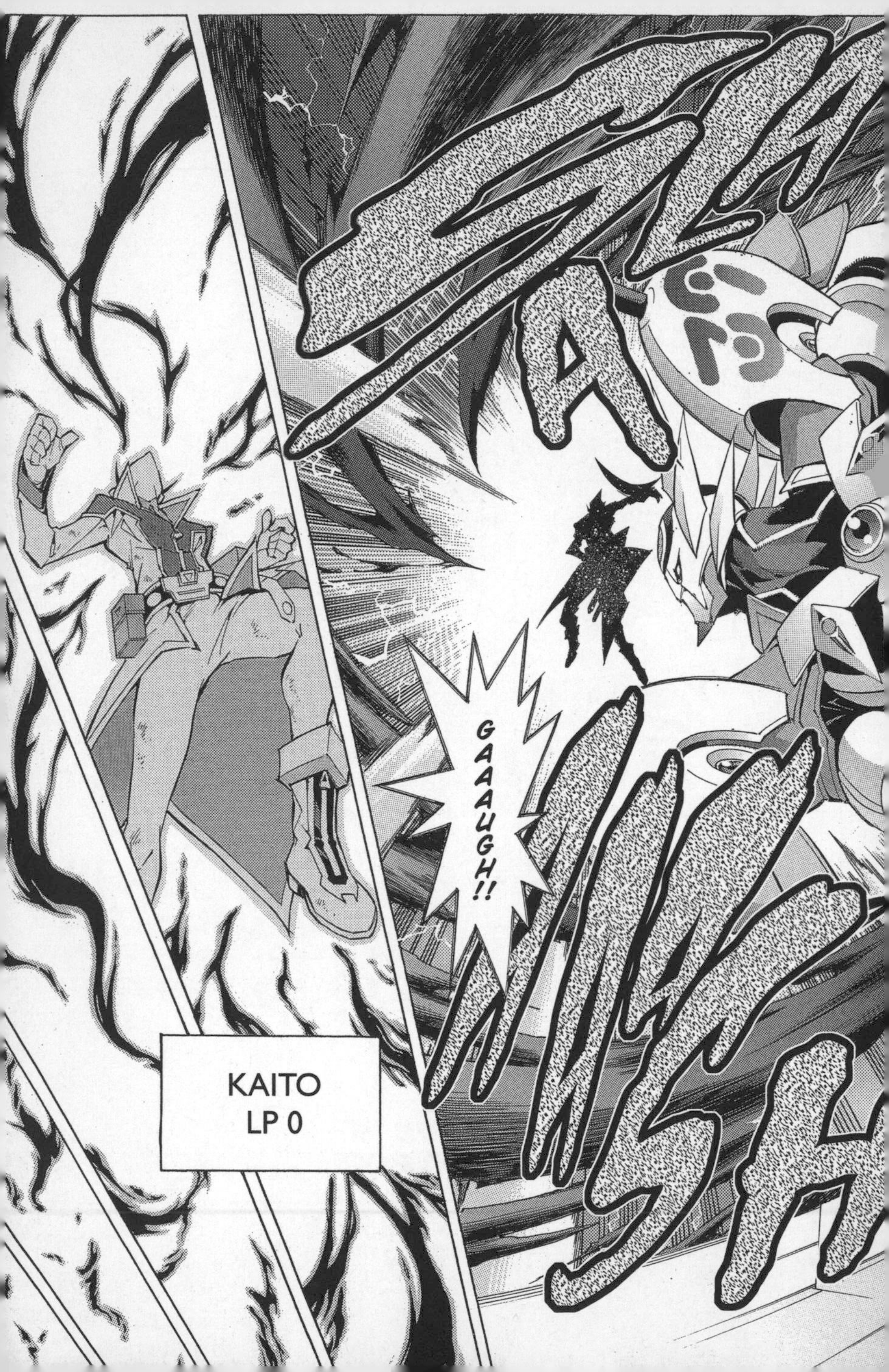
GAAAUGH!!
KAITO
LP 0

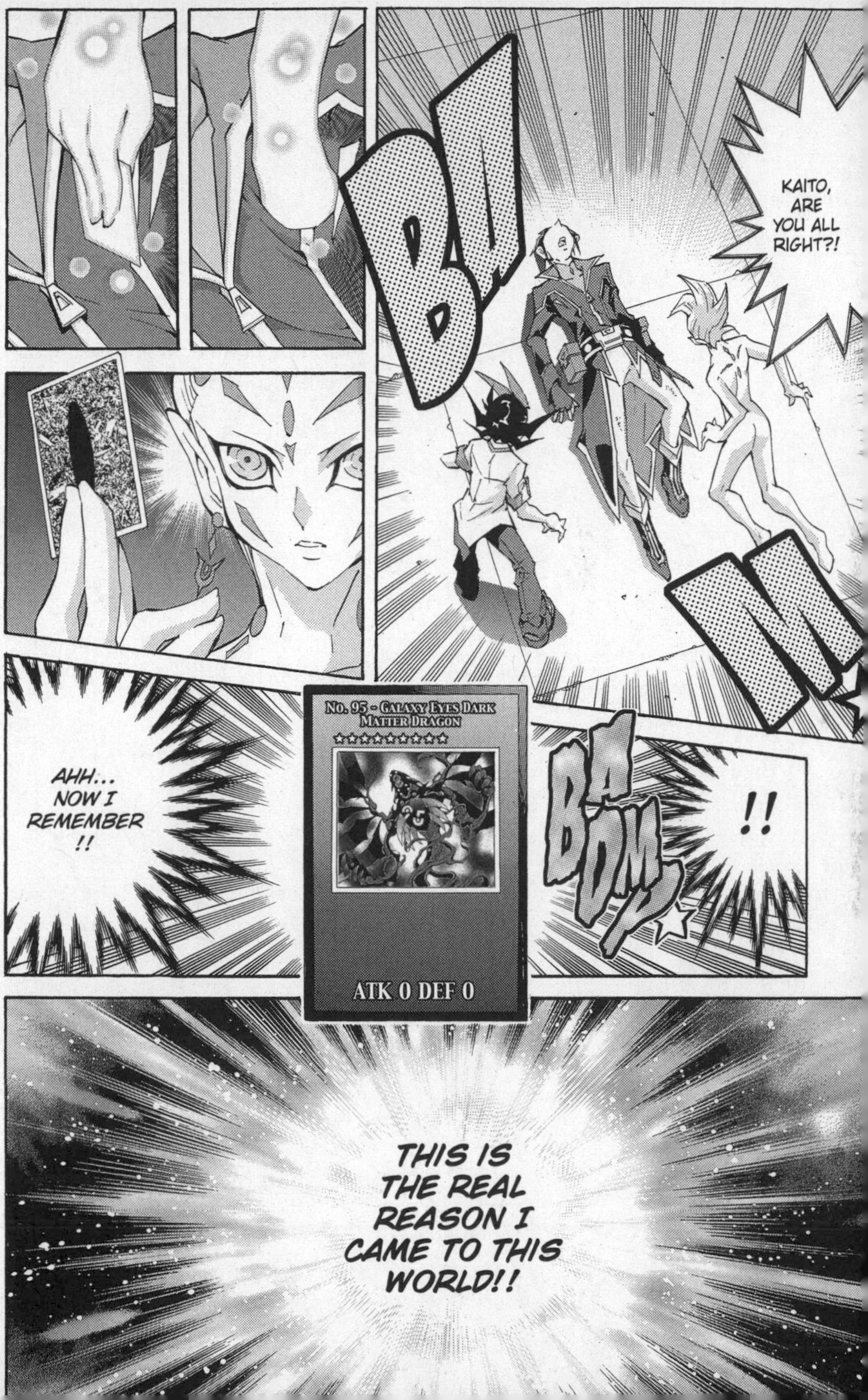

KAITO, ARE YOU ALL RIGHT?!
!!
No. 95 - Galaxy Eyes Dark Matter Dragon
ATK 0 DEF 0
AHH... NOW I REMEMBER !!
THIS IS THE REAL REASON I CAME TO THIS WORLD!!

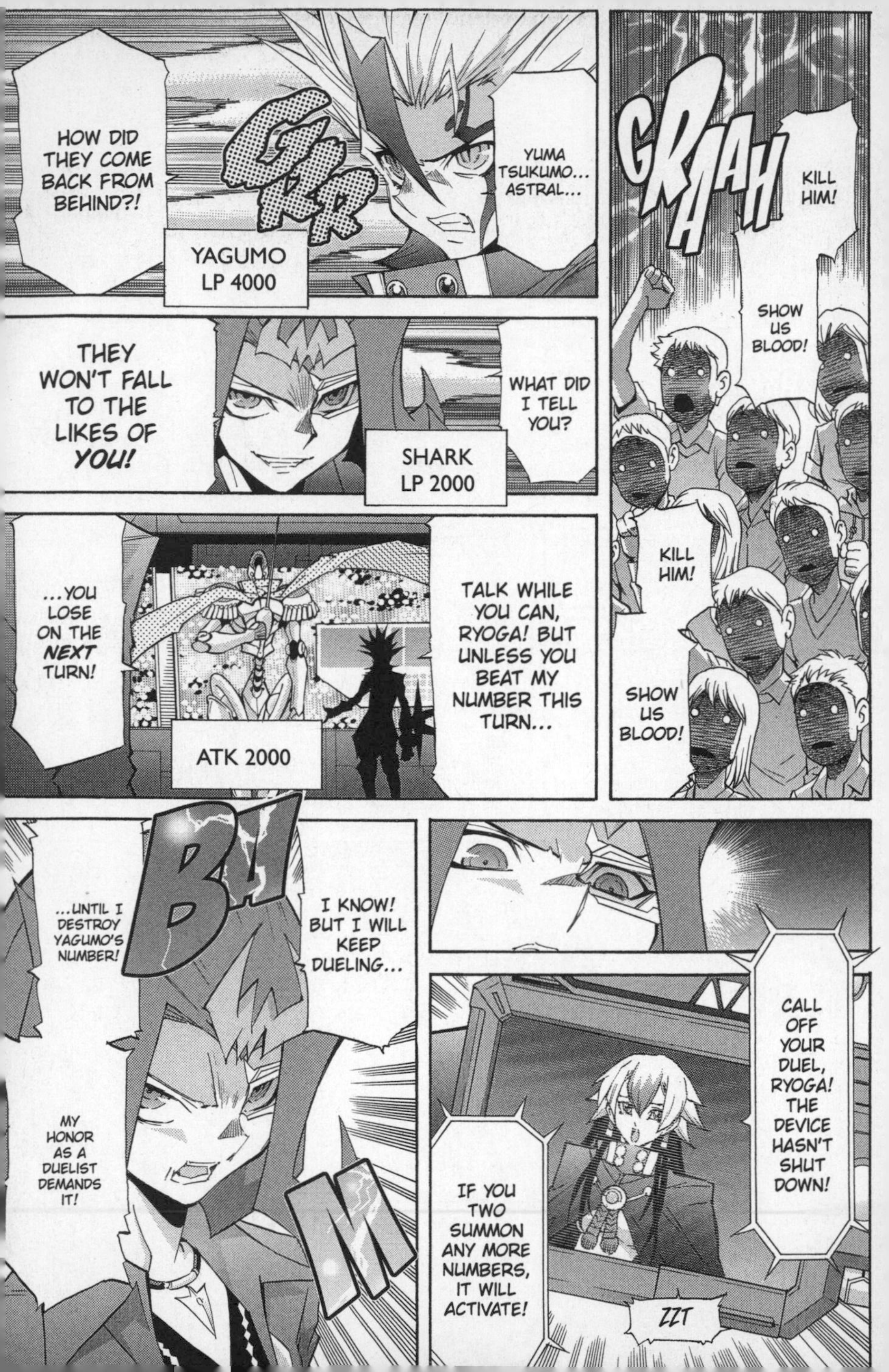
GRAAAH
KILL HIM!
SHOW US BLOOD!
KILL HIM!
SHOW US BLOOD!
YUMA TSUKUMO... ASTRAL...
GRRR
HOW DID THEY COME BACK FROM BEHIND?!
YAGUMO LP 4000
WHAT DID I TELL YOU?
SHARK LP 2000
THEY WON'T FALL TO THE LIKES OF YOU!
TALK WHILE YOU CAN, RYOGA! BUT UNLESS YOU BEAT MY NUMBER THIS TURN...
ATK 2000
...YOU LOSE ON THE NEXT TURN!
CALL OFF YOUR DUEL, RYOGA! THE DEVICE HASN'T SHUT DOWN!
IF YOU TWO SUMMON ANY MORE NUMBERS, IT WILL ACTIVATE!
ZZT
BUMM
I KNOW! BUT I WILL KEEP DUELING...
...UNTIL I DESTROY YAGUMO'S NUMBER!
MY HONOR AS A DUELIST DEMANDS IT!

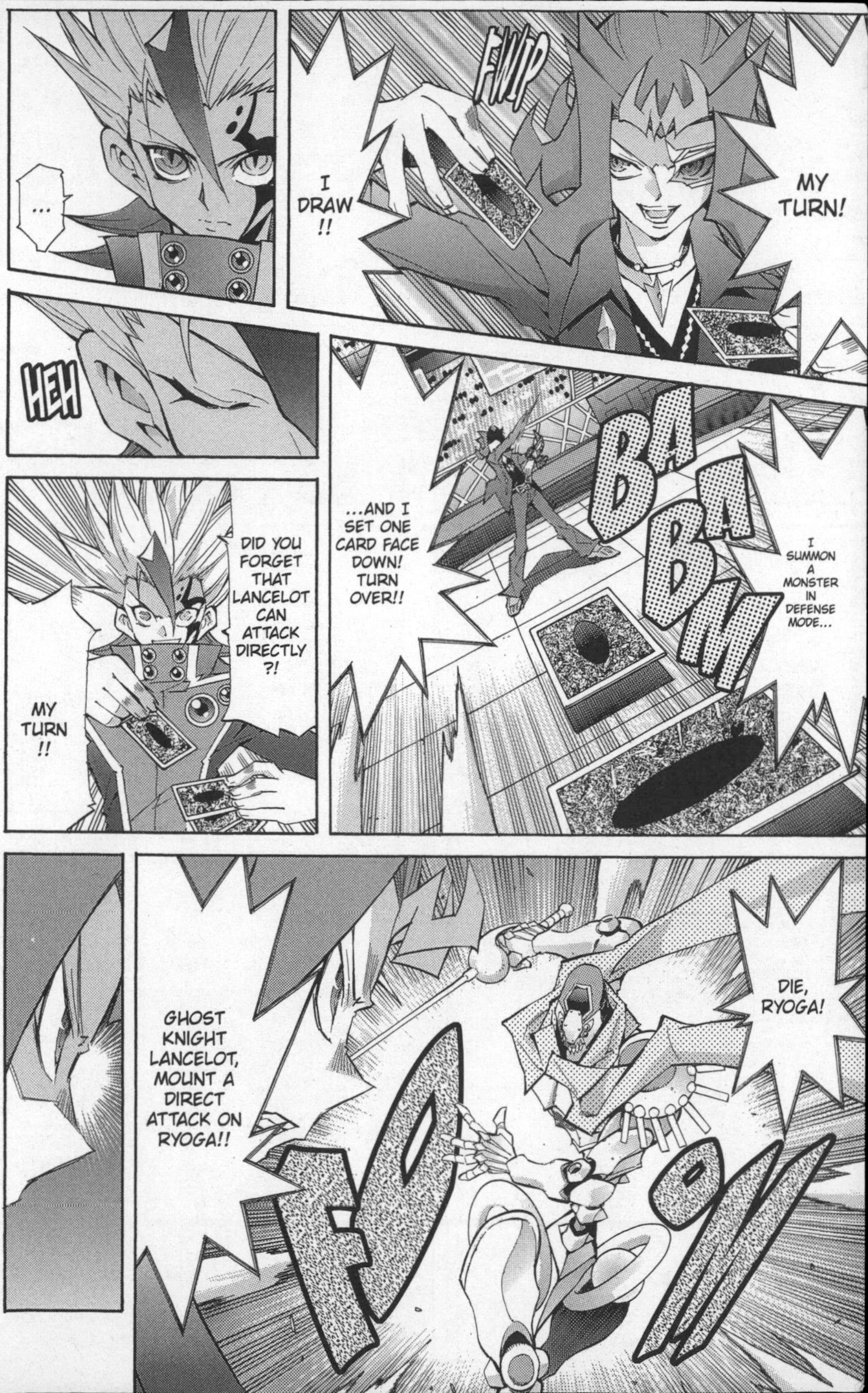
FWIP
MY TURN!
I DRAW!!
...
I SUMMON A MONSTER IN DEFENSE MODE...
BA BA BAM
...AND I SET ONE CARD FACE DOWN! TURN OVER!!
HEH
DID YOU FORGET THAT LANCELOT CAN ATTACK DIRECTLY?!
MY TURN!!
DIE, RYOGA!
GHOST KNIGHT LANCELOT, MOUNT A DIRECT ATTACK ON RYOGA!!
FOOM

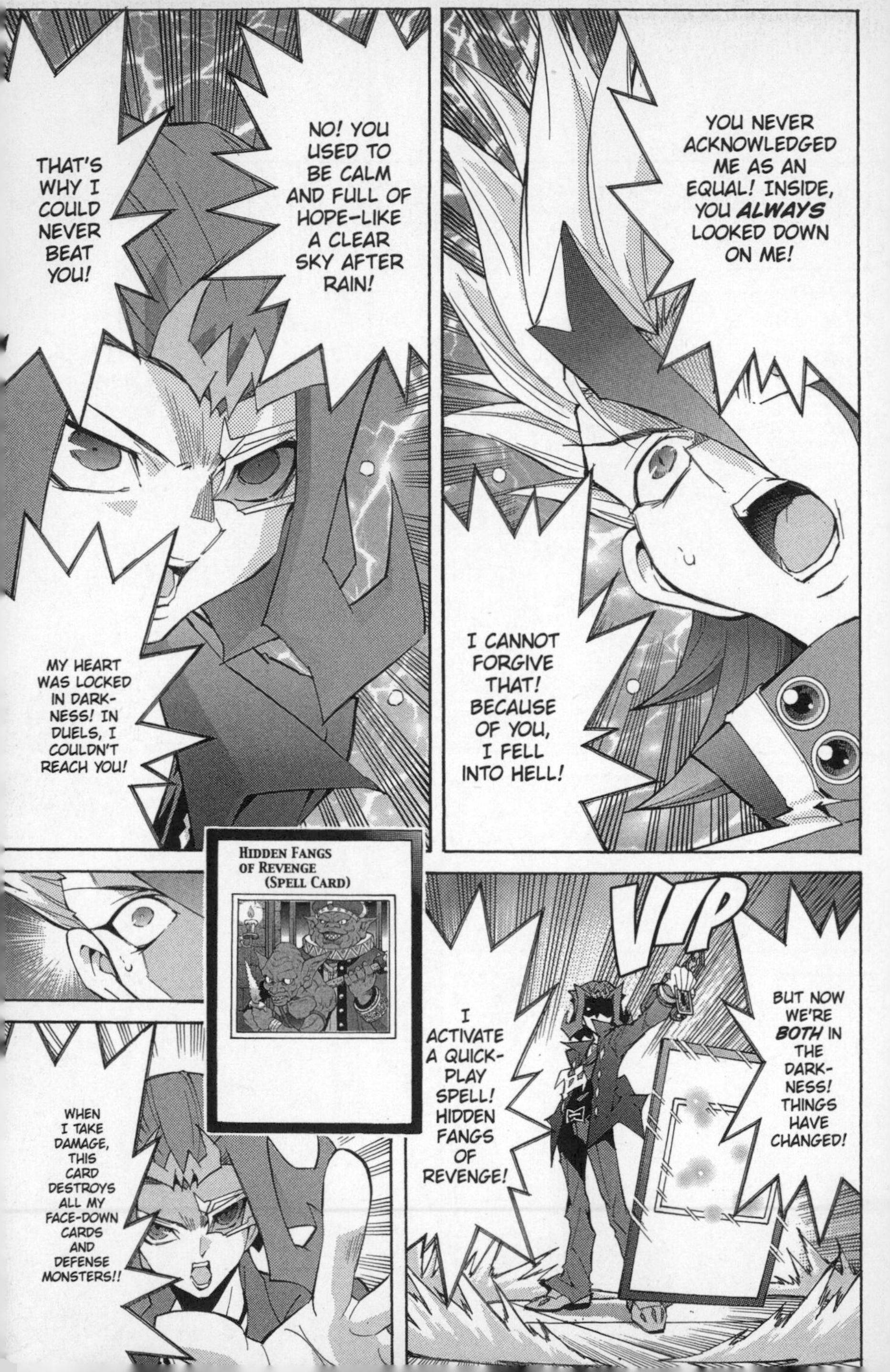
YOU NEVER ACKNOWLEDGED ME AS AN EQUAL! INSIDE, YOU **ALWAYS** LOOKED DOWN ON ME!
I CANNOT FORGIVE THAT! BECAUSE OF YOU, I FELL INTO HELL!
NO! YOU USED TO BE CALM AND FULL OF HOPE—LIKE A CLEAR SKY AFTER RAIN!
THAT'S WHY I COULD NEVER BEAT YOU!
MY HEART WAS LOCKED IN DARK-NESS! IN DUELS, I COULDN'T REACH YOU!
VIP
BUT NOW WE'RE **BOTH** IN THE DARK-NESS! THINGS HAVE CHANGED!
I ACTIVATE A QUICK-PLAY SPELL! HIDDEN FANGS OF REVENGE!
HIDDEN FANGS OF REVENGE (SPELL CARD)
WHEN I TAKE DAMAGE, THIS CARD DESTROYS ALL MY FACE-DOWN CARDS AND DEFENSE MONSTERS!!

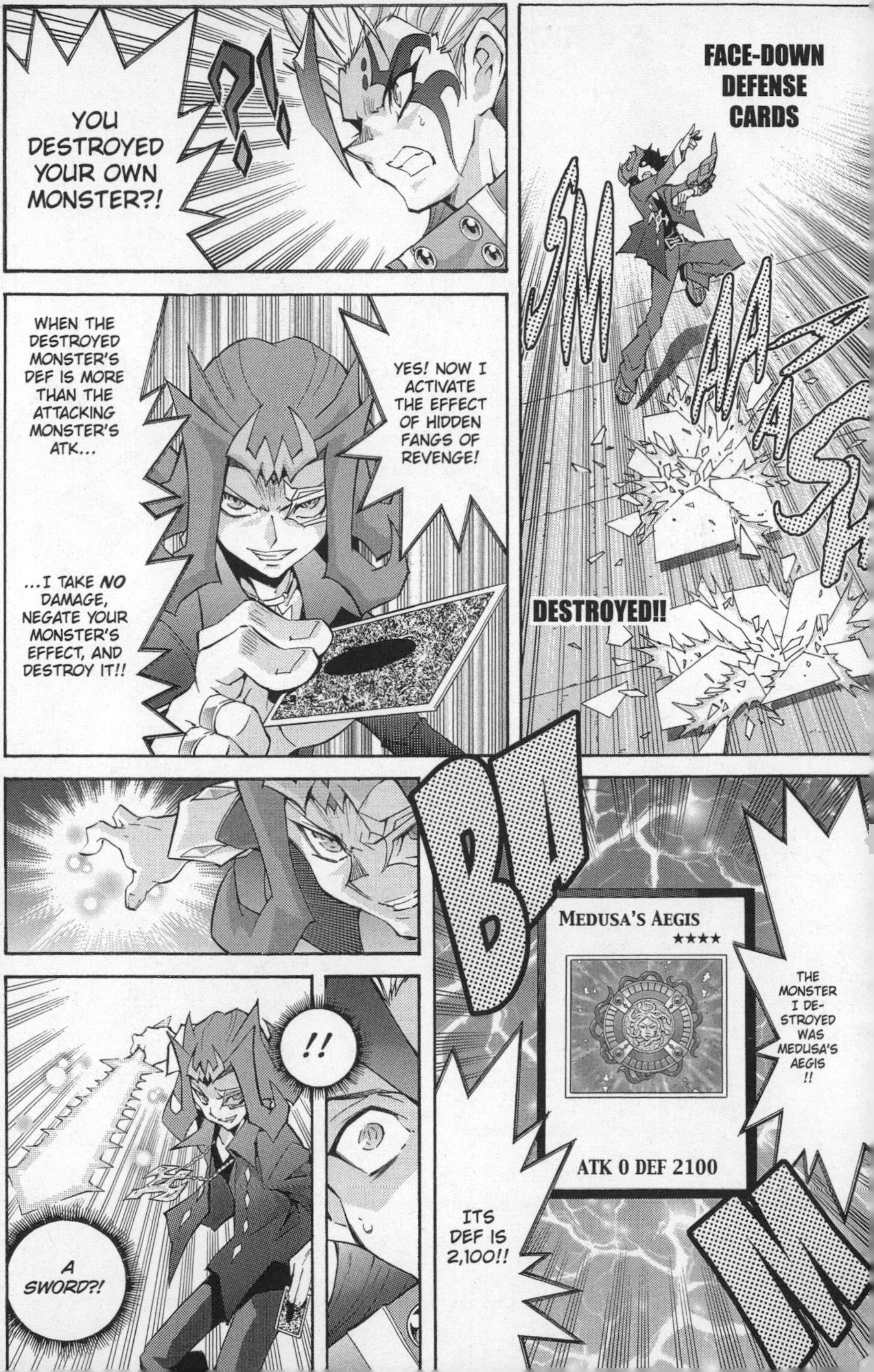
FACE-DOWN DEFENSE CARDS
SMAAASH
DESTROYED!!
YOU DESTROYED YOUR OWN MONSTER?!
YES! NOW I ACTIVATE THE EFFECT OF HIDDEN FANGS OF REVENGE!
WHEN THE DESTROYED MONSTER'S DEF IS MORE THAN THE ATTACKING MONSTER'S ATK...
...I TAKE NO DAMAGE, NEGATE YOUR MONSTER'S EFFECT, AND DESTROY IT!!
MEDUSA'S AEGIS
★★★★
ATK 0 DEF 2100
THE MONSTER I DE-STROYED WAS MEDUSA'S AEGIS !!
ITS DEF IS 2,100!!
!!
A SWORD?!

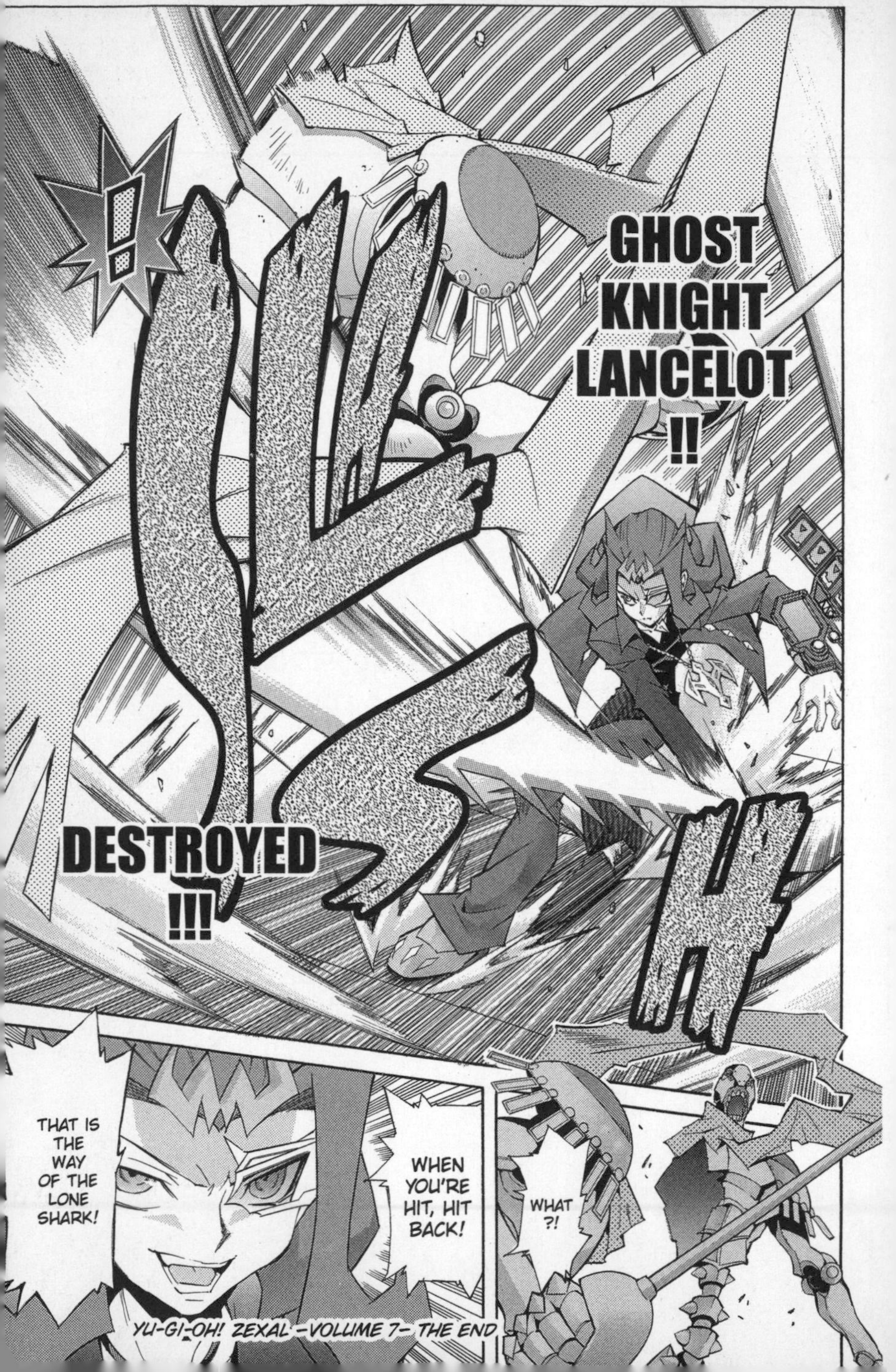
GHOST KNIGHT LANCELOT !!
!!
DESTROYED !!!
WHAT ?!
WHEN YOU'RE HIT, HIT BACK!
THAT IS THE WAY OF THE LONE SHARK!
YU-GI-OH! ZEXAL -VOLUME 7- THE END

STAFF
 JUNYA UCHINO
 KAZUO OCHIAI
 TOSHIAKI KATO
 MASAHIRO MIURA

 COLORING
 TORU SHIMIZU (COVER)

 EDITOR
 TAKAHIKO AIKAWA

 SUPPORT
 GALLOP

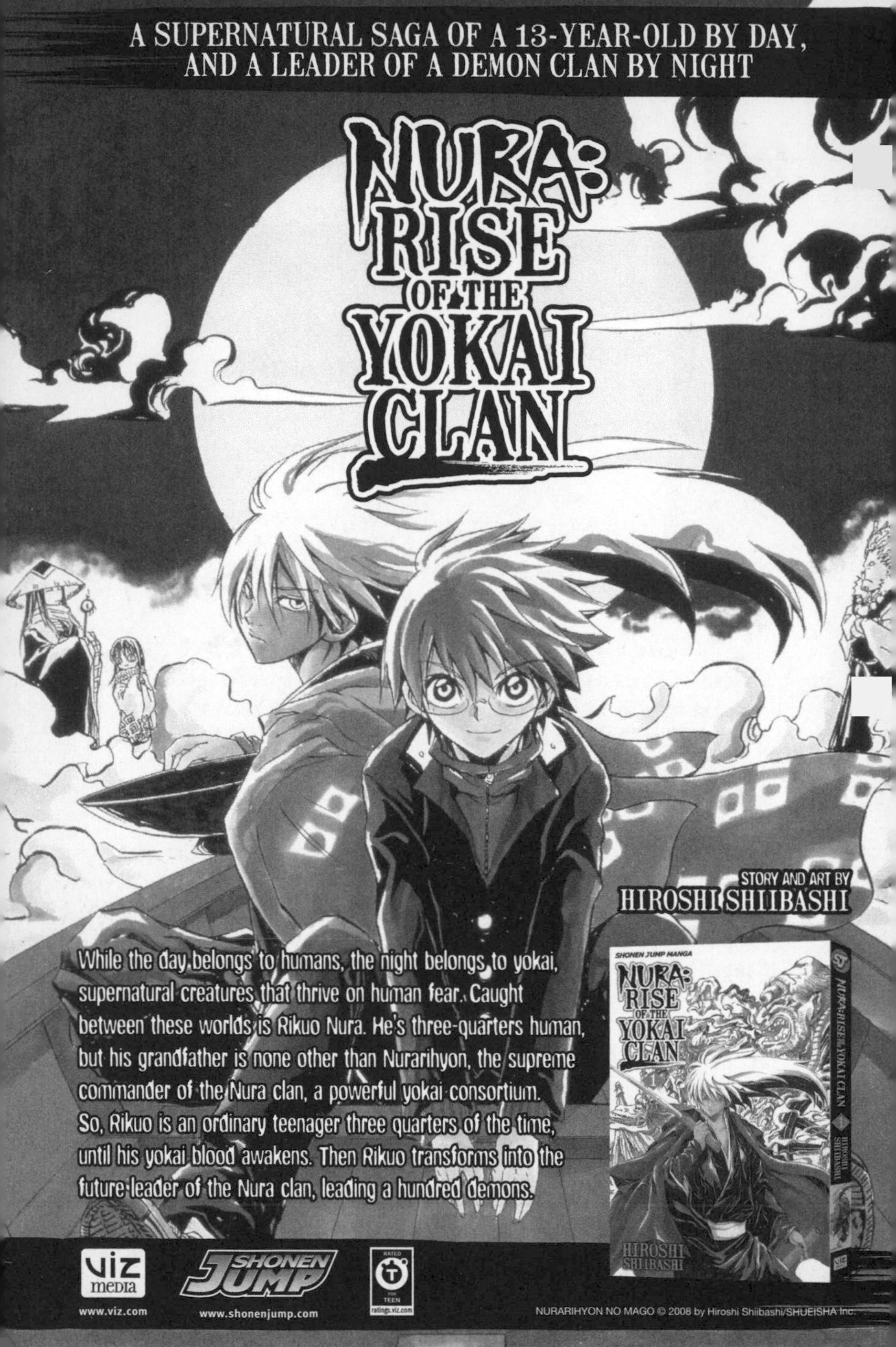
A SUPERNATURAL SAGA OF A 13-YEAR-OLD BY DAY, AND A LEADER OF A DEMON CLAN BY NIGHT
NURA: RISE OF THE YOKAI CLAN
STORY AND ART BY
HIROSHI SHIIBASHI
While the day belongs to humans, the night belongs to yokai, supernatural creatures that thrive on human fear. Caught between these worlds is Rikuo Nura. He's three-quarters human, but his grandfather is none other than Nurarihyon, the supreme commander of the Nura clan, a powerful yokai consortium. So, Rikuo is an ordinary teenager three quarters of the time, until his yokai blood awakens. Then Rikuo transforms into the future leader of the Nura clan, leading a hundred demons.
SHONEN JUMP MANGA
NURA: RISE OF THE YOKAI CLAN
HIROSHI SHIIBASHI
viz media
SHONEN JUMP
RATED T FOR TEEN
www.viz.com
www.shonenjump.com
ratings.viz.com
NURARIHYON NO MAGO © 2008 by Hiroshi Shiibashi/SHUEISHA Inc.

YOU AR[...]
IN THE WRO[...]!!

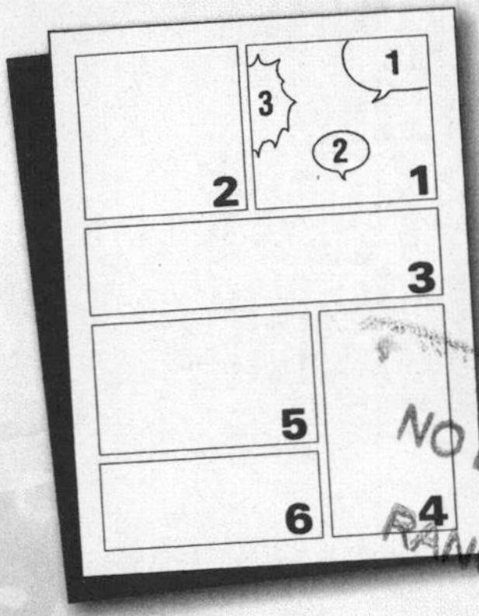

Whoops!
Guess what?
You're starting at
the wrong end
of the comic!

...It's true! In keeping with the original Japanese format, *Yu-Gi-Oh! ZEXAL* is meant to be read from right to left, starting in the upper-right corner.

Unlike English, which is read from left to right, Japanese is read from right to left, meaning that action, sound effects and word-balloon order are completely reversed... something which can make readers unfamiliar with Japanese feel pretty backwards themselves. For this reason, manga or Japanese comics published in the U.S. in English have sometimes been published "flopped"—that is, printed in exact reverse order, as though seen from the other side of a mirror.

By flopping pages, U.S. publishers can avoid confusing readers, but the compromise is not without its downside. For one thing, a character in a flopped manga series who once wore in the original Japanese version a T-shirt emblazoned with "M A Y" (as in "the merry month of") now wears one which reads "Y A M"! Additionally, many manga creators in Japan are themselves unhappy with the process, as some feel the mirror-imaging of their art alters their original intentions.

We are proud to bring you Shin Yoshida and Naohito Miyoshi's *Yu-Gi-Oh! ZEXAL* in the original unflopped format. For now, though, turn to the other side of the book and let the duel begin...!

—Editor